COST STRUCTURE AND THE
MEASUREMENT OF ECONOMIC PERFORMANCE

Productivity, Utilization, Cost Economics,
and Related Performance Indicators

COST STRUCTURE AND THE
MEASUREMENT OF ECONOMIC PERFORMANCE

Productivity, Utilization, Cost Economics, and Related Performance Indicators

by

Catherine J. Morrison Paul
University of California at Davis

Kluwer Academic Publishers
Boston/ Dordrecht/ London

Distributors for North, Central and South America:
Kluwer Academic Publishers
101 Philip Drive
Assinippi Park
Norwell, Massachusetts 02061 USA
Telephone (781) 871-6600
Fax (781) 871-6528
E-Mail <kluwer@wkap.com>

Distributors for all other countries:
Kluwer Academic Publishers Group
Distribution Centre
Post Office Box 322
3300 AH Dordrecht, THE NETHERLANDS
Telephone 31 78 6392 392
Fax 31 78 6546 474
E-Mail <orderdept@wkap.nl>

 Electronic Services <http://www.wkap.nl>

Library of Congress Cataloging-in-Publication Data

A C.I.P. Catalogue record for this book is available
from the Library of Congress.

Printed on acid-free paper.

Printed in the United States of America

To David

Contents

Preface

This text is a heavily revised version of my 1992 monograph, *A Microeconomic Approach to the Measurement of Economic Performance: Productivity Growth, Capacity Utilization, and Related Performance Indicators*, published by Springer Verlag Press. That monograph was out of print within a year, but was still in demand by the late 1990s, so it seemed a second edition was in order.

Like the original monograph, this text is designed to provide a comprehensive guide to students, researchers or consultants who wish to model, construct, interpret, and use economic performance measures. The emphasis of the treatment is on productivity growth and its dependence on the cost structure. The focus is on application of the tools of economic analysis – the "thinking structure" provided by microeconomic theory – to measure technological or cost structure, and link it also with market and regulatory structure, to provide a rich basis for evaluation of economic performance and its determinants.

Virtually everything that appeared in the first monograph is incorporated somewhere in the current text, so those who wish to use this version similarly will be able to do so.[1] However, both the field of production and productivity analysis and my own work have evolved significantly in the years since the first monograph was prepared. The text broadly follows this path, bringing in some recent applications of production theory while in the process drawing together threads of thought on economic performance representation and measurement from related literatures.

---

[1] An exception to this is the original chapter 8, which overviewed empirical evidence of the "productivity slowdown" which was a crucial focus of productivity analysts in the 1980s when that book was initially written. The empirical literature is referred to within the application chapters in this version, rather than providing the basis for a separate chapter.

The text overviews traditional productivity growth measurement techniques and adaptations to take into account various aspects of the technological or cost structure. In particular, it expands the standard growth accounting framework to accommodate various types of cost economies that may be evident in the cost structure, such as utilization and scale economies. Data construction procedures, theoretical foundations, and issues of econometric implementation are also outlined. These themes provided the foundation for the original text, and are further elaborated here.

In this monograph, however, the focus on the cost structure is pursued in more depth to consider additional cost economies or diseconomies affecting productivity patterns, including those from joint production, external factors such as spillovers from R&D and agglomeration effects, and characteristics of market or regulatory structure. Capital issues also are an overriding theme – from issues of "effective" capital or service flow as compared to stock (utilization, obsolescence, quality, composition, regulatory restrictions) to the more general notion of capital as a "knowledge" base deriving from, say, information technology, R&D or human capital. The potential for technical or allocative inefficiencies to affect measured performance is also addressed. These extensions are developed in the context of various literatures in which their impacts have been highlighted, including the macro/growth, industrial organization (IO) and efficiency literatures.

The emphasis here is on topics or questions of interest rather than theoretical tools for analysis. The basic productivity growth modeling and measurement practices that result in a productivity residual often called the "measure of our ignorance" are initially developed, and then the different aspects of technological, market and regulatory structure that might underlie this residual are explored. The ultimate goal is to decompose or explain the residual, via the multitude of impacts that determine economic performance of firms, sectors, and economies.

The chapters are organized with three broad goals in mind. The first is to introduce the overall ideas involved in economic performance measurement and traditional productivity growth analysis. Issues associated with different types of (short and long run, internal and external) cost economies, market and regulatory impacts, and other general inefficiencies that might impact these measures are then raised. Finally, some of the tools necessary to justify and implement these models are emphasized.

This organization emphasizes the *application* of the tools of economic analysis. Basic intermediate microeonomic theory is initially used to motivate most of the fundamental ideas underlying analysis of productivity growth and other crucial indicators of economic performance in the first chapters (Chapters 1-2 and most of 3). Chapter 1 provides the conceptual basis for traditional productivity measurement and the extensions in this text.

Chapter 2 overviews the traditional productivity growth literature and measurement procedures. Chapter 3 raises the possibility that short run capital constraints convolute measured productivity patterns so that they mis-measure true technical change and should be adapted to separately identify fluctuations caused instead by changes in capacity utilization.

Somewhat more advanced theoretical concepts, based on functional relationships that should be familiar to graduate students and in most cases upper level undergraduates, are utilized (with some qualification and explanation) in the next few application chapters (Chapters 4-8). These Chapters focus first on the combination of short and long run internal scale economies that affect observed cost efficiency (Chapter 4), and external factors or economies that may drive productivity and growth patterns (Chapter 5). Then market structure and its linkage to cost economies (Chapter 6), costs and benefits of regulatory constraints (Chapter 7), and the potential for technical inefficiency (Chapter 8), are brought in.

The primary theoretical, data and econometric tools providing the base for construction and empirical implementation of cost structure models are overviewed in the last chapters (Chapters 9-11). These chapters are therefore, to some extent, reference chapters, and direct the reader to the more rigorous economic and econometric theory literature for further details. Chapter 9 provides a summary treatment of the duality theory underlying production theory models, Chapter 10 addresses issues of data construction, and Chapter 11 targets some econometric issues of particular relevance to the types of applications overviewed in previous chapters of the text.

The material in this text is not meant to provide an exhaustive overview of contributions to the productivity literature and of methodologies underlying productivity and economic performance measurement. It is instead designed to feature the usefulness of a production-theory approach to the measurement of productivity and economic performance.

It essentially outlines one literature within which I have focused my research efforts for nearly two decades now, and some of its links to related literatures. It thus provides a foundation to facilitate understanding of the literature in this area, to generate and interpret associated empirical measures of productivity growth, and to carry out econometric estimation to identify and quantify important characteristics of production and performance.

The text is in some sense a "wrap-up" of the way my thinking about economic performance modeling and measurement has developed, guided by my colleagues and peers, co-authors, students, personal interests, and current policy concerns. My belief that a detailed analysis of the cost structure underlying production structure and performance is crucial for interpretation and use of any performance measures has intensified as I have utilized cost-oriented models for various applications over the years.

I believe that abstracting from the critical characteristics of the cost structure, which is done at least to some extent in most macroeconomic studies, analyses of market structure, and evaluations of "inefficient" production processes, makes interpretation and use of the associated measures problematic. I hope that this text shows why my thinking has moved in this direction, and perhaps even helps to synthesize some different perspectives, and encourage researchers to think more about cost structure.

Finally, I want briefly to mention a couple of people I would not have been able to do this without. I should first thank many people who have been supportive of me – both personally and professionally – over the past few years that have been particularly difficult ones for me. However, there are too many to mention. Certainly my family and many friends and colleagues have been enormously helpful. This has been particularly true as I have moved into a somewhat different field, and have begun to connect with many new friends and colleagues since I joined the University of California, Davis, Department of Agricultural and Resource Economics. I have met and been encouraged by many great new colleagues in my own department, others I have visited, and those who I have associated with at the USDA.

Particular thanks, however, go to two special people. My recent work with co-author Donald Siegel at Arizona State University West has been a great experience. Don not only has been a joy to work with and a wonderful support both personally and professionally, he is always there to provide help when needed – even when a book manuscript has to be in "yesterday"!

Even more heartfelt thanks, though, go to my best friend and husband David Paul, who makes life wonderful and provides a solid base for whatever I (and we) want to do. It's finally right.

Catherine J. Morrison Paul

Chapter 1

Introduction to the Conceptual Framework

The initial question to address when attempting to model and measure a concept like economic performance is "what does it mean"? Definition, construction, and use of measures representing performance require careful consideration of the underlying conceptual foundation. This in turn requires explicit recognition of the connection between productive performance or productivity and the cost structure. On this basis the theoretical formalization and implementation of appropriate measurement formulas, and interpretation and use of resulting performance measures, may effectively be pursued.

In the process of developing this conceptual framework, associated terminology such as "technical change", "efficiency", "utilization", "competitiveness", "market power", "distortions", and "spillovers" emerges. These words must also be precisely defined in order to be interpretable and applicable. Using them carelessly, or applying pat formulas or rules from basic micro-economic theory without thinking about what they imply, may result in misleading analysis. The "thinking structure" provided by our micro-production-theory foundations allows us to craft models to put these related ideas in context, and to link them to the goals of economic performance measurement, evaluation, and enhancement.

This text overviews many issues related to the conceptualization, construction, interpretation, and use of economic performance and productivity growth measures, with a focus on the cost structure and cost efficiency. By integrating many different characteristics of firms and markets into a cost-based microeconomic-production-theory framework representing firm behavior, we will develop a foundation for modeling and measuring many aspects of production and market structure and performance.

To accomplish this we have to begin with the basics, which are introduced in this chapter. Section 1 overviews the conceptual foundation for traditional productivity growth measurement and its components, and Section 2 extends this to consider various cost economies as embodied productivity or performance characteristics. The representation of such characteristics of firms' technology and behavior is motivated using basic production theory in

Sections 3 and 4. The connection of the cost structure to market and regulatory structures is outlined in Section 5. Finally, section 6 briefly overviews typical productivity growth measurement practices, as a base to consider the limitations of such measures for unraveling the multitude of characteristics associated with economic performance.

The following chapters pursue the issues and ideas raised in this introductory chapter in more detail, exploring cost-based production theory approaches to measurement of many interrelated performance indicators, their linkages to various branches of literature on economic performance, and underlying issues of theoretical background and empirical implementation. This allows consideration of many questions about the measurement and interpretation of performance indicators encountered by those who wish to construct and use such measures.

1.   WHAT DO "ECONOMIC PERFORMANCE" AND "PRODUCTIVITY" MEAN?

For a number of years now I have taught courses on the use of production theory models to assess firms' cost structure (input demand and output production given technological conditions and optimizing behavior), and to evaluate their resulting economic and productive performance. I typically begin such a course with the question in the title of this section. The answers indicate that the definition of these concepts depends, to a large extent, on the perspective of the respondent.

For example, a popular response to this question from my students is that economic performance is reflected in profitability or the market value of the firm. A high "score" along either of these dimensions implies something "good" for the associated entrepreneur or manager. However, *why* the product or firm is "valuable" in this sense is an important issue.

It could, for example, arise from over-pricing a commodity (and limiting its production), by taking advantage of market power in the output or product market. Paying workers low wages by exploiting labor market power also could generate high profits. In these instances profitability may be good for the firm (and thus its owners and managers), but bad for consumers or workers; it does not indicate the "greater good" overall that one might think is a more valid definition of productivity.

Similarly, from the perspective of workers, the terms "productive" or "good performance" may involve high wages, future potential or good working conditions. From the point of view of the consumer, it might have to do with the quality and price or "value" of a product.

These again simply represent *pieces* of the broader question of productivity and economic performance, which should have a more general welfare connotation. Greater productivity in this sense ultimately embodies all the individual components mentioned above for entrepreneurs or managers, workers, and consumers, and also may involve distribution changes. Untangling these different aspects of productive and economic performance is crucial for appropriate measurement, interpretation, and use of performance indicators.

More specifically, assessment of current and potential productive and economic performance fundamentally requires evaluation of the underlying production or cost structure, and changes in that structure from technical progress. A general (disembodied) advancement in knowledge, or output- or input-specific effects resulting in compositional adaptations may underlie such progress. This is the usual conceptual framework from which productivity growth is defined, measured and assessed.

Ultimately, technological progress implies getting more from what we have. Getting a bigger "pot" of goods for everyone as a whole means generating greater real output from a particular amount of resources or inputs. Productivity growth measures are thus based fundamentally on the idea of net output growth. If more output is possible from a given amount of inputs, or, equivalently, production of a given output level may be accomplished at a lower cost, this augmentation of efficiency is indicative of an increase in productive performance.

Productivity growth indexes, designed to reflect such net output changes, are perhaps the most common measures used to represent economic performance. These measures are built from various pieces of information that are sometimes individually used as economic performance indicators, including growth in production (output), employment, and investment. Combining these underlying components of the overall productive performance puzzle generates additional information about productive efficiency, but still results in a limited representation of the true broad array of productive and economic performance characteristics of interest to productivity analysts.

That is, productivity growth depends on all changes in output and input quantities and prices and their determinants, and thus on many characteristics of and changes in the economic climate in which the firm, sector, or economy operates. These are, both conceptually and empirically, difficult to untangle. Independently identifying these different aspects of economic performance allows us to highlight the different pieces of the puzzle. We can begin this process by motivating, step by step, the typical construction of traditional productivity growth measures (as pursued in depth in Chapter 2).

The first step is identifying a real increase in production levels, which involves separating output growth that can be explained by price increases from that which potentially represents augmented productivity or cost effectiveness. This requires isolating the real or physical increase in output from the inflation that is included in a value measure such as gross sales or gross national product (GNP). The resulting "constant dollar" (or other monetary unit) measure of production is as an indicator of true growth and therefore welfare, since it measures a "real" change in potential consumption rather than the dollar, or nominal, value of the product.

In turn, a portion of observed output growth may result from increased labor used for production. However, output growth will only affect overall welfare (per capita real product) if it arises from factors other than labor force expansion. Abstracting from this source of growth requires measuring augmentation of real or effective labor input, which involves identifying any wage or quality changes that might have also occurred separately from the pure quantity change.

When increases in labor use are "netted out" from output growth, it results in a measure of output per person or person-hour, interpreted as an indicator of enhanced output stemming from more "efficient" or "productive" labor. Although this labor productivity measure more appropriately reflects enhanced welfare from growth than does a measure simply reflecting production increases, other questions remain, such as: How much of this might be due to increased capital equipment per worker?

Such capital deepening indicates a boost in perceived labor efficiency due to input substitution, or changes in input composition toward a more capital-intensive technological process. An increase in the capital-labor ratio represents a shift in production processes, but not necessarily improved overall productivity. Since capital as well as labor is scarce (and thus costly), increased labor productivity arising from an expanded capital stock has a very different implication for overall welfare than if the increase had occurred without incurring additional capital costs.

Measurement of changes in the capital component of production raises issues similar to, but even more tricky than, distinguishing price and quantity changes for output and labor. This is due to its durable nature – the service flow must be distinguished from the stock. Also, once capital is included in the analysis it must be recognized that its effective contribution varies according to many factors, including changes in capacity utilization, capital composition, the skills embodied in the labor force, and regulatory constraints. These characteristics of the underlying production structure and other aspects of the economic environment in which the firm operates also affect our assessment of economic performance, and thus are important to capture, yet representation of their impacts quickly becomes complex.

2. PRODUCTIVITY GROWTH COMPONENTS

These types of production or cost structure issues complicate the implementation and interpretation of basic productivity growth concepts. Since the underlying question of productive and economic performance is "how much does it cost in terms of resource or input use to produce a certain amount of output", the appropriate framework for analyzing these complicating factors has its basis in the cost structure. This structure may, however, be quite complex, embodying many technological, market and behavioral aspects in addition to the fundamental questions about the representation of output and input growth alluded to above.

In particular, the measurement of productivity growth in terms of net output[2] has its conceptual basis in the notion of technical change that generates a general (or disembodied) shift in the output to input ratio over time. Such a change causes an increase in the output-cost ratio (output per dollar), or a decrease in the cost-output ratio (input cost per unit of output), and thus enhanced cost efficiency. If the costs represented are for a combination of labor and capital inputs, the net growth measure is typically denoted an index of multifactor productivity (MFP) growth.

One aspect of the production process issue that should be recognized to facilitate interpretation of MFP measures is the importance of additional input dimensions. Intermediate material use may change in addition to capital and labor input use. Purchased services, or outsourcing, rather than using in-house labor for production, may also be important to represent. Such input substitution or composition issues may have important implications for productive performance, and should be recognized.

Even with the contribution of all inputs taken into account, however, the resulting somewhat abstract notion of technical change represents only one component of the "productivity puzzle". In the "real world", we cannot carry out a controlled experiment like we can in our economic theoretical framework to identify this piece independently from the other aspects of the production structure that complicate performance measurement. Other identifiable changes in the technological and market structure that affect unit costs or the cost-output ratio can therefore be thought of as additional determinants of cost economies or efficiency. These should be separately distinguished to facilitate interpretation and use of the measures.

One such impact on costs was mentioned above in the context of input (such as capital) fixities or restrictions. This can be modeled by incorporating a difference between short and long run behavior due to short run capacity constraints, resulting in capacity utilization fluctuations. Such

---

[2] As discussed above, quantified in Section 6 and elaborated in Chapter 2.

fluctuations are based on the amount of output produced compared to some optimum potential given the inputs available. They therefore affect observed productive efficiency in terms of the cost per unit output.

That is, since such utilization fluctuations arise from short run constraints on capital investment, unit costs are higher than in a long run steady state when the firm is not producing at optimal capacity.[3] Cost economies may therefore arise from investing (or disinvesting) in a capital stock to the point where its level is consistent with current output demand. Then average costs will fall to their long run level given the existing technological base.

In the short run, therefore, capital constraints imply that inefficiencies from dis- or sub-equilibrium may exist, that impose costs on the firm. These cost changes have very different interpretations than those arising from technical change. Recognizing this dynamic aspect of the technological structure provides important insights about the appropriate interpretation of observed cost changes, facilitating measurement of its different underlying causes or components.

In addition, long run scale or cost economies may be reflected in the existing technology by a downward slope of the long run average cost function.[4] If such economies prevail, marginal cost falls below average cost, so output expansion will generate unit cost decreases (an improvement in the cost-output relationship), independently from technical change or other adaptations in the technology of or constraints facing the firm.

Such cost economies are embodied in the existing technological base, and thus are internal to production processes. They may be due to some type of fixity, such as entrepreneurial input that may be more effectively spread across a larger operation, or capital "lumpiness" such that only larger scale plants may use the most technically efficient type of machinery.[5]

Also, the possibility that cost economies may be derived from joint production is masked in the typical one-aggregate-output specification of the production process. In particular, economies of scope may arise, which reflect more efficient utilization of resources in the production of joint outputs. In reverse, specialization economies may prevail if machinery is very product-specific or specialty niche markets facilitate the production of high-cost but high-quality goods. Output *composition* may therefore be an important performance determinant.

---

[3] These notions will be formalized somewhat more below, and will be focused on in more depth in Chapter 3.

[4] Size economies may also be distinguished as economies arising when scale economies are generated with non-proportional input changes; this distinction is primarily made in the Agricultural Economics literature. This situation is more generally referred to as biased or restricted scale economies.

[5] Scale and other types of cost economies will be explored in more depth in Chapter 4.

Additional cost economies from intra- or inter-industry externalities or public goods could also affect the production structure and thus productive performance. That is, in addition to (internal) economies stemming from output and input decisions within the plant or firm, and thus affecting the slope of the cost function, external economies may be obtained that cause a downward shift of the function.

Such economies will clearly also affect the observed cost-output relationship, but have very different causes and consequences than internal economies. They may arise from various types of spillover effects, including those from R&D, expansion of the high-tech capital base, increased educational attainment, thick-market/agglomeration impacts, or public capital, as well as from technical change. General or disembodied technical change is thus only one of the many potential external factors that may cause shifts in cost curves, and that should be distinguished due to their very different implications for interpretation of productivity growth indicators.[6]

All of the production characteristics identified above are related to the technological and thus cost structure. As such, they can be represented in terms of standard cost-based microeconomic diagrams and theoretical models. Similarly to the sequential development in basic microeconomics courses, however, once the technological structure is represented via production and cost functions additional information about economic behavior and thus performance may be obtained by considering output decisions. This involves representing output demand and market structure.[7]

In particular, inefficiency could result from lack of competition, or market power. However, the impact of this is closely connected to the cost structure. If cost economies are evident, increasing concentration (or reducing competition, as generally defined) could instead stimulate efficiency.

Further market issues may involve constraints resulting from the regulatory structure. Regulations might be imposed to adapt for the lack of markets, in which case both their (non-marketed) benefits and costs (due to the binding constraint on cost-minimizing behavior) should be ascertained to determine their optimality, and associated cost and overall welfare effects.

---

[6] Note that these factors may have both internal and external effects. R&D may benefit a firm but have spillovers to competitors, suppliers, or demanders of their products. High-tech investment, and the resulting changes in input composition such that technical change is embodied in the capital stock, may increase efficiency of a firm but also provide greater potential for interactions among firms (thus, "information technology"). Other purely external cost savings may arise from, for example, public capital investment, or public investment in education. Many of these factors come under the rubric of "knowledge" capital, which has been emphasized in the endogenous growth literature to cause scale effects, in this case exogenous or external effects. This will be explored further in Ch. 5.

[7] This aspect of economic performance, which raises issues about output demand, imperfect competition and profitability, is developed further in Chapter 6.

Other regulatory issues arise with respect to market power issues such as "natural monopolies", where natural technological economies may result in large concentrated industries, and thus the potential to abuse market power.[8]

Finally, movements *toward* cost curves or production functions may be distinguished from those along, or due to shifts in, the curves. This implies increasing allocative or technical efficiency given the technological base. The potential for such efficiency increases is typically assumed away by the optimizing assumptions embodied in the production or cost function representation; the observed production point is assumed to lie on the function's boundary or frontier. Although one might think a sufficiently detailed production model would "explain" deviations from the frontiers in competitive markets, leaving little to be detected as general inefficiency, in some cases the assumption of efficiency may not be appropriate.[9]

All these pieces of the productivity puzzle should be conceptually, theoretically and empirically untangled to the extent possible, to facilitate the interpretation and use of performance indicators. Our task in this text is to outline a framework in which this can potentially be accomplished. To pursue this, in the following sections of this chapter we will provide a basic production theory representation of the fundamental concepts raised above. We will then look in more detail at the individual pieces of the puzzle identified here in subsequent chapters.

3. TECHNICAL CHANGE

To begin developing a structure for modeling, measuring, and evaluating economic performance and its determinants, let us start by defining more formally the most fundamental underlying concepts. The foundation for developing these concepts and their relationships is the micro-economic theory of the firm, based on the production function, which we will refer to as the micro-production-theory framework.

Explicit specification of the cost structure and cost economies requires adding to this technological basis by incorporating information on prices, specifying (cost minimizing) behavior, and recognizing the associated constraints and determinants underlying short and long run, internal and external cost economies. Further representation of overall economic performance involves appending additional layers to the model base, reflecting the market and regulatory structure, and potential inefficiency, that ultimately should be untangled from productive performance.

---

[8] Some regulatory issues are addressed in Chapter 7.
[9] This is further explored in Chapter 8.

The idea underlying specification of the production function is that it summarizes the state of technology – the maximum production of (aggregated) outputs technically possible given a particular amount of inputs. As alluded to above, "pure" productivity growth or technical change conceptually arises from a change or shift in the production function, so that more production is technically possible from the available amount of inputs.

We can formalize the production function in general mathematical notation as $Y(\mathbf{v},t)=Y(K,L,t)$, where Y is output, t is the state of technology or time,[10] and $\mathbf{v}$ is a vector of inputs. For now the relevant inputs are assumed to be capital, K, and labor, L to facilitate graphical representation.

This may be thought of as a "value added" production function since no other inputs are recognized. A corresponding gross output specification might include payments to materials and services such as intermediate processed materials, natural resources, agricultural products, purchased services, and energy inputs. However, this requires a multi-dimensional analysis, which we will defer to later chapters.

The production function relationship in a sense represents the "blueprints" outlining the technical features of the production process. This technological association between output and the productive inputs can also be summarized graphically using an isoquant map, where each isoquant, or "level surface" of the production function (for constant Y), indicates the different K-L input mixes technically capable of producing a particular quantity of output using the current technology.

Since productivity growth implies a decline in the amount of inputs necessary to produce any given amount of output, this in turn indicates a change in the production technology. This is typically the way productivity growth representation and thus measurement is motivated. As outlined above (and elaborated for most of this text) this structure has important limitations as a basis for economic performance measurement. It provides a starting point, however, for our exploration of such performance.

Changes in the technology are expressed by shifts in the isoquant map between time periods. Technological progress implies inward shifts in the isoquants; to produce a given output production level less capital and labor are required. This ultimately implies a reduction in input costs once prices and cost minimization are built into the model.

---

[10] Note that these "definitions" of t tend to be used interchangeably in this literature. Strictly speaking t is a time counter, but it represents general technical change occurring simply with the passage of time.

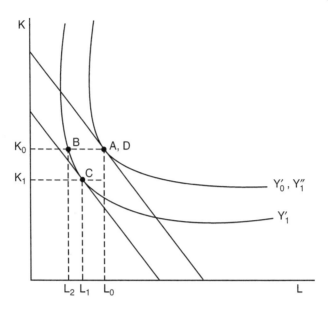

Figure 1. Technical Change as an Isoquant Shift

This situation can be diagrammed as in Figure 1. Say the firm wishes to produce a particular level of output Y' in period 0; denote this Y'$_0$ (so superscripts indicate quantity levels, and subscripts time periods). Productivity growth may be thought of as a change in the isoquant map so the Y' isoquant shifts toward the origin in period 1. After the shift, therefore, capital and labor are more "productive" since the same output, Y'$_1$=Y'$_0$ may be produced using less inputs (this input-based notion is "dual" to the production orientation).

Alternatively, the original isoquant may be renamed Y"$_1$ where Y">Y' and thus Y"$_1$>Y'$_0$. This indicates that more output may be produced, using the same amount of inputs, in period 1 than in period 0 (this is the "primal" perspective, based on output levels).

It is straightforward to add cost minimization to this so far purely technological representation. To produce the chosen level of output Y' in period 0, the cost minimizing firm chooses optimal capital and labor input demand levels – the point where an isocost line is tangent to the isoquant corresponding to Y'$_0$.

The isocost line represents the set of K-L combinations that cost a certain amount, say TC$_0$ (where TC denotes total costs) given input market prices p$_K$ and p$_L$. The cost minimizing choice, or equilibrium point (in the sense that as long as production of Y' is desired and technology and input prices are constant the firm is producing using optimum long run input levels) is thus at point A in Figure 1. K$_0$ units of capital and L$_0$ units of labor are demanded.

Cost minimization behavior implies a set of tangencies (a scale expansion path, SEP) between isoquants representing different outputs and their corresponding tangent isocost lines, which identify the lowest cost of producing any particular output level given current input prices and the state of technology. This correspondence is alternatively formalized as the (total) cost function representing the cost-output (TC-Y) relationship $TC(Y;\mathbf{p},t)$ or $TC(Y,\mathbf{p},t)$, or where both the technology (via the production function) and the firm's behavior (cost minimization) are incorporated, and t represents the current state of technology.[11]

This function is called "dual" to the production function since it equivalently represents the technology but does so in terms of cost rather than output levels. It summarizes the entire technological structure, including not only the purely technical aspects but also the behavioral factors resulting in observed output production and input use, and ultimately cost economies and efficiency.

The cost function allows further refinement of the dual productivity perspective. If (disembodied) technical change culminates in a shift in the isoquant map, so the Y' isoquant shifts toward the origin to become Y'_1, the corresponding equilibrium input demands become K_1 and L_1 (implying a total cost of $TC_1 = p_L L_1 + p_K K_1$). Now capital and labor are more "productive" since the same output may be produced using less inputs and therefore at less cost, so unit costs drop ($TC_1(Y',\mathbf{p},t) < TC_0(Y',\mathbf{p},t)$, so $TC_1/Y' < TC_0/Y'$). The effect of technical change can therefore be measured as the difference between the unit cost of producing Y' before and after the change.

From the output perspective the focus is on the isoquant going through the point (K_0, L_0), that is, $Y''_1(K_0, L_0) > Y'_0(K_0, L_0)$. This output comparison generates a measure of the implied technical change that is the primal productivity growth equivalent to the dual cost-based measure.[12]

Although this theory of productivity change is reasonably straightforward to motivate, empirical measurement of the implied concepts may not be so easy. If the world were adequately represented by this simple diagram we would just need to measure K, L, and Y, and develop a measure of the shift and implied change in input use or output production. However, numerous real-world complications cause difficulties in carrying out this task.

That is, this diagram may be used for motivation. But it is too simple to capture real-world complexities pertaining to the definition of the inputs and outputs, and the separate identification of this type of "technical change" from other adaptations in the technical, market, and regulatory structure suggested in the previous section.

---

[11] The cost function and its duality properties are discussed more formally in Chapter 9.
[12] Duality notions are elaborated in detail in Chapter 9.

Further refinement of the cost structure representation, however, facilitates capturing the effects of these complicated but potentially illuminating production structure characteristics. Representing the technological or cost structure more completely involves explicitly recognizing a number of such factors ignored in this simple diagram. To facilitate the formalization and ultimately measurement of such aspects of the cost structure, they may first be more directly conceptualized within a cost curve diagrammatic treatment.

4.   THE COST STRUCTURE

As developed above, the cost-output relationship derived from our standard isoquant diagram in Figure 1 is based on the scale expansion path defining $TC(Y;\mathbf{p},t)$, which embodies both the technological and behavioral structure (the production function and cost minimization). This path will change (or at least be renumbered in terms of cost levels) with technical change, since t is a shift variable in the cost function.

Additional impacts on the cost structure affect the cost-output (TC-Y) relationship through constraints on behavior. Perhaps the most basic of these is the distinction between short- and long-run behavior. As emphasized by Marshall over a century ago, and discussed in most Principles courses, if some factors are (quasi-) fixed in the short run (cannot be adjusted instantaneously in response to changes in the technology or input costs) this affects observed input use and thus costs. The observed cost relationship will adapt over time to reach the (long run) cost minimizing level represented by the SEP, or the cost function $TC(Y;\mathbf{p},t)$.

In terms of the isoquant diagram, this implies (for fixed K, for example) that the short run "scale expansion" path is a horizontal line at the given K value (say at K_0 in Figure 1). This line only intersects the SEP at one point (point A, where the short and long run cost curves are tangent, as formalized further below). The case of fixed L (due to long-term contracts, for example) follows analogously. If quasi-fixity instead prevails – short run adjustment is constrained by costs of adjustment – only partial adjustment of K toward its long run steady state (desired) level will take place.

If the firm is operating away from the steady state, unit costs are higher than after capital investment (or disinvestment) allows adjustment to an equilibrium point on the SEP. This short run dis- or sub-equilibrium also implies that capacity is not fully utilized, where full capacity utilization means the firm is producing its "optimal" or "capacity" output, given the current level of the capital stock (with only K fixed).

Under-utilization (over-utilization) will prevail if the capital level is too high (low) to reach the lowest possible cost of producing the currently demanded output. Thus, short run fixities must exist for utilization to be an issue, or the firm would simply sell (buy) inputs to reach the minimum cost point. Capacity utilization is also connected to costs and productivity. Utilization fluctuations have effects on short run efficiency (unit cost levels) that are conceptually distinct from those resulting from technical change.

Although these effects are difficult to untangle empirically, it is quite straightforward to identify them theoretically. If capital is fixed at K_0 (or at least cannot be changed to K_1 instantaneously), after technical change occurs short run production will not be carried out at an optimal (long run equilibrium) point. So, observed productivity growth will not reflect the full shift from K_0 to K_1 and L_0 to L_1. A deviation will thus emerge between produced and capacity output, and between actual and long run equilibrium costs.[13] Figures 1 and 2a together can be used to formalize this further.

First, define a measure of economic capacity utilization equal to one when full equilibrium exists for period 0 at points A in Figures 1 and 2a. That is, at point A the steady state output corresponding to the given capital stock K_0 (call this capacity output $Y^*_0=Y^*$) and the demanded level of Y ($Y'_0=Y'$) coincide by construction, so the capacity utilization measure, defined as $Y'_0/Y^*_0=Y/Y^*$, is equal to one.[14] By definition this equilibrium is associated with a tangency of the isoquant and isocost lines, and of the short and long run cost curves, since at this point the capital stock K_0 is consistent with minimum long run cost for output Y'.

In time period 1, after the technology has changed, production of the output level Y' requires less capital than before (K_1 instead of K_0) but reduction in the capital stock cannot be accomplished instantaneously. Assuming capital is completely fixed, in the short run, too much capital (K_0) is therefore used, and too little labor (L_2).

In Figure 1 this is represented by shifting the Y' isoquant in from Y'_0 to Y'_1 but not changing K_0, so a higher cost level is maintained (at point B) than would be the case with full cost minimization (at point C). In Figure 2a this sequence of events is reflected by a shift in the cost curves such that Y'_1 no longer corresponds to a tangency of the short and long run average cost curves in period 1, $SAC_1(K_0)$ and LAC_1.

---

[13] It should also be recognized that firms are doing the best they can, and are in thise sense not "inefficient", even if the long run equilibrium point is not reached due to fixity constraints. Note also that although the concept of utilization may include other inputs such as labor, in our two input diagram cost minimization is meaningless if both inputs are fixed. At least one variable input must be available to use to respond to technical change fluctuations or other changes in the economic climate facing the firm.

[14] These ideas are further elaborated in Chapter 3.

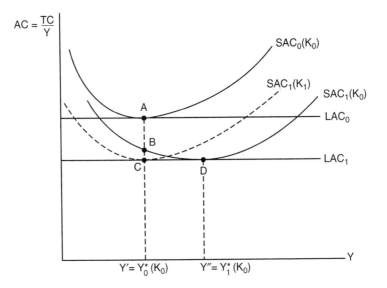

Figure 2a. Short and Long run Cost Curves and Technical Change, CRS

Thus, with the capital level fixed at K_0, the full potential decline in inputs and therefore costs permitted for a particular level of output by the change in technology is not represented correctly in the observed data. Instead (total and unit or average) costs corresponding to point B exceed those for point C. Also, $Y'_1 < Y^*_1$ where Y'_1 is capacity output given K_1 (by construction) and Y^*_1 is capacity output given K_0, in time period 1.[15] Note that $Y'_1 < Y^*_1$ implies both that $K_1 < K_0$ and $Y'/Y_1^* = Y_1/Y_1^* < 1$; under-utilization of the given capital stock prevails because the capital level is too high to be consistent with long run equilibrium given output production Y'.

If output demand remains at Y', adjustment of K will occur in the long run to K_1 (from B to C). This implies a movement along the isoquant corresponding to Y'_1 in Figure 1, and down the vertical line (as the SAC_1 cost curve shifts back along the LAC curve) at output level Y'_1 in Figure 2a. The long run cost efficient level of unit costs is thus reached, corresponding to the new technology level and given output demand.

---

[15]A similar argument can be made in the context of profit maximization. In this case output is not fixed after a change in the technology, but the short run profit maximization point will not, in general, correspond to the tangency of the short and long run average cost curves. Again, therefore, capacity output differs from that produced, and capacity utilization deviates from unity. In fact, when produced output differs between the two periods in question for this or any other reason (such as a change in demand), the analysis becomes somewhat more complicated, and difficult to motivate in a two-dimensional diagram, but the essential points remain valid. These extensions will be elaborated later in this text.

In reverse (the primal perspective), if the firm retains its inputs and increases production to its potential level given the new technology, capital fixity does not pose a problem. This implies that the firm will move from A to D, assuming output level Y''_1 may be sold. This raises two more issues.

First, as discussed further in the context of measurement procedures below, for an empirical application both output and input changes will be embodied in the data. Again, the controlled experiment of changing t given Y' (dual), or given K_0 and L_0 (primal) cannot be accomplished with observed data, which reflects a combination of underlying factors.

Untangling these components of the changes underlying productivity growth measures not only requires careful data analysis, but ultimately econometric modeling once production characteristics such as capital fixity are accommodated, since they cannot be separately distinguished directly from the data. A model corresponding to the diagrams used above must be constructed for measurement of the different implied pieces of the puzzle.

Secondly, when output production changes are brought in to the analysis (for the primal perspective), another facet of the production or technological structure that may convolute interpretation of standard primal productivity growth measures becomes potentially important – long run scale economies. Such economies are captured in the SEP or $TC(Y;\mathbf{p},t)$ functions, since they involve a movement along, rather than a shift in, the existing cost function. Scale economies imply a change in the TC-Y relationship resulting only from changes in the scale of production (movement between isoquants) rather than in the production function or isoquant map.

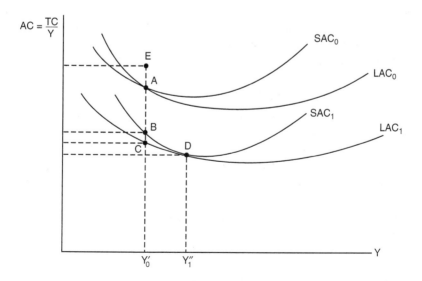

Figure 2b. Technical Change in a Cost Curve Diagram, NCRS

This difference may be motivated using Figures 2a and 2b. Figure 2a is drawn under the assumption of constant returns to scale (CRS), which is evident from the flat LAC curves. However, if non-constant returns to scale (NCRS) or scale economies exist, this curve will have a U-shape, as in Figure 2b. In this case, as pursued further in Chapter 4, C and D are at different AC=TC/Y levels; the TC/Y ratio at point D is lower than that at point C.

Thus, although scale economies do not affect the cost-side technical change measure (it is evaluated at a given output level), they will be embodied in the primal measure. The cost economies exhibited from point C to D, should be attributed to scale economies rather than to technical change.

If other external economies such as R&D or educational levels also cause shifts in the isoquant map and thus the cost function, they should appear as arguments of the cost function in addition to t, and their independent impacts on the cost-output relationship identified. This requires econometric modeling, since conceptually these impacts are observationally equivalent; they are diagrammed analogously to the technical change impact above.

Finally, note that this entire basic theoretical treatment has assumed that firms will be technically efficient (on an isoquant) and allocatively efficient (at the cost minimizing point on the SEP) unless there is a specific constraint pushing the firm off the SEP. However, if production or input demand decisions that violate these efficiency assumptions are made this would provide another reason for observed productivity change – moving toward an isoquant from a technically inefficient point, or toward the SEP from an allocatively inefficient point, to approach best practice production processes.

This implies that the curves drawn are "envelopes" of the true data points, say for different firms or countries, if such inefficiencies exist. The actual data points in Figure 2b will, for example, all lie on or above the drawn cost frontier. So if a firm is producing at, say, point E in period 0, part of the observed cost change between periods 0 and 1 may involve moving closer *to* the associated frontier rather than shifting *with* the frontier.

As noted above, in traditional productivity analysis inefficiency issues have not been pursued in depth, since one might think competitive forces would motivate (long run) efficiency, at least on average. Also, it is often the case in empirical application, particularly for developed economies and when a detailed production model is used for analysis, that little remains to be explained by "inefficiency". But, this still adds another layer to the reasons productivity growth might potentially be observed, that should be identified separately from other productive characteristics for construction of interpretable performance measures.[16]

---

[16] As noted above, this literature is overviewed in Chapter 8, which provides only a brief introduction to the efficiency literature but includes references for further exploration.

5.   MARKET AND REGULATORY STRUCTURE

Although technological or cost structure and resulting productive performance is the main focus in this text, economic performance is also based on other aspects of production processes such as market and regulatory structure.

Market structure issues are typically thought of as output-side rather than cost-side. That is, they are based on the output-demand structure facing the firm or industry, although they may also involve input supply if, for example, monopsony or oligopsony power allows input price endogeneity. Regulatory structure issues sometimes involve the creation of markets for non-marketed goods. They may also have to do with constraints on production technology and behavior to inhibit (or provide incentives for) certain behavioral patterns (input use or output production).

The incorporation of market structure may be developed by appending output demand information and resulting output supply decisions to the input choice or cost function framework represented in the figures in the previous sub-section. For a competitive firm (in the output market) this requires, as in intermediate microeconomics courses, adding a horizontal line representing a given output price to Figure 2b. Only period 1 is diagrammed for simplicity, and short- and long-run marginal costs (SMC and LMC), which provide the basis for output supply decisions, are explicitly represented (the S and L subscripts denote short and long run, respectively).

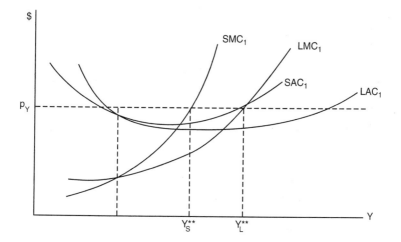

Figure 3a. Adding Output Price to the Cost Diagram (perfect competition)

The output supply decision – whether short- or long-run – is based on the p_Y=MC optimization condition from the theory of the firm (where p_Y is output price and MC is marginal cost). This results in the long run profit maximizing level of output Y** in Figure 3a for time period 1. This optimum level of output is different than the "optimum" discussed in the context of capacity utilization; it is based on profit maximization given an output price rather than representation of the cost-minimizing level of output for a particular capital stock level.

This extension can be formalized as transforming the cost function into a profit function, which depends on p_Y rather than Y, so output choice may be represented. This is also, however, theoretically equivalent to adding the p_Y=MC condition to the information contained in the cost function[17]. Profit maximizing behavior is not inconsistent with cost minimization for a particular output level, since that output level could have been based on profit maximization. It just adds another dimension to the behavioral model.

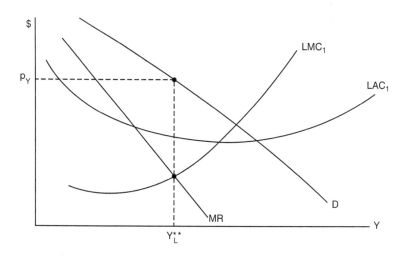

Figure 3b. Adding an Output Demand Function to the Cost Representation

More interesting implications for economic performance analysis emerge when an imperfectly competitive market structure prevails, reflected in a downward sloping output demand function. If, for example, monopoly power exists, as in Figure 3b for the long run, the firm's decision is based on equating marginal revenue (MR, the firm's marginal benefits) and marginal costs. However, *social* marginal benefits are reflected on the market demand curve, which indicates consumers' valuation of the product.

---

[17] This provides the basis for the main structural model developed in Chapter 6

A similar distinction may be made for inputs with upward sloping supply curves to the firm, so that marginal and average factor cost differ. In this case the marginal social cost of the product, in terms of resource use, is reflected by the average cost on the input supply function, but the firm will respond according the the marginal factor cost.

Since the MR=MC equality for output implies lower production and higher profit levels than the p_Y=MC equivalence, this is typically considered an inefficiency resulting from market power that includes both a deadweight loss and a redistribution from consumers to the firm in terms of profits. This therefore should be taken into account when evaluating economic performance and efficiency.

However, additional insights about the evaluation of such market power and its implications emerge from the linkage between the technological or cost and market structure. In particular, the firm may face a downward sloping demand curve, and yet make no (or very low) profits. This results if the market structure is monopolistically competitive.

In addition, there is a close linkage between the additional profitability implied by market power, and the negative marginal profits resulting from a p_Y=MC condition if scale economies exist. That is, if the technological structure embodies scale economies, MC<AC (where AC is average or unit costs), so if p_Y=MC losses will be made. Thus, in the presence of scale economies, one would expect a departure from the usual marginal condition that should not necessarily be considered market power, or at least an abuse of market power.

Short and long run MC must also be distinguished for appropriate evaluation of market structure and power. Although a competitive firm would be expected to produce according to the p_Y=MC rule in both the short and long run, this could mean negative short run profits if demand were sufficiently low. Ultimately, in order to be economically viable, at least zero profits must be generated.

The non-negative profit condition must also recognize all valid economic costs, such as returns to both capital and entrepreneurial input. Thus, the implications of behavioral assumptions such as the p_Y=MC condition should be carefully scrutinized when using these models to generate measures and guide policy about market power.

This discussion also has implications for some types of regulation, since industries experiencing scale economies are likely to also be concentrated. The rationale for considering this "bad" (or economically inefficient), and thus a justification for imposing regulation to counteract the problem, requires a full assessment of the underlying cost structure for support. Technological, market, and regulatory structure are inextricably entwined.

Additional impacts of regulatory structure may stem from the existence of public goods, non-marketed products (such as pollution), and informational constraints.[18] In this case the implied "market failures" may be accommodated by regulation. However, the resulting regulation may not be fully optimal, since competitive markets are not generating the final solution, thus imposing both private and social costs.

Evaluating such situations requires representing the costs of the constraints. For example, restrictions on pesticide use due to concern about their environmental impacts, or on food safety to protect consumers, impose economic costs on the producing firms. Recognizing both these costs, and the corresponding marginal benefits that are typically not measured (the "output" of a cleaner environment is not reflected in measured output), may be important for evaluation of the economic performance of some firms or industries, as well as providing evidence about the associated social costs.

This requires including the inputs subject to constraints in the cost function similar to the case of capital constraints. This implies both additional dimensions to the input specification and some restrictions on optimization that will inhibit adjustment of the inputs subject to regulation to their long run desired levels given the perceived input prices, as for K above.

The extra costs will, however, not disappear in the long run, since the input level is not under the control of the firm. Thus, the extra cost associated with the constraint (keeping the firm above the long run cost curve) should be interpreted as a direct cost of regulation; the effective long run cost curves are shifted up.

All of the notions raised above have their counterparts in intermediate microeconomic theory, as is evident by the diagrammatic treatment and motivation in terms of basic production, cost and profit functions. However, if this structure is to be used as a foundation to measure the various factors inderlying firm technology, behavior, and resulting economic performance, it must be further formalized and econometrically implemented.

In this text we will develop an implementable theoretical framework in which the technological, market and regulatory characteristics driving economic performance may potentially be incorporated and measured. This involves formally extending the structural theoretical model we have begun to conceptualize in this chapter to reflect these additional factors, and to identify their independent impact on productivity growth measures. To begin moving in this direction, we now proceed to an initial overview of standard techniques for measurement of such productivity growth indicators.

---

[18]Such that, for example, subsidizing export market in the short term when information gathering takes place is justified. Food safety issues also fall into this category, since markets do not exist due to lack of consumer information about potential hazards.

6.   BASICS OF PRODUCTIVITY MEASUREMENT

Although many limitations of the basic technical change/productivity growth framework from Section 3 have been raised, this framework remains the springboard from which productivity growth measurement is typically motivated. To initiate our development of productivity growth measures we will thus start with this structure, assuming the simple model is appropriate.

Economic models provide a foundation to guide our thinking about *what* needs to be measured. Our initial motivation for measurement should thus stem from Figure 1. Our productivity growth question becomes: "Between any two time periods, can we identify the output increase possible from a given amount of inputs, or the input diminution possible for a given amount of output?"

As we have alluded to above, to accomplish this we have to impute what happens with one change, as we have pictured, from data that includes many changes. That is, both inputs and output will have changed between two data points (say, for subsequent years). Thus, it is necessary to impute what output (costs) would have been if inputs (output) had remained the same to generate the primal (dual) measure. This is complicated by additional factors that must be distinguished for effective interpretation of productive and economic performance, which provide the focus of both nonparametric econometric productivity growth analyses.

Essentially, our question thus becomes one of how a basic isoquant diagram may be translated into empirically implementable measures.

For the primal output-based notion of productivity growth, we need to develop a structure to measure the difference between Y'_0 and Y''_1. This reflects the potential production levels associated with the technologies available in periods 0 and 1, using period 0 input levels K_0 and L_0. Indexes representing such a comparison are typically specified in terms of rates of output growth between two time periods.

Initially, this takes the form of measuring $d\ln Y/dt$, where dt denotes a change in technology or time, t_1-t_0 and $d\ln Y$ is $\ln Y''_1$-$\ln Y'_0$, and where the logarithmic difference by definition reflects a rate of growth.[19] That is, if t_0 is 1997 and t_1 is 1998, we measure the percentage change in output between 1998 and 1997 as $\%\Delta Y \approx \ln Y_{1998}$-$\ln Y_{1997}$. (where Δ implies a discrete change and the logarithms place the computation in a continuous format, so these two expressions are approximately equal).

---

[19] Note that this (and the following) treatment ignores the distinction between discrete and continuous measures. In most cases the theoretical framework is specified in terms of continuous time but application to the data, of course, requires the use of discrete numbers. The potential biases from this will be small if fluctuations in the data are not substantial.

This measured difference does not, however, necessarily represent the concepts of interest in Figure 1. It is not the observed output change between two periods that underlies productivity growth, but the change corresponding to a given vector of inputs (net output growth). Since observed data do not hold inputs fixed, the measure must be adapted to capture the output change independently of input growth (or possibly other changes in the production structure implicitly assumed fixed in the analysis).

More formally, say productivity is represented by an output to input ratio Y/V (where V is a measure of aggregated K and L inputs). Then productivity growth should be reflected by the change in this ratio over time, $(\ln Y''_1 - \ln Y'_0) - (\ln V_1 - \ln V_0)$, rather than just the growth rate of output.

This may be motivated by the logarithmic derivative from the production function $Y(V,t)$, $\partial \ln Y/\partial t = d\ln Y/dt - d\ln V/dt \approx \%\Delta Y/\Delta t - \%\Delta V/\Delta t$.[20] This expression removes the impacts of changing input use, and of substitution among inputs if V is not a single input, from the implied measure of efficiency change. Thus a measure of 0.02 means output could have increased by 2% with no input increase. It is therefore broadly consistent with the graphical development of the concept of productivity growth above, and provides the basis for the traditional growth accounting productivity growth measure developed in Chapter 2.[21]

Similarly (and equivalently), a dual cost measure of productivity growth can be specified as $\ln TC_1 - \ln TC_0 = d\ln TC/dt$, where TC_0 is the minimum total cost associated with Y'_0, and TC_1 corresponds to the cost level on the new isocost line tangent to the Y'_1 isoquant. Again, this cost change reflecting productivity growth should correspond only to the impact of technology change with all other exogenous factors constant. It must be independent of observed changes in output and the prices of inputs.

Therefore, in practice, these changes must be purged from the observed total cost change analogously to the adaptation of the output measure. This results in the cost diminution expression: $\partial \ln TC/\partial t = \%\Delta TC/\Delta t - \%\Delta Y/\Delta t - \%\Delta P/\Delta t = d\ln TC/dt - d\ln Y/dt - d\ln P/dt$, where TC is total costs $TC(Y,P,t)$, P is aggregate input price and $d\ln P/dt$ is a weighted average of P changes.[22]

[20] The theoretical basis for this expression, as well as that for the corresponding dual measure below, is developed in detail in Chapter 2.

[21] Note that productivity growth measures with a strong index number basis sometimes measure this more similarly to the capacity utilization indicators as Y''_1/Y'_0 (adjusted for changes in V). This exponentiation of the usual measure $(\ln(Y''_1/Y'_0) = \ln Y''_1 - \ln Y'_0 = d\ln Y/dt)$ avoids some approximation problems. Thus it is more precise than the usual logarithmic measure. See Diewert and Morrison [1990] for further discussion.

[22] The treatment here provides only a motivation for the idea and does not deal with the differences between derivatives and differentials, or continuous and discrete time, in a rigorous manner. In addition, the cost expression is often written without the $d\ln Y/dt$ component, implying constant returns to scale, as we will see below. The issue here is the

Similarly to above, a resulting measure of -0.02 would indicate costs could have declined by 2% with no change in input prices or output production.

Productivity growth measures are thus expressed in the form of a residual of output growth or cost decline less the impacts of specifically recognized exogenous changes that should not be included as efficiency determinants. This measure ideally reflects only changes in technology, but, as developed so far, does not recognize any changes in the production structure except input level and price changes (and thus substitution).

The resulting measure is therefore denoted a "residual" measure that subsumes any other productive characteristics ignored in the simple graphical analysis of Section 3. This productivity growth residual, often termed the Solow residual if measured from the primal perspective, has thus been called a "measure of our ignorance".

This implies a serious lack of interpretability of the measure. This limitation has stimulated much productivity research devoted to decomposing the residual "technical change" measure to purge it of other identifiable changes in the market or production structure, such as those we have raised in Sections 4 and 5 of this chapter. That is, to interpret this measure as technical change, as suggested by the original theoretical motivation, we must separately identify production characteristics such as capacity utilization and scale economies. Accomplishing this takes a form analogous to that for substitution, and will be dealt with through adjustments to the traditional measure in subsequent chapters.

For example, the basic theoretical framework developed in this chapter can be used to introduce, albeit in a limited way, the idea of adjusting productivity growth measures to identify the impact of capacity utilization. Essentially the observed output change is not only a combination of output and input growth (recognized in productivity growth measures), but also input *use* or "effort" levels (utilization). We must therefore determine how much potential output change to allocate to the fixity or utilization effect, to reproduce just the technical change impact.

More specifically, based on the notation developed above, observed output growth will be a combination of the difference between Y'_0 and Y''_1 (productivity growth) and the difference between observed and capacity output, Y and Y^*. The latter should not be attributed to technical change. To identify this we need a way to compare different levels of output, based on two observed data points. One of the Y output levels, Y^*, must thus be imputed as a steady state value, which is unobservable.

---

idea of adjusting for observed changes that are held constant in the theory. The technical distinctions will be dealt with more carefully in Chapter 2, and a more formal theoretical basis overviewed in Chapter 9.

To measure this we need to construct a Y/Y* ratio (capacity utilization measure) to indicate the difference between actual and potential equilibrium output, given all available input stocks. This involves finding a way to measure the tangency between the short- and long-run average cost curves, and thus the corresponding output level Y*, to compare to observed output. Similarly, on the dual cost side, taking account of capacity utilization requires assessing the *costs* associated with these output levels.

It is difficult to construct a justifiable economic measure of capacity utilization without an empirically implementable structural model of firm behavior in which to determine the shapes of short and long run cost functions, and thus to identify Y*. Such an adaptation of productivity growth measures must therefore be theoretically conceptualized, empirically implemented, and the associated indicators measured. This is true for any production or economic characteristic that we wish to extract independently from the overall "measure of our ignorance".

The remainder of this book is devoted to conceptualization and formalization of implementable models of the production and economic characteristics identified above, that can be used to generate measures of the different "pieces of the economic performance puzzle", and thus facilitate measurement and interpretation of economic performance.

7.   FURTHER REMARKS

This chapter has overviewed the conceptual and basic theoretical foundations for modeling and measuring economic performance. We will now start using this base to develop an integrated framework in which to assess relationships among various aspects of economic performance. We will first elaborate the traditional methodology for productivity growth measurement, to determine to what extent this framework facilitates interpretation of the measures and analyses of the theoretical linkages among performance indicators. We will then discuss restrictions embodied in the traditional approaches, and methods of adapting the procedures to more appropriately deal with these issues. As we proceed, we will continue to explore how a structural model of firm behavior can provide a framework in which consistent measures of economic performance indicators and their determinants can be obtained.

Chapter 2

Traditional Productivity Growth Measurement

The word "productivity" has widely varying connotations because the word is used so extensively and loosely. Although it is generally understood that increased productivity is somehow advantageous, most people would find it difficult to clearly define the notion of productivity growth.

The concept of productivity stems from the amount of output that can be produced from a given amount of input. Productivity growth can, therefore, result in an increase in the output that can be produced for a given level of input, or a decrease in the input (and therefore costs) necessary to produce a given amount of output, as outlined in Chapter 1. In this sense productivity growth is desirable; the efficiency of production has increased, so society can obtain more goods given available scarce resources. This straightforward idea is, however, not as easy to formalize and measure as it is to express, since observed changes in output production and input use have so many underlying determinants.

In this chapter we look at traditional methods of productivity growth measurement and their theoretical basis, to see in more detail what is really being represented by the resulting measures. We consider what interpretation is possible from these measures and what limitations are implied, to provide a basis for extensions of the traditional methods and linkages with other performance indicators in the following chapters.

In the first section we outline the earliest and most easily computable measures of productivity growth, single factor measures. The simplicity of these measures, however, generates interpretation problems. Possibly the most fundamental problem stems from ignoring substitution between factors of production. Refinement of these methods to include substitution, resulting in multi- or total-factor productivity growth measures, is elaborated in Section 2. Nonparametric extensions to this "growth accounting" basis for productivity growth measurement, to recognize various aspects of production structure entangled in the productivity growth residual, are overviewed in Section 3.

We begin to move toward direct representation of these production characteristics, within a full implementable micro-production-theory model, in the formalization of productivity growth as a technical change measure in Section 4. The fundamental duality between the output (primal) and cost representations of technical change is explored in Section 5, with a view toward linking other aspects of the technological structure in subsequent chapters. Section 6 then begins to delve into refinements of this framework to incorporate complexities associated with "real world" technical change and productivity, including distinctions between disembodied and embodied, and neutral and non-neutral, technical change.

1.   SINGLE-FACTOR PRODUCTIVITY MEASURES

One of the difficulties that is immediately obvious when attempting to measure productivity is finding relevant definitions of "output" and "input". Sometimes a firm produces only one type of product. Even in this case, however, "goods" or "bads" that could potentially be termed output may be produced using the inputs hired. For example, pollution may be produced, causing society to be worse off. For a full accounting of the production of a firm, therefore, these bads must be taken into account. From the input perspective, firms may purchase equipment that does not produce output for sale, but does reduce pollution produced, satisfy legal regulations, or otherwise provide a contribution that is not explicitly linked to measured production of goods and services. These contributions are, however, assets for society that perhaps should be taken into account when considering the productivity of the firm's inputs.

Many firms also produce multiple outputs using the same inputs. In this case it is difficult to measure output effectively because changes in the composition of output may affect input use independently of true productivity growth. This is particularly true when joint products exist (output complementarities that cause scope economies prevail, as discussed further in Chapter 4).

The standard method of dealing with this problem is to aggregate the various outputs into a single output quantity index. This may be justifiable under some conditions, but becomes increasingly questionable over periods of substantial relative price and quality change. The problem is further aggravated when productivity is measured for a large sector of the economy, so outputs must be aggregated over a number of firms or even industries.[23]

---

[23]Issues of aggregation and measurement are dealt with in further detail in Chapter 10.

Defining the relevant input base is also a problem. The first issue that arises is what inputs should be taken into account. To avoid double counting of materials inputs (particularly for macro aggregates), productivity accounting is often based on value added output, which is defined as the contribution of capital and labor inputs. By construction, therefore, capital and labor become the only inputs under consideration.

Researchers often expand this base to encompass the concept of gross output, particularly for more micro studies, which includes intermediate materials as part of the input measure. Often the inputs recognized for such a treatment are capital, labor, energy and non-energy intermediate materials. However, inputs such as purchased services, or outsourcing, have become increasingly consequential and may be important to identify separately.

Other inputs also might well be separately distinguished, including expenditures explicitly targeted to increase future production or demand such as R&D and advertising. Different types of capital and labor may also be identified, such as high-tech capital or skilled labor, which raises issues of input composition (and embodied technical change) within the standard input categories.[24]

For productivity growth measurement, which inputs provide the basis for comparing output and input growth is an important issue. However, single factor measures focus on the productivity of a single input, which implicitly suggests that this is the only scarce input. Such measures ignore substitution of this input for others in response to relative price changes, and differences in technical efficiency and input composition at different scales of output production. More complete multifactor measures, embodying changes in the use of other inputs, provide more clearly interpretable indicators of overall productivity but are more complex to motivate and construct.

Often the choice of input for measurement of single-factor productivity growth is determined by the application the productivity measure is designed for. For example, if wage negotiations are being held, the productivity of labor might be important. Since labor is the focus of the negotiations, the scarcity of that input, and its resulting level of compensation, is the primary consideration. Even in this case, however, if labor productivity increases are attributable to capital investment, resulting in more or better machines per worker, the firm engaged in the negotiations will have reason to argue that this augmentation of productivity should be reflected in the return to capital rather than labor.

---

[24] Any capital input is, however, difficult to measure effectively, due to its durable nature; service flows for the capital stock, and its associated rental values, must be imputed (see Chapter 10).

Therefore, although single-factor measures may sometimes be relevant, application and interpretation of single factor measures is often questionable. We must distinguish these simpler measures from more comprehensive measures in order not to make inappropriate conclusions. That is, in most cases one would not want to interpret increases in labor productivity as representing an overall increase in welfare. It may instead be due to changes in input composition from relative technological efficiency or price changes.

One of the first applications of single factor productivity (SFP) measurement was in agriculture, where productivity is motivated in terms of yield per acre, or the output possible from a given amount of land. [25] This single factor measure is constructed by measuring quantity of agricultural product or output as Y, and acres of land as A, and computing the index Y/A as a measure of the productivity level.

Productivity therefore is said to have increased when this ratio rises, which implies a positive value for the measure %Δ(Y/A)/Δt $\approx$ dln (Y/A)/dt = dln Y/dt-dln A/dt (where t denotes time). This productivity growth measure (the "residual" that remains when changes in A are removed or accommodated, as motivated in the preceding chapter) appears easily interpretable since it expresses growth in terms of percentage changes between time periods. It embodies, however, many different market and technological changes that may have occurred between two time periods but are attributed simply to the productivity of land in this simple measure.

More specifically, in terms of input substitution, this single factor measure implicitly considers land the only scarce input; it ignores changes in everything other than acreage as causes of the full output growth (or decline) observed between time periods. Thus, increases in the use of labor, fertilizer, capital machinery or any other input will be picked up as unidentified causes of the output increase, or a component of the residual.

These changes are due, however, to well-defined characteristics of the production process – additional use of other scarce inputs. Therefore, even if yield per acre increases it is not possible to say whether productivity as a whole has increased, since this measure focuses on only one component of costs and thus efficiency. As emphasized above, this seriously limits the interpretability of the measure as a welfare indicator.

Similar problems pertain to the later energy productivity emphasis of technocracy advocates in the 1920s and 1930s[26] and net energy analysts in the 1970s-1980s. Their focus was to determine the efficiency of energy use, which required constructing measures of the output to energy (E) ratio Y/E.

---

[25]See Ruttan [1954,1956] for an early example of this type of exercise.
[26]See Berndt [1982] for an interesting analysis of this perspective.

Productivity or efficiency growth in this context can be said to have increased if dln Y/dt-dln E/dt is positive.

Again, although this concept is useful for some types of analysis, it does not reflect a full accounting of productivity changes because it focuses solely on the scarcity of energy. It does not recognize the substitution of other types of scarce resources for energy by firms, which generates this increase in Y/E. Therefore, no matter how expensive it is in terms of use of other inputs, any small saving in energy use is considered an improvement in performance. Clearly, this is a limited economic performance indicator.

As noted above, labor productivity measures are also single-factor productivity measures, although they are still sometimes interpreted as if they were more general indicators. Labor productivity growth is defined as an increase in output per labor hour or laborer (L). Formally the productivity level is defined as Y/L and productivity growth is therefore dln Y/dt - dln L/dt. This measure again disregards the fact that part of an increase in Y/L could be a result of, for example, moving toward more capital-, land- or energy-intensive production, none of which is necessarily indicative of better economic performance.

Conflicting interpretations may be consistent with increasing measured "productivity" in this context. For example, as suggested above, increases in wages relative to the price of capital or energy might cause substitution away from labor. Resulting higher labor productivity might be interpreted by some as a justification for further wage increases, rather than a *result*, in this circumstance, of a compositional change induced by increases in wages above labor's initial marginal product, resulting in a decrease in labor use.

In this case workers as a whole may not truly benefit from their increasing productivity. That is, the standard reasoning that labor productivity calculations measure the "fruitfulness" of labor, so people are by definition better off when labor productivity increases (implying less work is necessary to obtain the same amount of goods and services), may not be entirely legitimate.[27] The marginal person is simply more "productive" because employment is reduced and diminishing returns exists.

Finally, output per unit of capital (K) is sometimes computed as a utilization indicator. The underlying idea is that if Y/K increases, the firm is utilizing capital more heavily and therefore approaching its maximum potential. Peaks in this measure can therefore be thought of as points where capacity output is reached given the available capital stock. Although this single factor measure is generally motivated more in the context of capital or

---

[27]Note that not only productivity analysts but also labor economists have recognized the interpretation problems with single factor productivity measures. This is evident, for example, by comparing Rees [1980] and Griliches [1980].

capacity utilization than productivity, the measure clearly has productivity growth connotations – in this case capital productivity.

Although these indexes (and related measures which may be defined for other inputs if they are separately distinguished) are limited in their individual interpretative power, in combination they provide a basis for decomposition of output growth into the different forces causing that growth. That is the focus of much of the "growth-accounting" productivity literature, including publications from statistical agencies such as the Bureau of Labor Statistics in the U.S (BLS). In these studies it is quite common to specify single factor productivity growth measures for all recognized inputs, in order to decompose the overall picture of changes in production processes.[28]

Such indexes might, for example, indicate increases in labor productivity over the past couple of decades, but also that much of this may be attributed to increased capital intensity (and also ultimately capital composition changes toward more technically efficient high-tech capital, as discussed further in subsequent chapters). Determining whether this reflects an increase or decrease in overall or multifactor productivity requires combining the single factor measures, which is the purpose of multifactor productivity measures.

For a graphical illustration of SFP measurement, consider Figure 4 (U.S. BLS [1983], Chart 4) which shows output (Y), hours (L) and output per hour for U.S. manufacturing, 1948-81.[29] The explanation for output growth provided by the purging of labor growth is evident from the lower output per hour (Y/L) than output (Y) growth rate after about 1960. Until that time L was quite flat (in terms of its secular trend, although it exhibited cyclical fluctuations). Further adaptation for capital use provides additional insights about these patterns, since growth in capital tended to be faster than in output, suggesting increased capital intensity and a source of labor productivity increases, as seen in the next section.

---

[28]Harper and Gullickson [1989] use an extended version of the growth accounting methods outlined below, based on share weights from a parametric translog estimation process, to assess the contribution to multifactor productivity growth of capital, labor, energy, materials and purchased services. See also U.S. BLS [1983] for an assessment of the contributions of different inputs to productivity growth.

[29] Although this example is already somewhat dated, it provides an example that is consistent with the extension to multifactor measures in the next sub-section. This publication was one of the first government statistical publications I am aware of that pursued this important extension. It also provides a very clear treatment of how these types of numbers are constructed, interpreted and used.

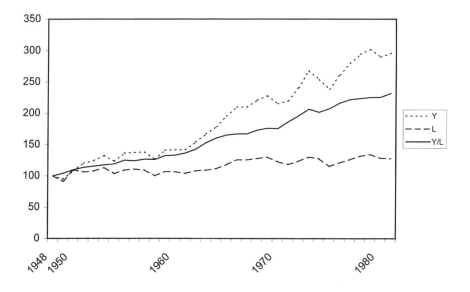

Figure 4. Manufacturing Sector Y, L and Y/L

2.   MULTIFACTOR PRODUCTIVITY MEASURES

None of the single factor productivity growth measures are particularly illuminating as a measure of overall productivity change. The measured productivity growth residual is a combination of technical change and other responses that we might want to isolate independently. These include not only substitution but also changes in capacity utilization, and internal and external cost or scale effects. Although ultimately it will be useful to identify the contribution to the residual of these various technological, behavioral, and market factors, the most obvious difficulty in interpreting productivity growth measures is that of input substitution.[30]

To eradicate the portion of the productivity residual that can be explained by substitution, the contributions of different inputs are generally combined by weighting their growth rates by their revenue shares, resulting in the overall measure of productivity growth:

2.1) $\varepsilon_{Yt} = \partial \ln Y / \partial t = d \ln Y / dt - \Sigma_j S_j \, d \ln v_j / dt,$

---

[30]Note that other components of the technology, like returns to scale, might also be included in this residual. This will be discussed further later.

where v_j is the quantity of input j, S_j is the share of input j in the value of output, $p_j v_j / p_Y Y$, p_j is the price of v_j, and p_Y is the price of Y.[31] This residual measure, which is designed to represent what one might mean by an overall increase in productivity given scarce inputs, has alternatively been denoted an index of growth in total- or multi-factor productivity (MFP). I will adopt the latter terminology, which is also used by the BLS.[32]

Note that with some rewriting (2.1) becomes:

2.2) $\varepsilon_{Yt} = \Sigma_j S_j [d\ln Y/dt - d\ln v_j/dt]$,

as long as the shares sum to one. Since the components of this measure in the square brackets represent single-factor productivity growth rates, this makes it clear that MFP growth is a weighted average of individual single factor productivity growth. Therefore, if the single factor measures grow at the same rate, this implies a common rate of productivity growth.[33] Otherwise, inputs with a lower share have a smaller impact on the overall measure.

Some further manipulation explicitly indicates how the single factor measures embody both technical change and input substitution. Since $d\ln Y/dt = \varepsilon_{Yt} + \Sigma_j S_j \, d\ln v_j/dt$ from (2.1), for example, if $d\ln L/dt$ is subtracted from the left hand side of this expression, and $\Sigma_j S_j \, d\ln L/dt$ (where $\Sigma_j S_j = 1$) is subtracted from the right hand side, this becomes:

2.3) $d\ln Y/dt - d\ln L/dt = \varepsilon_{Yt} + \Sigma_j S_j [d\ln v_j/dt - d\ln L/dt]$.

The labor SFP measure therefore represents the effects of both overall technical progress and substitution, through the change in the v_j to L ratio (input composition). This reflects the potential for labor productivity growth to arise from increased investment in capital plant and equipment (or more intensive use of any other input) relative to labor.

The multifactor productivity index ε_{Yt} is often termed an accounting measure of productivity growth because econometric estimation is not required to compute the necessary components of the index. Straightforward

---

[31] The distinction between revenue and cost shares will be discussed in later sections.

[32] Note that the single factor productivity measures cannot be interpreted directly as a decomposition of the multifactor measure since the single-factor measures do not share-weight the input growth. The substitution implications reflected in the share-weights are required for decomposition of determinants of output change. This slight inconsistency between the single factor and multifactor procedures has the potential to generate some confusion, and also raises questions about the measurement of the shares.

[33] This could result from the existence of Hicks neutral technical change, so isoquants do not "twist" when they change over time. Further discussion of technical change neutrality and biases is provided in Section 6 of this chapter.

accounting or data analysis methods can be used to construct measures of the prices and quantities of inputs and output, so they can simply be added.

U.S. BLS [1983] estimates of the MFP measure and its components for U.S. manufacturing from 1948 to 1981, provided in Table 1, are graphed in Figure 5. The measures graphed in this case are Y/L and Y/K, along with the combined multifactor measure. Note that Y/K is quite flat (in terms of the secular trend, although quite a lot of cyclical variation is evident), indicating that capital growth has kept up with output growth much more that has labor growth (as seen above). More observed output growth is explained by input increases than was apparent in the labor productivity measures, so the MFP measure falls below that for labor productivity.

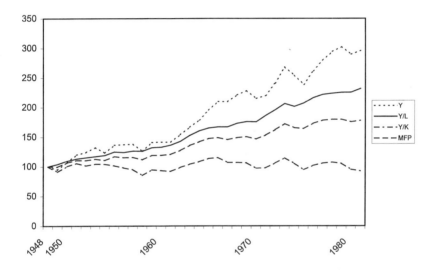

Figure 5. Manufacturing Sector Y/L, Y/K and Multifactor Productivity

The indexes themselves, in Table 1, provide a somewhat different perspective. The measures presented in the tables comprise the different components of an overall "growth accounting" framework. Such a decomposition is often termed "sourcing" the output growth into its components, or decomposing the growth rate. Note that the indexes are normalized to 100 in 1977. Normalization (to 100 or 1) is typical of aggregate indexes presented for productivity computations, since the growth rates in real terms may be directly inferred from these indexes.[34]

---

[34] The information presented in the figure above was instead normalized to 100 in 1947, to facilitate interpretation of the observed trends.

The quantity indexes represent real Y, L, and K independent of price changes that are contained in their dollar values. They are constructed, however, so that the value is maintained. That is, the quantity indexes are implicitly created by index number procedures, so that $p_Y \cdot Y$ remains equal to the measured dollar value of output for each year.[35]

Table 1. SFP and MFP Indexes

Period	Y	Y/L	Y/K	MFP
1948	35.8	45.1	94.4	56.2
...				
1965	69.8	74.5	107.3	82.8
1966	75.1	75.3	108.7	83.7
1967	75.0	75.3	101.1	81.8
1968	79.1	78.0	101.1	83.7
1969	81.7	79.3	100.5	84.6
1970	77.0	79.1	91.8	82.3
1971	78.7	83.9	92.4	86.0
1972	86.2	88.2	99.9	91.1
1973	95.9	93.0	108.2	96.8
1974	91.0	90.8	99.6	93.0
1975	85.4	93.4	89.4	92.2
1976	93.6	97.5	96.1	97.1
1977	100.0	100.0	100.0	100.0
1978	105.3	100.9	101.5	101.0
1979	108.2	101.6	99.5	101.0
1980	103.6	101.7	90.0	98.6
1981	105.9	104.5	87.5	99.9
			-2.6	
Annual %Δ				
1948-73	4.0	2.9	0.6	2.2
1973-81	1.2	1.5		0.4
			-2.6	
1948-81	3.3	2.6	-0.2	1.8

Although the L and K growth data provide some information about factors underlying observed output growth, and thus facilitate refining the productivity growth measure to represent net input use, many other potential "pieces of the puzzle" are clearly embodied in the resulting MFP measures.

For example, these measures are based on a value-added framework, which avoids recognizing substitution among L, K and intermediate inputs.[36]

---

[35] Some discussion of index number procedures for such aggregation (aggregating inputs using Divisia or Törnqvist index number formulas) appears later in this chapter, and further elaboration of aggregation methods and index numbers is provided in Ch. 10.

[36] Note that if the analysis focuses only on the K and L inputs the measure of output should be consistent with this assumption; it should be a value-added output measure with the contribution of materials inputs removed.

Often, however, multifactor measures *are* based on a broader definition of inputs, in order to include as many of firms' costs and substitution possibilities as possible, thus augmenting interpretability.

Another issue that is important to raise in the context of MFP measures, due to their reliance on input shares, concerns the deviation between total costs and revenues. Such discrepancies may arise due to fixities (SMC≠LMC), non-constant returns to scale (MC≠AC), or imperfect competition (p_Y≠MC). Mis-measurement or mis-specification of inputs may also occur, so that not all costs are taken into account; R&D, advertising, land acquisitions, inventory holdings and other costly choices made by the firm may be ignored. The revenue shares will then not add to one.

This problem is sometimes dealt with simply by constructing the capital measure as a residual. Any revenues not reflected in returns to other inputs are therefore imputed to some type of return to the capital stock. This is somewhat justifiable for accommodating problems related to ignoring inputs, such as land and inventories that may be considered components of the capital stock. But theoretically it imputes any returns to other market or technological characteristics, such as market power and scale economies, to the capital stock, which is not valid.

When this issue is not resolved by data construction, it may in some cases be finessed simply by working with cost rather than revenue shares. If total costs are defined as the sum of the payments to all the factors under consideration, the sum of the cost shares will then equal one by construction. However, the measure is then implicitly based on a cost-side, rather than output-side, productivity growth perspective. The latter is the conceptual motivation underlying single-factor productivity measures and the usual extension to multifactor techniques. The resulting measure is also not, strictly speaking, correct; the cost motivation implies that dln Y/dt should be weighted by the revenue to cost ratio. This distinction between cost (dual) and output (primal) measures will be developed below.

The residual measure of multifactor productivity growth ε_{Yt} thus embodies the impacts of many aspects of the technological and market structure, even though substitution effects are recognized. This is the basis for its characterization as a "measure of our ignorance", as emphasized in Chapter 1.

The assumptions about production processes motivating the construction of the MFP measure implicitly incorporate a number of restrictions, and raise many important issues that should be clarified. Some of these arise from the refinements involved in developing the MFP from the SFP measures, since share weights are required for the analysis. The growth rate no longer is based on a simple increase in a quantity ratio (such as Y/L).

Untangling the impacts of the various restrictions implied by standard MFP growth measurement procedures is not straightforward. These simple accounting measures are based only on data manipulation, and thus rely only on the information available from the raw data. But numerous factors potentially affecting productivity are not directly observable.

In particular, relaxing the implicit assumptions of instantaneous adjustment, constant returns to scale and perfect competition, which are embodied in the accounting measures, requires either heroic assumptions about the appropriateness and consistency of *ad hoc* measures, or a parametric framework. Adapting for other phenomena, such as the impacts of changes in regulation, has been accomplished somewhat more effectively in the accounting framework, although a more complete structural model is useful to facilitate measurement and interpretation. We will now turn to a brief overview of attempts to deal with these issues within the confines of the nonparametric approach, before turning to a parametric framework.

3. GROWTH ACCOUNTING: ADAPTATIONS TO THE NONPARAMETRIC FRAMEWORK

Many economic factors affect firms' technological and cost structure. Perhaps the most complete studies incorporating these factors into nonparametric measures, in the sense of spanning a broad range of issues, were carried out by Denison [1979, 1985]. In this section we briefly overview the types of adaptations to the standard measures to identify the impacts of these factors suggested by these and other related studies.

The general framework Denison developed and used for a number of studies is a further extension of the "growth accounting" notion outlined above. This methodology is designed to decompose total output growth in the economy into different potential determinants. The idea is that the resulting components "explain" evidence of output increases in the economy, purging the "measure of our ignorance" of any identifiable factors that affect the production process, so whatever is left may be called technical change.

Early research in this area attempted such an adaptation of productivity growth measures by characterizing their impacts directly in terms of the factor inputs, and adjusting the data accordingly. This was the basis for dissension among a group of researchers in the 1950's when the large productivity growth residual found by Solow [1957] was "explained" by some researchers by direct adjustments of capital measures.[37]

---

[37]For example, see Jorgenson and Griliches [1967].

In most cases, however, these adjustments tend to be rather *ad hoc*. Therefore it was fairly easy for dispute to emerge among productivity growth analysts about the appropriate adjustment methodology.

Denison built on the earlier work on adaptation of input measures by first re-specifying labor and capital input measures to reflect characteristics such as the composition of the labor force, and then computing a residual called the "semi-residual" that is based on these "effective" input measures. He subsequently identified more than twenty additional factors that could affect productivity growth, which he proceeded to use to adjust this semi-residual to obtain a final measure of "advances in knowledge".

Unfortunately, as we have seen, a multitude of different factors may affect input effectiveness and firm behavior (and therefore measured output) independently of technical change, and they are extremely difficult to isolate reliably from the raw data. Some measures of these factors can be obtained directly from published statistics such as national income accounts, although they may not directly be based on relevant economic reasoning, or be consistent with other measured components. In addition, factors such as returns to scale, the contribution of education to labor input, and obsolescence of capital, are notoriously difficult to measure directly.

Methodological problems therefore emerge from the weak conceptual, theoretical and empirical basis of many of the adjustments. These problems are confounded by the close interrelationships among many of these characteristics, which causes difficulties generating consistent and theoretically justifiable estimates of their independent impacts. The validity of many of the resulting measures is therefore subject to question, although Denison carries out as careful an analysis as is possible without a structural model of the production process.

Denison's output growth measurements are based on the observed growth in real national income (net national product at factor cost). One distinction he makes for this growth rate is between potential and measured output growth; potential output growth may increase faster than measured growth if unemployment is high. Measured growth is then allocated to various factors. For example, under the heading of total factor input, three factors of production are identified; labor, capital, and land. These in turn are divided into different characteristics. Labor is sub-divided into the contributions of employment, hours (average hours, efficiency offset, inter-group shift offset), age-sex composition, and education. Capital components include inventories separately from nonresidential structures and equipment.

Other identified contributions include improved (farm and non-farm) resource allocation, legal and human environment (pollution abatement, worker safety and health, and dishonesty and crime), economies of scale, and irregular factors (weather in farming, labor disputes, intensity of demand).

Clearly the magnitudes of the impact of many of these factors are problematic to assess effectively, although whether the impact is positive or negative might be relatively easy to determine.

Denison attempts to eliminate double counting, but because the adjustments are not based on a structural model he may not accomplish this goal due to problems with consistency. For example, as Norsworthy [1984] points out, his adjustments for cyclical effects seem incomplete since the residual retains a strong cyclical pattern after the adjustments, and his treatment of capital and depreciation "makes his framework unsuitable for analyzing the impact of capital on economic growth or on labor productivity growth". The problem arises from the National Accounts perspective, where the economy is viewed as producing income rather than output and therefore depreciation costs are excluded.

This is a real problem since capital's role in productivity fluctuations, in terms of the related impacts of capital accumulation, restrictions on adjustment, and capacity utilization, is critical for assessing economic performance. The interactions among such factors as cyclical effects, utilization, and investment also cannot be identified in such a framework, causing potentially serious difficulties maintaining consistency.

A related consistency problem has to do with returns to scale. Inputs are measured as if constant returns to scale exist, and then a scale adjustment is made based on an assumed level of returns to scale and the implied cost change associated only with output increases. However, since "scale effects" can appear from either short or long run responses to output changes, differentiating short run effects (which have to do with fixed inputs such as capital), and long run or true scale effects, is difficult to do without a structural framework. In addition, biased scale effects, resulting in input compositional changes as the scale of operations increases, may further confuse this separate representation of scale economies.

One researcher who questioned this particular aspect of the Denison procedures but from a somewhat different basis is Usher [1975]. Usher argues that technical change embodied in the capital (and labor) stocks are not correctly identified, and that the scale economies measure of about 12% per year is suspect for an entire economy, which will bias the estimated contribution of technical change or "advances in knowledge". He therefore rejects the results of Denison's study, while agreeing that the concept itself is useful for generating information crucial for an understanding of economic performance and for motivating policy. [38]

---

[38]In particular, he states that "The problem is of considerable importance because our prescriptions for generating economic growth from now on are likely to be conditioned by our understanding of the causes of the growth we have already enjoyed. We are more

Kendrick [1979] and Kendrick and Grossman [1980] have used procedures similar to Denison's, and therefore retain problems inherent in the growth accounting approach. However, some differences facilitate interpretation and comparison.

For example, Denison's treatment is at the national level, with a focus on the level of national income, whereas Kendrick's analyses are based on industry level data and therefore on output production. Kendrick and Grossman also use unadjusted capital and labor inputs as the basis for analysis and then incorporate changes in effective K and L, such as changes in labor force composition and capital quality, as part of the explanation of growth. As Norsworthy [1984] points out, however, there is still "probably considerable double counting among the quantitative effects he assigns to various causes".

In sum, these researchers have included numerous factors that one might think affect productivity growth and have attempted to assess their impact, which is critical for interpretation of overall productivity change. However, due to the lack of a structural framework for analysis, the adjustments have little theoretical basis and likely involve serious consistency problems.

The importance of a structural model for analysis of productivity growth has been emphasized in much of Dale Jorgenson's work. In Jorgenson [1988], for example, he states that: "the decline in economic growth would be left unexplained without an econometric model to determine the rate of productivity growth ...". This is consistent with Norsworthy's somewhat stronger conclusion that

"The neoclassical framework is, in reality, the only basis for aggregating the various factors of production into a measure of multifactor input... Consequently, insofar as these investigators depart from the neoclassical framework, they may be accused of using *ad hoc* procedures that will necessarily render their measurements inconsistent and incomparable with measurements using that framework."

Some of the adaptations identified by Denison, Kendrick, and others have been provided a more complete theoretical basis within such a neoclassical, econometrically implementable framework, although resulting productivity growth adaptations still tend to be simple, and based primarily on accounting methods or straightforward index number manipulations.

---

likely to promote education and scientific activity as means for fostering continued economic growth if we believe that observed growth has been due for the most part to technical change than if we believe that it has been due to capital formation or other changes which can be thought of as movements along a given production function".

For example, the differential impacts of investment in research and development (R&D) from other types of capital have been summarized by Grilichcs [1988, 1991], and incorporated by many other researchers within a structural model of firm decision making. These studies essentially recognize that R&D and other categories of productive capital have different characteristics, including price trends, time paths of investment, and depreciation, so they should be separated in models of firm behavior.

Some of this can be accomplished simply by including R&D as another type of capital (see Lichtenberg [1992] and Brynjolfsson and Hitt [1994]). However, the contribution of R&D, like high-tech capital investment might also have spillover and lagged effects that are important to recognize. Assessing these characteristics effectively thus requires a model that allows explicit consideration of R&D investment behavior separate from other capital investment, lags in obtaining the benefits of such investment, and external spillovers from R&D expenditures.[39]

Similarly, a distinction between the productivity impacts of pollution abatement capital (or other regulatory capital such as that required by safety standards) and "standard" capital has been made by Gray [1984], Norsworthy, Harper and Kunze [1979], and Conrad and Morrison [1989].[40] These studies recognize that pollution abatement capital is not "productive" in the usual sense for the capital stock; instead of producing measured output it produces a cleaner environment, resulting in biases in traditional productivity measures. An econometric model is useful here not only to motivate how the adjustment for regulatory requirements on capital should proceed, but also to identify the interactions between responses to such regulation and other types of firm decisions, neither of which is possible using growth accounting procedures.

These few examples indicate, although in a limited fashion, the importance of a structural model to motivate productivity growth adaptations for characteristics of the production process other than technical change which are possible to identify and measure. Much of the remainder of this text will be devoted to pursuing how the development and use of such a structural model might be accomplished.

---

[39] See Griliches [1991], Alston *et al* [1995], and the associated references for further elaboration. Also see Chapter 5 for more discussion of external effects and spillovers resulting from "knowledge capital" inputs such as R&D and high-tech capital investment.
[40] These studies and issues will be discussed in more depth in Chapter 7.

4.   TECHNICAL CHANGE AND PRODUCTIVITY

We began this chapter by defining productivity growth as the difference between the growth rates of output production and input use, or a percentage change in the output to input ratio. The underlying idea is that this difference reflects a change in technology that allows more output to be produced from a given amount of inputs. Developing the theoretical linkage between technical change and productivity growth involves formalizing this concept of productivity using a production function representation of the technology, and considering its implications for the definition of technical change.

Solow [1957] was one of the first researchers who explicitly outlined the use of a production function for modeling and measuring productivity growth.[41] This development is based on a production function of the form $Y(\mathbf{v},t)$, where t represents technology, generally proxied by a time counter, and $\mathbf{v}$ is a vector of J inputs with elements v_j. Using this function, we can express changes in output over time dY/dt as:

2.4) $dY/dt = \Sigma_j \, \partial Y/\partial v_j \; dv_j/dt + \partial Y/\partial t$.

Dividing this by Y to put the expression in proportionate terms, recognizing that $\partial Y/\partial v_j$ is by definition equal to the marginal product of input j (MP_j), and rearranging, results in:

2.5) $(\partial Y/\partial t)/Y = \partial \ln Y/\partial t = \varepsilon_{Yt}$

$= (dY/dt)/Y - \Sigma_j MP_j v_j/Y \; [(dv_j/dt)/vj] = d\ln Y/dt - \Sigma_j MP_j v_j/Y \cdot d\ln v_j/dt,$

where ε_{Yt}, interpreted as technical change, captures the output change not accounted for by changes in inputs and their composition.[42]

Further substitution requires recognizing that optimizing behavior implies that in equilibrium MP_j will be equal to p_j/p_Y.[43] This can be motivated by

---

[41]This is often jointly attributed to Tinbergen [1942].

[42] Such expressions, particularly in the earlier literature, have often been written with a "dot notation" where a dot (•) over a variable represents its time derivative. We will instead maintain our use of the logarithmic derivative to represent a percentage change over time to be explicit about the derivative we are taking, to be consistent with the notation used for elasticities, and to limit the amount of notation used.

[43]Notice the dependence of this derivation on instantaneous adjustment so $p_j=VMP_j=MP_j \cdot p_Y$, the value marginal product of input j, for all inputs. This implies full capacity utilization. This assumption will be relaxed once we consider the impact of fixity and therefore non-optimal capacity utilization. The equality also depends on perfect competition because

minimizing costs (TC=$\Sigma_j p_j v_j$) subject to an output constraint (Y(**v**) = $\bar{Y}$, where $\bar{Y}$ is a particular output level), resulting in the first order conditions $p_j=\lambda\bullet(\partial Y/\partial v_j)$ (where the Lagrange multiplier λ represents the change in the objective function with a relaxation of the constraint or marginal cost, MC). The profit maximizing equality MC=p_Y completes the equilibrium condition.

Alternatively, direct minimization of profits specified in terms of inputs ($\pi=p_Y\bullet Y(\mathbf{v})-\Sigma_j p_j v_j$) results in the first order conditions $p_Y\bullet(\partial Y/\partial v_j)=p_j$. Therefore, for a profit maximization model with perfect competition and instantaneous adjustment, (2.5) becomes

2.6) $\varepsilon_{Yt} = \partial \ln Y/\partial t = d\ln Y/dt - \Sigma_j\ p_j\ v_j/p_YY \bullet d\ln v_j/dt$

$$= d\ln Y/dt - \Sigma_j\ S_j\ d\ln v_j/dt\ ,$$

which reproduces the MFP growth expression we have been working with. Technical change can therefore be provided a formal definition that coincides with our conceptual idea of productivity growth, given certain assumptions about behavior and markets.

An even more specific and simple derivation of this equivalence of the productivity residual and a technical change measure results if the production process can be represented by a Cobb-Douglas (CD) production function. This simplicity is due to its underlying restrictive substitution assumption; by construction price and demand changes exactly offset each other to keep the shares constant in a CD function. This is a straightforward result obtainable by specifying the production function as:

2.7) $Y = A\ \Pi_j\ v_j^{\beta j}$,

so that $S_j = (\partial Y/\partial v_j)\bullet v_j/Y=\beta_j\bullet A\bullet\Sigma_j v_j^{\beta j}\ /Y = \beta_j$, where A represents technical change, as in Solow [1957]. Thus, the production function can be written as:

2.8) $Y = A\ \Pi_j\ v_j^{\ Sj}$, so $\ln Y = \ln A + \Sigma_j\ S_j\ \ln v_j$.

Taking derivatives, this implies that $d\ln Y/dt = \partial \ln A/\partial t + \Sigma_j\ S_j\ d\ln v_j/dt$, so $\partial \ln A/\partial t = d\ln Y/dt - \Sigma_j\ S_j\ d\ln v_j/dt = d\ln Y/dt - \Sigma_j\ \beta_j\ d\ln v_j/dt$. $\partial \ln A/\partial t$ therefore captures the technical change component earlier denoted ε_{Yt} – the percent output shift in the production function due to technical progress from (2.6), with constant shares represented only by a parameter.

---

we are relying on the equality of the value of the marginal product, $p_Y\bullet MP_i$ = VMP_j, and the marginal revenue product $MP_j\bullet MR = MRP_j$.

More general productivity growth specifications can be obtained by assuming a "flexible" functional form for the production function that allows a less restricted representation of input substitution. The transcendental logarithmic (translog) function developed by Christensen, Jorgenson and Lau [1973], for example, places no *a priori* restrictions on substitution elasticities and can be interpreted as a second order Taylor series approximation (in logarithms) to an arbitrary production function. The translog function (a 2nd order version of the CD) implies a Divisia index for the specification of shares rather than just a constant share.[44]

5.   PRIMAL AND DUAL MEASURES

A further extension to productivity growth measurement, motivated by developments in duality theory from the late 1970s, is to a cost-side rather than an output- or primal-side measure. The idea underlying the cost measure is that if a given output may be produced using less inputs once productivity growth has occurred, that output may by definition be produced at lower cost. Cost diminution for a given output level is "dual" to output augmentation for a given set of inputs. Based on this conceptualization and the representation of productivity growth from the production function already developed, we can easily develop an expression for dual productivity growth from the cost function.

The formalization of a cost diminution measure of productivity change is based on the definition of a (total) cost function TC(**p**,Y,t) as the lowest production cost possible for a given technological base (represented by the production function), a particular level of output, (Y), time or the state of technology (t), and the vector of input prices (**p**). The potential change in costs resulting from a change in t (between two periods) holding Y and **p** fixed (which is how we have motivated the cost-side productivity growth measure in words and graphs), can be written as $\partial TC/\partial t$ (or, in proportional terms $\partial \ln TC/\partial t$). Using the cost function, we may write this as

2.9) $(\partial TC/\partial t)/TC = \partial \ln TC/\partial t$

---

[44]The "exact" or "superlative" correspondence between the translog function and the Divisia (or Törnqvist when discrete) index was recognized by Diewert [1976]. This index is simply a share-weighted sum of growth rates, like the aggregate input measure in (2.6). For the discrete Törnqvist index, the share weights are generally measured as the sample mean between two successive data points. Direct use of the translog function allows assessment of the determinants of the shares, since the shares depend on the marginal products, which in turn depend on all arguments of the production function. See Chapter 10 for further discussion of index numbers.

$$= \text{dln TC/dt} - \text{dln Y/dt} - \Sigma_j \, p_j v_j / \text{TC} \cdot \text{dln } p_j/\text{dt} = \varepsilon_{TCt} \, .$$

Similarly to the development of the primal-side measure above, this is based on taking the total derivative and substituting:

2.10) $\text{dTC/dt} = \Sigma j \, \partial \text{TC}/\partial p_j \, dp_j/\text{dt} + \partial \text{TC}/\partial Y \, dY/\text{dt} + \partial \text{TC}/\partial t.$

Since constant returns to scale (CRS) are traditionally assumed (we will generalize this later), the cost function can be written as $\text{TC}(p,Y,t)=Y \cdot \text{AC}(p,t)$, where $\text{AC}=\text{TC/Y}$ is average or unit costs. This implies that $\text{dln TC/dt-dln Y/dt} = \text{dln (TC/Y)/dt} = \text{dln AC/dt}$, which is often used as the basis for the construction of equation (2.9) rather than total costs.

CRS also implies $\varepsilon_{TCY} = \partial \ln \text{TC}/\partial \ln Y = \partial \text{TC}/\partial Y(Y/\text{TC}) = 1$, which causes the (scale) cost elasticity term that otherwise would multiply the dln Y/dt term to drop out.[45] Finally, a duality theory result known as Shephard's lemma says that for a cost function satisfying standard regularity properties, $\partial \text{TC}/\partial p_j = v_j$, where v_j is the cost minimizing demand for input j, which allows substitution for the $\partial \text{TC}/\partial p_j$ terms. It turns out that, with CRS, this dual concept of productivity growth is equivalent to the original primal specification of productivity growth. This can be illustrated as in Figure 6.

Consider a firm with a CRS technology but with some inputs fixed in the short run. The firm in equilibrium may be thought of as producing at the point where the given short run average cost curve (SAC_0) is tangent to the long run curve (LAC_0), at output level Y_0.[46] When technical change occurs between two periods, the cost of producing any output level falls. This is represented by a downward shift in the long run average cost function.

In reverse, at given input levels, more output can be produced. This output level, Y_1, is determined by the tangency between the new short run average cost curve (SAC_1) and the corresponding long run curve (LAC_1). In this case (with CRS) the potential total cost decrease (in proportional terms) represented by the difference between AC_0 and AC_1 at output level Y_0 is equivalent to the possible proportional increase in output from Y_0 to Y_1 given TC_0. This reflects the duality of the two productivity growth notions.

---

[45]Note again the importance of constant returns to scale for these derivations. Ohta [1975] outlined the adjustment to these measures when CRS does not exist. This was extended by Morrison [1985a,1986a]. These refinements to the traditional framework will be taken into account in subsequent chapters (especially Chapter 4).

[46]Recall that the long run equilibrium is not defined here for a perfectly competitive profit maximizing firm that has a constant returns technology. Some hand waving must therefore be done to motivate the reasoning behind long run behavior of the firm, unless we allow for one of these three restrictions to be relaxed. This is often accomplished by assuming the firm is a cost minimizing entity, producing output level Y_0 at the lowest cost possible.

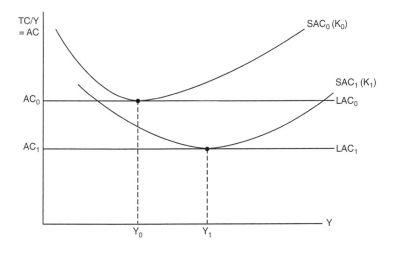

Figure 6. Duality of Primal (output) and Cost Productivity Growth Measures

Ohta [1975] demonstrated this result analytically using the expressions for primal and dual (cost) productivity growth (2.6) and (2.9). To summarize his argument, first note that if input costs are defined as $TC = \Sigma_j p_j v_j$, $d\ln TC/dt = (dTC/dt)/TC$ can be written as $(\Sigma_j v_j dp_j/dt + \Sigma_j p_j dv_j/dt)/TC$, or

2.11) $d\ln TC/dt = \Sigma_j p_j v_j/TC \, d\ln dp_j/dt + \Sigma_j p_j v_j/TC \, d\ln v_j/dt$.

Substituting this into (2.9) yields:

2.12) $-\varepsilon_{TCt} = -\partial\ln TC/\partial t = d\ln Y/dt - \Sigma_j p_j v_j/TC \, d\ln v_j/dt = \varepsilon_{Yt}$,

recognizing that $p_Y \bullet Y = TC$ with perfect competition, constant returns to scale and long run equilibrium, which for the moment are maintained hypotheses.

These primal and dual productivity growth expressions have provided the basis for measurement of MFP growth from both accounting (nonparametric) and econometric (parametric) perspectives, since the accounting practices can theoretically be justified by empirically estimable production and cost functions. The theoretical basis has also provided a stepping stone toward extension of the measures to relax some of the assumptions that the simple formulations maintain, including instantaneous adjustment (full capacity utilization), as we will do in later chapters.

6.   TECHNICAL CHANGE DETERMINANTS

The development of productivity growth as a technical change representation above is based on the notion of disembodied technical change, which is sometimes construed as "manna from heaven". It is not connected with specific inputs (although if it is non-neutral, inputs may be affected differentially), or to specific firm behavior (say, expenditure on high-tech capital or R&D). It simply reflects progress occurring over time, due perhaps to increased management skills, or some other general trend.

However, many aspects of technical change have an input-specific nature. More elaborate notions of technical change may be developed to recognize this and provide a more complete (but more complex to implement) technical change representation. These include the distinction between embodied and disembodied technical change, the recognition of non-neutral or biased technical change, and the consideration of specific technology determinants such as R&D, education, or investments in high-tech capital.

To provide a basis and link for these related extensions, we will first target specific technical change factors that may be important separately to distinguish for interpretation and "explanation" of productivity growth measures. Most of these factors have a more input-specific basis than the simple notion of renumbering isoquants to represent increases in net output.

Many of them involve capital issues, such as vintage or obsolescence and composition (quality, or proportion of high-tech capital), that will be pursued further in Chapter 3. Some, as will be elaborated in Chapter 5, also may have external as well as internal aspects, or, as discussed further in Chapter 10, involve capital measurement and aggregation. All, however, may be important to capture for representation and interpretation of factors underlying productivity growth and its measurement.

First, issues involving embodied technical change have been addressed from many perspectives. Often Solow [1957] is cited as not only providing the foundation for the literature on disembodied technical change, but also emphasizing the distinction – as well as the connection – between the notions of disembodied and embodied technical change. The literature exploring these linkages is extensive and diverse. Perhaps the most cited and comprehensive recent treatment is Hulten [1993].

The distinction between disembodied and embodied technical change, as motivated by Solow, is essentially "whether technical progress is due primarily to improvements in the design of new capital ('embodiment'), or is mainly "disembodied" and thus independent of the rate of capital formulation" (Hulten, p. 964). In this sense, it is typically treated as a capital vintage question, and thus is fundamentally connected to the representation of capital, which is a central theme in this text.

In this form, it has often been argued that technical change embodied in capital has little empirical impact on output growth, and thus productivity.[47] As noted by Hulten [1993], however, if one treats this as a quality issue, where quality is reflected in price instead of quantity, much more impact becomes apparent.[48]

The embodiment issue can also be addressed as a compositional issue that may be accommodated by identifying different types of capital which may have different marginal products, such as high-tech compared to more standard equipment. This is implicitly the focus of recent literature, including Hulten [1993], where increased computerization and thus "power" of the capital stock, rather than simply age, is the basis for adapting capital characteristics. This compositional question has also been addressed by disaggregation of the capital input into its high-tech and "other" equipment components, such as in Morrison [1997].

This has a similar motivation to the notion of constructing an efficiency index, which would reflect, in this case, the proportion of high-tech capital in the capital aggregate, or, as in Hulten [1993], captures the relative prices of these capital components. This concept is, in turn, analogous to adapting labor input measures for educational attainment (or the contribution of human capital), and thus extracting information on quality-adjusted or "effective" labor input, as commented on further below.[49] The idea of efficiency indexes representing capital vintages (but implemented in terms of different capital types), is used by Hulten [1992] to separately identify embodied from disembodied technical change effects.

It also may be important, as emphasized by Solow [1957], and pursued in much of the subsequent literature, to differentiate between technical change embodied in investment or in the entire capital stock. The treatment in Hulten [1993] involves such a distinction; an efficiency index for investment is constructed that feeds into the capital stock measure as investment takes place and the vintage of the capital stock changes. This procedure allows the productivity growth residual to be decomposed into a disembodied component and two separate capital-related components, one related to the capital flow and one to the stock. Such a decomposition is one basis for untangling different pieces of the "productivity puzzle".

---

[47] See Baily and Gordon [1988], for example. Also see Jorgenson [1998] for a detailed overview of the literature on capital investment and growth..

[48] This has been found, for example, in studies like Cole *et al* [1986] and Gordon [1990]. Such models are often based on hedonic analysis, as discussed in Triplett [1987].

[49] These approaches, as noted above, have aggregation implications, and also may involve external as well as internal effects. See Jorgenson, Fraumeni and Gollop (1987) for an example of the former, and Morrison and Siegel (1997b) for the latter, treatment.

This type of distinction may be provided with additional structure by translating it into a parametric model, through theoretical development of technical change and productivity concepts in terms of production and cost functions as above. Lee and Kolstad [1994], for example, attempt a similar distinction between flow and stock embodiment effects within a cost function-based model. The stock effect in this case is motivated as a factor augmentation issue, which is in turn closely related to biased technical change (as is discussed further below).

This brings us to the second primary issue raised above – neutral as opposed to non-neutral technical change. If the measures developed in this chapter are constructed using nonparametric methods, only the overall productivity residual may be distinguished from the cost or production side. However, with a parametric model, the ε_{Yt} or ε_{TCt} elasticities may embody both an average and input-specific effect (as formalized in the next section).

That is, neutrality (often termed Hicks neutrality) of technical change implies that all inputs are affected equi-proportionately by technical change. This is not, however, likely to be the case in general, since a particular type of technical advance may be more likely to conserve on a specific input, such as labor or energy.

These differentials may, in fact, even be induced by changes in relative prices; if the price of energy increases dramatically it might be thought that technology would be developed to save energy relative to other inputs. Technical change biases capture these disparate possibilities for conservation of inputs with a change in technology. Technical change may, for example, be input j-using, -saving or -neutral depending on whether the change in the use of input j is larger, smaller or the same as average input (cost) change.

It is important to recognize that these biases reflect *relative* changes in input use, since technical change may well reduce the use of all inputs. The bias is often, therefore, thought of in terms of input share changes; a decline in an input share reflects proportionally greater reductions in demand for that input than for others.

More formally, if the approximation to the production or cost function is of the second order, t may affect proportional marginal products ($\partial \ln Y / \partial \ln v_i$) differently; it may be the case that $\partial^2 \ln Y / \partial \ln v_i \partial t \neq \partial^2 \ln Y / \partial \ln v_j \partial t$. Both of these second order derivatives will appear as part of the overall output response to technical change, or the theoretical productivity residual $\partial \ln Y / \partial t, = \varepsilon_{Yt}$.

Similarly, it may be that $\partial^2 \ln TC / \partial \ln p_i \partial t \neq \partial^2 \ln TC / \partial \ln p_j \partial t$, or $\partial S_i / \partial t \neq \partial S_j / \partial t$ (using Shephard's lemma), and both these effects will be captured in $\partial \ln TC / \partial t = \varepsilon_{Ct}$. If all the input-specific effects are the same (proportionally), the overall output (cost) changes captured in ε_{Yt} (ε_{TCt}) will be equal to the input-specific impacts. However, if discrepancies in efficiency augmentation across inputs occur, the total technical change measure will be a weighted average of the individual impacts.[50]

This suggests that as the isoquant map changes with a change in t, the isoquants somehow "twist" so some inputs' relative efficiencies increase more than others. The resulting input-specific changes in efficiency are still essentially considered disembodied, since they simply happen with a change in t. However, this extension has implications for the representation of embodied technical change, since one would expect such patterns to be apparent if embodiment exists. That is, if, in addition to changes from price responses, technology affects relative efficiencies, this has implications for how the corresponding inputs might be represented in efficiency units to "explain" overall evidence of technical change.

If represented from this technological perspective, embodied technical change is sometimes modeled as factor-augmenting, as in Lee and Kolstad [1994]. For some functional forms and augmentation specifications, however, as pursued further in the next section, this is observationally equivalent to input-specific technical change biases. More generally, biases are a combination of substitution and augmentation factors.

This discussion raises questions about whether efficiency changes will be reflected in input prices or quantity levels. Efficiency increases suggest that standard price and quantity indexes derived from the total value of the input (typically capital) overstate price increases and thus understate (quality-adjusted) stock augmentation. If measured properly, the implied increases in capital input may account for some of the measured residual.

This idea may be used as in Hulten [1993] to separately identify different production components underlying the usual residual use of efficiency indicators, based on relative price changes for different types of capital. Another essentially equivalent procedure alluded to above is to directly adjust the input quantity (or price) measures by the efficiency indexes to reflect "efficiency-" or "effective-" units. This disallows separate representation of their effects as components of the overall residual, but facilitates appropriate measurement of disembodied technical change separately from factors explainable by input characteristics.[51]

---

[50] Since this derivative must be computable a functional form must be specified for the cost function and econometric estimation carried out. This is particularly the case if the exogenous determinants of the biases are of interest; certain functional forms simply yield a parameter as the bias estimate. Identification of biases is not directly possible from the data; distinguishing the differential impact of technical change across inputs requires more structure. See the next section for further elaboration.

[51] The direct adaptation of the inputs into their effective levels, as distinguished from decomposing the residual to reflect the "causes", or "explanations" or "sources" of growth

Finally, note that exploring possible embodiment of technical change in capital (and labor) inputs may be facilitated by disaggregation to reflect their compositional changes more explicitly. This would allow differential t-effects across types of capital, for example, as in Morrison [1997]. Investment in traditional capital may in this context be distinguished from investments in "knowledge" capital or other specific types of capital, to refine our representation of technical change and productivity determinants.

For example, as noted above in the context of growth accounting approaches, R&D expenditures may yield and thus explain advances in knowledge and, in turn, productivity. However, building this directly into a theoretical and ultimately econometrically implementable analysis requires explicit recognition of this "input", thought about how to represent the "price" of R&D, and recognition of risks and lags in the returns to R&D. One might also think high-tech capital would have a different "knowledge"-base implication than more "standard" capital, and thus should be separately distinguished by either a high-tech index, or decomposition across capital types (See Berndt and Morrison [1995] and Morrison [1997]).

Similarly, educational attainment of the labor force may be incorporated. This also may be interpreted as a capital issue, in this case human capital. As above, this may appear as a direct adjustment (via an efficiency index) to the data to represent increased "effectiveness" of the labor input, and thus explain some of the residual (Jorgenson *et al* [1987]). It is instead sometimes brought in as an additional human capital input, more along the lines of Hulten [1993] (see Mankiw, Romer and Weil [1992] for example). Recognition of the composition of the labor force by disaggregation into different educational categories might also be attempted, as in Berndt, Morrison and Rosenblum [1992], and Morrison and Siegel [1998a].[52]

These alternative perspectives provide somewhat different interpretations, but all are entangled. They are all attempts to somehow tease out changes in relative input efficiency, effectiveness, characteristics, or composition, in terms of either the price per constant quality unit or the "quality" of a particular constant dollar quantity, from the more general or disembodied notion of technical change.

---

was a focus of the 1960s debate among productivity experts such as Denison, Jorgenson and Griliches referred to above. See Jorgenson [1998] for further details of this debate.

[52] In these studies four educational "classes of labor", and thus their differing relative efficiencies, relation to t, and substitution across inputs, are explicitly recognized.

7. TECHNICAL CHANGE BIASES

Formal expressions for the technical change biases mentioned in the previous section can be constructed based on the developments by Sato [1970] and Binswanger [1974].[53] These treatments are based on the Hicksian concept that, with a value-added production function, technical change is labor-saving -using or -neutral depending on whether the marginal rate of substitution increases, decreases, or stays constant with a change in t while holding the capital-labor ratio constant. Resulting adjustments in factor shares are the basis of the definition of technical change biases.

A Hicksian-style definition of a technical change bias for the dual cost framework with multiple inputs is based on the relative factor share change allowing for substitution effects:

2.13) $B_{jt} = \partial S_j/\partial t = p_j v_j/TC \, (\partial \ln v_j/\partial t - \partial \ln TC/\partial t) = S_j \, (\varepsilon_{jt} - \varepsilon_{TCt})$,

where $S_j = p_j v_j/TC = \partial \ln TC/\partial \ln p_j = \varepsilon_{TCj}$ (using Shepard's lemma, $\partial TC/\partial p_j = v_j$), is the short run share of variable j in total costs, and $\varepsilon_{jt} = \partial \ln v_j/\partial t$.

The $(\varepsilon_{jt} - \varepsilon_{TCt})$ part of expression (2.13) is the primal Uzawa-Watanabe substitution term $B^U_{jt} = \partial \ln S_j/\partial t$, which is used to define technical innovation as input j-saving -neutral or -using when B^U_{jt} is less than, equal to, or greater than zero. Clearly, since $S_j > 0$, this also implies the same relationship for B_{jt}.

Two identifiable components to the total input j share response to technical change (for a given level of output) are represented by this measure. These components are the average percentage reduction in inputs ($\partial \ln TC/\partial t$) and the percentage change in demand for the jth input ($\partial \ln v_j/\partial t$). Thus, if $B_{jt} < 0$ the reduction in v_j from a change in t is greater than average; technical innovation is relatively input j-saving, and decreases costs particularly at the expense of employment of input j.

This highlights the interpretation of the bias as a *relative* change in input use. The second term in the parentheses, ε_{TCt}, is the overall proportional change in costs with technical change. The first expression in parentheses, ε_{jt}, signifies the input-specific change which may be greater or less than the neutral impact. If ε_{jt} and ε_{TCt} are equal, the proportional changes in v_j and TC are equal and technical change is neutral with respect to input j.

If this is true for all inputs, technical change is Hicks neutral. Even if technical change is non-neutral, however, the sum of the biases must be zero because overall the relative changes must cancel out. By definition *average* technical change must be neutral so the shares must sum to one.

---

[53] See Berndt and Wood [1982] for a good discussion of technical biases. Also see Gollop and Roberts [1983] for a related discussion including consideration of regulatory variables.

The empirical complexity of these bias terms depends on the functional form used for the cost function and therefore demand (or share) expressions, and whether the function used is a restricted cost function, allowing for the difference between short and long run (as in the next chapter). The simplest specification of biases arises when the functional form is such that the share equation is the natural expression for analysis.

This implies that a translog functional form, which as noted above is a 2nd order log-linear form (as compared to the 1st order log-linear CD form) may be useful. The logarithmic form of the translog cost function, so that ln TC = f(ln p_j, ln Y, t) suggests a natural adaption of the specification of demand equations is to construct the model in terms of shares (as mentioned above, Shephard's lemma implies ∂ln TC/∂ln p_j = (∂TC/∂p_j)•p_j/TC = $v_j p_j$/TC = S_j).

It turns out, in fact, that the specific expression for this share with the translog function is quite simple. Depending on the exact form of the function used for analysis (see Chapter 11 for further discussion of functional form issues) it looks something like:

2.14) $S_j = \partial$ln TC/∂ln $p_j = \alpha_j + \Sigma_{k \neq j} \gamma_{ij}$ ln $p_i + \gamma_{jj}$ ln $p_j + \delta_{jY}$ ln Y + δ_{jt} t,

where the α_j, γ_{ij}, γ_{jj}, δ_{jY} and δ_{jt} terms are parameters, and $\partial S_j/\partial t = \delta_{jt}$; the bias term is just a parameter. When concavity is imposed[54] this expression becomes simpler (for the CD form it becomes simply the parameter α_j) but is not likely to represent the production process well because often this requires restricting factor substitution parameters to zero. The measurement of biases is thus quite straightforward in the translog case, although econometric estimation is required to estimate δ_{jt}, and analysis of the determinants of the bias is not possible because it is not a function of the arguments of TC(•).

It is useful to note also that bias measures have a converse interpretation. $\partial S_j/\partial t = B_{jt}$ can be redefined as ∂^2lnTC/∂ln$p_j\partial t = \partial^2$lnTC/$\partial t\partial$ln$p_j = \partial\varepsilon_{TCt}/\partial$ln$p_j = B_{tj}$.[55] B_{jt} can thus alternatively be expressed as the effect on total cost diminution of a change in p_j. More specifically, when technical progress occurs, ∂ln TC/∂t is negative. Now if p_j increases and B_{jt} is positive (negative) then the effect of this price change is to reduce (increase) the rate of cost diminution from that which would have prevailed with neutrality.

---

[54] See Berndt and Wood [1982] for further elaboration. This simplification of the model to force it to satisfy regulatory conditions has often been imposed by Jorgenson (see Jorgenson [1988]). It may be useful to note for now that the most troublesome input factor in terms of curvature violations is capital in that study; 33 of the 36 industries violate curvature conditions. This may imply that the treatment of capital is invalid in the instantaneous adjustment framework and a short run model such as those suggested for measuring capacity utilization would be preferable.

[55] This equality uses Young's theorem on the symmetry of second derivatives.

This justifies the assertion often made in studies of biased technical change that an increase in the price of input j diminishes the rate of (multifactor) productivity growth if technical change is input j-using. Thus, if technical change is labor- capital- and energy- using, as is often found, increased prices for any of these three inputs will reduce multifactor productivity growth although increases in materials prices, since the bias is negative (materials-saving) will augment productivity growth.

This converse interpretation of the biases can more explicitly be illustrated by using the translog form to identify the dependence of the dual cost rate of technical change $\partial \ln TC/\partial t = \varepsilon_{TCt}$ on the biases. For the translog function the elasticity becomes

$$2.15) \quad \varepsilon_{TCt} = \partial \ln TC/\partial \ln t = \delta_t + \Sigma_j \, \delta_{jt} \ln p_j + \delta_{tt} \, t,$$

where the δ_{jt} terms are the biases, since $\partial \varepsilon_{TCt}/\partial \ln p_j = \partial S_j/\partial t = \delta_{jt}$. This term thus represents both the change in productivity growth with a change in the price and a change in the share of input j in response to technical change.

To provide additional interpretation of technical change biases it is worthwhile briefly to explore the linkages between biases and factor-augmenting technical change, since the distinctions between the two are sometimes confused. Augmentation of a factor is defined when technical change causes the "effective" amount of that factor to increase given its measured level; in terms of efficiency units more of the input exists. Conversely, this can be interpreted as a decreased price of a certain amount of services from the more efficient input, similarly to the equivalence of price and quantity adaptations for characteristics or embodied technical change discussed in the previous section.

If augmentation is expressed as a constant exponential rate, this implies

$$2.16) \quad v'_{jt} = v_{jt} \exp^{\lambda jt}, \text{ or } p'_{jt} = p_{jt} \exp^{-\lambda jt},$$

where " ' " refers to augmented or effective units and λ_j is the exponential rate of augmentation for input j. This imposes a particular form in which t enters the production or cost function. Berndt and Wood [1982] show, for example, with factor augmentation in a translog function, that the technical change parameters are related to the augmentation rates according to: $\delta_t = -\Sigma_i \, \alpha_i \lambda_i$, $\delta_{jt} = -\Sigma_i \, \gamma_{ij} \lambda_i$, $\delta_{Mt} = -\Sigma \, \gamma_{jt}$ and $\delta_{tt} = -\Sigma_i \, \gamma_{it} \lambda_i$ (where i indexes all inputs in the model but j denotes all inputs except intermediate-material inputs).[56]

---

[56] This assumes the materials share equation is deleted from the estimated system of equations, as required due to singularity of the system, from the fact that shares sum to one. See Chapter 11 for further discussion of this issue.

Therefore the bias coefficients are a complex combination of both augmentation and substitution among inputs.[57]

In this framework Hicks neutral technical change exists when all augmentation rates are equal. Harrod-neutral and Solow-neutral technical change are alternative versions of neutrality in which only labor- or capital-augmenting technical change occur, respectively. These imply, with λ_L only deviating from zero for the Harrod neutral case, $\delta_t = -\alpha_L \lambda_L$, $\delta_{jt} = -\gamma_{jL} \lambda_L$, $\delta_{tt} = -\gamma_{Lt} \lambda_L$. Therefore the biases δ_{jt} depend on the augmentation rate of labor and the substitution possibilities between input j and labor. Analogous conditions are inferred by the assumption of Solow neutrality.

"Value-added" neutrality is also sometimes distinguished, where capital and labor are augmented while materials (and any other identifiable inputs) are not. Leontief neutral technical change occurs when capital and labor augmentation rates differ and Leontief/Hicks neutrality occurs when the rates are the same. The associated biases depend on the augmentation rates and the substitutability of labor and capital with the other inputs.

Although, except in the case of Hicks neutrality, the relationship between biases and augmentation is reasonably complex, the concepts are closely related and intimately linked to the notion of overall technical change. That this latter assertion is true for biases is obvious from equation (2.15); ε_{TCt} can be expressed directly in terms of δ_t, δ_{tt}, and the bias terms. A similar association holds for the augmentation parameters, since the augmentation rates directly capture the change in effective input use between two time periods. As Berndt and Wood [1982] show, the relationship between ε_{TCt} and the augmentation rates is straightforward; $\varepsilon_{TCt} = -\Sigma_j S_j \lambda_j$.

Finally, it should be noted that the augmentation framework is not unique to a specification of technical change. Any quality adjustment that might be relevant to an input can be written in a form similar to (2.16). In particular, if (2.16) is rewritten as:

2.17) $\ln v'_{jt} = \ln v_{jt} + \lambda_j t$, or $\ln p'_{jt} = \ln p_{jt} - \lambda_j t$,

it looks very much like a simple hedonic expression for capital (see Chapter 3). In fact, the factor augmentation model is a simple quality-adjustment or hedonic model that just takes the impact of t into account. If any other quality-adjustment is made such as for utilization or characteristics determining its technical efficiency, it can be interpreted similarly.

---

[57] For an early treatment of biases and their relationship with augmentation see David and van de Klundert [1965]. They show that whether greater augmentation of capital than labor implies a capital-using bias, for example, depends on whether the elasticity of substitution between capital and labor exceeds or falls short of one.

8. FURTHER REMARKS

The theoretical and potentially empirical developments in this chapter provide us a basis for modeling and measuring technical change, and thus for further extensions and refinements to accommodate important technological and market structure affecting economic performance in subsequent chapters. Our first step in the following chapter is to explore the impact of short run fixities on production structure and associated productivity measurement. This involves representing the impact of short run input fixities in terms of costs, which in turn raises issues of capacity utilization, and of the dependence of measured productivity fluctuations on input constraints and utilization.

Chapter 3

The Short Run, Capital, and Capacity Utilization

One of the first issues that arises when attempting to disentangle the determinants of productivity growth is distinguishing between short and long run costs. This in turn raises other capital-related questions, particularly about capacity utilization and its representation.

Capacity utilization is closely connected to short run behavior, since existing capital stocks (or other quasi-fixed inputs) determine the amount of available capacity. If such fixity constraints were not binding, capacity would adjust to be fully utilized at each point in time. Since this is typically not possible, utilization effects and resulting short run cost changes must be distinguished from potential long run cost levels or cost efficiency in order appropriately to characterize true (secular) technical change trends from cyclical fluctuations. This requires measuring "effective" capital stocks, or the flow emanating from the existing capital stock.

That is, if greater production causes higher capital utilization, this reflects one aspect of efficiency, but only of a short-run nature. It thus should not be interpreted as evidence of long run productivity or efficiency trends. Since such utilization fluctuations are reflected in observed economic data, they must be untangled theoretically and empirically to determine what is really happening to economic performance. This may not be simple to accomplish.

The linkage between capacity utilization and productivity growth is emphasized in U.S.BLS [1983, pp 27-28]:

"Short-term fluctuations in aggregate demand result in cyclical changes in the utilization of capital and labor, and these too are reflected in the BLS measures of multifactor productivity. ... To the extent that labor is a quasi-fixed factor and there is labor hoarding, firms tend to underutilize (overutilize) the work force during periods of recession (expansion), ... In the case of capital, firms mainly adjust their inputs to meet changes in their short-run production needs by changing the utilization of existing stocks. The magnitude of the adjustments for the utilization of capital inputs is therefore likely to be larger than that for labor."

Although the combination of returns to these two production characteristics embodied in standard productivity growth measures is recognized in this study, no clear method for dealing with the problem is offered. A decomposition is instead attempted by calculating growth rates between cyclical peaks, with the suggestion that the remaining fluctuations arise from changes in utilization.

This approach, although quite common, is *ad hoc*. It is not clear whether the identified peaks are comparable, or even whether the capacity utilization definition underlying their measurement has any economic basis. It therefore does not effectively represent the concept of utilization presented above. It is clearly more desirable to formalize the linkages between productivity growth or technical change and capacity utilization within a more complete theoretical model of the technological and cost structure.

Such a framework, however, soon becomes too complex to be empirically implementable using the standard nonparametric productivity growth estimation procedures overviewed in Chapter 2. Data manipulation and ad-hoc methods must be set aside in deference to econometric methods that allow our economic "controlled experiment" to be carried out to empirically distinguish the individual pieces of the puzzle.

In this chapter we first consider the conceptual basis for an economic notion of capacity utilization (CU), and how this relates to the traditional motivation and measurement of CU indexes. In Section 2 we then develop the production theory basis for primal representation of capacity output and utilization separately from other aspects of observed productivity growth. Corresponding dual CU measures are developed in Section 3, via the construction of shadow values. Section 4 overviews the dynamics underlying input fixities, in the context of adjustment costs and dynamic duality. Finally, Section 5 discusses links between the CU framework and models focusing more directly on capital obsolescence and other determinants of the capital service flow as distinguished from its stock level.

1.   SHORT RUN FIXITIES AND CU

As we have discussed in the preceding two chapters, productivity growth measures are designed to reflect enhanced possibilities for output production from a given input vector as technology progresses over time, or the potential for generating a given output at lower cost. Capacity utilization also refers to a comparison of output (or cost) levels, but refers to the amount of output actually produced in the short run compared to some optimum long run potential given the input stocks or "capacity" at hand. It thus reflects cyclical rather than secular trends.

In engineering terms "capacity output" is often defined as the technically maximum production rate of a machine, say, if worked continuously, and thus at "full capacity utilization". This production level has little economic significance, however, if reaching it requires paying prohibitive labor, energy or maintenance costs.

One would think a more useful *economic* definition of full capacity utilization might be when the firm is in a steady state given the current level of the capital stock (or other inputs subject to adjustment constraints), and thus of "capacity". The firm's manager would not choose to change the current output level given the available capital stock, or the capital level at current output demand levels, since unit costs would be higher than in full equilibrium. In this scenario under-utilization (over-utilization) exists if the capital level is instead too high (low) to attain the lowest possible costs of producing the existing output level at observed input prices.

This reasoning indicates that some input such as capital must be fixed in the short run for utilization to be an issue, or the firm would simply sell (buy) enough to reach the minimum cost or long run equilibrium point for the prevailing output demand level. Measuring capacity utilization therefore involves identifying the input constraints which result in non-optimal use of the existing capacity, the levels of the fixed inputs, and the extent of the resulting constraints imposed on production processes.

The associated notion of capacity output reflects the "best" or equilibrium output level based on available input stocks, according to economic optimization. This may be conceptualized using an isoquant diagram, as for technical change in the previous chapter.

With only capital as a fixed input, capacity output is defined by the isoquant for which this stock is consistent with minimum costs (a line at this stock level crosses the scale expansion path, SEP). Representing the utilization of the existing capacity then involves comparing this capacity output to the actual production level.

Most approaches to capacity utilization measurement are based on developing such an "optimal" measure of capacity output, Y^*, and comparing this to actual output Y by forming the ratio Y/Y^* to generate a capacity utilization index. The differences among many of the alternative traditional measures, and between these and more economic theory-based measures, depend on the methods used to conceptualize and measure Y^*.

The procedures used to compute standard traditional capacity utilization measures vary, but tend to be mechanical. They typically disregard the fact that capacity is ultimately an economic concept due to its dependence on firm behavior. Instead they are based on some physical notion of the "maximum" output the capital stock is technically capable of producing.

In this context, "slack capacity" or under-utilization of capacity implies wasting "potential" production from the existing capital stock.

There are, however, a number of problems with this idea of a physical maximum, which limit its interpretability as the basis for a utilization measure. First, potential or maximum capacity is generally defined only in terms of the existing capital stock, rather than a combination of inputs.[58] This essentially specifies capacity in the context of capital- rather than capacity- utilization, which implies that capital is the only important fixed input.[59] More generally, since capacity utilization reflects overall firm behavior, it depends on all fixed factors facing the firm.[60]

For example, utilization of labor (especially overhead or non-production labor), and possibly other input stocks available to the firm, might be of interest to incorporate in a definition of capacity-, as contrasted to capital-, utilization. Utilization then becomes a multi-dimensional problem. If salaried employees are sitting semi-idle at their desks, it may be feasible to induce more production without an additional outlay in terms of wage bill, implying that labor inputs may currently be underutilized. Such a scenario requires some labor fixity due to, say, hiring, firing and training costs, which is often summarized by the expression "labor hoarding", as suggested by the BLS quote above.

In reverse, capacity utilization measures are sometimes based on the use of only one *variable* input. Foss [1963], for example, used the ratio of actual electricity consumption to the maximum possible electricity consumption, where the latter is obtained using the rated horsepower capacity of electric machinery, to construct a measure of capital utilization. Labor use per unit of capital is also important, however, to determine capital utilization; the combination of capital and *all* other productive inputs determines how effectively the available capital stock is "utilized".

The idea of physical maximization is also often simply not well defined. For example, is the capacity of a machine determined by its production if it were run 24 hours a day? One full shift? Two? Running a machine at full speed all the time may not even be a sustainable situation because of down time for repair and maintenance, or high costs of labor to support such a round-the-clock production schedule. Should this be allowed for?

---

[58] This distinction must be made as long as more inputs exihibit fixity than just capital, so capacity depends on all the fixed inputs.

[59] Betancourt and Clague [1981], for example, focus primarily on capital utilization.

[60] Note that we will develop the theoretical basis for capacity utilization below based only on one capital quasi-fixed input. This is done, however, for simplicity only. The production theory framework generalizes to more fixed inputs in a quite straightforward manner. See Morrison and Berndt [1981] for one example of such a treatment.

Similar questions arise if fixity of labor and thus the maximum physical contribution of labor is the basis for the definition of capacity. For example, to determine this maximum the relevant *measure* of labor is unclear. If we try to include all unemployed laborers past the "natural" rate, we need to determine what this rate is; it could be argued that "maximum" implies it is zero. We might even want to take into account other potential laborers who do not show up in the unemployment statistics. Also, this maximum could be based on a more than a 40-hour work week – but how much more?

These problems in determining the input-base for – and definition of – the physical maximum capacity output, suggest that this may not provide a very comprehensible basis for measurement. Unfortunately, however, standard published capacity utilization indexes generally have this type of mechanical measurement orientation, which limits their interpretation.[61]

One of the most common measures of capacity utilization in the U.S. is the Federal Reserve Board (FRB) measure. This is an eclectic measure taking many things into account. Construction of the FRB CU measure is based on FRB industrial production data, McGraw-Hill survey data, and capital stock and expenditure data. Survey data by industry is used to generate a series of "long term trends" in capacity, which are then correlated with industrial capacity measures generated using estimates of gross capital stock and survey data on capacity expansion, and aggregated.

This measure does not strictly rely on a physical or engineering notion of capacity, but it is not clear what it does rely on. It is based on an absolute rather than an economic evaluation of the optimum use of available capital, and on statistical and judgmental data analysis rather than economic theory.

The Wharton capacity utilization index poses other types of problems. This measure uses a "trend through peaks" approach, where the peaks are based on a maximum output (Y) per unit of capital (K) measure. The utilization index is based on linking together the peak Y/K points to determine the potential output that could have been attained between these maximum points. After the last peak the numbers are extrapolated.

This measure has definitional and thus interpretational problems because the maximum Y/K ratio may be altered by changing underlying economic conditions, which affects the appropriate comparison peak level. Although these other conditions may well be important they are not taken into account in this single factor measure that ignores scarcity of other factors. Because the measure is not based on analysis of the production structure in general,

---

[61] See Schnader [1984], Corrado and Mattey [1997] and Shapiro [1989] for further elaboration.

the numbers are difficult to interpret because the peaks are not equal and there is no explanation of why they differ, yet all are called "1.0". [62]

Another single-factor capacity utilization measure sometimes constructed depends on defining the potential Y* in terms of the full employment level of output.[63] Such an index is typically based simply on determining a maximum labor input level, although it may incorporate other inputs that are assumed important to employ "fully". When only labor is taken into account, problems analogous to those for the single-factor Wharton measure are clearly applicable. Even if more inputs are considered, the problem of defining full or maximum labor (or other factor) employment remains.

Survey methods have also often been used to measure capacity utilization. In the U.S. the index historically published by the Bureau of the Census is representative of this type of measure. Others include the McGraw-Hill and the Bureau of Economic Analysis measures.

These measures are based on survey questions that sometimes make a distinction between "preferred" and "maximum" capacity levels. Responses resulting from these more economics-oriented questions often result in a capacity utilization ratio that exceeds one. Managers indicate that production would be closer to optimal if current output levels were reduced, which implies that they recognize the economic impact of fixed input constraints.

Responses to such questions have, however, generally been ignored; published measures are based on the notion of maximum capacity. In addition, an underlying problem with constructing indicators using survey responses is that different firms apply disparate interpretations to the survey questions, especially when the definition of the concept involved is somewhat nebulous. Therefore, it is difficult to develop an explanation of or interpretation for the resulting measures.

A number of problems with standard mechanical capacity utilization measures therefore cause difficulties for their interpretation and use. The overall problem is that the "maximization" problem is not well defined. However, since economic theory is based on the notion of optimization (subject to constraints), it provides an important basis for formalizing how the idea of capacity utilization might better be developed and applied.

---

[62] The aggregate Wharton measure never reaches 1.0 because it is a summation of indexes constructed for each industry separately and at least some of these will fall short of one.

[63] See, for example, Okun [1962] and Fromm *et al* [1979].

2. A PRIMAL ECONOMIC CU REPRESENTATION

Dis- or sub- equilibrium input demand decisions, constrained by quasi-fixed capital (or labor) stocks, differ from those in the long run when full adjustment of quasi-fixed factors to their steady state levels is attainable. Short run constraints due to costs of adjustment result in deviations of shadow or implicit economic values of quasi-fixed inputs from their corresponding market prices. Such deviations reflect the extent of the existing subequilibrium, in terms of the costs of discrepancies between short run and steady state capital (capacity) or output levels that provide the basis for defining non-optimal capacity utilization.

Constructing economic measures of capacity utilization thus involves explicitly representing the constraints on or fixity of stock inputs, and determining what production level would "optimally" be supported by these fixed factors. If output demand differs from this capacity level, utilization of the fixed factors deviates from full capacity utilization.

More specifically, capacity output is determined as the production level that would be consistent with a steady state given the levels of fixed factors (or "capacity"). This economic capacity output may be denoted Y^*, so capacity utilization Y/Y^* equals one when capacity is fully utilized. Y^* is not, however, a "maximum" level, in the sense that this ratio can exceed, as well as fall short of, one; in the short run capacity can be over- as well as under-utilized in the economic sense.

Such a Y^* level is defined as the production level where the fixities the firm faces are not binding, or where short run production costs incurred are also minimum long run costs. With constant returns to scale (CRS) this is the minimum point of the short run average cost (SAC) curve, which is tangent by definition to the flat long run average cost (LAC) curve. If nonconstant returns to scale (NCRS) prevails, the tangency of the SAC and LAC curves remains the relevant point determining Y^*, as shown in Figure 7. If the corresponding output were demanded the firm would be in a steady state, even though the tangency is not at the minimum point of the SAC.

The idea of measuring the output corresponding to this tangency point as the "target" capacity output was suggested by Klein [1960] and Hickman [1964], following Cassels [1937] who first noted that the minimum point on the cost function (long run in his treatment) was an important indicator of capacity. Their reasoning was quite straightforward; if one wishes to ascertain how CU affects other economic characteristics like investment behavior or prices, the steady state notion makes more sense than does a mechanical physical concept.

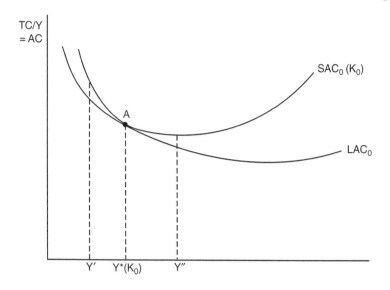

Figure 7. Capacity Utilization in a Cost Diagram

At that time, however, measurement of the steady state capacity output was not considered straightforward. The short run cost curves as well as the long run envelope must be estimated, which requires relatively sophisticated economic theory and econometric methods. [64]

Developments in the theory of cost and production have provided a useful basis for parametric measurement of these curves. Restricted or variable cost functions explicitly represent fixities, and so represent short run costs. That is, if a total cost function of the form $TC(\mathbf{p},Y,t)$ is specified, this implies that costs depend only on the prices of all inputs, including any input that might potentially be thought of as fixed.

If, however, capital (K) is fixed in the short run, then short run costs are dependent on both the price and the level of capital. If the price of capital changes no adjustment in K is possible, so use of the other factors (and thus variable costs) will not be affected. Therefore, if fixities exist a restricted cost function of the form $VC(\mathbf{p},Y,t,K)$ more appropriately represents short run costs, where short run total costs are defined as $TC=VC(\bullet)+p_K K$, $VC(\bullet)$ is variable costs, $p_K K$ is fixed costs, and $\mathbf{p}$ no longer includes p_K.[65]

---

[64] See Berndt, Morrison and Wood [1983] for further historical background and discussion of empirical work in this area, and Morrison [1987b] for an application of these ideas. Also see Gordon Winston [1977] for an integrated micro and macro analysis that focuses on this notion of microeconomic capacity, and Perloff and Wachter [1979] for a related treatment.

[65] We have now begun saying "fixed" rather than "quasi-fixed". This suggests that no adjustment is possible in the long run, whereas quasi-fixity implies some adjustment is feasible, which requires a more dynamic treatment (as developed further below).

Using these functions (and the duality theory more formally outlined in Chapter 9), $Z_K = -\partial VC/\partial K$ can be defined as the shadow value of capital. This reflects the value to the firm of having an additional unit of capital, in terms of the potential reduction in variable input costs for production of the given output. A corresponding "shadow cost function" may thus be defined as $TC^* = VC(\bullet) + Z_K K$.

Note also that such a shadow value may be defined more generally for any determinant of costs that is restricted in some way or for which Shephard's lemma is invalid for some other reason. That is, for any input market that is not functioning "perfectly", so that the input demand curve cannot be identified by reproducing the SEP representing optimal input demands for any given output level and input prices, including the input price as an argument of the cost function becomes inappropriate.

Including the price in the cost function implicitly suggests that costs may be defined as $TC = \Sigma_j\, p_j v_j^*(\mathbf{p}, Y, t)$, where v_j^* are the input levels solved for on the scale expansion path (SEP) from the cost minimization problem. Thus, optimal input demand may be represented as $\partial TC/\partial pj = vj^*$, which is a simple version of Shephard's lemma.

This implies full equilibrium in the factor market. If, however, fixities or regulations cause markets to respond sluggishly, if at all, this does not appropriately represent the market and the shadow value reflects the true marginal valuation of the input rather than its market price. The quantity level rather than price thus should appear in the cost function.

This will also be true with other market "imperfections" such as monopsony, in which case the firm responds to the marginal factor cost rather than the market price or average factor cost. We will return to these notions in subsequent chapters, but it is worth noting at this point that shadow values serve an important role for any case in which markets may not be functioning optimally.

Returning to the specific issue of short run fixities, note that in a steady state, the shadow and total cost functions will coincide because capital will be purchased or sold until its market price is equal to its shadow value to the firm; $p_K = Z_K$. However, in the short run this will not happen. If full equilibrium is unattainable the fixity constraints will be reflected by a difference between Z_K and p_K, and thus short- and long- run costs.

To reproduce a steady state or long run, we could set either the shadow and total cost functions or p_K and Z_K equal in this simple model with only one fixed input. If this were done and a corresponding value of K solved for, the resulting value would be the long run desired or steady state level of capital (K^*) given the output level and input prices faced by the firm. This establishes the long run cost curve.

Conversely, the $p_K=Z_K$ equality could be used to solve for Y given K (and the variable input prices). The resulting Y value would then be the steady state or capacity output level (Y*), consistent with the tangency between the SAC curve defined for the existing K, and the LAC curve. [66]

An alternative motivation for this equality more clearly expresses the tangency between the SAC and LAC curves in terms of the definitions of the curves themselves. Briefly, when the SAC and LAC curves are tangent, short run marginal cost (SMC) must equal long run marginal cost (LMC). This can be formalized using the definitions

3.1) $SMC = dTC/dY \,|_{\Delta K=0} = \partial VC/\partial Y$, and

3.2) $LMC = dTC/dY = \partial VC/\partial Y + \partial VC/\partial K \cdot dK/dY + p_K \cdot dK/dY$,

where " | " denotes "given", and $TC(\mathbf{p},Y,t,K,p_K) = VC(\mathbf{p},Y,t,K) + p_K K$. Equating SMC and LMC and using the definition $Z_K = -\partial VC/\partial K$ thus results in the same steady state condition as before: $Z_K = p_K$.

Once a functional form for $VC(\mathbf{p},t,Y,K)$ and thus $Z_K(\mathbf{p},t,Y,K)$, is specified and estimated econometrically, the resulting parameters may be used to compute $Y^*(\mathbf{p},t,Y,K)$ from this steady state condition even though Y* cannot be identified directly from the data. Thus, parametric techniques allow imputation of the optimal "long run" or capacity output value from observed short run data. [67]

Since this output level reproduces the tangency point of the short and long run average cost curves and thus reflects the economic notion of capacity output, the corresponding primal economic capacity utilization measure becomes $CU_y = Y/Y^*(\mathbf{p},t,Y,K)$. [68] Thus, if demand is less than the output corresponding to the tangency of SAC and LAC, the measure reflects the existence of excess capital: $CU_y<1$. However, as noted above, if output demand exceeds that supported in the steady state by the existing stock of K, overutilization exists and $CU_y>1$, contrary to the mechanical measures that always fall short of one.

---

[66] It is important to emphasize again that "capacity" in this example depends only on the fixed level of capital. However, other inputs might also be fixed, such as labor or other capital inputs, as will be developed further below.

[67] See Morrison [1985a] for an example of this, applied to the U.S. motor vehicle industry. Note, however, that the diagrams were reversed in this paper in the final version, so the figure said to be representing the CRS model is actually NCRS and vice versa.

[68] Y can either be given to the firm, which is assumed in the cost function, or can be the optimal short run profit maximizing value of output the firm chooses. This profit maximizing value, Y', will not normally be equal to the capacity output level.

This is the sense in which such an economic measure represents optimal rather than maximal use of the given stock. In addition, the determinants of utilization are explicitly represented since Y^* is a function of all arguments of $TC(\cdot)$, facilitating the use and interpretation of the resulting CU measures.

The difference between the cases where $CU_y < 1$ and $CU_y > 1$ can be illustrated in Figure 7. If K_0 is the given level of capital, perhaps remaining from the previous year when the firm was in equilibrium with output demand at a different level, the corresponding short run average cost curve is SAC_0. The long-run curve representing optimal variation of all inputs to output demand changes is represented by LAC_0.

Since the only point where K_0 is an optimal (steady state or long run) level of capital is at point A, where $Y = Y_0$, this level of output is $Y^*(K_0)$. If output demand jumps to a higher level ($Y' > Y^*$) and K cannot immediately adjust, then K_0 is overutilized. Costs are higher in the short run than is necessary in the long run for production of the given output level, because excessive variable inputs must be used to produce Y' with the now-scarce capital input ($Z_K > p_K$). Another unit of capital stock has a high implicit value in terms of its potential for allowing movement around the isoquant toward the SEP. If demand instead falls below Y^* ($Y'' < Y^*$), then there is excess capacity; too much capital, and therefore fixed costs, exists to produce at the lowest possible cost for that level of output ($p_K > Z_K$).

It should again be emphasized that fixity of inputs other than capital can be represented in this framework, and a corresponding measure of CU_y defined. If, for example, labor is quasi-fixed due to short-term contracts, the shadow value of labor ($Z_L = -\partial VC/\partial L$) will also differ from its market price (p_L), and the firm's capacity will depend on the given stock level of L in addition to that for K. L rather than p_L will therefore appear as an argument of the variable cost function, which in this case reflects non-labor as well as non-capital costs.

Thus the position of the SAC_0 curve depends on both inputs, and Y^* is then defined when both $Z_L = p_L$ and $Z_K = p_K$. This can be computed by setting total costs $TC = VC(\mathbf{p}, L, K, Y, t) + p_K K + p_L L$ equal to shadow costs $TC^* = VC(\mathbf{p}, L, K, Y, t) + Z_K K + Z_L L$, and solving for Y, as in Morrison [1982].

More generally, with multiple fixed inputs TC may be defined as $VC(\mathbf{p}, \mathbf{x}, Y, t) + \Sigma_k p_k x_k$ and TC^* as $VC(\mathbf{p}, \mathbf{x}, Y, t) + \Sigma_k Z_k x_k$, where $\mathbf{x}$ is a vector of fixed inputs x_k, p_k is the market price of x_k, and $Z_k = -\partial VC/\partial x_k$. CU_y is still defined as the output level satisfying the equality $TC^* = TC$, although the more quasi-fixed variables are taken into account the more possible combinations of their values could potentially satisfy this equality.[69]

---

[69] Berndt and Fuss [1989] have discussed in detail the problems arising when trying to compute capacity utilization measures with multiple inputs and multiple outputs. Since

Capacity and capital utilization are thus distinguishable in this situation, whereas when only capital is fixed they coincide. This should be kept in mind throughout this text, although in most cases developments focusing on short run behavior will be motivated in a fixed-capital-only context.[70] This is done only for simplicity of exposition; all the results carry over to more complete specifications.

Note finally that an explicit short-run long-run model has implications for the linkage of some kinds of capital investment models to the notion of capacity utilization. If $Z_K > p_K$ the value of capital on the margin is greater than its market price, stimulating firms to purchase additional capital. This idea provides the basis for construction of the investment indicator known as Tobin's q, which compares the implicit or shadow value of a firm (measured by its stock market value in most cases) to its market replacement value (the book value of the firm). This comparison is carried out by generating the ratio Z_K/p_K, which will exceed one when the shadow or implicit value of the firm is greater than its market price.

Although this highlights the similar foundations of investment indicators such as Tobin's q and our CU_y and Z_K measures, there are some differences between standard Tobin's q measures and the measure based on the shadow value concept, Z_K/p_K. First, Hayashi [1982] has shown that average and marginal Tobin's q will coincide only when constant returns to scale exist, and Tobin's q computations are typically based on average values, whereas the shadow value notion is explicitly marginal. Even studies that recognize the relevance of a shadow value or marginal comparison often depend on an *ex-post* or residual computation of this implicit price of capital rather than a parametrically computed shadow value using the definition $Z_K = -\partial VC/\partial K$.[71]

The denominator of the q-ratio is also computed in different ways. For average computations it is often assumed to be appropriately represented by a firm's book value. However, reported book values depend on accounting rather than economic principles. Construction of the p_K value for measurement of Z_K/p_K should instead explicitly be based on an *ex-ante* concept of the user cost of capital, as outlined in Chapter 10.[72]

---

total and shadow costs can be the same when shadow and market prices of each individual input deviate, for example, as long as they counteract each other, a unique measure of Y* may not exist in this context.

[70] This less complete capacity utilization idea is more correctly called capital utilization. This distinction has been emphasized in investment and capital utilization studies such as Bernstein and Nadiri [1988c], and Nadiri and Prucha [1998].

[71] This is the basis of *ex-post* measures of capital in general, where the value of capital services is defined as $p_Y Y-VC$, where p_Y is the price of Y, which reflects the "profits" of the firm after variable costs are paid.

[72] A useful discussion of the measurement of both the *ex-ante* and *ex-post* price of capital is in Hulten [1986].

Investment and stock market values are generally thought of as important indicators of economic performance that are closely related to utilization. Unfortunately most investment theories, including Tobin's q, have not had very much success at tracking or predicting trends in investment.[73] The idea of Z_K/p_K as an investment indicator suggests, however, that dual or cost-side CU measures may contribute substantial interpretative power to our analysis of utilization fluctuations, their implications about investment patterns, and their linkage with cyclical and secular patterns of productivity growth.

3.   A DUAL CU MEASURE

Since the output-side or primal capacity utilization measure is fundamentally based on comparing shadow and market values of stock inputs, it might well be asked directly what the cost consequences are of being away from capacity output rather than just what output deviation is implied. This is the underlying motivation of the Tobin's q or investment incentive ratio Z_K/p_K. This cost or dual perspective also facilitates the development of a cost-side capacity utilization measure CU_c.

An important implication of this dual concept is that if short run average cost curves are rather flat, a primal capacity utilization measure may differ considerably from unity, but could still be consistent with a relatively low short run costs of the deviation. This provides insights about how critical suboptimal utilization may be to firms.

In addition, since it is not necessary to solve for or impute the level of TC* from a steady state equality as it is for Y*, the former are typically more straightforward to calculate. They may even be computable using data such as those underlying construction of Tobin's q measures (and thus Z_K), although as mentioned above the average data typically used for such an exercise raises interpretability problems.

The dual cost capacity utilization index, like the primal measure, is conceptualized in terms of the deviations between shadow and market prices of fixed factors. It thus represents the extent of subequilibrium, or the nature of the constraint, in terms of its cost impacts. If the shadow value for an input exceeds its market price the input in question is being overutilized, and if this is true for all fixed inputs a general case of overutilization prevails. This suggests that a dual capacity utilization measure can be constructed as TC*/TC=CU_c, where, as above, TC* is shadow costs and TC is total costs.

---

[73] See Berndt [1990] Chapter 6 for a detailed discussion of different investment theories and their empirical implementation.

This measure indicates the overall deviation of shadow values from market prices and therefore represents the extent of adjustment pressure toward equilibrium for the firm. It will always deviate from one in the same direction as the primal measure if curvature properties for the variable cost function are satisfied (see Chapter 9). If TC*>TC, for example, the shadow value of capital (with capital the only fixed input) exceeds the market price, so not enough capital exists to produce the demanded output in the steady state and Y>Y*. However, it is generally the case that the cost measure is less volatile than the output measure, as might be expected.

Morrison [1985a] has shown that constructing this index is equivalent to computing the elasticity of costs with respect to K, similarly to defining the cost-side productivity growth measure as the cost elasticity with respect to t. That is, with one quasi-fixed input, ε_{TCK} = ∂ln TC/∂ln K = (K/TC) • ∂(VC+p_KK)/∂K. The equivalence of this expression with CU_c can be easily derived given the definitions of TC and Z_K above as:

$$3.3)\ CU_c = TC*/TC = (VC+Z_KK)/(VC+p_KK) = [TC - K(p_K-Z_K)]/TC$$

$$= [1-K(p_K+\partial VC/\partial K)]/TC = 1 - \varepsilon_{TCK}\ ,$$

with only capital fixed. With multiple quasi-fixed inputs this is adjusted only slightly to read: $CU_c = 1-\Sigma_k\varepsilon_{TCk}$, where k enumerates the fixed factors x_k.

In short run subequilibrium, ε_{TCK} will not equal zero ($Z_K\neq p_K$), and thus $CU_c\neq 1$. This is true of course only if the elasticity is evaluated from the perspective of the observed short run data; if it were evaluated at K* or Y* the measures would collapse to their steady state values ($\varepsilon_{TCK}=0$ and $CU_c=1$), as elaborated further below.

This definition of the dual cost capacity utilization index can be used to highlight the relationship between ε_{TCK} or ε_{TCk} and the elasticity of costs with respect to output, $\varepsilon_{TCY}=\partial$ln TC/$\partial$ln Y. Establishing this linkage is important for adjusting productivity growth measures for the impact of subequilibrium, to distinguish short-run or cyclical productivity growth fluctuations from long-run or secular trends.

This step requires explicit recognition of how elasticities measured in the context of subequilibrium differ from those in full (steady state) equilibrium. This is represented for the cost-output relationship (long run scale or cost economies, as developed further in Chapter 4) by the expression for the long run elasticity of costs with respect to output:

$$3.4)\ \varepsilon^L_{TCY} = (Y/TC) \cdot dTC/dY = (Y/TC) \cdot (\partial TC/\partial Y + \partial TC/\partial K\ dK/dY)$$

$$= d\ln TC/d\ln Y = \partial\ln TC/\partial\ln Y + \partial\ln TC/\partial\ln K$$

$$= \varepsilon_{TCY} + \varepsilon_{TCK} = 1 \text{ , so}$$

$$\varepsilon_{TCY} = 1 - \varepsilon_{TCK} = CU_c$$

where $\varepsilon^L{}_{TCY}$ is the long run scale effect (the inverse of the returns to scale measure), and CRS is assumed so $\varepsilon^L{}_{TCY} = d\ln K/d\ln Y = (dK/dY)Y/K = 1$ and thus $dK/dY = K/Y$. This expression can be extended with multiple quasi-fixed inputs to $\varepsilon_{TCY} = 1 - \Sigma_k\varepsilon_{TCk} = CU_c$.

The $\varepsilon^L{}_{TCY}$ elasticity may be derived by taking the total differential of TC, and recognizing the exogenous nature of all arguments of the function except K as the firm moves toward long run equilibrium. It may also be motivated by substituting $K^*(Y)$ in the TC function to explicitly represent the dependence of long run capital adjustment on observed output demand. $\varepsilon^L{}_{TCY}$ thus represents the shape of the long run cost curve, imputed from the short run, and thus total cost economies after all adjustment has taken place.

The short run cost elasticity with respect to output coincides with CU_C when CRS exists.[74] Capacity utilization can therefore be thought of as a short run scale effect; when capacity is overutilized, costs in the short run increase more than proportionately with output, although they increase proportionately in the long run.

Expression (3.4) will provide the foundation for a number of extensions of the standard cost-based production theory model in this and subsequent chapters. Therefore, it is useful at this point to make a few additional comments and qualifications about its construction, interpretation, and use.

First, note that the cost capacity utilization measure CU_c provides useful interpretation for analysis of short- as compared to long-run behavior, and also for interactions between scale economies and capacity utilization. In this context short run scale or cost economies are reflected by the shape of the short run cost curves (represented by ε_{TCY}), and long run economies by the shape of the long run curves (in $\varepsilon^L{}_{TCY}$, as is pursued in Chapter 4).

Also, the cost elasticities (and thus CU_c) are directly dependent on derivatives of the cost function, rather than being solved for as with Y^*. Thus these indexes facilitate computation of utilization biases (discussed in the next section), allowing further representation and interpretation of what economic factors underlie CU fluctuations.

---

[74] It is worth noting here that this value also reflects the ratio between marginal and average costs at this point, since $MC/AC = (\partial TC/\partial Y)/(TC/Y) = (Y/TC) \cdot (\partial TC/\partial Y)$.

One qualification about the construction, interpretation and use of such measures, however, has to do with where they might empirically be evaluated, as alluded to above. The derivation of the long run values imputes them from the perspective of the short run, since the data by definition reflect short run behavior. Such imputation requires some type of approximation since discrete changes are involved. That is, as for any type of elasticity computation, since we are ultimately using discrete data to approximate continuous or point derivatives, which necessitates some approximation of the point estimate.

Alternative perspectives on what type of approximation is most appropriate may result in different conclusions about the construction and interpretation of these measures. For example, Fousekis [1999] argues that since the derivation of expressions such as (3.4) at least implicitly requires the use of a chain rule approximation to the total derivative, they should be evaluated at the imputed long run. This raises important questions, however, about: (a) which "long run" approximation we are referring to; (b) whether it makes sense to impose the long run via a theoretical "envelope theorem", or to use imputed future values rather than the current existing state of the world as the perspective from which the long run is viewed; and (c) what the empirical differences are among the different approximations.

That is, (3.4) can be considered a "combination" elasticity, viewing long run adjustment from the point of the short run. The conceptual basis for this is clear: given current input prices and output demand, we wish to impute what investment will be required to move to a steady state. The intuition underlying the decomposition in this expression is explicit as well as advantageous for interpretation. The full long run cost-output elasticity is a combination of the short run effect (along the short run cost curve), and an adjustment toward the long run based on the current state of disequilibrium. The empirical approximation of such a measure to one based on evaluation of the entire expression at K^* is also close.

An alternative to using (3.4) to represent the long run, as alluded to above, is simply to evaluate the elasticity at K^*. The conceptual basis for this approximation to ε^L_{TCY} is similar. The long run is defined where a steady state is reached through investment to K^* given Y and p_K. The theoretical justification for this is also definitive, since use of the chain rule implies substitution of K^* into the cost function, suggesting evaluation at that point.

However, since the resulting ε^L_{TCY} measure simply collapses to its long run value, the determinants of the extent of subequilibrium are not separately identified. Also, evaluating the elasticity at a long run equilibrium point that must be imputed may cause estimates to be somewhat volatile if this imputation is at all empirically sensitive, by contrast to using as a base the already observed short run values from which adjustment will take place.

A third possible approximation involves imposing the envelope condition at the observed Y, K values. This in turn imposes the $p_K = Z_K$ equality, therefore requiring evaluation of the elasticities at Z_K rather than p_K. This is theoretically valid. Again, however, this disallows consideration of the "wedge" separating the short and long run measures, since it simply reproduces the long run elasticity. Also, the conceptual basis is limited; the firm will respond to an existing disequilibrium by investing (disinvesting) in K given observed p_K values rather than the reverse. Finally, in terms of empirical content, such an approximation tends to deviate from the first two approximations, which are often quite close (see Morrison [1999]).

Thus, although there are important issues to think about when estimating and evaluating (3.4) and its components, the "combined elasticity" framework seems a preferred approach for constructing long run elasticities from short run observed data.

One other point to raise, which we will return to, is that problems emerge when applying the type of model we are developing to aggregate data. The potential for "aggregation biases" plagues any type of analysis in which representation of an "aggregate technology" (aggregate production or cost function) is attempted, as emphasized at least as far back as Solow [1957].

This is particularly true when scale economies are incorporated, which is implicitly the case also in a short run context since in subequilibrium firms will be operating on a sloped section of the SAC curve. Production theory models are based on representation of the technology of a firm, and unless all firms are producing according to a CRS technology, it is not clear how to aggregate firms and obtain an interpretable measure of returns to scale.

It *can* be determined, however, whether scale characteristics are important for representing the data even if interpretation is not transparent. Also in some cases it seems justifiable (at least empirically) to rely on the assumption that patterns for a "representative firm" are being captured, even if there is heterogeneity across units within the aggregate (see Morrison and Siegel [1998c]).

It is also worth emphasizing that typical uses of capacity utilization measures as economic indicators of expansion/contraction or inflationary forces are signficantly facilitated by using the economic framework for capacity utilization (from either the dual or primal perspective). In particular, a deviation of capacity utilization measures either above or below one has clearly interpretable consequences.

For example, CU is often used as an investment indicator, but if the measure never exceeds one, as in traditional measures, its validity in this context is not easy to establish. Using economic measures, if CU_y or CU_c are greater than one investment will take place because the stock constraint is binding; the shadow value of the fixed input(s) exceeds its market value.

Similarly, product price increases will likely occur because of inflationary pressures, and productivity growth (especially with respect to fixed inputs) will appear higher than in actuality due to the over-utilization of these inputs.

These economic responses will be stimulated when $CU_c>1$ and $CU_y>1$, not when the capacity utilization ratio somehow "gets too close" to one, as is sometimes suggested for the traditional measures. The linkages among the CU indexes and common applications of the measures are therefore much better defined within the economic theoretical model than for more mechanical traditional measures.

Finally, although the dual CU measure is based on the overall cost consequences of fixity, associated input-specific effects are also identifiable with the cost framework. Similarly to the treatment of technical change, the short- as compared to long-run input-specific effects may be framed in the context of utilization (fixed input) biases (see Morrison [1988b]).

Such biases reflect the (relative) change in inputs when a fixed input constraint is relaxed. It may be the case, for example, that when capital stocks are reduced due to low capacity utilization, the cost-share of energy declines. In this case investment is energy-using relative to other inputs.

More generally, say capital is fixed in the short run, and the share of input j tends to decline if the capital input increases. Then expansion of the capital stock may be said to be input-j-saving in the sense that adding more capital reduces the demand for input j relative to other inputs. Alternatively, this suggests that if the stock of capital is a binding constraint (demand is too high for a steady state given the capital stock), over-utilization of capital implies extra-normal use of input j.

Following this reasoning, a "subequilibrium" or utilization bias can be defined similarly to that for technical change as:

$$3.5)\ B_{jk} = \partial S_j/\partial \ln x_k = p_j v_j/TC\ [\partial v_j/\partial x_k \bullet (x_k/v_j) - \partial TC/\partial x_k \bullet (x_k/TC)]$$

$$= S_j \bullet (\varepsilon_{jk} - \varepsilon_{TCk})$$

where $\varepsilon_{jk} = \partial \ln v_j/\partial \ln x_k$. ε_{TCk} will be negative if $Z_k>p_k$ so more of input x_k would be desired to reach a steady state, and vice versa for $p_k>Z_k$. In the former case, $B_{jk}<0$ implies that ε_{jk} must be strongly negative – inputs k and j must be substitutes. Thus an increase in x_k relaxes the fixed input constraint but reduces costs extra-proportionately with respect to v_j. It is input j-saving because the constraint on input k was initially accommodated by over-using substitutes. The reasoning is reversed if x_k and v_j are complements. Again, however, note that this is a relative rather than absolute direction of change.

All inputs might be "saved" in terms of reducing their levels; the *bias* has to do with the relative or proportionate change.

(3.5) can be interpreted as a utilization bias since over-utilization of fixed x_k imposes extra costs on the firm for substitutes. Over-utilization of capital equipment may, for example, cause substitution of extra labor-hours relative to other inputs to accommodate the lack of capital, or additional reliance on partly processed raw materials so machinery limitations are less binding.

In the former scenario under-utilization of capital would impinge particularly on labor employment in the short run, due to the tendency to substitute excessive existing capital. Conversely, if labor is a gross complement with capital, as suggested by the existence of short run increasing returns to labor in some industries,[75] labor may benefit in the short run from output stagnation and resulting excess capacity.

The symmetry of biases mentioned in the context of technical change biases also holds for utilization biases, which facilitates interpretation. For example, $\partial S_j / \partial \ln K$ can be redefined as $\partial \varepsilon_{TCk} / \partial \ln p_j$; biases with respect to fixed capital also represent the impact of a change in p_j on the cost elasticity with respect to capital.

Since the elasticity $\varepsilon_{TCk} = \partial \ln TC / \partial \ln K$ is the basis for the CU_c measure, this further supports the interpretation of these measures as utilization biases. In this case, if the utilization bias implies that investment is energy-using, this not only indicates that increasing capital causes the share of energy to rise, but also that higher energy prices reduce capacity utilization. This can be further illustrated using the translog functional form by constructing an explicit expression for ε_{TCk}, analogously to that for ε_{TCt} in (2.15).

Note also that utilization biases can be specified in an augmentation framework, as in (2.16) or (2.17) for the analogous technical change measures, when utilization is represented directly as a determinant of capital quality (as in a hedonic expression). When utilization is more aptly recognized to be a result of input fixity, this specification is inapplicable.[76]

Finally, note that technical change biases such as those in Chapter 2 may also be defined in a restricted or variable cost function framework with fixed inputs. However, these measures, as for any others constructed based on the restricted model without explicit representation of long run adjustment (as in 3.4, for example), must be interpreted as short run measures.

---

[75] See Morrison and Berndt [1981]. Note that this is most likely to be the case for skilled workers, and substitution may exist for production workers, although in total complementarity may be observed.

[76] As noted below, this type of exercise has implicitly been carried out by Jorgenson and Griliches [1967], but problems arise for computatin of the utilization index. The index must be exogenous to be used in this way, which causes interpretational difficulties.

4. FIXITY, ADJUSTMENT COSTS AND DYNAMICS

A framework that facilitates computation of shadow values and explicit determination of the arguments of the shadow value function is important for analysis of capacity utilization and investment, and ultimately of the relationships between these indicators and productivity or economic performance. The variable or restricted cost function framework developed in this chapter, which includes fixed inputs as arguments of the cost function, and which we will expand further in this text, provides such a structure.

This type of framework is an extension of the production theory basis for investment modeling, generally termed the "neoclassical" approach, to explicitly include short run fixities. The resulting model therefore can be used to measure short-, and impute long-run behavior. Related conceptually important aspects of the production structure that may also be useful to represent include dynamic adjustment and expectations formation.

The problem of dynamic adjustment arises when one asks *why* fixity might occur, and *how* adjustment takes place if levels of quasi-fixed inputs deviate from their steady state values. In the literature, input fixities are generally attributed to some type of adjustment costs. The idea of adjustment costs is that for stock inputs the speed of adjustment may be associated with costs that increase on the margin (the function is convex). This makes instantaneous adjustment prohibitively expensive (if even possible), which is, in a sense, a formalization of the old adage "haste makes waste".

Such adjustment costs may occur for most inputs, and may be internal or external. Internal adjustment costs may be associated with expenses for ordering or bolting down machinery. This is internal in the sense that variable inputs (hired within the firm) may be required to put capital in place rather than to produce output. External costs may be incurred due to upward sloping input supply curves. These costs are external in the sense that they stem from increased outlays to the supplying firms. In response to increased demand for their product (particularly for "rush jobs or emergency orders), firms producing and supplying the machinery may have to increase overtime and therefore charge more for their product, or they may need to have more field people available (at extra cost) to install or maintain the machinery.

These internal and external adjustment costs could also arise for inputs other than capital. For labor, for example, hiring, firing, and training costs can be considered internal costs; funds that otherwise could be used to pay labor for producing output are instead used to set up a personnel or training department. An upward sloping supply curve for labor could also be generated – therefore causing external adjustment costs – if it takes longer to train more marginal recruits or it becomes increasingly expensive to transport them to the area in which the firm is located.

Incorporating adjustment costs in a model makes it more complete, and also provides the basis for an investment equation that determines how much adjustment will take place in each period. This typically takes the form of an Euler equation, resulting either explicitly or implicitly from an intertemporal optimization problem. It also implies that inputs are not completely fixed in the short run (except perhaps the "very" short or "immediate" run) but instead partially adjust (they are "quasi-fixed").

This changes our short run analysis, and complicates defining and interpreting capacity utilization somewhat. That is, current adjustment must be taken into account because "fixed" input stocks are moving toward their desired levels. Investment is therefore included as an argument of the shadow values of (quasi-)fixed inputs, and thus of the CU measure.

Adjustment costs cause additional complexities for the modeling of firm behavior because expectations of the future become important when current behavior depends on anticipated values of exogenous variables. This is particularly the case when the optimization problem is explicitly based on the present value of a stream of future costs (or profits), rather than just on imputation of the implied long run level of fixed inputs given current economic conditions.

This problem emerges due to the link between time periods over which optimization decisions are being made, from stocks that carry over. The firm's manager knows that next period he/she will be stuck with the decisions made now with respect to the stock inputs. Future plans therefore will take into consideration potential changes in the economic climate that are likely to affect output production and costs next period. If only a temporary change in exogenous variables is perceived very little adjustment might thus be expected to take place, whereas if the change is permanent, movement toward a new long run level of the stock based on this change is more likely.

Although taking expectations into account is important, little work on capacity utilization has dealt with this. Morrison [1985b], however, has shown that, as might be expected, the present-valued and current-valued optimal levels of capacity utilization will not coincide when future expectations are important. For example, say the firm expects increased demand over time and wishes to begin to expand the scale of operations in anticipation of this. Then, from current behavior it may seem that the firm is operating with excess capacity ($CU_y < 1$) but in terms of a present value computation of future profits it could be at an optimal level.[77]

---

[77] See Morrison [1985b] for a further formalization of this problem and empirical results for U.S. manufacturing.

Expectations have typically been incorporated into the production theory framework via the stochastic or econometric specification, in particular by "instrumenting" prices (and possibly output) to represent deviations of future expectations from currently observed values using instrumental variables (IV) or generalized method of moments (GMM) techniques. Other approaches to this may involve directly incorporating adaptive or rational expectations (see Morrison [1986b]). However, in a model with the structural complexity of the production theory models developed in this text, the expectations problem is often largely swept under the rug. Therefore we will bypass it for now (for further discussion see Chapter 11).

Even without the further complication of representing expected prices and output, however, incorporating adjustment costs and therefore dynamics results in a model that is empirically quite complex and thus potentially difficult to estimate (or at least to generate robust results from).

The most direct adaptation of our model to incorporate dynamics is to include investment levels ($\Delta\mathbf{x}$) as arguments of the restricted cost function, and thus explicitly to recognize that costs are higher due to internal adjustment costs when investment is taking place. That is, more variable inputs (and thus costs) are necessary to produce a given amount of output when investment is occurring, since some inputs are targeted toward carrying out the investment (such as ordering, bolting down, and training). This results in a restricted cost function of the form $TC = VC(\mathbf{p},K,\Delta K,Y,t) + p_K K$ for one quasi-fixed input K.

This function has properties similar to the standard restricted cost function, although ΔK appears as an argument of the associated variable input demand and shadow value expressions, and an Euler expression representing capital investment may be constructed as: $p_K = -\partial VC/\partial K - i\partial VC/\partial \Delta K + \Delta K \partial^2 VC/\partial K \partial \Delta K + \Delta\Delta K \partial^2 VC/\partial(\Delta K)^2$ (where $\Delta\Delta K$ is the second difference of K, $\Delta(\Delta K)$, and i is a long run discount rate).[78] This model is further elaborated in Chapter 9.

The "dynamic dual" approach often attributed to Epstein [1981] provides a somewhat more formal and rigorous treatment of the dynamic structure.[79] This approach emphasizes the general role of input adjustment lags by including investment decisions directly in the present value optimization problem, resulting in a value function of the form $J(\mathbf{p},\mathbf{x})$ where $\mathbf{p}$ is a vector

---

[78] See Berndt, Fuss and Waverman [1980], Morrison [1985a], and Morrison and Siegel [1998b] for example).

[79] Empirical applications of such a model include Vasavada and Chambers [1986], Howard and Shumway [1988], Luh and Stefanou [1991], and Fernandez *et al* [1992], for example, who used this approach to incorporate adjustment lags for inputs in aggregate U.S. agriculture, in the dairy industry, in the measurement of agricultural productivity, and in representating scale and scope elasticities, respectively.

of input and output prices (since this is typically based on a profit maximizing rather than cost minimizing model). The empirical tractability of the value function (since variable factor demand, investment and output supply equations are obtained directly as derivatives of this function), combined with the duality relationships between the production and value functions that justifies its use, makes this an attractive framework for analyzing firms' investment decisions. This framework is developed in more depth in Chapter 9.

The importance of recognizing the role of adjustment costs and thus quasi-fixity rather than fixity of factors is that the resulting models are explicitly dynamic in structure. This contrasts with the short run static models developed earlier in this chapter, where the short run is estimated and the long run is imputed but investment behavior toward the long run is not directly represented. The additional richness of the dynamic models facilitates some types of analysis but does come at the cost of additional conceptual and theoretical, and thus empirical, complexity.

5.   CAPITAL COMPOSITION AND SERVICES

Another capital issue associated with determining the flow of services from a particular amount of capital stock, and thus closely connected to the notions of shadow values and utilization, is that of obsolescence. This is in turn related to issues of capital composition and characteristics, such as vintage or the extent of high-tech or energy-efficient capital.

Accommodation of such issues is sometimes accomplished very similarly to the way we have dealt with fixity issues above, in the context of shadow values. The associated service flow (as contrasted to stock) variant on this is to adapt the measure of the capital *quantity* to reflect changes in its implicit "valuation" or composition. These are, in a sense, dual notions.

Further elaboration of these ideas may be accomplished using hedonic price or quantity models, where the characteristics of inputs (in this case capital) are explicitly identified as determinants of a "true" quality- or composition- adusted price or quantity. In this section we will overview some of the approaches and literature that address these types of issues.

One of the first literatures to deal with such questions in a framework similar to that we have been developing focused on the impact of energy price changes on the measurement of capital services. Researchers in this area attempted to document that energy price changes contributed to the productivity slowdown of the 1970s, even though much research suggested that its cost share and thus effect on production processes was too small to have generated a significant impact.

One viewpoint on this was that energy price shocks may have had an *indirect* impact on capital obsolescence, and thus on the appropriate representation of capital services for productivity growth measurement. For example Baily [1981], Berndt [1983], Berndt and Wood [1984] and Hulten *et al* [1989] focus on how increased energy prices in the 1970s may have caused less energy efficient capital equipment to become obsolete, resulting in increasingly overstated measures of capital service.

Baily suggests that the capital obsolescence issue arises due to limited evidence on scrapping of old capital or on technological changes embodied in the capital stock, which should be incorporated in the capital measure. He argues that standard capital data understated growth of the effective capital stock in the 1950s and 1960s and overstated growth from the late 1960s on, due to investment patterns after World War II and changes in the production structure in the 1970s and 1980s.

In particular, he believes that in the 1950s and 1960s substantial investment was for capital that "supplemented and modified the capital already in place", whereas technological advances of the 1970s, some of which may have been stimulated by high energy prices, made much of this capital obsolete. This therefore caused scrapping and low economic value of the remaining capital stock, which was not reflected in standard K measures that equate service flow with stock.

In this scenario, much of the investment during the 1970s and 1980s was required simply to replace the obsolete capital, and to respond to changing energy prices and satisfy environmental regulations, so net investment in productive capital was overstated.

Baily supports his argument that capital growth has been exaggerated largely by analysis of Tobin's q measures. As outlined in section 2, these measures are designed to reflect the market value of capital as compared to the replacement cost. Baily contends that q has been below unity since 1968 and declined steadily since the late 1960s. Thus, if capital is evaluated at the implied shadow price, the total value of the capital stock is much lower than that reflected in standard measures.

This is similar to adjustments by q to deal with fixity, since it is based on the notion of valuing K at Z_K rather than p_K to reflect service flow (utilized capital rather than the available stock level, if based on our model from previous sections). However, Baily interprets this in terms of obsolescence rather than the effect of fixity or utilization. The distinction between the two is not straightforward, particularly with an all-encompassing measure of firm value such as Tobin's q. This raises an important issue for interpretation of shadow value measures; different causes of deviations from market price may be observationally equivalent.

The obsolescence adjustment can be given a stronger theoretical basis by employing a hedonic function that either specifies the effective (shadow) price as a function of the measured price and exogenous changes that will affect obsolescence, or the effective quantity as a function of the measured quantity and these changes. This allows distinctions among different hypotheses about what might be causing measures of the valuation or quantity of a particular input changing (here capital).

As noted above, the price (value) and quantity perspectives on this problem may be thought of as dual notions, as was briefly touched on in the context of factor augmentation for technical change in Chapter 2. Since the shadow value of capital might vary for many reasons other than obsolescence, and obsolescence may best be conceptualized as a quality-adjustment to the capital quantity, obsolescence adjustments tend to be formulated in terms of direct quantity level rather than valuation adjustments. This suggests obsolescence can appropriately be considered a mismeasurement rather than stock/flow problem for data construction.

Issues confronted when attempting to appropriately specify "effective capital" are, however, broad and pervasive. They involve not only utilization and obsolescence but also characteristics including (but not limited to) the vintage, the high-tech nature, and the energy efficiency of the capital stock. Ideally, therefore, one might want to build a combination of such differential capital characteristics directly into the model.

One way to pursue such quality-adjustments to obtain the effective service flow of the stock of capital and their impacts on production processes involves a synthesis of hedonic and production theory modeling approaches. In turn, this general approach simplifies to more standard quantity and price adjustments, for adaptations such as those for utilization, as special cases.

One basis for such a synthesis has been provided by the theoretical treatment by Lau [1982], which was further developed by Berndt [1983] and Berndt and Wood [1984].[80] Their methodology is based on incorporating a scalar index of quality in the production function for each input that should be quality-adjusted.

If, for example, capital is the only input for which the effective and measured units differ, the production function $Y(K,v)$, where v is again a vector of J variable inputs, becomes $Y(K,b_K,v)=Y(K',v)$, where K' is the quality-adjusted or effective stock of capital and b_K is an index of capital quality . The production function therefore explicitly depends on b_K, which can be a function of whatever exogenous variables are thought to affect quality; $b_K = b_K(h_K)$ where h_K is the vector of these characteristics.

---

[80] A similar approach was used by Hulten *et al* [1989] to adjust for obsolescence for a number of specific types of machines.

The quality adjustment (more rigorously elaborated in Berndt and Wood [1984]) can take various forms. For example, they explicitly incorporated the dependence of overall capital quality on fuel efficiency by recognizing the dependence of the fuel efficiency of new investment goods in each time period on the expected price of energy during that period, (p_{Et}).

This results in a distributed lag specification that depends on the price of fuel prevailing in all previous periods when currently used capital equipment was initially purchased:

$$3.6) \quad K'_t = K_t + \Sigma_\tau \, (p^*_{EK,t-\tau}/p^*_{EK,t})^\sigma \, K_{t,t-\tau} \, ,$$

where p^*_{EK} is the value of the expected life cycle relative fuel-capital equipment services price function, $K_{t,t-\tau}$ is the amount of vintage $t-\tau$ investment surviving to time t, and σ is the substitution parameter of a constant elasticity of substitution (CES) sub-production function between fuel and capital equipment.

Since the production function depends on K', the dual restricted cost function will also depend on this effective capital service flow. Thus, to implement this model in a restricted cost function framework, VC(**p**,Y,t,K) is adapted to VC(**p**,,Y,t,K') = VC(**p**,b_K,Y,t,K). This function can then be estimated and used to establish the effects of quality-adjusting capital on indicators of firm behavior and productivity growth.[81]

The effect on traditional productivity growth (ε_{Yt}) measurement of quality-adjusting the capital stock can be expressed quite simply in terms of accounting methods if no fixity, scale economies or markups exist. In this case K' may be simply substituted for K in the computation of costs, shares and changes in the capital stock.

This results in an error bias term which depends on the ratio of K' to K, $B_K = K'/K$, where B_K is called the quality-conversion ratio for capital.[82] This results because if $K' = B_K K$, dln K'/dt = dln K/dt + dln B_K/dt. Thus, if the correct measure of productivity growth based on the effective capital stock is $\varepsilon_{Yt}' = $ dlnY/dt - $\Sigma_j S_j$ dlnv_j/dt - S_K dlnK'/dt, and the standard measure is $\varepsilon_{Yt} = \varepsilon_{Yt}' = $ dlnY/dt - $\Sigma_j S_j$ dlnv_j/dt - S_K dlnK/dt, the relationship between ε_{Yt} and ε_{Yt}' becomes $\varepsilon_{Yt}' = \varepsilon_{Yt} - S_K$ dlnB_K/dt (where the last term is the error bias from incorrectly assuming that $B_K = 1$ in the standard measurement procedures).

---

[81] For estimation the hedonic function may be estimated in the system of equations, as in Morrison and Nelson [1989]. However, due to the complicated nature of the Berndt-Wood hedonic expression, different assumptions about the parameters were made and a grid search was made to find the highest likelihood, rather than using standard systems estimating procedures.

[82] β_K clearly is related to the index of capital quality b_K, although they only coincide if the production function can be written in the form Y=f(b_KK,v)=f(β_KK,v)=f(K',v).

For the Berndt-Wood energy price adjustment taking fuel-efficiency-induced obsolescence into account, increased obsolescence rates after energy price increases in 1973 are reflected in a negative $d\ln B_K/dt$ term, and productivity growth is thus understated using standard measures of capital services. This quality-adjustment of the capital stock had a large empirical impact on productivity growth indexes for U.S. manufacturing in the Berndt-Wood study. This was increasingly true in the late 1970s as the effect of inflated energy prices in the earlier part of the decade became compounded.

Berndt and Wood found that for most years before 1971 the existing capital could be exploited more heavily than originally planned because relative energy prices were actually decreasing. Thus, costs of utilizing the capital stock were less than expected. However, after 1971, and especially post-1973, effective capital services taking obsolescence into account eventually became only about 80% of those measured without the obsolescence adjustment. This implies that growth rates of real capital input were generally overstated over this time period, and the productivity downturn exaggerated.[83]

The adaptation of economic performance indicators becomes more complicated, however, when it is recognized that the adapted value of K, K', also figures importantly in estimation of the production structure by parametric methods. It thus is inherently connected with the representation of capacity utilization and scale economies. When these characteristics of the production structure are incorporated in the estimating model, therefore, a complex pattern of dependence on factors determining obsolescence results.

This is even more evident when other production characteristics affecting capital quality are taken into account. Morrison and Nelson [1989], for example, attempted also to include vintage and embodied technical change effects explicitly as determinants of effective capital services or the "quality" of capital. A somewhat different methodology was used, however, than that developed by Berndt and Wood, since their model is difficult to implement empirically for even one quality-adjustment factor, and is not feasible analytically to implement with more factors.

---

[83]In particular, Berndt and Wood show that using the standard multifactor productivity growth measure a slowdown of 0.39 percent was found, but for the adjusted measure this became 0.30 percent. The traditional measure thus overstates the slowdown by approximately 25 percent, but the slowdown still remains after obsolescence is accounted for. A significant amount of "smoothing" of the productivity growth measure also occurs within the 1973-81 period. As Berndt and Wood [1987] state for the 1973-75, 1975-78, and 1978-81 periods: "the traditional measure first understates productivity growth by 0.52 percent (.16-.68 percent), then overstates growth during the recovery by 0.25 percent (1.18-.93 percent) and finally understates growth in the second OPEC price shock by 0.19 percent (.96-.77 percent)." For further elaboration see Berndt and Wood [1984, 1987].

Morrison and Nelson specify a more standard hedonic expression for K'. In this treatment the dependence of obsolescence on fuel efficiency (measured by current values of p_E), vintage or embodied technical change (reflected in the purchase year or vintage of the capital stock, v), and the passage of time or disembodied technical change impacts (incorporated by a standard time counter, t), is represented by $K' = g(b_K, K) = g(b_K(p_E, t, v, K), K)$.

Various assumptions about the functional form of this relationship can be made. Morrison-Nelson worked initially with a linear function but found the interactions between the arguments of the K' function were important, so a functional form similar to a generalized Leontief was used. Empirical results for 22 coal-fired electricity generating plants suggest that productivity growth declines in the 1970s were not as severe as those measured using standard methods, because obsolescence caused the productive capital stock to grow less slowly than implied by the traditional measures.

Special cases of these types of models have also provided, at least implicitly, the basis for utilization adjustments such as those in Jorgenson and Griliches (JG) [1967]. JG attempted to "internalize" capital utilization by measuring capital in the production function as utilized capital, or "true" capital services, rather than just assuming capital services were proportional to the stock. This was accomplished using the Foss [1963] CU estimates mentioned above. JG multiplied the estimated capital stock by Foss's electric motor utilization index (U) for manufacturing to generate a measure of capital, K', that can be written as $K' = K \cdot U$ or $\ln K' = \ln K + \ln U$. K' was then assumed to be the relevant, effective or quality-adjusted capital stock for the production function, which can be written as Y(K',L,t).

Note that this is similar to the standard adjustments of labor quantity measures for educational attainment to generate a measure of "effective" labor input discussed in the previous chapter. Such an adjustment to the data is typically based on the notion that effective labor input is $L'=H \cdot L$ (where H is a human capital or education index), so $\ln L' = \ln H + \ln L$.

The K' (or L') expression(s) can be written in a slightly more general form such as $\ln K' = \ln K + \kappa \ln U$, which is a simple hedonic expression for capital with the κ parameter determining the impact of utilization on capital. It might well be thought that $\kappa<1$ rather than being equal to one, since the electricity-based index might vary more than an aggregate measure utilization of capital. If so, the JG procedure is too restrictive but can be extended using hedonic methods to estimate κ.[84]

---

[84] This can be thought of as recognizing a type of "embodied" as contrasted to "disembodied" technical change, as briefly overviewed in the last chapter. Compositional and other changes in the capital stock could result in extra-efficiency of capital independently of an overall isoquant shift. This distinction has been the basis of some controversy. For a

This is in a sense a direct quantity adaptation of the capacity utilization adjustments discussed earlier in this section. The Foss index reflects electricity usage, which may be thought of as a proxy for variable input usage underlying the measurement of the shadow value of K and CU.

That is, if the Berndt and Baily ideas of using shadow valuation of the capital stock to reflect changes in utilization or obsolescence are combined with this, one might think that an appropriate measure of U might be based on the Tobin's q measure Z_K/p_K. This approach would reproduce a steady state in terms of capital usage implied by the *ex-post* capital user cost. More specifically, the adjustment of $p_K K$ to $(Z_K/p_K) \cdot (p_K K) = Z_K K$ would take the form $(Z_K/p_K) \cdot (p_K K) = p_K K'$, where $K' = K \cdot Z_K/p_K = K \cdot U$.

The JG model can thus be considered a quantity perspective on the utilization issue, based on an exogenous U measure, the direct adjustment of the quantity level, and the assumption that U is the only characteristic distinguishing K' from K. If, however, utilization is considered the only cause for a deviation of Z_K from p_K, it is preferable to recognize the endogentity of the shadow value and thus CU rather than use an *ad hoc* CU measure to pre-adjust the data. This is even more apparent if fixities for other inputs are evident, so capacity and capital utilization do not coincide.

Also, if other capital characteristics are important (such as vintage), these arguments could be used to generalize the hedonic function for K'. The resulting K' measure could then be used as an argument of VC($\cdot$), resulting in a Z_K measure that identifies fixity and resulting utilization separately from other potential determinants of capital "effectiveness", now built into the quantity measure. This could allow us to identify and include aspects of the production structure that otherwise would be difficult to untangle.

In reverse, if the JG utilization adjustment is thought to be valid, and therefore appropriately captures the impact of fixity, measuring Z_K with their utilization-adjusted K' as an argument of the model might capture other "quality" issues such as obsolescence. However, using both an *a-priori* adjustment of the capital data for utilization and separate estimation of Z_K to reflect fixity and thus utilization implies double counting.

One other capital composition issue that is useful to raise here briefly is about components of the capital stock that might not be "productive" in the sense of producing observed output. One example of this is pollution abatement capital that is regulated to be in place to produce a cleaner environment rather than measured product. Since the firm does not have a choice about this input, measured capacity utilization could differ depending on how much of the capital stock is not a choice (and "productive") variable.

---

useful overview of the literature and recent empirical application distinguishing between these two different factors affecting efficiency, see Berndt and Kolstad [1987].

This may potentially be accommodated by augmenting output measures to reflect the contribution to a cleaner environment, by including the extent of "regulatory capital" R as a characteristic of K', or by recognizing changing capital composition by separate measurement of this capital component (this type of issue is dealt with in more depth in Chapter 7). Morrison [1988b] has, for example, used the last of these approaches to characterize the differential contribution (shadow value) of R as compared to "other" capital stocks.

This approach allows consideration of how capacity utilization might depend on R by computing elasticities of CU measures with respect to the level of R. The results in Morrison [1988b] indicate that pollution abatement regulation has a negative impact on capacity utilization, and thus on the (shadow) valuation of the capital stock overall. That is, given a constant output level, increasing R implies more capacity to utilize but no growth in output demand to raise utilization, so productivity measures will be biased.

As suggested above, such a disaggregation of identifiable components of the capital stock provides another path to separate out the "returns" to or the "quality" of the capital stock reflected in shadow values or by adjustment to "effective" capital units, which fundamentally involves the characteristics or composition of the input.

6.   FURTHER REMARKS

The development of the concept of capacity utilization in this chapter highlights the economic foundation of this production characteristic. We have seen that utilization is tied to short run fixities for inputs such as capital, and thus a deviation between the shadow and market price of the input, or of short and long run costs. Constructing and implementing a model that embodies this kind of structure facilitates exploring the interrelationships among economic performance indicators such as investment, utilization and productivity.

In the next chapter we will pursue further extensions of our cost-based production theory model for representation of economic performance, by linking utilization-induced short run "scale" economies (the slope of the short run cost curve) to long run scale economies and other cost economies associated with the shapes of cost curves.

As we develop and extend our model to incorporate these kinds of "real world" production structure characteristics, the richness and interpretability of the model is expanded. However, potential difficulties with computing and interpreting the resulting economic measure also arise.

For example, as alluded to above, Klein [1960] raised questions about whether economic measures of capacity output might suffer from aggregation problems. That is, capacity outputs for firms might all be increasing. Yet industry capacity output may not be consistent with the sum of the firm's individual capacity outputs because of, say, downward sloping product demand, or upward sloping input supply curves. This raises a problem for empirical implementation of the production theory framework for CU measurement.

All researchers doing applied economic analysis with aggregate data face this sort of problem, and the solution is not at all clear. The difficulty should, however, be kept in mind, and we will return to it in various contexts as we proceed through subsequent chapters.

Since the theory of the firm provides the basis for analysis of production and cost functions, strictly speaking econometric estimation should be carried out with micro data. However, even when such data are available, noise in the data, difficulty classifying firms by industry, and important systematic problems like materials bottlenecks and other supply constraints for the industry convolute use of the data. Aggregate data that is "cleaner" and has less noise may thus be preferable in some ways.[85] In addition, many questions of interest to economists involve overall patterns in an industry or economy, which may not be answered by analysis of heterogeneous micro units. Therefore, the "fix" is not clear, although increasingly researchers are constructing and using quite micro data for analysis (see Chapter 11).

---

[85] This has been pointed out, for example, by de Leeuw [1962]. The interaction between micro capacity issues and their aggregate macroeconomic counterpart has been explored by Winston [1977].

Chapter 4

Short and Long Run Scale and other Cost Economies

In addition to utilization fluctuations, long run scale economies (diseconomies) provide another technological reason cost efficiency might increase (decrease) independently of technical change. Such economies derive from the potential for larger scale production to proceed at lower unit costs. This could possibly be due to some type of long-run "fixity" such as spreading entrepreneurial skill, managerial labor, or massive indivisible "chunks" of (more efficient than small-scale) capital across a larger productive base. Such technological characteristics are commonly represented by a U-shaped long run average cost (LAC) curve.

The concept of scale economies may therefore be explored in the context of the cost-output relationship, represented by the elasticity $\varepsilon_{TCY}=\partial \ln TC/\partial \ln Y$. However, scale economies are a somewhat restricted notion. Their interpretation in terms of returns to scale suggests proportional adjustment of inputs and long run behavior. It buries issues of multiple outputs and output composition. It also ignores the potential endogeneity of input prices that could affect costs as output (and thus input use) expands. All these production characteristics will, however, be captured in the cost-output elasticity measure.

That is, in basic production theory models derived from a cost function of the form $TC(\mathbf{p},Y,t)$, the cost economy measure ε_{TCY} reflects scale economies since it represents the proportionate cost increase necessary to support a given proportionate output expansion. If a one percent increase in output requires (in the long run) a one percent increase in all inputs and thus in costs, constant returns to scale would be implied and $\varepsilon_{TCY}=1$. If scale economies exist, then costs do not increase proportionately to output, and $\varepsilon_{TCY}<1$.

However, in the more comprehensive model we are developing, additional issues arise when defining and interpreting ε_{TCY}. For example, as seen in the previous chapter, if some input(s) such as capital is restricted or fixed in the short run, the ε_{TCY} measure may reflect short run behavior and thus utilization changes. Similarly, with sequential optimization (for example due to two quasi-fixed inputs with different adjustment speeds), this two-stage process must explicitly be built into the ε_{TCY} measure.

If input-specific scale effects differ from the overall cost impact, scale biases also exist. In turn, with multiple outputs economics may arise due to changes in output mix or composition. This implies jointness in production and resulting scope economies (or, in reverse, economies of specialization, or scope diseconomies).

In addition, pecuniary economies (or diseconomies) may exist if input prices are dependent on the amount purchased. In this case ε_{TCY} will depend on the marginal factor cost instead of the observed average factor cost p_j. If, for example, monopsony prevails, greater output levels will only be possible at higher factor costs, so the associated factor price increases will appear in ε_{TCY}.

These technological and pecuniary economies that will be embodied in the cost economy measure ε_{TCY} are conceptually different than the standard notion of scale economies, and should be distinguished. Although the theoretical specification of and measurement techniques for these aspects of the production process vary, they are closely related, and thus difficult to untangle empirically. However, to appropriately interpret and use measures of these different components of technological economies and economic performance, it is often useful to pursue such a decomposition of their effects.

This chapter outlines these adaptations and extensions to our framework for modeling and analyzing economic performance. In the first section the total cost consequences of different production characteristics of firms such as fixities, scale and scope economies and input-market-power are identified. In Section 2, a decomposition of productivity growth measures recognizing these determinants of cost efficiency is overviewed. Section 3 outlines the theoretical foundation for representing scale biases. Section 4 discusses the impacts of multiple outputs (4a), multiple quasi-fixed inputs (4b), and finally the representation of imperfect input markets (4c). All these components are motivated as separately identifiable components of overall cost economies, and thus of economic performance or cost efficiency measures.

1.   COMPONENTS OF THE COST-OUTPUT RELATIONSHIP

The cost-output elasticity from the cost function, $\varepsilon_{TCY} = \partial\ln TC/\partial\ln Y = \partial TC/\partial Y \cdot (Y/TC) = MC/AC$ may reflect various production characteristics affecting marginal and average costs. In a long run framework, where the cost function is of the most standard form, $TC(\mathbf{p},Y,t)$, this elasticity is typically interpreted as characterizing cost-side scale economies. If the value of this elasticity exceeds one, diseconomies prevail. Output expansion results in higher unit costs. That is, the LAC curve slopes up, so LMC>LAC. The reverse is the case for scale economies; ε_{TCY} <1 and LMC<LAC.

This measure of scale economies is typically interpreted as an indicator of returns to scale, which implicitly presupposes that all inputs adjust by the same proportion. However, this will not be true if scale biases exist, in which case isoquants "twist" as the firm moves up the existing isoquant map to higher output levels. This is sometimes motivated as indicating "size" economies.

In addition, if some factors are quasi-fixed, as explored in depth in the previous chapter, the constrained inputs will not be changing (at least proportionately). The "scale" economy measure must then be interpreted as one restricted by the fixity constraints, and thus reflecting movement along short- rather than long- run cost curves.

Interpretation of this as a scale economy measure becomes further convoluted if multiple quasi-fixed inputs and thus sequential optimization exist, or multiple outputs subject to some type of jointness are produced (suggesting scope economies or diseconomies). If production decisions affect other economic factors facing the firm, such as input prices, this will also be embodied in the overall cost economy measure.

Distinguishing among these potential cost economy characteristics, or factors underlying observed cost efficiency (cost per unit of production), can be motivated conceptually as an attempt to untangle movements along, movements between, and shifts in isoquants and cost curves. This requires formalization of the interactions that cause cost and output levels to change non-proportionately. This is not straightforward theoretically, and is even more complex empirically. But the different effects have distinct theoretical attributes and implications for interpretion of input demand and thus productivity patterns. Therefore, a structural model facilitating their separate identification is important for economic performance analysis.

Accommodating these characteristics as part of economic performance or productivity measures requires explicitly representing them as parts of the ε_{TCY} measure using our cost-oriented framework. Then, to identify the cost characteristics separately from technical change in a productivity growth measure, both a "correction" to the measure, and a decomposition of the primal-side measure to identify its separate components through the duality relationship, may be carried out (as in the next section). We will proceed in this direction step by step to clarify the interrelationships involved.

The initial determinant of productivity growth we theoretically isolated from other aspects of productive efficiency is technical change. Technical change has a precise definition; it has been motivated as a shift in the isoquant map so that any output level may be produced with a smaller amount of inputs (and therefore costs). As we have indicated, this "controlled experiment" is possible to carry out in a diagram, but is much more difficult to measure using real world data in which other efficiency characteristics are also affecting costs of production.

That is, as the isoquant map is shifting, other production characteristics are also changing that are difficult to separately identify with real-world data, such as concurrent "twists" along with shifts in the curves. In this case technical change is non-neutral or biased, causing differential proportional impacts across inputs, as discussed in Chapter 2. Again, this is not readily identifiable as a technological effect without an econometric model, since input composition may also be changing due to input price changes, and other kinds of exogenous economic forces.

Changes in economic conditions such as input prices, and resulting alterations in the composition of input demand (and thus costs), do not imply any change in technology or scale or have any necessary linkage with increasing efficiency. They simply reflect economic forces that are exogenous to the firm's behavior, and the associated optimal (cost-minimizing) responses. This reasoning provided the motivation in Chapter 2 for dividing out the impacts of substitution from single factor measures of technical efficiency to generate a more interpretable multifactor measure of true productivity growth. However, when additional production characteristics "muddy the water", it becomes more difficult to separately identify such characteristics in economic performance measures.

Further, scale economies arise when movement *between* isoquants causes a less than proportional increase in inputs and therefore costs, independently of any change in the isoquant map itself. This will result in lower unit costs of production due strictly to technological forces operating as the scale of production expands – a movement *along* the scale expansion path and thus the long run cost curve. This additional component of overall efficiency or "productivity growth", should be independently represented if the technical change portion of cost efficiency changes is to be correctly identified.

Again, biases may also occur if scale changes affect inputs differently, therefore saving on some more than others (or production is non-homothetic, as discussed in the next section). These further complicating factors cannot easily be separately identified from shifts in the entire isoquant map and thus the cost curves without a parametric treatment which theoretically and statistically reproduces the experiment we carry out in our diagrams when representing one change in isolation.

As seen in Chapter 3, input fixity may cause cost responses to output changes to differ from those possible if movement to a new equilibrium were to take place. This results in a possibly inefficient (in terms of lowest possible or best practice) method of production in the short run, even though in the long run there is potential to reduce costs further given the current technology. Less than optimal capacity utilization therefore can cause elevated production costs even when optimal short-run behavior is exhibited.

If multiple (say, two) quasi-fixed inputs exist, this implies a nested set of cost curves representing the short-, intermediate-, and long-run, as developed further in Section 5. These "runs" are defined such that both quasi-fixed inputs are fixed (or partially adjusted) in the short run; the most variable quasi-fixed input is adjusted fully by the intermediate run; and the most costly to adjust input is at its steady state value by the long run. Adjustment constraints therefore imply distinctions between layers of short and long run behavior and thus cost curves, in turn suggesting sequential optimization. This again cannot be identified directly from observed data that by definition reflects short run responses, but requires parametric or econometric analysis.

In addition to these pieces of the puzzle already discussed or at least inferred in previous chapters, other aspects of cost economies will also be reflected in the ε_{TCY} measure. As elaborated in Section 4, when multiple outputs are produced, scope economies will cause changes in "other" outputs to shift the cost curves defined in terms of one type of output.

If, for example, scale economies are defined in terms of output Y_m, jointness will imply that interaction terms with other outputs (say Y_l) will appear in the ε_{TCYm} measure (they are shift variables in the cost function diagram defined in terms of Y_m). If, instead, scale economies are defined by production of all outputs, a combination of such interaction terms will appear in the ε_{TCY} measure since it reflects a change in "overall" output.

Other shift factors (interdependencies) will arise if input prices are not exogenous. As discussed further in Chapter 6 in the context of market power in input markets, for example, if the price of input j depends on the demand for v_j, and thus on output production, the cost function should be written with $p_j(v_j)$ or v_j as an argument.

If the former treatment is chosen, an endogenous variable (v_j) is incorporated in the cost function, which implies a second-stage response of p_j, which would shift the cost curve expressed in terms of a given p_j. If v_j is included in the function, Shephard's lemma no longer applies to this input so an adapted optimization equation must be defined to reflect the market power implied by the dependence of p_j on v_j. The total cost function must then include variable costs defined in terms of other inputs, plus a $p_j(v_j)v_j$ term (similarly to the treatment of capital fixity in Chapter 3, which also causes Shephard's lemma to be invalid). Changing output would therefore have a second order effect on the demand for v_j, and thus on p_j, affecting the cost-output relationship.

All these impacts on the cost-output relationship must be identified separately for appropriate interpretation of cost efficiency. Such a decomposition of the ε_{TCY} measure is pursued in steps in the following subsections. First, however, we will determine how the resulting ε_{TCY} measure may be distinguished from technical change.

2. COST ECONOMIES VS. TECHNICAL CHANGE

To formally motivate the theoretical connection of productivity growth measures to the various types of cost economies reflected in the ε_{TCY} measure, we can begin with the cost-side specification of productivity growth reflected in equation (2.9), and the duality connection identified in (2.12), summarized here as (4.1):

4.1) $\varepsilon_{TCt} = \partial\ln TC/\partial t = d\ln TC/dt - d\ln Y/dt - \Sigma_j\ p_jv_j/TC \cdot d\ln p_j/dt$

$$= -d\ln Y/dt + \Sigma_j\ p_jv_j/TC \cdot d\ln v_j/dt = -\varepsilon_{Yt} \ .$$

If, however, $\varepsilon_{TCY} = \partial\ln TC/\partial\ln Y$ differs from one, which will be the case if any of the cost economies overviewed in the previous section exist, (4.1) becomes an invalid measure of technical change. It is based on an erroneous assumption that generates an error bias.

That is, as discussed briefly in Chapter 2, (4.1) is based on the assumption that the total cost function can be represented by $TC = Y\cdot AC(\mathbf{p},t)$ so $\varepsilon_{TCY} = 1$ and $d\ln AC/dt = d\ln (TC/Y)/dt = d\ln TC/dt - d\ln Y/dt$. However, if $\varepsilon_{TCY} \neq 1$, this becomes $d\ln (TC/Y)/dt = d\ln TC/dt - \varepsilon_{TCY} (d\ln Y/dt)$.

We will initially explore the theoretical basis for correcting (4.1) to recognize $\varepsilon_{TCY} \neq 1$, and the associated decomposition of the overall primal productivity growth measure to distinguish cost economies and technical change. We will then begin adding refinements to the ε_{TCY} measure to separate out capacity utilization and scale economies in this section, and then to incorporate the more complex (and less commonly recognized) interactions alluded to above in following sections.

More specifically, to correct for $\varepsilon_{TCY} \neq 1$ if this occurs because of scale economies, the residual ε_{TCt} must be adjusted to

4.2) $\varepsilon^A_{TCt} = d\ln TC/dt - \varepsilon_{TCY}\ d\ln Y/dt - \Sigma_j\ p_jv_j/TC \cdot d\ln p_j/dt$

$$= -\varepsilon_{TCY}\ d\ln Y/dt + \Sigma_j\ p_jv_j/TC \cdot d\ln v_j/dt$$

$$= \varepsilon_{TCt} + (1 - \varepsilon_{TCY}) \cdot d\ln Y/dt,$$

as shown in Morrison [1992b], where A represents "adjusted", and the second equality is from the Ohta [1975] derivation of the equivalence of cost- and primal- side productivity growth measures ε_{TCt} and ε_{Yt} in Ch. 2.

The last term of (4.2) captures an "error bias" resulting from the inappropriate assumption that $\varepsilon_{TCY}=1$ in (4.1). If the deviation of ε_{TCY} from one is due to nonconstant returns to scale, the adaptation can be interpreted as reflecting the fact that $MC \neq AC$. Therefore, if output changes, its valuation should be at marginal rather than average costs.[86]

That is, ε_{TCt} differs from ε^A_{TCt} by $(1-\varepsilon_{TCY}) \cdot dln\ Y/dt$. This correction shows to what degree standard nonparametric procedures for measurement of technical change are invalid when cost economies exist. However, if a cost function appropriately incorporating cost economies were specified, the resulting elasticity measure ε_{TCt} would accommodate these characteristics of the production process, and thus separately identify technical change.

Also, since cost economies may not in most cases be identified without a full model of the cost structure, nonparametric procedures are unlikely to be justifiable for measuring cost-side productivity growth. Primal measures will still be valid, but will preclude separate identification of cost economies and technical change as two independent aspects of overall productivity or economic performance.

More specifically, even with the error adjustment a difference arises between the primal and cost measures. Since the primal measure is $\varepsilon_{Yt} = dlnY/dt - \Sigma_j(p_j v_j/p_Y Y) \cdot dlnv_j/dt$, and $\varepsilon_{TCY} = MC \cdot Y/TC = p_Y Y/TC$ with perfect competition, the correspondence between the primal and dual productivity growth specifications now must be adapted to read $-\varepsilon_{Yt} = \varepsilon^A_{TCt}/\varepsilon_{TCY} = \varepsilon^A_{TCt}'$.

This adaptation stems from the fact that the shares weighting the output growth rates in the cost measure are in terms of costs, and with nonconstant returns to scale costs no longer equal returns (revenue, $p_Y Y$). From the equality $\varepsilon_{TCY} = MC \cdot Y/TC$ above, $p_Y Y = TC \cdot \varepsilon_{TCY} = MC \cdot Y/AC \cdot Y = TC$. Thus, if the denominator of (4.2) is multiplied by ε_{TCY}, which implies dividing the entire expression by ε_{TCY}, the equivalence of the cost and primal measures again emerges.

This modification is typically attributed to Ohta [1975], whose focus was clarifying the duality relationship rather than providing the basis for separating components of productivity growth measures. It is only appropriate, however, if the cost-side measure has already been adjusted for $\varepsilon_{TCY} \neq 1$ so there is no error bias. Conceptually the definition of ε^A_{TCt}' as a product of two cost derivatives is a decomposition of the primal measure into two parts – the effects of technical change and of cost economies – since the output-oriented measure reflects both characteristics of production.[87]

---

[86] Recall that $\varepsilon_{TCY} = MC \cdot Y/TC = MC \cdot Y/AC \cdot Y = MC/AC$, so the adjustment by ε_{TCY} restates the change in output in terms of its correct marginal value.

[87] Note that the primal measure does not have a bias correction because the assumption $\varepsilon_{TCY}=1$ was not used for construction of the measure.

The first reason we explored for $\varepsilon_{TCY} \neq 1$ was fixity constraints in Chapter 3. In particular, we found that $\varepsilon_{TCY} = 1 - \Sigma_k \varepsilon_{TCk}$ for multiple quasi-fixed inputs when CRS prevails, or $\varepsilon_{TCY} = 1 - \varepsilon_{TCK}$ if capital only is fixed. Incorporating the deviation between short run costs and minimum long run costs so that technical change is correctly measured requires adjusting the weight on the growth in output by this ε_{TCY} as in (4.2).

For this adaptation, as in the general case of cost economies, the dual and primal measures no longer coincide. Reproducing the primal from the cost-side expression now implicitly requires defining the shares in terms of the shadow values of the fixed inputs. That is, although the adjustment is still motivated in terms of ε_{TCY}, this elasticity now has a specific form in terms of the subequilibrium impact. $\varepsilon_{TCY} = 1 - \varepsilon_{TCK} = TC^*/TC$ with only capital fixed, so dividing the shares by ε_{TCY} results in specifying the shares in terms of TC* instead of TC. In turn, we can decompose the primal measure into its individually identifiable technical change and capacity utilization impacts as formalized below, resulting in $-\varepsilon_{Yt} = \varepsilon^F_{TCt}/\varepsilon_{TCY} = \varepsilon^F_{TCt}'$, where F now specifies that this adjustment is in terms of "fixity" effects.

Specific interpretation of the adjustment factor is important for both interpretation and appropriate use of the measures, since in some cases, including that for fixity, *additional* adjustments must be made to standard productivity measures to correct for the erroneous assumption that $\varepsilon_{TCY} = 1$. In the presence of fixities, for example, it must be recognized that if the quasi-fixed input shares (both cost and revenue) are evaluated at p_k, observed changes in these inputs are not being weighted at their correct marginal values. In fact, they should be valued at their shadow values Z_k for construction of both the dual and primal measures.

This is another variant on the theme that the correct valuation of inputs or outputs for productivity or economic performance analysis should be in terms of their true marginal economic benefits (or costs). If markets are working perfectly (instantaneous adjustment rather than fixity in this case) the market price is a justifiable approximation to this marginal value. However, if this is not the case, due to adjustment constraints, market structure, or other deviations from "perfect" markets, this should be accommodated.

As discussed already in Chapter 3 this is the role shadow values play. In the case of fixed capital the deviation between Z_K and p_K is due to adjustment costs. In other cases, the "wedge" between the observed market and true marginal valuation may be due to other market imperfections.

To formally motivate this, if $\varepsilon_{TCY} \neq 1$ because of fixity and thus non-optimal capacity utilization, the assumptions underlying (4.1) are further violated. As seen in Chapter 2, the construction of (4.1) relies on Shephard's lemma, which is used to substitute v_j, the cost minimizing demand for input j, for $\partial TC/\partial p_j$ for all inputs.[88] If any input x_k is fixed, however, this is not valid because the firm cannot choose its cost minimizing level. Thus, VC and TC do not change proportionately with output even with long run CRS; costs change extra-proportionately in the short run due to input constraints.

Computation of the shadow value representing these excess costs typically requires parametric analysis, although it is sometimes represented as an *ex-post* measure of capital computed as the residual $p_Y \cdot Y$-VC. This is only valid in the case of only one quasi-fixed input, perfect competition and constant returns to scale (as discussed further in Chapter 11). If these assumptions are violated, the Z_k cannot be estimated nonparametrically; the returns to these different characteristics of the production process cannot be untangled by just data manipulation. This is true in general for measurement of ε_{TCY}, as suggested above, since this cost elasticity is not likely to be observable even if only one extension of the base model is accommodated.

In sum, if fixities exist so the assumption that market prices approximate the marginal products of inputs cannot be made, $\varepsilon_{TCY} = 1-\Sigma_k\varepsilon_{TCk} = CU_c \neq 1$ because $Z_k \neq p_k$, and the shadow values Z_k rather than p_k are required for valuation of the x_k inputs. The corrected dual cost productivity measure computed from the variable cost function then becomes:

$$4.3)\ \varepsilon^F_{TCT} = -(1-\Sigma_k\varepsilon_{TCk})\ d\ln Y/dt + \Sigma_k Z_k x_k/TC \cdot d\ln x_k/dt + \Sigma_j p_j v_j/TC \cdot d\ln v_j/dt$$

$$= \varepsilon_{TCt} + \Sigma_k\ \varepsilon_{TCk}\ (d\ln Y/dt - d\ln x_k/dt)\ ,$$

using the second equality of (4.2), which reduces to

$$4.4)\ \varepsilon^F_{TCT} = -(1-\varepsilon_{TCK}) \cdot d\ln Y/dt + Z_k K/TC \cdot d\ln K/dt + \Sigma_j\ p_j v_j/TC \cdot d\ln v_j/dt$$

$$= \varepsilon_{TCt} + \varepsilon_{TCK} \cdot (d\ln Y/dt - d\ln K/dt)$$

with only capital fixed.[89] The last term in this expression is again an error bias that occurs now if instantaneous adjustment is assumed when subequilibrium really exists. Note that the bias depends on the relative growth rates of output and the quasi-fixed inputs since the $\varepsilon_{TCk}=0$ assumption affects the weights on both these components of the measure.[90]

---

[88] See Chapter 9 for more detail about the underlying duality theory.

[89] This is developed in more detail in Morrison [1992b].

[90] Equations (4.2) and (4.3) are based on an output-side computation of the cost measure, where dln TC/dt has been substituted. Alternatively, the cost side measure can be

After the error bias correction is made, to identify potential productivity separately from the effects of disequilibrium, we can derive:

$$4.5) \; \varepsilon^{F'}_{TCT} = \varepsilon^{F}_{TCT} / (1 - \Sigma_k \, \varepsilon_{TCk}) = -d\ln Y/dt + \Sigma_k \, Z_k x_k / TC \cdot d\ln x_k/dt$$

$$+ \Sigma_j \, p_j v_j / TC \cdot d\ln v_j/dt = -\varepsilon_{Yt} \; .$$

This cost elasticity combination disentangles $-\varepsilon_{Yt}$ to identify independently the technical change (ε^{F}_{TCT}) and fixity $(CU_c = 1 - \Sigma_k \varepsilon_{TCk})$ impacts.

It should be emphasized that, although the first adjustment (for the error bias) corrects for erroneous assumptions in the unadjusted measure, the second adaptation or decomposition instead facilitates interpretation. Depending on the context, either ε^{F}_{TCt} $(\varepsilon^{A}_{TCt}$ more generally) or $\varepsilon_{Yt} = -\varepsilon^{F'}_{TCt}$ $(\varepsilon^{A'}_{TCt})$ might be a more appropriate representation of productivity growth.

The point of the decomposition to generate a primal-side equivalent is to highlight the changes in the duality relationship, and the independent factors incorporated in MFP measures based on a cost framework, rather than to identify the "best" or "correct" measure. In many cases, however, the additional interpretation potential of the cost-based treatment is useful for analyzing economic performance.

More specifically, in some circumstances one might think short run constraints due to fixity are a valid element of observed cost changes that should be jointly incorporated in an indicator of productivity growth. However, in most cases identifying the individual contributions of technical change and utilization or fixity (or other aspects of cost economies) to observed changes in "productivity" would seem desirable. The decomposition of ε_{Yt} from the cost side then provides more interpretative potential than the primal measure,

Further qualifications are required if both nonconstant returns to scale (NCRS) and fixities exist, since adjustments must be made for both of these aspects of cost economies. The decomposition of ε_{TCY} into these different production structure characteristics must first be established; then adaptation of the productivity growth measure can be carried out similarly to (4.2). Re-valuing the output change appropriately at its marginal value accommodates changes in output that should not be attributed to technical change, whether they result from scale economies or subequilibrium. The shadow value adaptation must also be made to accommodate fixity constraints.

---

calculated directly, although the adjustment is not as straightforward. See Morrison [1992b] for further elaboration and additional adaptations to include dynamic adjustment.

Let us denote the long run cost elasticity with respect to output $\varepsilon^L_{TCY} =$ dln TC/dln Y = η. With homotheticity (no input scale biases so the SEP is a ray from the origin), η will also reflect the long run elasticity of any input with respect to output. In particular, dln K/dln Y = (dK/dY) $\bullet$ Y/K = η with full adjustment to the long run. Manipulations equivalent to those in (3.4) result in $\varepsilon_{TCY} = \eta(1-\varepsilon_{TCK})$ (or $\eta(1-\Sigma_k\varepsilon_{TCk})$ with multiple fixed inputs) so the cost economy measure has two identifiable components representing returns to scale and capacity utilization.

More specifically:

$$4.6)\ \varepsilon_{TCY} = \eta(1- \varepsilon_{TCK}) = \varepsilon^L_{TCY} \bullet CU_c = (MC \bullet Y)/TC^* \bullet TC^*/TC \ ,$$

where $\eta = \varepsilon^L_{TCY} = (MC \bullet Y)/TC^*$ is the inverse of the primal returns to scale measure, $(1-\varepsilon_{TCK}) = CU_c = TC^*/TC$ is the cost side measure of capacity utilization with only one quasi-fixed input, capital (K), and the last equality is from Morrison [1992b].

This becomes more complex when nonhomotheticity exists, since in this case $\partial TC/\partial K \bullet (\partial K/\partial Y) \bullet (Y/TC)$ cannot be written as $(\partial TC/\partial K) \bullet K/TC =$ ∂ln TC/∂ln K because $\partial K/\partial Y \bullet (Y/K) \neq \eta$, so $\partial K/\partial Y \neq \eta$ K/Y. In particular, when this simplification is disallowed, (3.4) becomes:

$$4.7)\ \varepsilon^L_{TCY} = dln\ TC/dln\ Y = \partial TC/\partial Y \bullet (Y/TC) + \partial TC/\partial K \bullet \partial K/\partial Y \bullet Y/C$$

$$= \varepsilon_{TCY} + \varepsilon_{TCK}\varepsilon_{KY} = \eta,\ so$$

$$\varepsilon_{TCY} = \eta - \varepsilon_{TCK}\varepsilon_{KY} = \eta[1- (\varepsilon_{KY}/\eta)\ \varepsilon_{TCK}]$$

(an analogous result can easily be developed if additional fixed inputs exist). This creates further difficulties untangling the differential scale effects, as well as complicating the computation of CU_c since it now becomes a combination of the scale effects; $CU_c = (1-[\varepsilon_{KY}/\eta]\ \varepsilon_{TCK})$.[91]

Finally, these performance components can be illustrated diagramatically. Figure 8 identifies three types of cost changes that may be reflected in productivity measures when subequilibrium and scale impacts are ignored.

Assume the firm was initially in equilibrium at point A in time period 0 at the tangency of the short run average cost curve SAC_0 (defined for a fixed capital stock K_0) and the long run average cost curve LAC_0. Between periods 0 and 1 technical change caused these curves to fall to SAC_1 and LAC_1.

---

[91] See Morrison [1985a, 1988c] for further details and an empirical application.

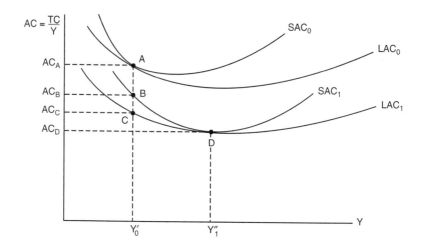

Figure 8. Components of Cost Economies

The primal response (technically possible output change given the same input use as before) is to produce Y_1'' at average cost AC_D. This average cost is lower than AC_A due to a combination of technical change and scale economies, and fixity is not an issue since this output involves the same input use as before. Thus these individual effects from these production structure characteristics are not independently observable.

Cost-side measures will instead reflect the individual "pieces of the puzzle" – the cost economy (unit cost) impacts of fixity constraints, scale economies and technical change. This is why they can be used to decompose the output-side measure into identifiable components representing these different aspects of cost economies, or production structure characteristics.

The first theoretical issue raised above to correct and decompose the primal productivity growth measure was to derive the error bias adjustment. This step cannot easily be motivated in diagrammatical form, however, because the existence of NCRS (the U-shape of the LAC curve) and fixity (the steeper slope of the SAC curve) is incorporated in the diagram.

If, however, it was assumed that the LAC curve were flat, and that full adjustment could be accomplished, points B, C and D would clearly not be represented correctly. Such a diagram and the corresponding analytical derivations would be erroneous. The error bias corrections, therefore, simply generate a correct diagram.

Even if the points were correctly measured, however, the duality relationship indicates that inappropriate conclusions could result if either the primal or dual measures were not appropriately interpreted. For example, in the short run at the given output level Y_0' the measured cost decline would be only to AC_B. If the assumptions of full equilibrium and CRS were made, it would be assumed from cost measures that the change from AC_A to AC_B reflected the full potential decline.

However, when subequilibrium and NCRS are recognized, the interpretation changes. Movement from AC_B to AC_C stems from adjustment of the fixed inputs (the full long run potential unit cost change). An additional unit cost decline to AC_D would be permitted if potential scale economies (to capacity output) could be taken advantage of. The complete primal side productivity change will therefore not be captured unless these potential cost declines are represented.[92]

For the primal measure, if instantaneous adjustment is assumed when it is unjustified, the movement from Y_0' to Y_1'' will be misrepresented because the market price is greater than the shadow value of capital in the short run. Therefore, the weight on capital growth will be incorrect, resulting in over- or under- representation of productivity growth depending on whether capital growth during this period was positive or negative. Assuming CRS also limits interpretation, because the entire movement from AC_A to AC_D will be assumed to be a result of technical change.

Expression (4.7) therefore facilitates both the error bias correction as in (4.4) and decomposition of the full potential change in output and costs via independent indicators of technical change, capacity utilization and scale economies identifiable from the full ε_{TCY} measure, analogously to (4.5).[93] This permits justifiable interpretation of measured productivity growth and its various production structure characteristics in terms of cost efficiency.

Note also that input-specific effects that may or may not be proportional underlie these overall cost impacts representing cost efficiency and productivity. For the case of scale economies, variations in input-specific scale patterns imply nonhomotheticity, and thus scale biases, or more generally biased cost economies, as is explored in more detail in the next section.

---

[92] Note, however, that all these measures are point estimates, evaluated at the observed input-output combination. The elasticity measures therefore indicate the potential change, but in a continuous rather than discrete manner.

[93] Alternative decomposition frameworks such as that proposed by Fuss and Waverman [1986] have also been used. Although clearly analogous to that used here, the motivation and interpretation differ somewhat.

3.   SCALE BIASES

We have motivated the representation and measurement of technical change, shadow values of fixed inputs (and thus capacity utilization), and scale economies as various type of cost elasticities. To reiterate briefly, if the cost function is of the form $TC(\mathbf{p},Y,K,p_K,t) = VC(\mathbf{p},Y,K,t)+p_KK$ (with one quasi-fixed input K), the derivative of this function with respect to t ($\partial TC/\partial t$) reflects the impact of t changes independently of other factors affecting costs. The derivative with respect K ($\partial TC/\partial K = \partial VC/\partial K+p_K$) represents the (net) shadow value of capital, p_K-Z_K. The derivative with respect to Y ($\partial TC/\partial Y$) captures the slope of the short run cost curve, or, if K adjustment is appended to impute the long run (based on the idea of a chain derivative, $\partial TC/\partial Y + \partial TC/\partial K\bullet[\partial K/\partial Y]$), the long run curve. Expressing these derivatives in percentage (logarithmic) terms restructure them as the elasticities $\varepsilon_{TCt}=\partial\ln TC/\partial t$, $\varepsilon_{TCK}=\partial\ln TC/\partial\ln K$, $\varepsilon_{TCY}=\partial\ln TC/\partial\ln Y$ (K fixed), and $\varepsilon^L_{TCY}=d\ln TC/d\ln Y$ (with K adjustment).

In addition, in Chapter 2 we overviewed the concept of technical change biases, and in Chapter 3 developed utilization biases. The underlying notion of biases is that input-specific responses to whatever change in the economic environment we are addressing (t or K changes) may differ proportionately from the overall (input cost) change.

The most commonly discussed type of biases, technical change biases, imply that Hicks neutrality (the proportional change in costs is the same as that for each input, implying that the shift of isoquants is parallel) is not a legitimate assumption. Technical change instead augments or reduces the use of some inputs relative to others.

That is, input-j-saving implies that this input is becoming relatively "productive"; less of input v_j is required in terms of proportions or cost-shares, so its measured SFP rises. In reverse, this implies that the input which is being "used" more heavily has become technically more efficient relative to its price. The input's marginal product is enhanced so more is used at given input prices.

Typically, for example, if technical change generates greater capital intensity because the productive power of capital units is being augmented, at given input prices technical change will be capital-using and labor-saving. This will result in greater labor productivity (labor use per unit output). In turn, it implies a "twist" of isoquants as the map shifts in.

Rather than reflecting the changing shape of isoquants as they shift, *utilization* biases derive from differential substitution of variable inputs with a given amount of capital. That is, on an isoquant diagram, they reflect the shapes of isoquants along a horizontal line (with K on the vertical axis) as this line crosses each isoquant.

At any point on an isoquant, its shape reflects the marginal technical rate of substitution of L (or other input) for K given a particular Y-K combination. The question the utilization bias addresses is: if the constraint on K is relaxed, so K changes on the margin, how does use of other inputs change? More capital means in general that less variable inputs are required for production, but the amount each input adapts to a change in K depends on its substitutability with the capital input. Differential adaptation among inputs implies that utilization biases exist.

This may also be interpreted as a short run "scale" bias, since at the corresponding point on the SAC curve changes in K given Y and in Y given K will have closely related cost effects. This has been shown in the context of the intertwined nature of the ε_{TCK} and ε_{TCY} measures, which implies that the short run input-specific effects, say ε_{jK} and ε_{jY}, will also be connected.

For the long run scale economy measure $\varepsilon^L_{TCY} = $ dln TC/dln Y = (Y/TC)•[∂TC/∂Y + ∂TC/∂K•(∂K/∂Y)] (or $\varepsilon_{TCY} =$∂ln TC/∂ln Y with no input fixity), differential input-specific effects will be embodied in the overall measure if the shapes of isoquants change as the firm adapts its scale of operation. This implies moving along the SEP for a given isoquant map. Different isoquant shapes thus imply that the SEP is not a straight line, in turn suggesting nonhomotheticity[94].

Since the notion of scale biases is closely connected to the homogeneity of the cost function with respect to output, and since confusion often arises about these concepts, before developing this further it is worth exploring briefly what homogeneity and homotheticity mean. In particular, scale economies have to do with the "distance" between isoquants as we move out on the SEP. (Relative) input specific impacts involve the slopes of the isoquants along a ray from the origin for different production levels.

As discussed more formally in Chapter 9, one "regularity" condition (or condition required for logical consistency) for a cost function is that it is homogeneous of degree one in input prices. If all input prices change by the same proportion (the slope of the isocost line is constant), the implicit level of costs for a particular output level just increases by the same proportion.[95]

---

[94] Briefly (as elaborated below), this is closely related to the homogeneity of the production function (constant or nonconstant output elasticities with respect to inputs) and thus cost function. Homogeneity of the cost function to any degree with respect to output (which will be one with CRS), or even homotheticity, results in constant long run input shares with scale changes. All inputs change proportionately to each other and thus to costs. Only in the case of nonhomotheticity will the input shares change for different output levels, causing a twist in the SEP. This was alluded to in the previous section in the context of a difference between the ε^L_{TCY} and ε^L_{KY} elasticities.

[95] I have found that a common misunderstanding of students about this relationship is exactly what should be multiplied by the proportional factor (say λ) to represent or test for it.

There is no such requirement for the cost-output relationship; that is, if Y is multiplied by a proportional factor λ there is no necessary cost implication. With CRS, however, costs will increase by the same factor; linear homogeneity (homogeneity of degree one) means output changes cause a proportional adjustment in inputs and thus costs. In the isoquant diagram this implies isoquant curves are evenly "spaced" – if we double inputs, the output represented by the corresponding isoquant doubles.

If instead homogeneity of degree λ exists, output increases cause costs to increase by λ times the proportional increase. With homotheticity, costs will increase by a function of the degree of homogeneity (thus "nesting" homogeneity, since homogeneity is more restricted). In both these cases, however, the isoquant slopes remain the same. Only the "spaces" between isoquants are dependent on the degree of homogeneity or homotheticity.

Only with nonhomotheticity does the isoquant map change shape at higher levels of production or scale. In this case as output expands different input combinations become efficient (for given input prices). For example, a large-scale plant may find its most efficient input combination is much more capital intensive than a small plant that cannot take advantage of the cost efficiencies embodied in large capital units.[96]

The direct link between returns to scale and scale economies is also broken, since the production-function-side notion of returns to scale requires proportional changes in inputs, whereas scale economies refers to the overall cost-output relationship where input-specific effects may exist. This is sometimes referred to as a difference between scale and size economies.

If nonhomotheticity and thus input-specific scale effects are exhibited characteristics of the production structure, this implies that the (long run) cost-output elasticity ε^L_{TCY} differs from the (long run) input-output elasticities ε^L_{jY}, as well as the (long run) capital-output elasticity ε_{KY} discussed in the previous section. The ε^L_{jY} elasticities are defined similarly to the cost-output elasticity but are based on a second-order derivative, since from Shephard's lemma $v_j = \partial TC/\partial p_j$, so $\varepsilon_{jY} = \partial \ln v_j/\partial \ln Y = (Y/TC)\partial^2 TC/\partial p_j \partial Y$.

With no input fixity this is the input-j-specific long-run output or scale elasticity. With K fixity, this becomes $\varepsilon^L_{jY} = (Y/TC) \cdot (\partial v_j/\partial Y + \partial v_j/\partial K \cdot [\partial K/\partial Y])$, similarly to the development of ε^L_{TCY} above. This clearly depends on both the substitutability of v_j and K through the $\partial v_j/\partial K$ derivative (holding Y fixed), and the long run K-Y relationship ε_{KY} (since $\partial K/\partial Y$ is defined in terms of the long run desired level of capital K*).

Since this is homogeneity in prices, *only* the price terms should be multiplied. This has no implication for the cost-output relationship; in particular Y is *not* multiplied by λ.

[96] Clearly this is also an issue of indivisibility which is often alluded to to motivate the notion of nonhomotheticity.

Scale biases have to do with the difference between the ε^L_{TCY} and ε^L_{jY} elasticities, which formally are expressed in terms of (long run) shares. Note that these shares are also based on cost-elasticities, similarly to ε_{TCt}, ε_{TCk} and ε_{TCY} – in this case with respect to input price. The elasticity (or logarithmic or proportional) form of Shephard's lemma is $S_j = \varepsilon_{TCj} = \partial \ln TC / \partial \ln p_j$.

More specifically, the differential impact of short run output fluctuations on individual inputs can be represented analogously to technical change and utilization biases, by determining the change in the share given a change in output demand. This Hicksian output- or "scale"- bias is:

4.8) $B_{jY} = \partial S_j / \partial \ln Y = p_j v_j / TC \cdot [(\partial v_j / \partial Y) \cdot Y/v_j - (\partial TC / \partial Y) \cdot Y/TC]$

$$= S_j (\varepsilon_{jY} - \varepsilon_{TCY})$$

where $\varepsilon_{jY} = \partial \ln v_j / \partial \ln Y$. This can alternatively be expressed as the Uzawa output bias: $B^U_{jY} = \partial \ln S_j / \partial \ln Y = \varepsilon_{jY} - \varepsilon_{TCY}$.

Although this bias may be thought of as a scale bias, when measured from a restricted cost function (K fixed) it reflects a short run change and thus does not represent true scale but instead returns to only the variable inputs. This results again because ε_{TCY} incorporates both CU and returns to scale.

For a true long run scale bias both ε_{jY} and ε_{TCY} must be measured in terms of their long run (K adjusted) values. This emphasizes the linkage between the notion of a (short run) utilization and (long run) scale bias, which both ultimately depend on the cost-output relationship but are expressed in terms of different adjustment and thus cost curves (or expansion paths).

The scale bias can be interpreted similarly to the technical change bias; ε_{TCY} represents the average- and ε_{jY} the input-specific- output effect. If, for example v_j is labor (L) and ε_{LY} is very small so $B_{jY} < 0$, this implies increasing returns to labor relative to other inputs. Short run increases in output are therefore input j (labor) saving. In this case stagnation of output demand (a recessionary contraction) implies an expansion in the share of labor, which will hurt workers less than if the decline in all inputs were proportional. Symmetry of bias terms further implies that $\partial S_j / \partial \ln Y$ can be redefined as $\partial \varepsilon_{TCY} / \partial \ln p_j$; $B_{jY} < 0$ also means that p_j increases augment cost economies.

Note also that since the biases are defined in terms of cost elasticities, the linkages between technical change, utilization, and scale can also be formalized as symmetrical relationships. For example, a "bias" term could be defined as $B_{Yt} = \partial \varepsilon_{TCY} / \partial t$. This measure indicates how ε_{TCY} adapts to a change in the state of technology, which in turn summarizes the combined change in capacity utilization and scale economies from technical change. The effect only on capacity utilization can be isolated by computing $B_{Kt} = \partial\varepsilon_{TCk}/\partial t$ (with only capital fixed).

Similar "biases" can be defined in terms of changes in ε_{TCY}, ε_{TCt} or ε_{TCk} with respect to Y or x_k. Athough the structural similarity of these measures to biases provides interesting implications for analysis, however, conceptually it seems more useful to motivate them directly in the context of second-order elasticities. The bias interpretation is somewhat ambiguous.

Finally, although the discussion in this section has focused on (short- and long- run) scale economies, when other aspects of cost economies are incorporated into the model the resulting input-specific elasticities ε_{jY}, as well as output elasticity ε_{TCY}, embody these components of the production structure. Therefore, for example, with multiple outputs both output-specific ε_{jYm} measures and the "full" output elasticity ε_{jY} may be constructed. This more general framework for cost economies is pursued in the next section.

4.   COST ECONOMIES MORE GENERALLY

As emphasized in the preceding section, many production characteristics may be captured as cost-elasticities with respect to arguments of the cost function. Perhaps the most fundamental cost elasticity measure stemming from our model is the cost-output elasticity $\varepsilon_{TCY} = \partial\ln TC/\partial\ln Y$, since this represents cost curves typically developed in TC-Y space in microeconomics courses. Differences among these cost curves arise from technical change (or other external shift factors, as developed in the next chapter) and fixities (differences between short and long run curves). Movements along the (short and long run) curves reflect all other aspects of (internal) cost economies.

As we have developed so far, internal cost economies simply reflect utilization changes (or economies) in the short run, and scale economies (or economies of size) in the long run. However, the production structure may also be characterized by other economies such as scope economies.

Incorporating such economies requires distinguishing among different types of outputs, since scope economies result from joint output production, which in turn has implications for analysis of the causes and consequences of vertical (or horizontal) integration. Multiple quasi-fixed inputs, and the interactions among their adjustment processes, may also complicate the representation of short- as compared to long- run cost economies.

Other observation-specific cost determinants such as multi-plant economies may also exist. Addressing this kind of issue requires disaggregated data for plants and firms. Spillover effects across firms or industries (such as agglomeration or thick market effects) may also occur.

Accommodating such production structure characteristics also requires disaggregation into sub-industries, or even plants (firms).

Endogeneity of some arguments of the cost function, in particular input prices due to input market imperfections, may also drive cost economies. In this case the associated market structure must be recognized in the model.

In this section we will address the potential for multiple outputs, quasi-fixed inputs, and multiple-plant firms to complicate our analysis of economic performance, as motivated by cost economy measurement. We will also touch on the issue of input market imperfections, although further development of this will be postponed to Chapter 6, which focuses on market structure and power issues. Spillover effects, which are by definition exogenous to the individual firm, will be addressed in the next chapter in the context of external economies.

4.1 Multiple Outputs

We can trace through the various production and market forces embodied in the overall cost economy measure by carefully considering how they might be represented within the structural model outlined above. The first extension to develop is how "output" Y, and thus "scale economies" are defined with multiple outputs.

The initial issue is how to adapt the cost function for this, which is quite straightforward. With multiple outputs the cost function becomes a function of a vector of M outputs Y_m, **Y**, rather than one aggregate output Y. It can therefore be written as: $TC = VC(\mathbf{Y},\mathbf{p},K,t)+p_K K$ in the case of one fixed input, K. The next question is more complicated, however; how does one define a "scale" measure such as ε_{TCY} in the context of multiple outputs, which implies multiple "scale" measures.

The answer is based on an idea similar to that underlying index number construction; it involves a weighted sum of the different effects. More specifically, the individual output effects $TC_m=\partial TC/\partial Y_m$ may be combined as in Baumol, Panzar and Willig [1982] (BPW) to generate an overall scale- (or more generally cost-) economy measure

4.9) $SG = 1/S(Y) = \Sigma_m Y_m TC_m(\mathbf{Y})/TC(\mathbf{Y})$.[97]

This is actually the inverse of the BPW measure, to make it more comparable to our cost-side measure developed above.[98] It can be rewritten even more analogously to ε_{TCY} above as $\varepsilon_{TCY} = \Sigma_m \partial TC/\partial Y_m \bullet (Y_m/TC)$.

---

[97] Much more detail and rigor about this measure and the many issues resulting from jointness that could complicate an analysis based on this measure may be found in BPW [1982].

Note that refinements overviewed above about the overall ε_{TCY} elasticity now pertain to each of the $\varepsilon_{TCYm} = \partial TC/\partial Y_m \cdot (Y_m/TC)$ measures. In particular, we may develop the measures in a long run as compared to short run context, as shown further below. It is also important to recognize that the elasticities must be represented in terms of total costs for appropriate interpretation.

In addition, information on scope economies is also embodied in this measure, since each $\partial TC/\partial Y_m$ derivative includes cross-terms with other outputs (as long as a sufficiently flexible functional form is assumed). That is, scope economies involve jointness of output production implied by cross-output terms in the cost function.

Following Fernandez-Cornejo *et al* (although they construct a dynamic measure, the static measure is analogous), a scope economy measure may be written as:

$$4.10) \quad SC = (\Sigma_m TC(Y_m) - TC(\mathbf{Y}))/TC(\mathbf{Y}),$$

where $TC(Y_m)$ is the minimum cost of producing output Y_m. Since the difference between TC for each output separately and combined simply depends on the cross-cost parameters γ_{mn}, this measure is ultimately dependent on the second derivatives $\partial^2 TC/\partial Y_m \partial Y_n$ ($= \partial^2 VC/\partial Y_m \partial Y_n$ with quasi-fixity).

Since $\partial TC/\partial Y_m$ is, for example, the marginal cost of producing Y_m, the second derivative $\partial^2 TC/\partial Y_m \partial Y_n$ essentially asks whether this marginal cost is less – or greater – if production of output Y_n is being carried out at the same time as Y_m. In the first case scope economies prevail (joint production is cheaper, due to some kind of "connectedness" of input use) and in the second case scope diseconomies, or specialization economies, are evident.

4.2   Multiple fixed inputs and "imperfect" input markets

Secondly, the case of multiple quasi-fixed inputs, or inputs for which Shephard's lemma does not hold for any other reason so that they appear in the cost function in terms of levels, should be addressed. As discussed in Chapter 3, basing analysis on a restricted or variable cost function model, total costs (TC) are defined as $TC = VC(\mathbf{p}, \mathbf{Y}, t, \mathbf{x}) + \Sigma_k p_k x_k$, where the x_k represent any inputs included in the function as a quantity that is subject to adjustment, and which thus form part of the definition of "restricted" costs.

---

[98] This is written in terms of $1/S(Y)$ instead of $S(Y)$ since BPW defined scale economies as the inverse of the cost-side scale measure, $1/\varepsilon_{TCY}$, in order to more closely relate it to the more standard primal expression for returns to scale. Either is appropriate as long as the interpretation is adapted accordingly.

If fixity of x_k is caused by adjustment costs as in Chapter 3, this distinguishes the short- from the long-run model. It may also imply that adjustment costs, and therefore partial adjustment, should be incorporated in the model via including Δx_k as another argument of the function. In either case, the issue is that the inverse of Shephard's lemma, $\partial VC/\partial x_k = p_k$, does not hold for x_k, and thus including p_k as an argument of the cost function is invalid. Instead the quantity level is included in the function so the shadow value $-\partial VC/\partial x_k = Z_k$ is defined, which only in equilibrium will be equal to p_k.

If multiple quasi-fixed inputs exist, additional $Z_k \neq p_k$ inequalities will appear in the short run. The movement to the long run is therefore somewhat ambiguous since adjustment of each input depends on the other's levels. The solution may, however, be solved simultaneously. Alternatively, sequential substitution may yield a good approximation to the final equilibrium point (see Morrison [1999]). In certain cases the combined adjustment process may also be solved analytically (see Morrison and Berndt [1981]). The path to the final equilibrium point is not, however, well defined (see Berndt and Fuss [1989]).

Other reasons may also, however, cause Shephard's lemma to be violated. In these cases also it may be more appropriate to incorporate the quantity level into the cost function with an implicit optimization equation based on the market price, which depends on what causes the deviation from full (perfect) market equilibrium.

For example, for fixed inputs this implicit deviation may be written generally in terms of an Euler equation of the form $p_k = Z_k + A(\bullet)$, representing the deviation of Z_k from p_k resulting from adjustment costs (in the general form $A(\bullet)$). If instead other market imperfections keep equilibrium from prevailing for an input, this may also be represented within the cost framework in terms of a similar optimum pricing expression.

If market imperfections in an input market cause $p_l \neq Z_l$ for input x_l, a pricing equation representing this deviation may be constructed by explicitly distinguishing marginal from average factor cost. The observed market price for x_l will be the average price p_l. However, if input prices are dependent on the associated levels – $p_l = p_l(x_l)$ – the marginal factor cost will be $p_l + \partial p_l/\partial x_l \bullet x_l$, rather than p_l (adding more x_l input requires increasing the price paid for all units of x_l since the firm faces an upward sloping factor supply curve).

This could result from input market power such as monopsony, or other pricing structure like volume discounts. The price endogeneity will affect cost economies since expanding the scale of production, and therefore input use, will cause a pecuniary diseconomy – an increase in the price of x_l – in the former case, and a pecuniary economy in the latter case.[99]

---

[99] See Morrison [1998c,e] for further discussion of this issue in the context of monopsony in the cattle market for the beef packing industry.

More specifically, in this case $TC = VC(\cdot) + p_k x_k + p_l(x_l) \cdot x_l$, and endogeneity of x_l implies $p_l = p_l(x_l(Y, \cdot))$. A difference thus exists between cost economies measured at given x_k, x_l levels, or with adjustment of these factors and thus of $p_l(x_l)$ recognized.

Note also that sequential optimization is implied, as in the multiple-fixed-input case. The adjustment of x_l may, however, be nearly instantaneous and therefore it should not be thought of as a "fixed" input, but just one for which a second-stage impact must be built into the model. For purposes of interpretation, we may still represent optimization behavior in terms of a series or sequence of "very short"- to long-run decisions.

In the (very) "short run", or based on the restricted cost function defined in terms of x_l and x_k, the cost economy measure may be defined as $\varepsilon^S_{TCY} = \partial VC/\partial Y \cdot (Y/TC)$, since only $VC(\cdot)$ explicitly depends on Y. As emphasized, although this may be motivated as reflecting movement along a short run cost curve, with "fixed input(s)" constant, if the input quantity x_l is included in the function due to a difference in the optimization assumption rather than short run fixity the underlying implication is somewhat different.

For x_l, since the conceptual basis for including it as a quantity in the cost function relies on the recognition of endogenous pricing behavior and a deviation from perfect markets (say, perfect competition), demand for x_l still adjusts at any point to current existing market conditions. The model is therefore characterized by full equilibrium in the x_l market, while recognizing that $p_l = p_l(x_l)$ and thus that the implicit optimization equation determining both price and quantity in this market.is $p_l + \partial p_l/\partial x_l \cdot x_l = Z_l$.

If we wish to represent responsiveness to a change in economic conditions, such as a change in Y for the cost economy elasticity, the direct measure based on $VC(\cdot)$ is evaluated at the existing level of x_l rather than embodying the resulting changes in the x_l market. If the output change is small (as is assumed for the marginal change represented by an elasticity measure), the envelope condition suggests that there will be little difference from incorporating full equilibrium response for this input (there will be no difference if the model is truly continuous). However, if there is a large discrete change, the x_l response (and associated $p_l(x_l)$ adaptation) should be directly appended to the cost economy elasticity ε^S_{TCY}. This notion is similar to reproducing long run from short run observed decisions in Chapter 3.

I have called the resulting elasticity expression an "intermediate run" elasticity (see Morrison [1998b,c,e]), since it explicitly incorporates this sequential optimization. Again, this does not necessarily imply a time lag in the adjustment process. The ε_{TCY} measure incorporating this step thus seems the most appropriate representation of what is typically thought of as "short-run" cost economies, although the distinction between the short- and intermediate-run measures facilitates interpretation about adjustment processes and the impacts of utilization changes.

As for the fixed input case, such a measure can be constructed in various ways, including substituting the "desired" optimal condition for x_l from the pricing expression into VC($\bullet$), or using a "combined" elasticity that directly appends the adjustment of x_l from a change in output such as 3.4. These approaches to the problem generally are very similar empirically (see Morrison [1999]), but the latter is conceptually the most appealing.

As noted in Chapter 3, this method simply relies on the chain rule of differentiation. Since the desired level of x_l depends on the output produced, the VC($\bullet$) function may be expressed as VC($\bullet$, Y, $x_l(Y)$), where ($\bullet$) represents all other arguments of the function. Thus, the cost elasticity becomes: $\varepsilon^I_{TCY} = (\partial TC/\partial Y + \partial TC/\partial x_l \bullet \partial x_l/\partial Y) \bullet (Y/TC)$, where the $\partial x_l/\partial Y$ elasticity comes from solving the pricing equation $p_l + \partial p_l/\partial x_l \bullet x_l = Z_l$. for the implied "desired" level of x_l, and taking the required derivative.

A similar argument may be used to represent the next layer of the sequential optimization process – to the long run taking capital adjustment into account. Accommodating such adjustment (from the intermediate run) is again based on the notion that the long run desired capital level is such that the shadow value and market price of capital are equilibrated. This implies solving the shadow value equation $p_k = Z_k = -\partial VC/\partial x_k$ for the desired level of x_k, and taking the derivative $\partial x_k/\partial Y$ to substitute into the expression:

$$4.9) \ \varepsilon^L_{TCY} = (\partial TC/\partial Y + \partial TC/\partial x_l \bullet \partial x_l/\partial Y + \partial TC/\partial x_k \bullet \partial x_k/\partial Y) \bullet (Y/TC),$$

Where pecuniary diseconomies (or economies) from changing p_l are included since $p_l(x_l)$ is part of TC and thus $\partial TC/\partial x_l$ incorporates this cost impact.

Note finally that the various aspects of cost economies addressed in this section may not only be conceptually but also empirically untangled if they are all taken into account in the estimation model, such as in Morrison [1998b,c], although increased complexity of the model may generate estimation problems such as convergence difficulties, especially with limited time series data.

4.3 Overall cost economies

A final aspect of cost economies to be raised before addressing their combined effects has to do with multi-plant economies, which may be represented by fixed effects in a panel data set. In this case the effects of such economies do not appear directly in the cost economy measure ε_{TCY}. However, if cross-effects between "dummy' variables representing plants that are in a multi-plant firm with other arguments of the function (especially Y) are included, this will have an associated effect on cost economy measures for designated observations.

Multi-plant economies suggest that cost economies may be derived from expanding the number of plants under the control of one firm. This could involve increasing (input and output) market power or borrowing power (more control in *financial* markets), or the potential to spread overhead costs for marketing and management across plants.

One might think that these effects would not necessarily depend on output levels, or have other cross-effects, and thus could appropriately be assumed to affect the level of costs but not the elasticities. That is if multi-plant economies vary across output levels they will affect the shape of the cost function and thus appear in the ε_{TCY} expression. If they are fixed effects they act as shift factors and do not affect the ε_{TCY} elasticity.

At this point we have addressed all the different aspects of cost economies we will pursue, so we may finally sum up the combined impact of these production characteristics. As overviewed above, since TC is defined as TC $= VC(\mathbf{Y},\mathbf{p},\mathbf{x},t) + p_k x_k + p_l(x_l) x_l$, cost economies reflected in the full $\varepsilon_{TCY} = \partial \ln TC / \partial \ln Y$ measure depend on the individual "short run" changes, $\partial VC / \partial Y_m$; the "intermediate" adjustment of the x_l input necessary to support output changes, $\partial x_l / \partial Y_m$; the "long run" adjustment of the capital stock to its "desired" level, $\partial x_k / \partial Y_m$; the interactions among the Y_m variables (scope economies), adjustments in p_l resulting from changes in x_l, $\partial p_l / \partial x_l$; and, finally, multi-plant economies (if the data are disaggregated across units and cross-effects are accommodated in the function). We therefore need procedures to untangle these different impacts on the ε_{TCY} measure.

To unravel the impacts of scale and scope economies contained in these measures, for example, the multiple-output cost economy measure may be written as SG $= \varepsilon_{TCY} = (\Sigma_m \partial TC / \partial Y_m \cdot Y_m)/TC$. The scope economy measure is SC $= -H(\mathbf{Y})/TC$, where H includes only the joint cost impacts of producing the M outputs, and thus only the cross-Y_m terms of the VC($\cdot$) function.

For example, for a GLQ (generalized Leontief quadratic) functional form such as in Morrison [1998c,e][100] and presented in Chapter 11, H($\cdot$) is $\Sigma_i p_i \cdot (\Sigma_m \Sigma_n \gamma_{mn} Y_m Y_n)$, so SC $= -\Sigma_i p_i \Sigma_m \Sigma_n \gamma_{mn} Y_m Y_n / TC$. However, if the equation for ε_{TCY} is fully expanded, it is easy to show that it includes the component $2 \cdot \Sigma_i p_i \Sigma_m \Sigma_n \gamma_{mn} Y_m \cdot Y_n / TC$. Therefore, although the existence of other productive outputs should be accommodated within a scale economy measure, the impact of jointness is also included in the cost economy measure since adjustment of the Y_m levels is embodied in $\Sigma_m \partial TC / \partial Y_m \cdot Y_m$.

Since negative γ_{mn} terms imply scope economies are present (complementarity exists between outputs so that increasing one output shifts the marginal cost of the other down), the cost economy measure ε_{TCY} will be lower than scale economies would indicate by $\Sigma_i p_i \Sigma_m \Sigma_n \gamma_{mn} Y_m \cdot Y_n / TC$.

---

[100] See Chapter 11 for further discussion of functional form issues.

ε_{TCY} may therefore be decomposed into a measure purged of jointness effects or "net" scale economies, $\varepsilon^n{}_{TCY}$, and one directly capturing jointness or economies of scope, $\varepsilon_{TCY} = \varepsilon^n{}_{TCY}$ - SC. In reverse, the scale economy measure purged of jointness can be represented as $\varepsilon^n{}_{TCY} = \varepsilon_{TCY}$ + SC. Since SC>0 if scope economies exist, $\varepsilon^n{}_{TCY} > \varepsilon_{TCY}$, indicating less economies when scope economies are purged from the total cost economy measure.[101]

Also, as alluded to above, ε_{TCY} will include in the $\partial TC/\partial x_l$ portion of the measure the component $(\partial p_l/\partial x_l \bullet) \bullet x_l$ from the definition TC = $VC(\mathbf{Y,p,x},t)$ + $p_k x_k + p_l(x_l) x_l$. Thus the cost economy measure is larger (less economies) if monopsony power exists, since the MC measures ($\partial VC/\partial Y_m$, underlying the ε_{TCY} elasticity) recognize the additional pressure on the input market.

The fact that expanding output requires a movement up (or possibly down) the x_l input supply function, resulting in a higher (lower) p_l, is captured in the MC which appears in the numerator of the cost economy measure. That is, it is still the case that $\varepsilon_{TCY} = \partial \ln TC/\partial \ln Y = \partial TC/\partial Y (Y/TC) = MC(Y/TC) =$ MC/AC even with all the adjustments above; the adaptations just affect the measurement of MC (and sometimes AC).

To further decompose ε_{TCY} to separately represent input price endogeneity, the difference of the marginal cost of the factor (MFC$_l$) from its average price (AFC$_l$=p$_l$) due to $\partial p_l/\partial x_l \bullet x_l \neq 0$ must explicitly be recognized as part of marginal cost. If MC is measured with $\partial p_l/\partial x_l$ set to zero, the pure *cost* measure not including pecuniary diseconomies $\varepsilon^C{}_{TCY}$ is defined, as elaborated in Chapter 6.

This process of unraveling the individual effects contained in the ε_{TCY} measure emphasizes their interactions and jointness. As for decomposing technical change and scale (cost) economies, this is more an interpretational issue than a measurement problem or bias.

Ultimately, total cost economies are of interest when evaluating the combined economies of production and assessing associated issues such as market power. However, if this measure includes the impacts of scope as well as scale economies, for example, it is useful to independently identify these cost economy components to facilitate appropriate interpretation and use of the measure. Representing these production characteristics explicitly also reduces the potential for generating biased performance estimates.

More specifically, as discussed in more detail in Chapter 6, measurement of cost economies is fundamental to a number of questions including the assessment of market power and its underlying determinants. Measuring such market power typically involves constructing "markup" (for output markets) or "markdown" (for input markets) price ratios. A definitive interpretation of what underlies MC is clearly important for such an exercise.

---

[101] As clarified further in the results section, the appropriate ε_{TCY} measure for construction of these measures would be $\varepsilon^S{}_{TCY}$, since the scope economy measure is based on VC($\bullet$).

That is, the usual interpretation of these measures is that if they deviate from one, something is "wrong" in the market. Firms are somehow taking advantage of a large presence in the market to make excessive profits by charging high prices for their products, or paying low prices for their inputs. However, whether this inference is appropriate depends critically on the existence of cost economies that cause marginal and average costs to differ.

To explore this a bit further, recall that the notion of overall benefit to the firm from the purchase of a marginal unit of x_l involves the shadow value of the input Z_l, and that in a "perfectly" functioning market this would be equated to p_l to determine the optimal level of x_l. The inference of an abuse of input market power is typically based on determining if p_l falls short of Z_l (or VMP_l), since the firm will respond to MFC instead of AFC=p_l if it faces an upward sloping input supply function, thus restricting input x_l use from its "efficient" or perfect market level. This suggests that excess profits are being made over the payments to that marginal unit of input. Evaluating whether true excess economic profits are being generated, however, involves representing returns in terms of average costs and revenues if cost economies exist.

Of course, these arguments are also complicated by additional aspects of the production structure incorporated in our model. For example, a deviation between MC and AC is *likely* to exist in the short run when some inputs are quasi-fixed. In this case increasing output allows more efficient use of the existing fixed factor (say, capital plant and equipment), or more efficient utilization of the existing capacity. The most "economical" or optimal production decisions must recognize this short run fixity.

The detailed interpretation of cost economies facilitated by a full structural model of production processes and costs is greatly advantageous for interpreting such cost-related issues. Such a structure therefore facilitates the use, as well as the interpretation and justifiability (unbiased-ness) of economic performance measures representing the cost and production structure.

5.   FURTHER REMARKS

Various cost economies, including those related to utilization and scale effects but also deriving from market imperfections or interactions among multiple outputs, fixed inputs, and plants, can be represented within our cost-based model to facilitate the measurement, interpretation and use of economic performance indicators. These internal aspects of the production structure should be separated from the impacts of exogenous forces such as technical change, or other phenomena that may be internal to industries or economies but external to individual firms.

In the following chapter we will pursue additional production structure topics and resulting refinements of the model to identify external, market structure, and regulatory effects. Although such models are much richer in terms of analysis of economic performance than simpler production models in which these aspects of the cost structure are ignored, their increasing complexity also raises estimation issues.

The amount of structure incorporated in our models by this time clearly precludes analysis of economic performance without parametric techniques. Although straightforward data manipulation is sufficient to construct the accounting measures of productivity growth presented in Chapter 2, and is sometimes used (with qualifications) to construct capacity utilization indexes such as those discussed in Chapter 3, the adaptations discussed in this chapter require econometric modeling. The multitude of interactions potentially embodied in total cost economy measures, such as biases and scope economies, cannot be captured by data analysis alone.

As we proceed to further refinements of the model, we should therefore keep in mind that although recognition of critical characteristics of any particular production process under evaluation is important, model simplicity also has its benefits. The relative "pros" of further model richness – the potential detailed representation of important real-world production characteristics and augmented interpretability and applicability of results – must be balanced with the cons – the increasing difficulties of estimating such a complex model, particularly using aggregated data.

Chapter 5

Internal and External Cost Economies, and Growth

The last chapter explored various cost economies that may be captured in the ε_{TCY} measure typically interpreted as a cost-side representation of scale economies. Deviations between short and long run scale economies (due to input fixities), and the impacts of jointness among quasi-fixed inputs and multiple outputs, and of market power in input markets, were elaborated. All these cost economies may be termed "internal". They involve movements along and shifts in (or movements between) cost curves representing the technology, that stem from decisions made within, or internal to, the firm.

Additional internal technical change impacts derive from investment decisions, in particular decisions to invest in different types of capital. These capital components may have a technology "attached" to them that should be taken into account in models of the technological structure. This may be accomplished by recognizing changing (capital) input composition and thus characteristics in data construction, by disaggregating input specifications into separate components, or by explicitly incorporating input characteristics such as capital vintage into the estimating model.

Such input compositional patterns may also have their external counterparts if they stimulate spillover effects. That is, impacts on cost efficiency, or the cost-output relationship, may be derived from "environmental" factors representing the economic "climate" the firm is operating within. External factors shift firms' cost curves and thus affect the cost of production independently of any decisions or action taken by the firm. They may be associated with regulatory, technological, public good and spillover effects.

"Pure" technical change – the motivation underlying our initial discussion of productivity and economic performance measures – may be thought of as one type of external cost economy. Technical change, as defined in this context, causes a disembodied shift in production and cost functions that is often motivated as "manna from heaven". It is not therefore attributable to any specific technical factor, but just identifies the existing technological base or climate.

Many other potential external cost impacts have a capital and public good orientation. In this context capital may take the form of human, physical, knowledge, or public capital, but invariably involves the notion of an expanding technological base. Such externalities also, at least implicitly, involve some type of scale or cost economies. They affect the cost-output relationship by driving downward shifts in cost curves.

In much of the endogenous growth literature this connection to scale economies is quite explicit. Knowledge factors are assumed to generate "returns" that augment scale economies over and above those to standard measured inputs. Thus, even if the technology is constant returns to scale (CRS) in measured internal inputs, the external, public, or spillover effects may stimulate overall increasing returns to scale or scale economies. In the cost context these may generally be thought of as cost economies that shift cost curves rather than causing movements along the curves.

These types of external effects have been the focus of many studies, most addressing one type of externality but sometimes incorporating a combination of possible spillover effects to assess their independent impacts.[102] Whether or not it is made explicit, however, the notions of externalities and spillovers encompass a broad range of closely linked effects, which are also related to utilization and internal scale economies discussed in the past two chapters, and to technical change from Chapter 2. In a sense the idea of external or spillover technological effects provides an explicit vehicle for representing "technical change" rather than leaving it loosely defined as a disembodied time trend, which is essentially what "t" becomes in the standard technical change literature.[103]

In addition, the literature on external effects links economic *growth* to productivity; externalities capture one reason that productivity growth may be self-enhancing and thus cause long-term growth. Since many studies in this area stem from the endogenous growth literature, and thus have a basis in the macroeconomic literature, they have not often been directly connected to the traditional productivity growth literature. However, their joint focus on internal and external utilization and scale economies suggests that the micro-foundations provided by a production theory-based model may be used to synthesize the notions raised in the macro literature with traditional productivity growth analysis.

In this chapter we will explore the notion of external cost economies, linking a cost-based treatment with the macro-oriented literature in this area.

---

[102] Note, however, that some of these spillovers may be closely related, such as knowledge capital and agglomeration effects, so including both may involve double counting.

[103] In fact empirically it is often the case that a standard time trend t representing technical change becomes insignificant when other external knowledge factors are explicitly built into the analysis.

Again, the ultimate goal is to identify the types of production characteristics that one might want to incorporate in a empirically implementable model, firmly grounded in production theory, of economic performance patterns in a particular sector of an economy – or in this literature, often entire economies or across nations.

Section 1 provides a formalization of the general idea of external effects in the cost function context. In Section 2 this is applied to one type of external effect – from public capital expenditures. Section 3 links such models to the endogenous growth literature, with its focus on knowledge capital. Section 4 discusses in more depth the macro literature that provides a basis for the treatment of external effects, and its connection with the cost-oriented microfoundations models we have been developing, focusing on the treatment of utilization and scale economies. These linkages are explored further, in the context of the literature on agglomeration effects, in Section 5.

1. A MODEL WITH EXTERNAL EFFECTS

Incorporating external effects into the cost function framework developed in the previous chapters results in a function of the form $TC=VC(\mathbf{p},\mathbf{Y},\mathbf{x},\Delta\mathbf{x},\mathbf{r})+\Sigma_k x_k p_k$, where the variables are defined as before: VC is a variable cost function depending on vectors of the J prices of the v_j variable inputs ($\mathbf{p}$), M outputs ($\mathbf{Y}$), K quasi-fixed (internal) capital factors ($\mathbf{x}$), investment in these factors (representing adjustment costs, $\Delta\mathbf{x}$), and B external scale factors ($\mathbf{r}$, where t may be included as of the components of this vector). Total cost (TC) includes also short run fixed costs through the x_k levels and their market prices, p_k, but does not include costs of the external factors since they are not chosen or paid for by the firm but instead determine the economic "environment" in which the firm operates.

The r_b variables can take a number of forms. They may also have various homogeneity properties (relationships with output levels),[104] and thus contributions to overall efficiency or returns.

For example, the (external) impacts of regulation, further discussed in Chapter 7, may cause costs of production to be higher than would otherwise be the case for any particular output level. This cost impact could derive from incentives to aid in protecting the environment, contributing to (workplace or consumer) safety, reducing market power, or accommodating some other type of public externality or "market failure" the firm would otherwise not choose to pay for.

---

[104] See Morrison and Schwartz [1994] for further discussion of these properties.

Such regulations determine the "regulatory environment" the firm is operating in, so variables representing these impacts may be included as arguments of the production, and therefore cost, function. They may also have level effects or be connected to output levels (in the sense that, for example, a certain amount of pollution abatement capital is necessary to negate the pollution impacts of a certain amount of output).

Other types of "public goods" that could affect firms' costs may be considered part of the capital base the firm may draw from. For example, public capital or infrastructure, such as roads, may augment a firm's productivity since internal resources need not be devoted to production of such an "input" to production. In terms of direct internal costs, additional roads may reduce transportation expenses (gas, trucks), or augment workers' ability to get to the workplace and therefore be more productive at work rather than devoting energy and time resources to a commute. Public education may also embody similar characteristics; human capital provided by government funds may contribute to the "effective" labor input. Measures representing the availability of these types of infrastructure may therefore be used as r_b variables to identify their impacts.

External effects can also be generated from spillovers across sectors due to "knowledge" factors. That is, the contributions of human-, R&D-, or high-tech capital- investment might have different – and more generally knowledge-expanding – impacts on productive performance than "ordinary" capital investment.

This idea is fundamental to endogenous growth models, in which knowledge stemming from, say, an expanding technological base (more high-tech capital), research (R&D), or human capital (education or training) augments productivity by some type of synergy that causes it to be an "engine of growth".[105] Such knowledge capital is assumed to generate additional returns over its private benefit due to spillover effects, and therefore has public (external) as well as private (internal) consequences. The amount of these types of capital existing in the industry as a whole, therefore, may affect sub-sectors of the industry.

Expanding the boundaries of this to accommodate spillovers across countries – in the form of knowledge, or possibly just the impacts of competitiveness or increasing the scope of intermediate inputs – suggests that increasing openness of trade also may contribute to cost efficiency. The extent of trade may therefore also be an important part of the "environment" facing the firm that will affect its productive and thus cost structure, and therefore be the basis for defining and including an associated r_b variable.

---

[105] See Greenwood and Jovanovic [1998] for one recent example of an attempt to disentangle these different types of "engines" or drivers of growth processes.

Agglomeration or thick-market effects may also cause spillovers that reduce production costs and thus augment productivity and growth. These may be due to either demand-side (consumer) or supply-side (supplier) impacts. In this case, measures of weighted aggregates of consumer or supplier activity levels may be r_b variables. Changes in the quality or variety of intermediate goods may also be thought of as supply-side effects that may contribute to growth independently of other technological factors.

Most of these potential forces causing spillover effects also have their internal counterparts. That is, a firm may have to maintain training, R&D, and high-tech investment efforts in order to "keep up" in an industry. In fact, "creative destruction" resulting in obsolescence of knowledge (see Caballero and Jaffe [1993]) has been suggested to cause stagnant firms to fall behind by perhaps 4% per year.[106] This suggests that measures of R&D, human capital (or "effective" labor adjusted for education), and high-tech capital may also need to be included as v_j or x_k variables separately from other capital inputs (or capital adjusted for vintage effects or other characteristics) for analysis of economic performance.

For now, however, the important issue is that these factors have public as well as private impacts that may enhance the overall "productivity" or contribution resulting from their associated expenses over and above the private marginal product or cost-share. Thus, the overall pervasiveness of these knowledge capital "inputs" in the industry or economy should be recognized in analyses of sectors at lower levels of aggregation. They stimulate "increasing returns" in the sense that the external impact ("trickle-down" effect from higher aggregation levels) augments the internal impact. External effects stemming from spillovers thus have a more synergistic effect for the average firm in the industry than that just stemming from private investment.

The general intuition underlying this type of external effect is well motivated by Benhabib and Jovanovic [1991]. They state that: "if firms with more capital also have more productive knowledge and if this knowledge spreads to other firms, then unless one can somehow measure knowledge and control for it, an increase in the capital stock of one firm will appear to lower the production costs of other firms".

External effects from human capital may thus imply that a general expansion of knowledge and problem-solving ability, or facility with more high-tech methods of production, arise from greater labor force education.

---

[106] In particular, they say that "in an average sector at an average year a firm that does not invent sees its value relative to that of the industry erode by about 4%." Such knowledge obsolescence is also asserted to be "clearly an endogenous function of the number of new ideas, rather than an exogenous function of time."

More human capital embodied in the work-force of a particular industry will then affect individual firms or sub-industries. If not measured as part of the "effective" labor input, this should be represented separately in the function representing the firms' costs.[107]

External impacts could potentially also be associated with some type of network effect. It doesn't help a business, for example, to be hooked up to the world-wide-web if other firms are not, or to have a FAX machine if supplier and consumers of the product do not have corresponding machines! Thus, the high-tech capital accumulation of related firms in the industry, or consumers and suppliers, will affect the costs of an individual firm.

In the following section we will motivate the cost-side representation of external effects in the context of public capital, as in Morrison and Schwartz [1994, 1995, 1996]. In subsequent sections we will discuss related literatures on external effects, and how our model can similarly be used to provide insights about external effects on cost efficiency. That is, the framework from Section 2 provides a micro-foundations basis from which we can explore the more macro-orientation of these literatures on external factors such as knowledge capital and agglomeration effects.

Also, for expositional purposes, we will abstract from some of the refinements raised in the previous chapters to reduce the problem to one more similar to those typically found in this literature. In particular, we will restrict the model to allow for only one output, Y, ignore adjustment costs ($\Delta \mathbf{x}$) so the dynamic nature of the model does not cause additional complexities, and also, as we have done in previous chapters, assume only one internal quasi-fixed input, private capital (K_p). We may also restrict this for simplicity to one external factor, r_b, which for the development in the next section we will think of as public or "government" capital (K_g), although we will also develop our model in a more general fashion to facilitate the transition to combinations of external factors in later sections.

With these qualifications, the resulting total cost function may be expressed as $TC(\mathbf{p},Y,K_p,K_g,p_K)$. This cost function is dual to a production function of the form $Y(\mathbf{v},K_p,K_g)$. The production function orientation is typically used to analyze external effects in the macro literature.

The duality between the two functions is clear, however. As usual, the cost function is based on adding the behavioral assumption of cost minimization for a given set of input prices, subject to the technological possibilities summarized by the production function, to represent input demand responsiveness for a particular technological base.

---

[107] The overall impact of knowledge may be separately identified from other factors affecting performance, rather than just subsumed in the labor measure, thus allowing more direct interpretation of what is underlying productive performance.

This duality facilitates linking the cost to the more standard primal approaches, and motivating the idea of environmental factors such as K_g appearing in the cost function. That is, if the existence of a stock of public capital allows firms to produce their output more efficiently – with less private inputs – public capital is in a sense substituting for private resources. This "input" should therefore appear in the production function even though the firm does not demand, and pay for, the resource itself. In turn, this allows the firms to produce at less input costs, and therefore at greater cost efficiency, so it will appear also as an argument of the dual cost function.

2.   RETURNS TO PUBLIC CAPITAL

The restricted cost function VC($\bullet$) can be used as a vehicle to evaluate the contributions of both the private and public (or external) capital stocks via shadow values. A shadow value analogous to that for private capital, $Z_{Kg} = -\partial VC/\partial K_g$ (or, more generally, $Z_{Kb} = -\partial VC/\partial r_b$), may be constructed to represent the potential cost-savings from an additional unit of public capital. This represents the private "returns" in terms of resource savings for a firm or sector, or in reverse (the primal side) the potential augmentation of output production resulting from government expenditures.

This notion of returns to public capital is similar to that for private capital embodied in the shadow value for K_p, $Z_{Kp} = -\partial VC/\partial K_p$. This suggests that shadow value measures for the capital types may be compared to determine the relative "productivity" of or "returns" to private as compared to public capital investment.

This idea was a motivating force for the literature on public infrastructure investment that was particularly topical in the early 1990s. Researchers in both academic and policy circles were interested in whether a lack of public infrastructure investment, and the resulting decline in services due to deterioration (particularly relative to output growth), was having a stagnating effect on productivity in developed countries.[108]

Two of the most cited actors in this debate were Aschauer [1988, 1989, 1991] and Munnell [1990a,b, 1992]. Aschauer's early work in this area was based on a simple aggregate production-function framework. Aschauer's work suggested that productivity growth was closely linked to public infrastructure investment, and that in fact the returns to public investment, in terms of its measured marginal product, substantially exceeded the returns to private investment.

---

[108] A useful summary of this literature is Hulten and Schwab [1993b].

Many other researchers, including Holtz-Eakin [1994] and Hulten and Schwab [1991, 1993a], strenuously questioned these results. Most found that the marginal returns to K_g investment were much smaller, or even in many cases trivial, when adaptations were made to the early simple models. Models based on less aggregated data, a more detailed structure (such as the cost-oriented models in Morrison and Schwartz [1994, 1995, 1996]), or time-fixed-effects, for example, were found to yield ambiguous measures of returns to public capital. Very little consensus was ever found, which has often been attributed to problems of (spatial) spillovers from and endogeneity of public infrastructure investment that are notoriously difficult to deal with.

A cost-oriented model is useful for such an analysis since it allows a much more detailed consideration of substitution and scale factors underlying the measured benefits than does a simple aggregate production function model. It also facilitates direct assessment of the net returns to public capital through a cost-benefit-type analysis.

In a sense, the shadow value computation is a cost-side version of the marginal product, as pursued more explicitly below. The relevant question that arises with respect to investment in public capital is therefore what the returns are in terms of productivity enhancement (or reductions in resource use) for firms in an economy, compared to the outlays for such investment.

Addressing this question requires computing a measure to compare the shadow value and the price of investment. As seen in Chapter 3, the Tobin's q-type measure Z_K/p_K, or in this case the measures Z_{Kp}/p_{Kp} and Z_{Kg}/p_{Kg}, allow consideration of the benefit-cost relationships underlying optimal investment in these two types of capital. At least one important question arises here, however, in addition to the measurement of the Z_{Kp} and Z_{Kg} shadow values, which may be computed within a cost framework of the type we have been developing. This has to do with the construction of the market price measures p_{Kp} and p_{Kg}.

In particular, a firm or even industry does not observe a price of public capital since is not a factor they choose and pay for (except indirectly through taxes, perhaps). However, there is clearly a social cost associated with investment in infrastructure. This cost has to do with the direct expenses incurred for such investment, which may be difficult to obtain data for. It may also involve the relative "efficiency" of public as compared to private spending, as discussed in Morrison and Schwartz [1996]. Comparing relative returns to different types of capital also requires putting firms' costs in a more appropriate comparison framework, for example taking taxes into account that are a private but not public cost. Such analysis is facilitated, as well as the underlying issues highlighted, by the cost framework.

To compute the net private benefits for firms (or industries), it seems most justifiable to treat p_{Kg} as zero. In this case net returns to investment in the different types of capital, at least in terms of private returns, may alternatively be represented by the ε_{TCk} (ε_{TCKg} and ε_{TCKp}) total cost elasticity. Then $\varepsilon_{TCKp} = (p_{Kp}-Z_{Kp}) \cdot (TC/K_p)$, but $\varepsilon_{TCKg} = -Z_{Kg}(TC/K_g)$. Public investment therefore, from the (private) perspective of the firm, has an unambiguously positive impact (external economies exist) as long as its shadow value (or marginal product) exceeds zero.

These measures can be used to represent the various factors affecting the cost-output relationship (and thus evidence of cost economies and productivity growth) in this scenario, via the overall cost economy measure of the previous chapter with the additional external factors recognized as shift factors. The resulting "total cost economy" measure "sources" the components driving the observed cost-output relationship into short run fixity, long run (internal) returns to scale, and external economy effects. It can be expressed as:[109]

5.1) $\quad \varepsilon^T_{TCY} = Y/TC \,[\partial TC/\partial Y + \partial TC/\partial K_p \cdot dK_p/dY + \partial TC/\partial K_g \cdot dK_g/dY]$

$$= \varepsilon_{TCY} + \varepsilon_{TCKp}\varepsilon_{KpY} + \varepsilon_{TCKg}\varepsilon_{KgY}, \text{ so}$$

$$\varepsilon_{TCY} = \varepsilon^T_{TCY} - \varepsilon_{TCKp}\varepsilon_{KpY} - \varepsilon_{TCKg}\varepsilon_{KgY}, \text{ or, more generally}$$

$$\varepsilon_{TCY} = \varepsilon^T_{TCY} - \Sigma_k\, \varepsilon_{TCk}\varepsilon_{kY} - \Sigma_b\, \varepsilon_{TCb}\varepsilon_{bY},$$

where $\varepsilon_{TCk} = \partial \ln TC/\partial \ln x_k = (p_k-Z_k)x_k/TC$, $Z_k = -\partial VC/\partial x_k$, $\varepsilon_{TCb} = \partial \ln TC/\partial \ln r_b$ $= -Z_b r_b/TC$ ($p_b=0$ since r_b is external), $Z_b = -\partial VC/\partial r_b$, and ε_{kY} and ε_{bY} are defined as the long run "desired" levels of the x_k and r_b factors (x^*_k and r^*_b), determined when $\varepsilon_{TCk}=0$ or $\varepsilon_{TCb}=0$, respectively (where the net private marginal benefit of an additional unit of the capital stock becomes zero).[110]

---

[109] Note that in the studies referenced (5.1) was denoted a "total scale economy" representation. This connects it more closely to the idea of scale economies generally used to motivate the production function-based literature, overviewed in the next section. However, it veils the additional interpretation possible from a cost perspective of scale economies, that distinguishes a movement along the long run cost curve from a shift in the curve from external forces. Both will affect the observed cost-output relationship but both also have particular interpretations that are facilitated by identifying them separately in terms of the more generic term "cost economies".

[110] This represents the point where the cost-savings accruing to factor increases are "used up".

This cost-output or scale relationship ε^T_{TCY} essentially translates the production-based concept of returns to various capital components into one of cost efficiency or cost-based "returns". Such returns are generated from not only short run (private capital) fixities but also from public capital. Or, more specifically, the sources of cost-output changes are decomposed into (a) movement along the short run cost curve (from ε_{TCY}); (b) movement to the long run curve due to private capital investment (from ε_{TCKp} and ε_{KpY}); and (c) the potential to take advantage of shifts in cost curves due to external forces – in this case public capital investment.

That is, if $Z_{Kp} > p_{Kp}$ (so additional investment in K_p would "pay"), $\varepsilon_{TCKp} < 0$ and $\varepsilon^T_{TCY} < \varepsilon_{TCY}$ (returns to internal and external factors together exceed those available in the short run). Similarly, if $Z_{Kg} > 0$ (K_g provides positive net marginal benefits), this will be another source of a deviation between ε^T_{TCY} and ε_{TCY} such that $\varepsilon^T_{TCY} < \varepsilon_{TCY}$. Further, $\varepsilon_{TCKg} \cdot \varepsilon_{KgY}$ measures the efficiency deriving from changing environmental factors – the cost savings accruing to increases in K_g (from Z_{Kg}) adapted for the "returns" to this factor (contribution to growth, ε_{KgY}), to generate a full measure of the potential benefits of increases in K_g.

These representations of cost and scale economies and returns to (both types of) capital therefore stem from a different perspective than those resulting from production function models. The typical motivation of the production function models, as overviewed further in the following section, is in terms of a Cobb-Douglas (CD) production function. In this case the parameters of the function represent $\varepsilon_{YKp} = \partial\ln Y/\partial\ln K_p$ and $\varepsilon_{YKg} = \partial\ln Y/\partial\ln K_g$ (or, more generally, $\varepsilon_{Yk} = \partial\ln Y/\partial\ln x_k$ and $\varepsilon_{Yb} = \partial\ln Y/\partial\ln r_b$) elasticities.

Such parameters, capturing the marginal product in proportional terms, are often interpreted as "returns" to the individual inputs. Overall returns to scale in the primal sense are then represented by the sum of the capital-oriented parameters ($\varepsilon_{YKp} + \varepsilon_{YKg}$ for example, capturing total returns to capital rather than the more typical $\varepsilon_{YKp} = \partial\ln Y/\partial\ln K_p$ private capital contribution) plus those corresponding to other inputs in the CD function.

Relating this representation of capital returns and its connection with returns to scale to that captured in the dual cost measures ε_{TCk}, ε_{kY}, ε_{TCb}, and ε_{bY} is somewhat involved due to the additional behavioral information embodied in the cost elasticities. For example, for the private capital inputs, the ε_{Yk} elasticities from the production function measure returns to the x_k inputs in terms of the technological possibilities for increasing output when x_k is increased on the margin, holding other arguments of the function constant. These elasticities (parameters of the CD function) are generally assumed to fall short of unity, due to diminishing returns. On the cost side, this is somewhat loosely related to the ε_{TCk} elasticities, and more closely related to the ε_{kY} elasticities.

To see this, first note that elasticities such as $\varepsilon_{TСk}$ and ε_{TCb} only exist for quasi-fixed (internal) factors or factors not chosen by the firm in the short run, since $\varepsilon_{TCk}=0$ ($p_k=Z_k$) for inputs that are instantaneously adjustable to their desired levels. The shadow value-based measures ε_{TCk} and ε_{TCb} thus indicate returns to changing the x_k and r_b factors in terms of the cost-savings derived from investment behavior toward their long run optimal levels.

Consider the case of no external factors. If $Z_k>p_k$ for any x_k, net cost savings from investment are positive ($\varepsilon_{TCk}<0$, so there are cost incentives for investment in x_k). This measure is related to the ε_{Yk} elasticities in the sense that ε_{Yk} is based on the marginal product $MP_k = \partial Y/\partial x_k$, the ε_{TCk} elasticity is based on the shadow value $Z_k = -\partial VC/\partial x_k$, and $p_Y \cdot MP_k = p_k = Z_k$ in equilibrium (where p_Y is output price). Thus, increased output given input costs, or reduced costs for a given output level, represent the marginal benefit of investment in x_k. These benefits may be compared to the marginal cost p_k to determine the associated *net* benefits.

This is different than the purely technological version of returns embodied in the ε_{Yk} elasticities, and implied by the ε_{kY} elasticities. These elasticities represent different phenomena. ε_{Yk} indicates how much more output can *technologically* be produced given an increase in x_k (holding other inputs constant), and ε_{kY} shows the increase in x_k that would be desired (in the sense of long run cost minimization) given an increase in output demand and the state of technology. Both the ε_{Yk} and ε_{kY} elasticities thus portray information about the existence and determinants of overall scale economies. This will be connected more explicitly to the idea of returns to scale, in the context of the macro-oriented literature, in the next sections.

In the meantime, note that the returns to K_g investment in terms of private production costs may be represented by Z_{Kg}, the optimality of existing K_g levels (through the net returns to the sector under investigation) by the q measure Z_{Kg}/p_{Kg} or ε_{TCKg}, and the relationship of K_g to observed cost economies by a combination of ε_{TCKg} and ε_{KgY} elasticities (as in Morrison and Schwartz [1996]). The measures of cost-savings, Z_{Kg} or ε_{TCKg}, may in turn be decomposed into their input-specific components, representing the impacts of public capital investment on input composition and thus substitution effects. This can be accomplished using measures analogous to the utilization biases developed for capital in Chapter 3 (which provide the basis for the analysis in Morrison and Schwartz [1995]).

Thus, a rich set of patterns of public capital impacts on productivity and economic growth may be captured and evaluated using the cost-based approach we have been developing.

3.   "KNOWLEDGE CAPITAL" AND SPILLOVERS

The endogenous growth literature addresses further scale issues related to capital returns and externalities. The underlying notion is the potential to generate increasing returns through knowledge accumulation, deriving from the social effects of knowledge capital investment, which in turn drives productivity and long run growth. As Caballero and Jaffe [1993] put it: the "public stock of knowledge that accumulates from the spillovers of previous inventions is…a fundamental input in the technology to generate new ideas".

This broad notion of knowledge may involve indirect effects related to the expansion of knowledge capital factors such as education (human capital), research, and capital-specific technology. These effects may result in increasing returns to capital in a social sense, even if decreasing returns are evident for private capital. The ideas providing the basis for this literature are closely related to those found in earlier productivity and growth literatures, but specifically target these types of synergistic effects.

That is, the traditional productivity growth literature, at least from the time of Jorgenson and Griliches [1967] and Christensen and Jorgenson [1969], recognized the embodiment of technical change in labor and capital inputs as an important *explanation* of the Solow residual. This in a sense endogenizes economic growth in the treatment of inputs. Thus, as Jorgenson [1998] states: the growth literature of the 1980s was a "renewed thrust toward endogenizing economic growth" that "acquired startling but illusory force by channeling most of its energy into a polemical attack on the deficiencies of the 'exogenous' theories of growth…."[111]

These apparently disparate views thus both embody the endogenous nature of enhanced productivity through accumulation of human and technological capital. The endogenous component is seen as part of productivity or growth that should be separately identified. This highlights the importance of carefully measuring the quality or characteristics of labor and capital, and representing their service flow as compared to stock nature. As discussed in previous chapters, various perspectives on this issue have emerged in the productivity and growth literatures. However, the underlying issue is essentially the same.

In endogenous growth models the impacts of knowledge accumulation are generally represented by an efficiency function that is separable from a stationary production function. Such a function facilitates interpreting the additional capital contribution as external to private production processes – in most studies arising from indirect effects or some type of spillovers.

---

[111] The issue of what is "new" with "new" growth theory was addressed also by Nelson [1997].

Again, these spillovers typically stem from the self-enhancing nature of knowledge or agglomeration effects. They are external or exogenous to sub-sectors of the economy, but endogenous to overall growth of the economy since the external effects are internalized at the macro level. The external factors thus generate "returns" in terms of output augmentation given existing input or resource levels, which contribute to long run growth.

The macro-oriented production function approach focuses on first-order effects, and thus typically is motivated in terms of a CD function divided into its efficiency- and stationary production function- components:

$$5.2) \quad Y = A_0 \, g(\mathbf{r})f(\mathbf{x,v}) = A_0 \, \Pi_b \, r_b^{\gamma b} \, \Pi_k \, x_k^{\alpha k} \, \Pi_j \, v_j^{\beta j},$$

where Π indicates a product over the variables, A_0 represents the Solow technical change shift variable, and as above $\mathbf{x}$ is a vector of quasi-fixed (internal) capital factors and $\mathbf{r}$ is a vector of external capital components.[112]

This model is first-order in the sense that it does not incorporate cross-effects – only first-order terms are included in the function. It thus precludes analysis of substitutability or any type of biases. It presupposes (if estimated directly) very restricted relationships among the variables. A second order or "flexible" approximation is instead required to capture second order effects, or interactions among the arguments of the functions.

The simpler CD structure facilitates estimation, and in the macro context first order effects may be more important to represent due to aggregation problems. However, much of the richness of the model and potential implications from the data are swept under the rug by assumption in such a framework. This is an important problem for the analysis of economic performance, since many interesting questions about productivity and growth involve behavioral patterns and their underlying determinants.

For example, based on (5.2) and with only one private capital input K, the standard measure of "returns" to capital, based on a first derivative, is simply a parameter; $\alpha_K = \partial \ln Y / \partial \ln K = \varepsilon_{YK}$. The returns accruing to the broader capital base including knowledge incorporated in the r_b factors is a combination of the associated parameters: $\alpha_K + \Sigma \gamma_b$.

The efficiency or scale effects associated with the external factors may be separately identified and measured, and the overall productivity or growth effect includes returns to all internal and external or knowledge capital.

---

[112] A similar framework was also used by Fulginiti and Perrin [1993] to incorporate the impacts of prices as technology changing variables in a production function framework, where the production function becomes $Y(\mathbf{v},\tau)$, and where τ is a vector of technology-changing variables reflecting the economic environment. In this case the model is interpreted in terms of a variable-coefficient CD form, since the shares (which in a standard CD would be parameters) end up depending on the τ variables.

However, analysis of the determinants underlying these returns, or changes in input composition, are precluded by the first order specification.

This model is in the spirit of Romer [1986, 1987] and Lucas [1988] when the r_b variables are motivated as knowledge capital variables, although Hulten and Schwab [1993a] apply a very similar structure to analysis of public infrastructure as an additional external capital input (as discussed in the previous section).

One important example of a knowledge capital variable that may appear in this framework is human capital, typically represented as educational attainment. This was, for example, the main thrust of Mankiw, Romer and Weil [1992], that "takes Robert Solow seriously" and reconciles seemingly paradoxical evidence of labor productivity across countries and convergence of growth by incorporating human capital. This endogenizes characteristics of the labor input that will have independently identifiable impacts on production processes, and will have additional public or social consequences since it contributes to the general knowledge base.

This focus on the contribution of human capital to growth and productivity patterns again builds on a strong tradition. As stated by Jorgenson [1998]:

> The theme of making economic growth endogenous within the neoclassical framework was first enunciated by Schultz [1961]. Schultz envisioned a process of gradually replacing the Solow residual by specific sources of economic growth that could be rationalized by means of investment in human capital."

The second sentence here is quite useful for connecting the endogenous growth treatment, and associated microfoundations models of external effects (such as that outlined in the previous section), with the literature on endogenizing human capital by recognizing changes in quality, as in Denison [1962] and Jorgenson and Griliches [1967]. The focus of the endogenous growth literature is on separate identification of this efficiency component, and on the external synergistic or exacerbating impacts of growth driven by its contribution to scale (or cost) economies. This is clearly related to earlier treatments, but with a somewhat different motivation.

Some production function studies allowing for human capital in an empirical model have a micro-economic basis, such as Lichtenberg [1992]. However, such studies often also identify other aspects of knowledge capital within an integrated structure. Lichtenberg, for example, incorporates a measure of R&D into his model based on (5.2), to determine whether a combination of returns to "standard" inputs combined with those to R&D and human capital may generate overall increasing returns to scale estimates. In Lichtenberg [1993], he also focuses on the availability of information systems (high-tech) capital, as another form of knowledge capital.

In his treatment, the importance of human capital as an argument of the production function is connected to R&D and high-tech capital because they "contribute to the process of intellectual capital formation". His estimates of the γ_b parameters, and thus returns to these factors, are positive and significant.

This raises issues associated with the capital-labor relationship that may help to drive the joint impacts of human, research and physical knowledge capital. This has been addressed in a cost-based model of the type developed in the previous section by Morrison and Siegel [1997]. In such a model not only the differential cost effects of the various types of knowledge capital may be identified (from human capital, R&D and high-tech capital), but the input-specific interaction terms or substitution effects may also be taken into account.[113] In Morrison and Siegel [1998a], this was pursued further by dividing labor into educational categories to identify the differential impacts of capital components on labor demand and productivity. This brings an internal human capital dimension, that of labor composition and its internal and external determinants, into the picture.

The external (and internal) impacts of R&D on its own have also been addressed in a large literature summarized in Griliches [1991]. He refers to the associated endogenous growth treatments by indicating that there has been a "recent reawakening of interest in increasing returns and R&D externalities". He references a large literature originally based on gains from specialization, development of "know-how", and interactions, and later in terms of "learning by doing" (proxied by the size of the capital stock). Griliches indicates that there is a "whole array of firms which "borrow" different amounts of knowledge from different sources according to their economic and technological distance from them".

Other recent studies such as Baily and Schultze [1990] also indicate that although growth seems not to be attributable to private capital accumulation, external effects such as those deriving from R&D investment may drive growth patterns. Studies by Bernstein and Nadiri [1988a] and Bernstein and Mohnen [1994] have formalized these spillover effects from R&D, across industries and countries, in a detailed cost-oriented framework.

The additional importance of high-tech capital formation, and both its direct and indirect effects, has been recognized in micro-oriented empirical models such as those by Brynjolfsson and Hitt [1996]. They focus on high returns to computer capital as an engine of growth, since "industry-wide increases in the stock of knowledge affect output only insofar as the increases are uniquely related to embodied technical change of physical capital".

---

[113] Internal returns to high-tech capital, identified by decomposing capital investment and stocks into their high-tech and "other" equipment components, was instead the focus in Berndt and Morrison [1995] and Morrison [1997].

They find an "extraordinarily high implied gross marginal product" of computers, which they interpret as consistent with "excess net returns".[114]

The more macro-oriented treatments of external effects typically do not directly estimate the parameters of the CD production function but instead use index number theory to construct a Hall/Solow residual, as elaborated further below, so the shares are not actually held constant over the sample period. This results in a function expressed in terms of an aggregate of internal inputs. The models are generally also written in terms of growth rates rather than levels. Such a model still disallows consideration of second order effects, since the variation in the shares is not modeled.

Note, however, that in these types of models, and in their macro literature counterparts that do not focus on externalities (discussed in the next section), "effort" or utilization, and sometimes long run scale economies, are often recognized separately. The distinction between these internal effects, and among the internal and external impacts, are not made explicitly, since only a limited amount of structure may be identified within the first-order model. The dependence of utilization fluctuations on input fixities is therefore not built into the model; instead "effort" is typically proxied. Scale effects are often also estimated as an overall residual value capturing any characteristics that may cause fluctuations in the Solow residual.

That is, the macro literature tends to focus on why the Solow or Hall/Solow residual, expressed as output growth minus aggregate input growth as in Chapter 2, might fluctuate. The underlying motivation is that technical change might be expected to appear as a constant proportionate growth rate across time. Therefore, evidence of variation in this residual may be attributed to some type of cyclical impact (utilization or market power), or an additional long run scale trend. If external effects exist, they will also appear in the residual, but their impact should be separately identified for appropriate interpretation. This furthers the tradition of Hall [1990], who also mentioned scale effects arising from thick markets or agglomeration effects as a potential cause for variance of the residual.

Empirically oriented models of this genre include Caballero and Lyons' [1992] and Bartlesman, Caballero and Lyons' [1994] treatment of procyclical variations and agglomeration effects (see Section 5). Their analysis is based on a macro model similar to (5.2), specified in log-differences, with an extra factor representing a weighted average of other industries' activity.

---

[114] These findings are somewhat contrary to those resulting from models in which high-tech capital investment is considered an internal capital composition issue where different kinds of capital generate varying returns measured by shadow values and q ratios, as in Morrison [1997]. The literature on the productivity impacts of computers has largely been based on such analysis. Like most types of internal capital investment, it has often been found that high-tech investment seems to generate surprisingly low measured productivity impacts.

Barro and Sala-I-Martin [1994] focus more explicitly on the issue of intermediate goods and the potential growth of quality improvements, in the context of changes in the variety of intermediate inputs. This improvement in intermediate inputs is, however, assumed to be a direct result of technological progress from research. New goods are assumed to shut out old ones, which is another version of obsolescence or creative destruction. The model is similar to others expressed in terms of quality enhancement, but in this case focuses on the variety instead of quality dimension.[115]

Benhabib and Jovanovic [1991] also realize the potential importance of this (intermediate good) dimension of the problem independently of other external capital effects. However, their conclusions emphasize the difficulty of identifying this type of effect independently of a general "knowledge expansion" from accumulation of capital. They state that "growth in capital causes a growth in knowledge or a growth in the availability of specialized inputs, or both".

Links between growth and trade, or the openness of the economy, have been addressed in studies such as Ades and Glaeser [1994]. These authors focus on how "dynamic increasing returns" operate through larger markets enhancing growth by increasing the division of labor. They find empirical support for this hypothesis, at least for developed economies. This may also be connected with the labor skill/educational attainment literature in the sense that the mechanism works through increasing effectiveness of the labor force. In this context specialization and the division of labor causes growth through innovation and learning by doing. The issue of trade effects as an external environmental variable was also raised in Morrison [1998a] within a cost function-based model.

All of these studies of external effects represent efforts to explain the fact that internal (private) factors seem insufficient to explain all evidence of scale economies; external factors must play a role. However, as noted above, the macro models address the distinction between internal and external factors, and between the internal utilization and scale components from a different perspective. They do not recognize the rich structure for analysis of production structure and economic performance provided by production theory-based microfoundations models. This difference in perspective is further explored in the next section.

---

[115] Feenstra and Markusen [1992] also focus on the role of "new inputs" in a more micro framework, using a framework based on index numbers and duality theory.

4.   UTILIZATION AND SCALE INTERACTIONS

The microeconomic literature on productivity and economic performance we have been exploring, which may be considered the microfoundations for a macro-oriented perspective on productivity and growth, has explicitly addressed the importance of distinguishing between scale economies and utilization, and between these internal production characteristics and external factors. That is, cost-based production theory models allow representation of the underlying factors causing movements along short and long run cost curves (utilization changes and internal long run scale economies), and responses to exogenous changes in these functional relationships (from technical change or other explicitly defined external or exogenous factors).

Empirically identifying these separate relationships requires explicitly recognizing the quasi-fixity of inputs that determines the capacity available for production. In such a framework, that we have specified in this text in terms of a restricted cost function, utilization variations may be directly represented as the result of behavioral responses which may have differential input-specific aspects. Internal scale economies with various homogeneity properties including nonhomotheticity (and thus potential scale-biases across inputs) may also be explicitly allowed for and measured.

The resulting model of short- and long- run scale or cost effects provides a theoretical structure in which the characteristics of production important for determining economic performance may be evaluated. In particular, it may be used to formalize and interpret issues and hypotheses focused on in the macroeconomic literature based on Hall [1990], that also has provided a foundation for modeling external impacts.

For example, Hall [1990] suggested that returns to scale measures are upward biased by unobserved factor utilization. If all factors are assumed variable in the cost function framework, this is equivalent to assuming that observed cost/output variations occur along a long run cost curve. If the appropriate representation is instead a short run cost function with some inputs' adjustment restricted, the associated short run curve will be more steeply sloped at any point except the tangency with the long run curve. This provides an explicit framework for interpretation of such biases.

The literature in the Hall [1990] tradition, based on empirical implementation of a Solow residual model founded on (5.2), recognizes that utilization fluctuations and scale economies are an issue for evaluating productivity trends. It does not, however, allow direct modeling of such production structure characteristics. As alluded to above, such a treatment is typically expressed in terms of an aggregate of inputs and growth rates. That is, $Y(\mathbf{v},t)$ is written as $dY = dv + dt$, where dv is a share-weighted average (say, a Divisia index) of input growth ($\Sigma_j S_j \, d\ln v_j/dt$ in our notation), dY is output growth ($d\ln Y/dt$), and dt is the technology shift factor ($\partial \ln Y/\partial t = \varepsilon_{Yt}$).

The basic idea underlying the macro-oriented approach to untangling the productivity residual is similar to our motivation for accommodating utilization and scale economies in Chapters 2 and 3, and thus distinguishing them explicitly from the remainder of the "measure of our ignorance". Independently identifying these factors allows us to separate them from other factors appearing in the residual, and thus to explain a portion of the residual by decomposing it. If these production characteristics exist but are not identified separately, not only is interpretation of the residual limited, but measures of technical change, or of scale economies, will be biased.

In the macro tradition, however, utilization fluctuations are assumed to be embodied in "mismeasured" inputs. That is, variable utilization is assumed to cause mismeasurement of capital (and labor) inputs. The impact of cyclical changes are thus incorporated in measures of, say, scale economies based on this model. Unlike the microfoundations model in which this may be explicitly modeled as part of the production structure, in the macro literature this is dealt with using proxies for capital utilization and labor hoarding.

To explore this further, let us first be more explicit about the underlying framework used for estimation in the macro-oriented models. Following Hall [1990], these studies typically attempt to estimate a "scale factor" causing a deviation between revenues and costs, which is usually interpreted as a measure of markups or scale economies. This becomes a (scale) adjustment factor in a regression of dY on dv and dt, since the *ratios* of all the output elasticities (the parameters of the CD function) may be derived from the shares, but the scale factor must be estimated to identify the *levels*. More formally, $dY = \mu dv + dt$, where μ distinguishes revenue from cost shares.

Without the scale factor $\mu=1$ (or as discussed in our development of the microfoundations model, cost and revenue shares are equivalent if $\varepsilon_{TCY}=1$ and markets are perfectly competitive). A deviation from this equality thus may arise from either (short or long run) scale economies (MC$\neq$AC) or imperfect competition (MC$\neq p_Y$). The impact of imperfect competition has been a primary focus of this literature, since it is often connected to the procyclical nature of the residual (as elaborated in the Basu and Fernald [1998] survey article). Whatever the interpretation of the "scale factor" μ may be, however, it may be estimated by ordinary least squares (OLS) if dY, dv, and thus dt are constructed according to the Solow residual approach.

The focus on measuring μ is similar in spirit to the adjustment of ε_{Yt} by the ε_{TCY} measure, adapted to include utilization fluctuations in Chapter 3 and cost economies in Chapter 4. If a primal perspective is used to construct the nonparametric Solow residual in terms of revenue rather than cost shares, an adjustment for AC$\neq p_Y$ is necessary.

In the cost framework, in which behavior and the cost structure (technology) are explicitly represented, the utilization, scale, and ultimately also market power "causes" for the scale factor μ may be separately identified and their determinants evaluated. In the macro models, however, they are all allowed to become part of what is essentially another residual representing the difference between revenues and costs, which also is constant. That is, since only one "scale" factor μ may be measured in this framework, this may be interpreted as a combination of returns to scale and markups if both exist (so they are not separately identifiable), or as one of them if the other is assumed away.

These determinants of the deviation between revenues and costs have different implications for interpretation of productivity growth, as we have already discussed. But in this literature they are often treated as nearly observationally equivalent. For example, Basu and Fernald state that "if $\mu \neq 1$ we need to know the markup (or the closely related technological concept of returns to scale)", thus tossing them both in essentially the same basket.

However, separate identification of these production characteristics is crucial for assessment of economic performance. The only time they are directly related is if zero profits (and long run equilibrium) exist, possibly due to monopolistic competition, in which case the scale economy and markup factors exactly counteract each other (as discussed further in Chapter 6, as well as in Morrison [1992a,b, 1993a,c, 1994]).

As noted above, however, the importance of separately identifying the impacts of utilization fluctuations is recognized in the macro literature. For example, Burnside, Eichenbaum and Rebelo [1993] noted that including labor hoarding (or utilization) helps to "explain" measured scale economies. Similarly, Basu [1996] and Burnside [1996] focused on the role of capital utilization in representing cyclical fluctuations. Burnside also considered the potentially important role of industry-specific parameters when using aggregate data for estimation of the model.

Utilization is represented, however, through proxying it by some type of relationship with variable (intermediate) inputs. For labor, for example, Basu and Fernald [1998] say that: "increases in observed inputs can proxy for unobserved changes in utilization. For example, when labor is particularly valuable, firms will work existing employees both longer (increasing observed hours per worker) and harder (increasing unobserved effort)." Measurement error from unrecognized utilization fluctuations thus will generate a specific bias; "variations in utilization are likely to be (positively) correlated with changes in the measured inputs, leading to an upward bias in estimated elasticities" (Basu and Fernald). This must be accomodated to estimate the model.

The idea of labor (or capital) input "mismeasurement" underlying this motivation is clearly similar to identifying the service flows as compared to stocks of quasi-fixed inputs, which we have already seen is a critical issue for representing economic performance. The microfoundations framework puts this in an explicit form based on direct representation of the production structure, which has explanatory power. It is not necessary to find proxies for utilization based on materials input fluctuations, for example. A full set of short and long run cost impacts and substitution factors may be measured to identify the impact of short run fixities and resulting utilization changes.

The connection of the macro- and micro-oriented notions of utilization has been largely bypassed in both literatures, however. In fact Basu and Fernald indicate that the implication in some studies that "variable utilization" and "capacity utilization" are similar is "unfortunate". However, within the context of the production function framework it can be seen that this distinction is essentially due to a primal as compared to dual perspective.

That is, Basu and Fernald indicate that "capacity utilization is about measuring output elasticities appropriately, while "variable utilization" is about measuring factor quantities appropriately". However, as discussed in Chapter 3, adjustment for utilization (or other production characteristics) may equivalently be accomplished from either the price or the quantity side, with the appropriate adaptation in interpretation. This adjustment obviously affects representation of the elasticity (or share) but also has implications for interpretation of the service flow stemming from the input stock level.

If the focus is on the production function and thus quantities, recognizing utilization fluctuations becomes a question of adapting the quantity measure. But this is essentially equivalent to adjusting the stock measure to represent the service flow by a value-oriented measure such as Z_K/p_K. This is actually similar to what is often done in these models, as elaborated below.

Similarly, effort or utilization changes for labor are analogous to labor valuation adjustments due to hoarding, by the shadow value for quasi-fixed labor. That is, labor hoarding implies quasi-fixity, which is – as is emphasized in this literature – necessary for effort fluctuations to exist.

Utilization is also often motivated in terms of adjustment costs, since "if there were no costs to increasing the rate of investment or hiring, firms would always keep utilization at its minimum level and vary inputs using only the extensive margin, hiring and firing workers and capital costlessly" (Basu and Fernald). This further connects the shadow value approach to that of variable utilization, or effort.

More specifically, labor services are often specified as a multiplicative relationship between the number of employees, N, hours worked per employee, H, and the effort of each worker, E. It is normally recognized that hours rather than numbers of workers are the appropriate data to use for this type of analysis, so the only additional adaptation involves determining, and multiplying by, the E factor. Similarly, capital services are seen to depend on the capital stock, K, multiplied by a capital utilization measure, Z. Rather than proxying Z and E, they could potentially be defined, using the cost structure of Chapter 3, in terms of the shadow value measures Z_K and Z_L, when both K and L are considered quasi-fixed.

To further link these perspectives and highlight the interelatedness of the different treatments, note that one proxy used for capital utilization in the macro literature is based on the Jorgenson and Griliches (JG) representation of utilization in terms of energy use. This is, for example, the procedure used in Burnside *et al* [1995]. This is directly related to the shadow valuation of quasi-fixed capital in terms of variable input use, as we have developed in Chapter 3.

Similarly, Basu and Kimball [1997] recognize that labor use also is important for representing utilization, by incorporating the idea that hours per worker proxies for capital utilization as well as for labor effort. This is again directly related to our shadow value Z_K, which represents changes in *all* variable inputs as capital utilization fluctuates.

Note also that the energy and labor use linkage with capital utilization may differ depending on their substitutability with the capital input, which we have seen can be represented within a cost-based model as input-specific utilization effects (or biases). That is, if the shadow values are estimated within a full model of the structure of production, their variable input-specific determinants are well defined in terms of second order elasticities since Z_K depends on all arguments of VC($\bullet$).

Another second order issue that is finessed in the macro approach to estimating scale effects is time-varying output elasticities. Again, if not only a cost- or production-elasticity with respect to t is estimated in such a model, but cross- terms are also incorporated, the potential for non-neutrality can be incorporated directly. If this is ignored, it will appear as an unidentified component of the residual, and thus bias the resulting estimation.

In addition, if the CD function is estimated directly, which requires estimating output elasticities for both K and L as well as the μ parameter, this raises issues of endogeneity and thus OLS biases (as well as potential multicollinearity in a one-equation model). As developed in Marschak and Andrews [1944] and commonly recognized in this literature, the error term is "likely to be correlated with a firm's input choices, leading to biased OLS estimations. The usual "fix" for this "transmission problem" is to use instruments for estimation. This works in principle, but, as also noted by Basu and Fernald [1998], "most plausible instruments have relatively weak explanatory power", and "the problem is much worse when using the same weak instruments to estimate multiple parameters".

Thus, it is more common to construct a Divisia index of the inputs, so that only the μ parameter must be estimated (and constancy of the CD parameters does not need to be imposed). However, if utilization fluctuations exist, this requires first proxying these changes, as noted above. Thus the estimation process becomes a two-stage procedure where the utilization proxy is measured separately and used to adapt the data. Also, instruments are still required to accommodate potential biases from misspecification. The macro model is thus linked to our cost-based production theory model, but limits interpretability due to its focus on 1st-order effects, and ability to estimate only one scale factor so proxies and instruments are required.

5. MICROFOUNDATIONS AND MACRO MODELS

The previous sections overviewed some of the macro literature on productivity and growth. Such studies have provided a basis for empirical application of the endogenous growth notions of knowledge capital factors, externalities and spillovers, and their contribution to scale economies. More microeconomic approaches to modeling and measuring economic performance, such as the framework we have been developing in this text, have also been linked to the macro-oriented treatment. Such a model may be thought of as providing the microfoundations of the macro models.

For example, the model framework discussed in the previous section provides the underlying framework for the incorporation and measurement of agglomeration effects in Caballero and Lyons [1992], and Bartlesman, Caballero and Lyons [1994]. They recognize that cyclical productivity fluctuations may occur due to "mis-measurement" of inputs such as labor, which is interpreted as "variations in effective labor". Internal scale effects are also incorporated as a potential contributor to productivity and growth trends. They find, however, that in a standard macro model of internal production processes such as those overviewed in the previous section, additional unexplained variation persists.

In particular, they note that "effort variations must not be related purely to own-input variations if it is to generate the type of external effect found here". In fact, they conclude that that "explanations of procyclical productivity based upon either (a) internal increasing returns or (b) unmeasured utilization tied to own-industry inputs are at best insufficient."

This returns us to the main thrust of this chapter – that external factors, perhaps relating to knowledge capital or (less specific) agglomeration effects, may augment short- (utilization) and long- run scale effects. Incorporating such factors thus allows further decomposition and interpretation of factors underlying productivity and growth.

Caballero and Lyons essentially use (5.2), with the r_b external factors representing the impacts of thick markets through weighted (by output produced or materials purchased) averages of consumer and supplier "activity". The underlying motivation is that agglomeration or thick-market effects may operate through knowledge spillovers resulting from activity levels of the customers and suppliers. They distinguish short and long run impacts via "within" (fixed) compared to "between" (random) estimates of the production function. They find significant impacts for such variables that help to explain scale economy measures, and particularly differences between such measures estimated using more or less aggregated data.

Morrison and Siegel [1998d] use such factors as environmental variables in a framework such as that developed in Section 1 of this chapter. The cost-oriented production theory framework allows explicit determination of which agglomeration effects may be operative over what period (by looking at short as compared to long run elasticities with respect to the r_b variables). It also facilitates identification of channels through which they operate (through substitution patterns from both technological relationships and management decisions associated with the r_b arguments of the cost function).

The Morrison and Siegel model allows for a complete specification of substitution patterns among variable and quasi-fixed inputs, nonhomotheticity, and nonneutral technical change – all of which could affect the residual in an unidentified fashion if not taken explicitly into account. Also, results for two alternative specifications, in which only capital, and both capital and labor, are quasi-fixed, are presented.

The results suggest that when agglomeration effects are ignored, and thus cost savings and substitution patterns from thick market effects are inappropriately represented as determinants of the slopes of the cost functions, measures of short and long run scale economies are overestimated. If not taken into account, the effects of shifts in the cost curves from these external factors are entangled and thus confused with measures of internal scale economies. These impacts tend to partially explain evidence of long run scale economies, and also to mute the measured effects of disembodied technical change (which becomes insignificant).

The findings are generally consistent with Bartlesman, Caballero and Lyons [1994]; they imply that measured scale effects may be partially explained by external agglomeration factors, and that long run growth is stimulated more by suppliers than consumers. However, contrary to the Bartlesman *et al* finding that short run fluctuations are caused by output agglomerations impacts, the results indicate that although output effects may only prevail in the short run, even in this time frame input or supplier-based externalities have a dominant impact.

Note also that the agglomeration factors may be interpreted as more general knowledge spillovers than those resulting from more directly specified knowledge capital factors such as human capital (H, education), research (R, R&D) and the technological base (IT, high-tech or information technology capital). Morrison and Siegel [1997], as mentioned above, have accommodated estimates of industry-level H, R and IT similarly to those for agglomeration factors as r_b arguments of the cost function. Their results provide similar evidence that external factors may provide more specific explanations of both estimated scale economies and technical change.

The interpretation of the results in Morrison and Siegel [1997, 1998d], based on estimation of the full cost framework, as compared to Bartlesman, Caballero and Lyons, using the basic production function model, can be elaborated by further considering the linkages between the estimated indicators arising from the alternative models.

The linkages between the primal- and cost-side measures, and their implications for returns to scale and to capital are based on standard production theory. First, as outlined in Section 3, the degree of returns to scale in the x_k, v_j variables is implied from the parameters of (5.2); it is measured as $\Sigma_k \alpha_k + \Sigma_j \beta_j = \Sigma_k \varepsilon_{Yk} + \Sigma_j \varepsilon_{Yj}$. In terms of costs, information on scale economies is provided by the $\varepsilon_{TCY} = \varepsilon_{kY} = \varepsilon_{jY}$ elasticities (with instantaneous adjustment and homotheticity), rather than as a sum of the elasticities.

With fixity of the x_k factors this relationship becomes more complicated, but also more informative, since the interactions are decomposed into short and long run responses. For example, long run returns to scale are measured as $\varepsilon^L_{TCY} = \varepsilon_{TCY} + \Sigma_k \varepsilon_{TCk} \varepsilon_{kY}$ (from (5.1) above, where the L superscript denotes long run). Also, as noted above, ε_{kY} represents the desired movement of x_k to its steady state level (where $\varepsilon_{TCk}=0$ or $Z_k=p_k$), resulting from a change in Y. Thus, the cost function framework provides additional insights into the behavioral and technological interactions involved in moving to a steady state and taking advantage of scale economies.

Appending the external factor effects to this relationship is analogous, although their externality somewhat obscures the behavioral motivation. This development is in the same spirit as adding the γ_b parameters to the sum of the α_k and β_j parameters from (5.2) to measure returns to scale, or combining the α_k and γ_b parameters to capture the returns to "total" capital.

Accomplishing the first of these goals from the cost side was already implied by the construction of (5.1). Applying this to the measurement of the total returns to capital, however, requires recognizing (a) the influence of r_b changes on desired K investment ($\varepsilon_{Kb} = \partial \ln K^* / \partial \ln r_b$, representing substitutability between K and r_b); and (b) the potential benefits generated by the positive marginal product of r_b when output expands ($\varepsilon_{bY} = \partial \ln r^*_b / \partial \ln Y$).

That is, if additional r_b would be desirable with an increase in output ($Z_b > 0$), and r_b is substitutable with K ($\varepsilon_{Kb} < 0$), less K is necessary to support an increase in output. Thus capital as a whole has greater returns than is evident from just considering private capital. The resulting measure of returns to capital as a whole becomes: $\varepsilon^T_{KY} = \varepsilon_{KY} + \Sigma_b\, \varepsilon_{Kb}\varepsilon_{bY}$.

This representation of returns results in a detailed "picture" of the interactions among internal and external capital factors, and among technological and behavioral responses, that are a foundation for growth. Such a decomposition in terms of utilization, internal scale economies, and external effects, as well as the associated potential analysis of second-order or substitution patterns from the "biases" associated with the r_b variables, may only be accomplished with the more detailed microfoundations models.

It is worth noting, however, that although studies such as Caballero and Lyons [1992], Bartlesman, Caballero and Lyons [1994] and Morrison and Siegel [1998d] find evidence of external effects, much of the empirical literature on productivity and growth minimizes the importance of externalities. For example, researchers have questioned results such as those found by Caballero and Lyons. They have raised issues of inappropriate data (Basu and Fernald [1995]), incorrect econometric technique [Burnside [1996]), and inadequate proxies for utilization (Sbordone [1997]).

Some micro studies also suggest that capital externalities are not an important determinant of growth. Gordon [1990], for example, argues that measured procyclicality results from the interaction of different types of measurement error including excess-capacity and labor-hoarding. This is a stark contrast to Cabellero and Lyons, in which significant external effects are said to rule out explanations of the variance of the Solow residual based on own-input variation.

Other researchers, however, indicate that although productivity patterns may not be attributable directly to physical capital, indirect effects are likely to be important. Baily and Schultze [1990], for example, focus on the impact of an expanding capital base, and find that their results "do not support recent work (assuming) capital externalities or increasing returns to capital" (but they restrict their model to physical capital). As they note, "Lucas has emphasized externalities from human capital, and Romer has recently stressed the externalities from technological capital in contrast to his earlier emphasis on externalities from physical capital. We agree with Romer and the large literature that finds substantial spillovers from R&D." They therefore, in a somewhat backhanded fashion, support the idea that externalities rather than actual physical capital may augment growth.

Similar support for the notion that capital has some type of indirect, external of synergistic effect in addition to its direct impact is provided in Solow [1988]. He expresses his "surprise" at the relatively minor role often found empirically for capital accumulation, and the resulting need to include some type of embodiment, since technological progress "could find its way into actual production only with the use of new and different capital equipment". He also says that this suggests that "the stimulation of investment will favor faster intermediate-run growth through its effect on the transfer of technology from laboratory to factory".

No empirical consensus about the importance of the intuitively crucial issue of external knowledge capital impacts has yet been found, therefore, in either the macro or micro literatures. However, both micro and macro approaches to the analysis of productivity and growth recognize the importance of "endogenous growth" factors that tend to have spillover effects across sectors. Theoretical and empirical treatments, from many perspectives, have attempted to identify the role of these factors.

As emphasized by Jorgenson [1998], there is a clear need for "a new empirical and theoretical consensus on economic growth". Much of the recent "massive accumulation of new empirical evidence, followed by a torrent of novel theoretical insights" (Jorgenson) has involved some type of recognition of the embodiment of an expanding technological base in human, research and high capital, and its potential for spillovers. Even though this difficult area of research has gained little synthesis or consensus as yet, hopefully we are moving toward such a convergence of different perspectives on these issues.

Finally, pursuing the link between the microfoundations and macro empirical literature further raises issues about the roles of each in understanding economic performance, productivity and growth. In the macro literature on productivity, utilization, internal and external scale effects and growth, the ultimate interest is in the economy as a whole. This is the justification for motivating the analysis via an aggregate CD production function. As stated by Basu and Fernald, "For many purposes, what matters is whether such a function provides at least a first-order approximation to the economy's production possibilities, even if an explicit aggregate function does not exist (as it rarely does)".

This top-down approach allows consideration of important overall questions and patterns that may not be dealt with using microeconomic data. Aggregation issues are also less stringent when attempting to capture overall patterns than when trying to identify the full production structure, as for the cost-based production functions we have been using. However, as emphasized in the previous section, the first order approximations are also seriously limiting as a basis for identifying and evaluating important production structure characteristics such as utilization and scale (or other cost) effects, and their interactions and determinants.

These problems are further exacerbated if we wish to expand the framework to model and measure external effects and market structure. There are too many "pieces of the puzzle" to identify them using a residual perspective rather than by modeling and measuring the underlying technology and behavior.

Estimating the full structural model and second order effects, especially with aggregate data, raises its own problems. The production theory or microfoundations cost-based analysis we have been developing in this text allows explicit modeling of factors that otherwise require proxies and instruments to attempt separate identification. It permits a full specification of cross- (or second-order) effects, and even of adjustment costs underlying quasi-fixity of factors. Elasticities representing cost and input-specific impacts from a wide range of market and technological factors can therefore be directly estimated within a system of equations representing the associated costs and input demand functions. However, these model complexities also cause estimation and interpretation difficulties.

In particular, the additional structure of these models is useful for some applications and causes difficulties in others because of the additional complexities of estimation and interpretation based on aggregates. Essentially, the intuition of these models is based on the level at which the goods are produced – the firm. Although this is true for both the macro and micro approaches, the production theory basis of the microfoundations treatments ties it even closer to the theory of the firm.

This in turn raises important issues of implementation and interpretation of the models when applied to aggregated data, particularly when second-order effects are the focus of analysis. That is, interpreting measures of short and long run scale effects as representing the slopes of the associated cost curves, and measuring input-specific impacts of changes in utilization, scale and external effects, requires that aggregate data may be interpreted as capturing patterns of a "representative firm".

To some extent we can rely on such an assumption (and there are some conceptual and empirical arguments for such an assertion as noted in Chapter 3). And if such characteristics as scale (cost) economies are clearly significant we can make the further argument that something important is being captured, even if we cannot directly interpret it as resulting from the curvature of a particular firm's cost curve. However, qualifications about the results of empirical analysis based on these models, should also be kept in mind. Trade-offs abound in economics!

6.   FURTHER COMMENTS

Issues of economic performance, productivity, and growth are fundamentally important in a number of different literatures. In this chapter we have overviewed some of the connections between the macro- and micro-oriented productivity literatures. Similar issues are addressed from alternative perspectives in these literatures, suggesting differences in the application and interpretation of these models.

The macro literature, for example, tends to begin with a first order model and top-down approach, and the micro with a second order model of firm behavior and thus, at least implicitly, a bottom-up approach. The former approach faces implementation issues from its simple structure, and the latter from its complexity. However, both provide important and potentially complementary theoretical and empirical approaches to analysis of productivity and growth, and its underlying utilization, internal and external scale economy (cost structure) and market structure components. Hopefully these literatures will begin to draw more on their potential complementarities to facilitate more synthesis and consensus in terms of both the theoretical frameworks and empirical implementations of such models.

In the meantime, we will move on to further discussion of market structure issues underlying measurement of economic performance. The notion of imperfect competition and its potential link to economic performance measures was touched on in this chapter as a determinant of deviations between prices and marginal costs of outputs. Although we have been focusing on the cost structure and thus have bypassed issues of output pricing, such behavior provide information on market structure and allocation across production sectors that may be important for assessment of economic performance.

In particular, imperfect competition may have implications for concentration in industries, and markups of prices, both of which have welfare connotations. These issues have been developed primarily in the industrial organization (IO) literature. We will address some of these issues, and the potential to evaluate them using the more cost-based framework for economic performance analysis provided in this text, in the next chapter.

Chapter 6

Market Structure and Economic Performance

In the preceding chapters we have largely ignored the output supply (and demand) side of the productive relationship, since our focus has been on the cost structure and its implications for productivity and economic performance. The quantity of outputs produced, and the resources used up in the process, determines returns to factors and ultimately the per capita product available for consumption. Analysis of the cost structure allows us to characterize optimum production, and thus real productivity.

Output quantity and pricing decisions, by contrast, have less of a productivity connotation, although product prices have implications for distribution and allocation, and quantity decisions that deviate from fully competitive outcomes may imply economic inefficiency. Also, if productivity analysis is based on revenues rather than costs, and the potential discrepancy between these values is ignored, real productivity fluctuations may be masked by pricing patterns. Performance characteristics related to output and input markets, and thus prices, thus need to be separately distinguished from the cost structure for appropriate analysis of productivity and welfare.

More specifically, in competitive markets, observed price and quantity outcomes occur when the marginal costs and benefits of an action – production of a commodity or purchase of a product – are equated. In such markets, as we learn early on in economics courses, market pressures work for the greatest good through economic efficiency. Resources are allocated to their "best" uses, and quantities of products produced respond to the implicit valuations of consumers via their observed demand levels.

However, many markets are characterized by some type of market "imperfections", or market power. That is, rather than simply responding to prices, producers may have some kind of power over the pricing mechanism. In this case they respond according to their private cost or benefit (marginal factor cost for an input or marginal revenue for an output) rather than the social value (the average factor cost or average revenue, and thus market prices). This affects both the income distribution (firms may generate non-zero economic profit) and the available quantity of products.

The realm of market power issues is typically that of industrial organization (IO) economists. Many earlier market power studies in the IO literature took the form of structure-conduct-performance (SCP) analysis, which focused on the links between prices and industry concentration (few firms and thus implicitly market power). More recently, new empirical industrial organization (NEIO) models have been used as a basis for modeling and measuring the impacts of monopoly and oligopoly power. Game theory models also became popular over the past decade, but they are typically not very amenable to empirical application.

Another perspective on market power issues has been evident in the macroeconomic literature, as we touched on in the last chapter. As noted there, deviations in the "scale effect" from one may, if revenues provide the basis for analysis so the shares are based on revenues, stem from both deviations of output price from marginal cost ("market power") and marginal from average cost (utilization or scale economies). The macro literature has not achieved a consensus about the prevalence of output price markups. But many studies have suggested that markups that are evident may stem from counteracting scale economies. Zero profitability seems to prevail in many markets, perhaps suggesting monopolistic competition may plausibly be assumed to represent market structure in many industries.

Most of these kinds of models and analyses deviate significantly from the cost-based structure we have been developing here. However, it does seem clear from all these perspectives that appropriate representation of (short and long run) marginal costs is crucial for representation and interpretation of market power measures. NEIO models provide a basis from which at least a partial synthesis of the literatures may be developed.

Some richness of the NEIO model structure must be assumed away in order to theoretically and empirically identify both cost *and* demand structure components. However, our micro- production theory model allows us to create a framework in which the crucial characteristic of market imperfections – e.g., the wedge between market prices and true marginal costs for outputs – may be incorporated. Further details of the market structure are possible to recognize in some cases if particular types of market power such as Cournot oligopoly seem justifiable to assume.

In this chapter we will focus on this aspect of the problem by outlining a model in which marginal output (or factor) costs (benefits) are measured via a cost-based production theory model. These measures are then used as the basis for constructing markup (markdown) measures that compare these marginal costs (benefits) with the associated marginal benefits (costs) of output production (input use), resulting from the output demand (input supply or pricing) functions facing the firm.

In order to assess the implications from the resulting models and measures for market structure and power we have to carefully consider their interpretations. In particular, the cost-based production theory model provides a useful framework in which to analyze the potential for cost economies to drive concentration patterns, and the resulting indications of market power. Thus, stepping from evidence of a deviation of marginal cost from price to the inference of abuse of market power must be carried out with care.

Potential "damage" to society as a whole from imperfect competition involves a number of production and market structure characteristics. Perhaps most fundamentally, the potential for and existence of market power "abuse" has to do with the determinants of true marginal cost, and how this relates to average cost as well as to output price. Careful consideration of both production and market structure characteristics is therefore crucial for appropriate interpretation of market power, its determinants, and its effects.

In this chapter we first (Section 1) overview the basics underlying empirical representation of market power in the IO literature. We focus on NEIO models based on modeling industry-structure and marginal cost, which provide a link to our cost-oriented approach to modeling and measuring production and market structure and performance. Section 2 discusses the implications of such models for the measurement and evaluation of productivity and economic performance. In Section 3 we consider the application of such models to representation of market power in input markets, and comment also on the related nonparametric literature in this area. Section 4 then raises the question: "is market power bad", in the context of the linkage between measured markups and the existence of excessive profitability or abuse of market power.

1. MARKET POWER MODELING

In previous chapters we have developed an implementable production theory-based framework, founded on the analysis of input use and costs, as a basis for the analysis of production processes and productivity. However, in these models either the assumption that output is given (no optimization behavior with respect to output is modeled), or that products are supplied such that $p_Y=MC$ (where p_Y is output price and MC is marginal cost, $\partial TC/\partial Y$, implying perfect competition) has been maintained. We have also primarily assumed that the marginal factor costs (MFC) of inputs are appropriately represented by their market prices – $p_j=MFC_j$ for any input v_j – so firms respond to these (exogenous) prices when making input demand decisions (Shephard's lemma holds for these inputs).

When imperfect markets or market power prevail (the firm does not respond to a given output or input price but instead has some control over the price since it faces a downward sloping output demand or upward sloping input supply function), this changes our analysis in important ways. We will first focus our investigation on the assumption of perfect competition in output markets, and what happens when it is not appropriate. This extension to imperfect competition in the context of product markets is the most familiar, and the most commonly addressed in the literature. However, market power in input markets may also be important to recognize for characterization of production processes in some sectors. We will explore these issues further later in this chapter.

The assumption that output is "given" is sufficient for analysis of cost-output patterns, since it is observed output that is relevant for representing real productivity trends. However, in many cases output supply (and pricing) decisions are important to represent for evaluation their impact on the production structure. In this case a profit maximizing assumption – that results in output being produced such that $p_Y=MC$ – is typically relied on to represent output supply decisions. This may be incorporated into parametric production models by explicitly modeling profit maximizing behavior (output choice) based on observed product prices, or into nonparametric treatments by assuming that marginal cost values required for index number computations may be approximated "closely enough" by market prices.

The $p_Y=MC$ condition only holds when firms have no output-market power. If firms have some monopoly (or oligopoly) power, this power is captured by a deviation between observed output price p_Y (or average revenue AR) and marginal costs MC (assumed to be equated to marginal revenue MR in this case). This is usually represented by a ratio of the markup of price over marginal cost, p_Y/MC (or by a Lerner-type index directly representing the deviation, $(p_Y-MC)/MC$). An adaptation to the usual analysis of the production structure and, therefore, the measurement of productivity growth (if they are based on measures of revenues), must be carried out when this ratio exceeds one (zero).

Evaluation of market structures resulting in imperfect competition, and associated evidence of the extent of deviations from perfect competition, has typically been the focus of industrial organization (IO) economists. This has been a separate field of economics since the late 19th century when concern about monopoly power grew in response to great increases in conglomerates.

Until the early 20th century most analyses focused on the polar extreme cases of competition and monopoly. Work by researchers such as Chamberlin [1933], however, on alternative "in between" types of imperfect competition such as monopolistic competition, focused on how differences in market structure motivate different types of pricing decisions.

By the 1950s, largely in response to Bain [1951, 1956] structure-conduct-performance studies were beginning to be a focus of the IO literature. These studies attempted to connect high concentration levels in an industry (few firms) to high prices from collusive behavior, with the motivation that this indicated economic inefficiency in these markets.

In such studies profitability and concentration ratios were measured and correlated, typically based on observed accounting data and cross-section variation. The resulting measures are obviously not based on a detailed representation of the cost structure; in fact it is assumed that price-cost margins and all other relevant indicators can be directly observed in the data.

Profit measures are based on accounting rather than economic profits.[116] Thus the notion of *economic* profitability is not well defined. This raises serious issues about interpretation of the results found in these types of studies. In addition, causation becomes an issue for a number of reasons; for example firms may be large *because* they are efficient.[117] Other issues of measurement, misspecification, causality, and simultaneity were also raised in the literature, and discussed at length in Schmalensee [1989].

A major problem with this type of analysis is the focus on profits rather than the components of profits – prices and costs. Prices and costs must both be measured carefully, especially when attempting to represent marginal values for the appropriate construction, use and interpretation market power measures. That is, the markup of price over marginal cost is designed to capture the deviation of price and marginal revenue (MR), and thus the slope of the product demand curve, assuming firms facing such demand curves set MC equal to MR rather than to p_Y. However, important problems arise.

First, this deviation has little to do with profitability; profits are based on comparisons of average or total revenue and cost values. If, for example, marginal costs fall below average costs (scale economies prevail), p_Y/MC will exceed one but little true economic profitability may be implied.

In addition, both MC and the motivation for the interpretation of $p_Y=MC$ as an indication of competitiveness must be carefully defined. For example, there may be a deviation between short and long run marginal costs. In an industry with high capital intensity, short run MC (SMC) may be quite low. However, for long run feasibility of the industry, firms must cover long run costs, including capital expenditures. Appropriate representation of cost measures is thus fundamental to appropriate interpretation.[118]

---

[116] There has also been some controversy about whether high accounting profits should be interpreted as good or bad performance. See Fisher and McGowan [1984].

[117] This was the view of Demsetz [1973, 1974]. For further details about this debate and more references to the historical and current literature, see Azzam and Anderson [1996].

[118] In addition to issues about short and long run costs and thus the appropriate MC measure, and cost (or scale) economies and thus the difference between markups and profitability, is

Associated with this is an important issue about the construction and use of the markup measures. Although for a perfectly competitive firm we argue in intermediate microeconomics classes that the firm will stay in production as long as p_Y exceeds minimum AVC (average variable costs), in the long run the price must at least cover ATC (average total costs) or the firm will leave the industry. Firms making pricing decisions rather than facing a given output price would therefore be expected to price such that at least their ATC is covered, if they are to stay in production in the long term.

The NEIO (new empirical industrial organization) literature began in an attempt to focus more on the appropriate representation of prices and costs, and their connection to optimization behavior of firms, and thus to provide a stronger theoretical basis for empirical representation of market power. Rather than emphasizing profit-concentration or price-concentration regressions, researchers such as Iwata [1974] began to compute the conjectural variation implied by a noncooperative equilibrium.

These models are based on the same fundamental notion as the SCP models; the gap between p_Y and MC provides the basis for analysis of market power. However, the NEIO studies begin to recognize that there is an associated deviation between market and shadow prices that is unobserved, and thus must be estimated from data on observed prices and outputs and a structural model of market behavior. The focus on econometric estimation rather than assuming observed prices and costs summarize all relevant information, motivated by the fact that marginal costs are typically not observed directly in the data, is a crucial characteristic of NEIO models.[119]

Many NEIO models, however, especially those which appeared early in the Industrial Organization evolution toward econometric estimation of price-cost margins, greatly limit their representation of the cost structure. Studies overviewed by Bresnahan [1989] such as Porter [1984], for example, recognize optimization processes but use the production theory model foundation to generate reduced forms for price and quantity determination with little attention paid to costs. Price and quantity are therefore the only endogenous variables. That is, as noted by Bresnahan, these methods "treat the comparative statics of the industry or market equilibrium in isolation … To the extent that price-cost margins are estimated, the inference is based on the supply behavior of firms".

---

the issue of "excess costs". That is, it has also been suggested that costs may appear higher in concentrated markets either because high prices attract inefficient producers, or because the availability of profits encourages unions to push for higher wages (see Karier [1985] for example). This is one basis for the literature on X-inefficiency (see Shen [1984] for one example).

[119] Bresnahan [1989] provides a useful and quite comprehensive overview of seminal NEIO studies and the distinction between these approaches and the SCP models.

These models did recognize, however, the importance of a measure of the "competitiveness of oligopoly conduct" (Porter) which falls between zero and one, with values farther from zero indicating less competition. The underlying optimization model from these studies is thus closely related to conjectural variations studies such as Iwata [1974], Spiller and Favaro [1984] and Gelfand and Spiller [1987] (as discussed in more detail in Bresnahan [1989]). Such models tend to focus more specifically on the behavior of the oligopolistic firms, and the measurement of the conjectural variations parameter.

A typical estimating equation from such an approach (as in Azzam and Schroeter [1995] and discussed in detail in Azzam and Anderson [1996]) is:

$$6.1) \quad p_Y = -(\theta/\eta) \cdot p_Y + MC ,$$

where θ is a weighted average of the firms' conjectural elasticities, η is the absolute value of the market demand elasticity $-\partial \ln Y/\partial \ln p_Y$, and MC is industry marginal cost (or a weighted average of firms' marginal costs).

This derives from the idea that for firm i that produces y_i, where total industry output is $Y = \Sigma_i y_i$, profits are $\pi_i = p_Y(Y) \cdot y_i - TC(y_i)$. The first order condition for profit maximization is thus $p_Y[1-(1/\eta)(y_i/Y)(1+\lambda)] = \partial TC/\partial y_i = MC$ (where λ_i is the conjectural variation of firm i, $d(\Sigma_i\, y_i)/dy_i$). Since the conjectural elasticity can be written as $\theta_i = dY/dy_i \cdot (y_i/Y)$, the first order condition becomes (6.1) after multiplying it by the firm's market share y_i/Y and summing across the I firms. $(\theta/\eta) \cdot p_Y$ therefore reflects the gap between the price and marginal cost, and thus is another indicator of the markup. This gap therefore depends on two pieces of the market structure puzzle; the market demand elasticity and the conjectural elasticity.

The measures underlying this representation of market and production structure can be can be constructed using a production theory-based model to identify the other components of the equation. For example, MC is often measured from a Leontief cost function, and substituted into (6.1). An econometric estimating model is usually constructed based on output demand and input share equations to represent the production structure and obtain estimates of the θ and η measures

One difficulty with this methodology is that the cost structure assumptions are typically so simplistic. Therefore the crucial issue of estimating the marginal cost to compare to the output price is largely finessed, although focused on more than in models representing only the price-quantity reduced form for a sector, such as Porter [1984].

The incorporation of a more complete econometric model of the cost structure, and thus of the level and determinants of marginal cost into these types of models, is typically attributed to Gollop and Roberts [1979], and

Appelbaum [1979, 1982]. These studies used duality models to represent input costs, and thus to explicitly identify the factor demand relationships underlying the cost structure. Such models are more along the lines of the models we have been discussing in this text. In particular, they are based on specifying cost and input demand equations. Information about the output demand function and a profit-maximizing condition representing output supply choice behavior are then appended, as we develop further below.

Including factor demand information in the IO output demand and supply model allows estimation of MC with much more precision and structure. This is particularly true since the output supply function will embody parameters from the cost structure, so there will be cross-equation restrictions between the factor demand and output supply relationships. As we have been discussing in this text, however, appropriate characterization of the cost structure in such a framework requires careful consideration of issues of capital measurement and fixities, and representation of other cost characteristics such as returns to scale.

If a full cost structure is used as a basis for the model, separate identification of θ and η tends to become difficult. Thus, for our production theory model below, we will bypass the conjectural variations framework and instead measure the gap as if it were based on a monopolistic rather than oligopolistic model. This simplification, like other issues of measuring production characteristics like scale economies, implicitly presumes that we are capturing average relationships, or the behavior of a "representative firm". It could also suggest collusive behavior, since if empirical implementation is based on aggregate data, so is the estimated demand elasticity.

Such a production model provides the basis for Morrison [1988c, 1992a, 1998b,e], which follows to some extent from Appelbaum [1979]. Although the focus on market structure is limited, the approach allows a more complete analysis of the patterns and determinants of the cost structure underlying the markup. The estimated markup is explicitly dependent on arguments of both the cost and demand functions, so elasticities can be computed with respect to the exogenous supply (cost) and demand variables.

Including market power into the model we have been developing in previous chapters requires first incorporating the output supply decision. This may be accomplished most simply by using a profit instead of cost function if perfect competition is assumed. In this case p_Y instead of Y appears in the function representing technological and behavioral optimization, resulting in $\pi(p_Y, \mathbf{p}, K, t)$ rather than $TC(Y, \mathbf{p}, K, t)$ (for our base model with one output, one fixed input and one exogenous technical change variable). Hotelling's lemma may then be used to construct the output supply equation $Y = \partial \pi / \partial p_Y$.

Analogously, profit maximization may be built into a cost function analysis by appending the equation $p_Y = MC = \partial TC / \partial Y$ to the equation representing input demand behavior, as in Mork [1978]. For either extension, output becomes a decision variable, at the cost of imposing the further assumptions of profit maximization and perfect competition in output markets over the cost function assumptions we already have specified.

If perfect competition exists, p_Y is exogenous to the firm's optimization decisions. Thus, in aggregate also we would observe $p_Y = MC$. If firms are making output supply quantity decisions in response to a given market output price, however, the cost-function-based equation from Mork encounters endogeneity problems, since the endogenous variable Y appears on the right hand side of the equation.

p_Y only becomes a choice variable if the firm faces a downward sloping output demand function so that p_Y and Y decisions are made simultaneously by choosing a point on the demand function. The optimization problem must then be adapted accordingly.

Incorporating imperfect competition requires recognizing that neither Hotelling's lemma or the corresponding $p_Y = MC$ equation from the cost function analysis holds when MR deviates from price ($p_Y = AR$), since firms will respond to the marginal rather than average value of output when making supply decisions. In this case $p_Y = p_Y(Y)$, so marginal revenue is $\partial TR / \partial Y = \partial [p_Y(Y) \cdot Y] / \partial Y = \partial p_Y(Y) / \partial Y \cdot Y + p_Y(Y)$ by the chain rule. The optimization equation then becomes: $MR = \partial p_Y(Y) / \partial Y \cdot Y + p_Y(Y) = MC$, or $p_Y(Y) = -\partial p_Y(Y) / \partial Y \cdot Y + MC$.

The "wedge" between p_Y and MC, and thus the deviation represented by a markup measure is therefore explicitly captured by the slope of the demand function $\partial p_Y(Y) / \partial Y$. There are a number of ways to measure this deviation.

One is simply to incorporate a parameter in an equation along the lines of Mork [1978] above, such that $p_Y = -\varphi Y + MC = -\varphi Y + \partial TC / \partial Y$, although this allows little structure, and therefore interpretation, of the φ term. Another, more along the lines of the NEIO literature discussed above, is to use the equation $p_Y = -\theta / \eta + MC$. However, in most cases it is not easy to identify both η and λ separately, especially with aggregate data (see the studies by Azzam for the development and use of such a model extended also to allow monopsony power). An alternative approach is to substitute an adjusted p_Y measure reflecting MR instead of $p_Y - p_Y' = p_Y(Y) + \partial p_Y(Y) / \partial Y \cdot Y = p_Y(Y) + \varphi Y$ – directly into the profit function, as discussed in the context of "poorly priced goods" in the next chapter, although again the φ parameters tend to become difficult to identify.

One promising option for incorporating market power is to explicitly add an inverse demand equation $p_Y = D^{-1}(Y, \rho)$ to equations underlying the optimization process, where ρ is a vector of demand function shift variables.

This requires specifying the arguments underlying the function, as well as a functional form for estimation, which raises the possibility of specification error. However, if feasible, it ends up as the most complete model of the production and market structure. This results in the equation

6.2) $p_Y = -\partial p_Y(Y,\rho)/\partial Y \cdot Y + \partial TC/\partial Y = -\varphi(Y,\rho) \cdot Y + \partial TC/\partial Y$

as a representation of output pricing (and implicitly supply) behavior, where $MC = \partial TC/\partial Y$ can be computed directly from the cost function $TC(Y,\cdot)$, and $\partial p_Y/\partial Y$ from the inverse demand function $D^{-1}(Y,\rho)$.

(6.2) therefore represents the optimal price, which, if estimated within a structural model can be compared with $MC = \partial TC/\partial Y$ to create the markup measure $p_Y/MC = [-\varphi(Y,\rho) \cdot Y + MC]/MC$. It can also be used to compute the Lerner price-margin expression more commonly used in the IO literature to represent market power: $(p_Y - MC)/p_Y = [-\varphi(Y,\rho) \cdot Y]/p_Y$.

The markup measure provides the basis for adaptation of productivity indexes for the existence of market power. The index also depends in an explicit manner on the exogenous cost and demand determinants. This dependence permits the responsiveness of the markup to different factors affecting the cost and inverse demand functions to be measured.

2.   MARKET POWER AND ECONOMIC PERFORMANCE MEASURES

A model of the form specified in the previous section was developed in Morrison [1992a] and applied to analyze the impact of market power on productivity growth measures by Morrison [1992b] for the U.S., Canadian and Japanese manufacturing sectors. In the latter study the adjustment of standard productivity growth computations is handled similarly to those for utilization and scale in Chapters 3 and 4. The adjustment of productivity measures to accommodate markup behavior, however, differs somewhat conceptually, because this adjustment is an output demand side adjustment, whereas those for scale and utilization economies are supply (cost) side adjustments. Thus it only becomes important when the foundation for the measurement of performance has an output orientation; it applies mainly to primal models of productivity growth.

Since the focus is on an output-demand-side adjustment, it is useful to further elaborate the construction and interpretation of the markup ratio before considering the adaptation of productivity growth measures for market power. In particular, is is illuminating to connect it to the product market explicitly through the output demand elasticity.

In the base "monopoly" model discussed in the previous section, output price deviates from marginal cost since it differs from marginal revenue. As discussed above, the difference between p_Y and MR is due to the wedge $\varphi \cdot Y = \partial p_Y / \partial Y \cdot Y$, from the definition of MR as: $\partial TR / \partial Y = \partial p_Y(Y) \cdot Y / \partial Y = p_Y + \partial p_Y / \partial Y \cdot Y$. Since the MR=MC equality can also be written as $p_Y = -\partial p_Y / \partial Y \cdot Y + MC = -\partial p_Y / \partial Y \cdot Y + \partial TC / \partial Y$, the markup of price over marginal cost can be represented in general by $Prat_Y = p_Y / MC = [-\partial p_Y / \partial Y \cdot Y + \partial TC / \partial Y] / (\partial TC / \partial Y)$ (where "Prat" denotes "price-ratio"). If this ratio (statistically) significantly exceeds one, market power may be inferred, with the deviation of the measure from one interpreted as the percentage markup.

Markup measures may also be constructed for multiple outputs. The marginal cost of any particular output may be defined as $MC_m = \partial TC / \partial Y_m$ analogously to the single output case above, as seen in Chapter 4. Also, the wedge from market power, $\partial p_{Ym} / \partial Y_m \cdot Y_m$, may be derived from the pricing equations, resulting in the output-specific markup or price ratio equations $Prat_{Ym} = p_{Ym} / MC_m = [-\partial p_{Ym} / \partial Y_m \cdot Y_m + \partial TC / \partial Y_m] / (\partial TC / \partial Y_m)$.

Constructing an overall markup measure is analogous to the development of the BPW cost economy measure in Chapter 4. Recall that this measure is written $\varepsilon_{TCY} = \Sigma_m \partial TC / \partial Y_m \cdot (Y_m / TC)$, or $\Sigma_m MC_m \cdot Y_m / TC$. Thus, a comparable price margin measure is $Prat_Y = \Sigma_m p_{Ym} \cdot Y_m / \Sigma_m MC_m \cdot Y_m$.

An important linkage to recognize here is that the markup ratio $Prat_Y = p_Y / MC$ (or $Prat_{Ym} = p_{Ym} / MC_m$) contains the same information as the standard Lerner measure of market power, which is in turn based on the firms' inverse demand elasticity.[120] That is,

$$6.3) \quad Prat_Y = p_Y / MC = [-\partial p_Y / \partial Y \cdot Y + \partial TC / \partial Y] / (\partial TC / \partial Y) = 1/(1 + \varepsilon_{PY}),$$

where $\varepsilon_{PY} = \partial \ln p_Y(Y, \rho) / \partial \ln Y$.[121] The size of the markup is therefore completely determined by the output demand elasticity, through the deviation between p_Y (AR) and MR. The level of marginal costs simply determines the output level chosen for evaluation of the markup.

The equivalence of the markup measure and the elasticity expression, like the capacity utilization and scale measures used before for adjustment of productivity growth indexes, is important for motivating its construction and use. This information can be used to formalize the difference between cost and revenue shares, and thus primal- and cost- side productivity growth measures, that results because $p_Y Y \neq TC$ with market power.

---

[120] This relationship and many related issues are discussed in Bresnahan [1989].

[121] MC=MR in short run equilibrium for the profit maximizing firm, where MR is marginal revenue, so the expression for p_Y / MC becomes $p_Y / (p_Y + Y \cdot \partial p_Y / \partial Y)$ $= p_Y / [p_Y \cdot (1 + \partial \ln p_Y / \partial \ln Y)] = 1/(1 + \varepsilon_{PY})$.

The relationship between revenue and costs in this case becomes $p_Y Y = TC \cdot (p_Y/MC) = TC/(1+\varepsilon_{PY})$.[122] The revenue value ($p_Y Y$) captures returns to all characteristics of the production process (including returns to market power), whereas TC includes only the market or *ex-ante* returns to inputs. Primal productivity growth measures, which are based on revenue shares (as seen in Chapter 2), therefore represent not only technical change (and scale and utilization effects) but also the impact of market power.

This idea has recently been the focal point of a number of macro studies of economic performance, as alluded to in Chapter 5, which are typcally attributed by Hall [1988a]. The adaptations to productivity growth measures used by these researchers are based on a similar conceptual motivation to that above, since the Solow residual equation (the expression defining ε_{Yt}) provides the foundation for measuring the markup in these studies. That is, the deviation between revenues and costs, and thus the share-weights on the inputs, are recognized as a potential distortion in the productivity residual, which is reflected in variance of the Solow residual.

Hall's approach to measuring marginal costs and therefore markups was discussed in the context of scale effects in the last chapter.[123] He used Solow's [1957] residual analysis of technical change, interpreted as overall productivity growth, to highlight the importance of evaluating output growth appropriately at its marginal value. This value is reflected, of course, if market power exists, by marginal cost (MC) rather than output price (p_Y).

The idea is that if the deviation between p_Y and MC can be identified by regression techniques, this component of measured primal-side productivity trends can be distinguished from that more clearly attributable to technical change or other productive factors. This decomposition requires estimating the markup of p_Y to MC, and using this ratio to adapt the shares for more appropriate measurement of the residual as an indicator of technical change.

Hall's implementation of the model was carried out for aggregate data, and was based on the assumption of a constant markup over time. His measurement procedures can be carried out using single equation methods, and typically focus only on estimation of a single scale factor which now is interpreted as a measure of market power. Although later studies in this literature also recognized utilization issues through proxies for "mismeasurement" of capital (and labor) inputs, the separate impacts of scale and market power are more difficult to establish in these models. The scale effect reflects any differential between revenues and costs.

---

[122] Using reasoning analogous to that developed in Chapter 4, it can be shown easily that this adapts to $p_Y Y = TC \cdot (p_Y/MC) \cdot CU_c \cdot \varepsilon_{TCY}{}^L = \varepsilon_{TCY} \cdot TC/(1+\varepsilon_{PY}) \neq MC \cdot Y \neq TC^* \neq TC$ if nonconstant returns and subequilibrium also exist so $\varepsilon_{TCY} \neq 1$.

[123] See Chapter 9 for more details.

The resulting measures may be used to "correct" the primal-side residual for the impacts of market power, but little scope for analysis of the interactions between different components of the production structure exists in this framework. Interpretation of the measures is limited because of the simplicity of the model, as discussed more generally in Chapter 5. [124]

By contrast, markup measures based on the richer structure of the production-theory-based models greatly facilitate formal representation of the components of the residual that may be separately distinguished. Representing the wedge between p_Y and MC via the equation $p_Y = -\partial p_Y(Y,\rho)/\partial Y \cdot Y + \partial TC/\partial Y$, suggests that we can represent the inverse output demand elasticity $\varepsilon_{pY} = [\partial p_Y(Y,\rho)/\partial Y] \cdot Y/p_Y$ directly. This elasticity may be computed from the estimating equation (6.2), which also requires measurement of the marginal cost from the rest of the model structure based on the cost function. Alternatively, if a full output demand structure is incorporated into the model, the markup indicator can be computed from the inverse output demand equation.

Once this markup – reflecting the "returns" to market power – is estimated, the measure may be used to explicitly separate its impact on the primal measure of productivity growth from the other productive performance factors (technical change, utilization and scale) represented from cost-side elasticities, similarly to Hall. [1988a].

That is, to use this to refine the productivity growth residual and identify its underlying determinants, we must consider what measures to use as weights for the output and input growth rates. In the microfoundations models these appear as elasticity components of the productivity growth expression, reproduced here in somewhat adapted form (and with $\varepsilon_{TCY}\neq1$) as:

$$6.4) \; -\partial \ln TC/\partial t = -\varepsilon_{TCt} = \varepsilon_{TCY} \, d\ln Y/dt - \Sigma j \, \varepsilon_{TCj} \, d\ln v_j/dt = \varepsilon_{Yt},$$

where $\varepsilon_{TCY} = \partial \ln TC/\partial \ln Y$ (=1 with CRS and instantaneous adjustment) and $\varepsilon_{TCj} = \partial \ln TC/\partial \ln p_j$ (= $p_j v_j/TC = S_j$ when Shephard's lemma is valid).

In previous chapters the possibilities that $v_j \neq \partial TC/\partial p_j$ ($S_j \neq \partial \ln TC/\partial \ln p_j$) due to fixities and thus subequilibrium, and $\varepsilon_{TCY} \neq 1$ from these fixities and/or cost economies were considered. The correction for market power has a somewhat different form, however, since the cost-side measure of

---

[124] Note also that if estimated empirically both the markup and returns to scale measures generated by this framework are extremely large and implausible for some industries, and the reasons for this are not evident (See Hall [1988a,b]). Further discussion of the empirical implementation of such models is provided in Chapter 9.

productivity growth ε_{TCt} is not based on assuming the equality $p_Y Y = TC$ is true. It depends only on cost elasticities.[125]

Instead the primal measure ε_{Yt} must be adapted, since the shares of inputs used to generate an aggregate input growth measure should be in terms of costs instead of revenue (output should be evaluated at its true marginal valuation to the firm, or MC, rather than its average value, p_Y). The adjustment to separate out the return to market power involves removing it from the denominator of the output shares, thus purging the market power effect from true productivity growth.

More specifically, since imperfect competition implies $(1+\varepsilon_{PY}) \neq 1$, and $(1+\varepsilon_{PY}) = MC/p_Y = TC/p_Y Y$, the share adjustment becomes $M_j = S_j \cdot (1+\varepsilon_{PY})$ where M_j is the revenue share $(p_j v_j / p_Y Y)$ and S_j is the cost share $(p_j v_j / TC)$. Therefore, the primal measure ε_{Yt} can be written as

6.5) $\varepsilon_{Yt} = -\varepsilon_{Ct} + \varepsilon_{PY} \cdot \Sigma_j S_j \cdot d\ln v_j / dt$,

This correction requires computing $\varepsilon^M_{Yt} = -\varepsilon_{TCt} = \varepsilon_{Yt} - \varepsilon_{PY} \cdot \Sigma_j S_j \cdot d\ln v_j / dt$, where $\varepsilon_{PY} \cdot \Sigma_j S_j \cdot d\ln v_j / dt$ may be considered the "error bias" in the usual primal measures of productivity growth, and M stands for the "markup correction". The bias therefore depends on the cost shares, the inverse demand elasticity (or markup), and the growth rates of the inputs.[126]

The empirical result of the adjustment by markups found by Morrison [1992b] is to smooth productivity growth fluctuations and counteract the productivity growth slowdown. This smoothing stems primarily from the time trend in the markup; markup ratios in the U.S. have been rising, so the traditional measures increasingly underestimate productivity growth. However, interactions among markups, subequilibrium, and scale economies raise additional issues. When corrections are made to accommodate all these production characteristics, the smoothing result is at least partially offset. This occurs because the cost characteristics imply minimal profitability, even with the existence markup behavior, consistent with Hall [1990].

---

[125] This also implies that markups do not affect the cost elasticities determining capacity utilization and scale economies.

[126] . This is analogous to the Hall [1988a] adjustment for market power, since his treatment simply evaluates the shares in terms of $MC \cdot Y$ instead of $p_Y Y$.

3. INPUT MARKET POWER: MONOPSONY

3.1 A parametric model

Although the most familiar market power issues dealt with both in standard textbooks and in the IO literature pertain to output markets, market power in input markets may also be important to represent. Monopsony (or oligopsony) power may provide the basis for an additional type of cost economies for large firms, as noted in Chapter 4.

This possibly might not be "bad" in a bilateral monopoly-type scenario. For example, producers of electric power may be monopsonists, but face energy input markets dominated by large refiners that therefore have some monopoly power. Inefficiencies deriving from the monopoly power could then be minimized by the countervailing market power forces, resulting in a reasonable "second best" solution. Similarly, supermarket chains that could potential take advantage of monopsony power may face meat product markets dominated by large producers in concentrated markets.

However, like in the monopoly scenario, deviations from competitive markets have their associated costs – in this case in terms of lower prices paid and quantities demanded for input producers in these markets. This may be particularly true if, for example, meat product producers in turn are able to take advantage of their monopsony power over the "little guy" – say, cow and calf producers, or local labor markets.

The meat packing industry does provide one currently topical example of a market that has generated significant attention about market power issues. In the meat packing industry large plants (and some very large firms) dominate the market, and purchase cattle from smaller calf/cow producers or possibly independent feeding lots. There has been significant concern about market power in this concentrated market since nearly 100 years ago, and in the past decade increasing concentration was again evident, stimulating further concern and economic analysis.

The case of oligopsony in this industry has been addressed in a number of papers referenced by Azzam and Anderson [1996], including Azzam and Pagoulatos [1990] and Azzam and Schroeter [1995]. These models closely follow the NEIO treatment of oligopoly behavior. A cost-oriented analysis, as developed for the monopoly case, can also be used to frame the problem in terms of monopsony in the market for input v_1 with some adaptations.

In this situation Shephard's lemma is severed for the input 1 market; $\partial TC/\partial p_1 \neq v_1$. Thus, to represent this deviation, the cost function may be expressed in terms of the level or quantity of v_1, similarly to the treatment of fixities (although the wedge is from market structure rather than fixity).

To incorporate this distinction between standard variable factors and those subject to some type of market "failure" that causes Shephard's lemma not to hold, we can denote the lth input as a component of the **x** vector, x_l, as in Chapter 4. This implies that the true marginal value of input x_l should be represented as a shadow value; it is not reflected in the market price since the market structure is not competitive.[127]

More specifically, if imperfect competition in the form of monopsony exists, and thus p_l is dependent on x_l ($p_l = p_l(x_l)$), profit maximization in the x_l market implies

$$6.6)\ MFC_l = \partial[p_l(x_l) \bullet x_l]/\partial x_l = p_l + x_l \bullet \partial p_l/\partial x_l = -\partial VC/\partial x_l = Z_l,$$

(where MFC_l is the marginal factor cost of factor x_l). To represent the associated input pricing behavior more directly this may be written as $p_l = -x_l \bullet \partial p_l/\partial x_l - \partial VC/\partial x_l$, where $VC = VC(Y,\mathbf{p},\mathbf{x},t)$, $Z_l = -\partial VC/\partial x_l$, the **x** vector includes both quasi-fixed inputs and those subject to monopsony power (any inputs that violate Shephard's lemma), and the **p** vector does not include prices of any **x** inputs.

Such an equation may be included as part of the optimization model to represent both input 1 demand behavior and any kind of pricing power. In this case – as for monopoly in an output market – price and quantity are determined jointly given the input supply function facing the firm.

(6.6) is a cost-side version of the usual $MFC_l = VMP_l$ equality for profit maximization in an input market when market power exists. The marginal benefit of an additional unit of the input (value of the marginal product, VMP, or marginal revenue product if market power also exists in the output market) is represented in this scenario by the dual cost-side value (the marginal shadow value of the x_l input, Z_l). The marginal cost of an incremental change in x_l (marginal factor cost, MFC_l) adapts the observed price per unit (average factor cost p_l) to a marginal value, due to the existence of a sloped input supply function and thus endogeneity of p_l.

This approach to representing input-side market power – or monopsony behavior – allows direct representation of the differential between the observed input price and the price the firm would be willing to pay for that quantity of input if it had no market power. This differential is simply the $x_l \bullet \partial p_l/\partial x_l$ component of the pricing expression $p_l = -x_l \bullet \partial p_l/\partial x_l - \partial VC/\partial x_l$; the market price will fall short of the shadow value by this amount.

---

[127] Alternatively, if an estimate of the actual marginal value of x_l, p'_l, may be obtained, it can be substituted into the cost function and its usual properties will be are retained. See Chapters 7 and 8 for further discussion of this approach, often attributed to Toda [1976].

This deviation can be thought of as the "markdown" of price below the shadow value if it is expressed in the ratio form $p_l/(-\partial VC/\partial x_l) = (-\partial VC/\partial x_l - x_l \cdot \partial p_l/\partial x_l)/(-\partial VC/\partial x_l)$, analogous to the usual measurement of the "markup" of output price over marginal cost p_Y/MC.

More specifically, the relevant "markdown" measure – representing the amount a plant facing an upward sloping input supply function would hold the price down below their true marginal benefit from the input – would be

$$6.7) \ Prat_l = p_l/Z_l = p_l/(-\partial VC/\partial x_l) = [-x_l \cdot \partial p_l/\partial x_l - \partial VC/\partial x_l]/(-\partial VC/\partial x_l),$$

since, similarly to the monopoly case, we have found that $MFC_l = p_l + x_l \cdot \partial p_l/\partial x_l = Z_l = -\partial VC/\partial x_l$, or $p_l = -x_l \cdot \partial p_l/\partial x_l - \partial VC/\partial x_l$.[128]

If this measure falls significantly short of one, markdowns are evident and monopsony power appears to be present. The magnitude of the deviation indicates the percentage markdown from the price that could feasibly be paid, given the marginal benefit to the plant of additional x_l input. The markdown measure therefore depends on the cost elasticity with respect to input 1 ($Z_l = -\partial VC/\partial x_l$), and the own elasticity of the (inverse) input supply function ($\varepsilon_{pll} = \partial \ln p_l/\partial \ln x_l = \partial p_l/\partial x_l \cdot (x_l/p_l)$, so $\varepsilon_{pll} \cdot p_l = \partial p_l/\partial x_l \cdot x_l$).

Including market power in this manner requires generating an input supply $x_l(p_l)$ (and thus inverse supply $p_l(x_l)$) equation to incorporate into the model. This could be as simple as a linear form relating p_l and x_l, so that $\partial p_l/\partial x_l$ is just a parameter (κ_l) that can be estimated directly within the pricing equation (like φ for the monopoly case). This implies the pricing equation takes the form $p_l = -Z_l - x_l \cdot \kappa_l$.

A somewhat more flexible representation may be accommodated by putting in squared and possibly cross-terms with, say, a t parameter, in order to capture simple curvature and trends. Ideally, however, the (inverse) input supply or pricing function $p_l(x_l)$ may be represented as a more complex relationship with curvature of the function and the role of "shift" variables (other arguments) of the function being determined by the data.

A number of comments are worth raising about the extension to a model with input market power. One has also implicitly been raised in Chapter 4 in the context of a multiple "fixed"-input model. In this case although x_l is not fixed, it appears in the VC function as a quantity level. In the estimation process, if the pricing equation, which also implicitly represents input demand behavior, is used as part of the estimating system, the optimal x_l will

---

[128] A similar but simpler specification of the markdown, and comparisons for the labor market between somewhat limited structural models (Cobb-Douglas with a focus on labor use) and Hall-type monopsony models is outlined in Hyde and Perloff [1994]. They use Monte-Carlo simulations to determine the power of tests of market power, and find that they are quite sensitive to the existence of returns to scale.

be reproduced by construction. However, for elasticity computations it must be recognized that the elasticity will be based on a given quantity of x_l rather than allowing input demand response to the exogenous change underlying the elasticity computation.

Analogous reasoning provided the basis for the distinction among the "short-", "intermediate-" and "long-" run elasticities in Chapter 4. This implies some type of representation of sequential optimization, and thus the construction of combined elasticities that allow us to capture the implied sequence of responses. In particular, to allow for the adjustment of x_l as in Chapter 4, the intermediate elasticity (to distinguish it from the short- or "immediate"- run elasticity based on the existing levels of all **x** factors) was written as: $\varepsilon^I_{TCY} = [\partial TC/\partial Y + \partial TC/\partial x_l \cdot \partial x_l/\partial Y] \cdot (Y/TC)$.

This is important for the interpretation of the ε_{TCY} elasticity, which is fundamental since it represents cost economies and provides the basis for cost-side productivity adjustments to represent the various possible cost-side factors affecting observed economic performance. It also motivates some additional distinctions among ε_{TCY} elasticities stemming not only from the short-intermediate-run distinction, but also from the fact that when output increases, x_l responses will have impacts on p_l which will appear as pecuniary (price-related) cost economies or diseconomies.

Essentially, if output expands, the implied increases in x_l in turn affect the price paid in a market where the price is not exogenous. This may be accommodated by building it directly into the model, as has implicitly been done here through the ε^I_{TCY} elasticity (since it is based on total costs). That is, the "short run" measure $\partial VC/\partial Y$ depends on a given quantity of x_l, so this is not an issue, but if the total cost (intermediate run) measure $\partial TC/\partial Y$ is appropriately characterized with $p_l(x_l)$ incorporated, the resulting measure will depend on MFC_l rather than p_l.

Thus, since the marginal price of the factor (MFC_l) differs from the average price $(AFC_l = p_l)$, part of the cost economy measure ε^I_{TCY} includes $x_l \cdot \partial p_l/\partial x_l$. If MC (or ε^I_{TCY}) is measured without this component ($\partial p_l/\partial x_l$ is set to zero), the pure *cost* measure *not* including pecuniary diseconomies, ε^C_{TCY}, may be defined.

Although the relationship between ε^C_{TCY} and ε_{TCY} does not have a simple analytical representation, their ratio is closely related to the $Prat_l$ measure. $Prat_l = (Z_l - x_l \cdot \partial p_l/\partial x_l)/Z_l$, and $\varepsilon^C_{TCY}/\varepsilon_{TCY} = MC^C/MC = MCrat = (MC - x_l \cdot \partial p_l/\partial x_l \cdot \partial x_l/\partial Y)/MC$ (where MC^C is the "pure" cost MC, which is equivalent to "short run" marginal costs $\partial VC/\partial Y = MC^S$, and MC is the full marginal cost including the p_l change). The relationship between MCrat and $Prat_l$ depends on the marginal valuation of x_l as compared to Y, adjusted for the pressure on the input market when x_l changes either independently (the $Prat_l$ measure) or as a result of a change in output (the MC measure).

For most purposes ε^I_{TCY} is the appropriate measure for cost analysis, since it represents the full range of cost impacts arising from output increases, including associated input price changes due to market power. However, for interpretational purposes it may be useful to evaluate the impact of "pure" cost economies separately from potential diseconomies resulting from market power in the input market. This allows input market impacts to be distinguished from other cost effects, through the decomposition of ε^I_{TCY} into $\varepsilon^I_{TCY} = MCrat \cdot \varepsilon^C_{TCY} \approx (1/Prat_I) \cdot \varepsilon^C_{TCY}$.

The productivity adjustments implied by this adaptation of the ε_{TCY} measure follow directly along the lines of those for utilization in Chapter 3 and cost economies more generally in Chapter 4. They all involve the adaptation of the residual by ε_{TCY} to reproduce the baseline technical change measure $-\varepsilon^A_{TCt} = \varepsilon_{Yt} \cdot \varepsilon_{TCY}$, from the equalities $\varepsilon_{Yt} = -\varepsilon^A_{TCt}/\varepsilon_{TCY}$, and $\varepsilon^A_{TCt} = \varepsilon_{TCt} + (1 - \varepsilon_{TCY}) \cdot dln\ Y/dt$ developed in Chapter 4.

The difference is in the specification, and implied decomposition, of the ε_{TCY} measure, which allows separate identification of the cost economies contained in ε_{TCY} and thus in the total primal measure. The differences between ε^S_{TCY}, ε^I_{TCY}, and ε^C_{TCY} may, thus, be explicitly specified and the impacts of monopsony power directly identified as part of observed cost changes embodied in productivity growth measures.

A final crucial point to emphasize about the cost economy and market power measures developed above is that they are all entangled. Further analysis of the welfare implications of such a complex combination of cost and market structure forces is pursued in the next section. For now, however, it is worth noting that when both monopoly and monopsony (or, if conjectural variations are brought in, oligopoly and oligopsony) power is evident, "standard" markup or Lerner indexes are not fully appropriate to represent market power in the output market.

This interpretational issue arises because the actual marginal cost measure depends on the marginal factor cost of the input subject to monopsony power (MFC_I) rather than the observed average price (p_I). Evaluation of market power therefore requires joint consideration of potential imperfections in both the output and the input markets. This involves identifying, and ultimately separating, the impacts of monopoly or oligopoly (the deviation between marginal cost and price), and monopsony or oligopsony (the distinction between marginal cost at given input prices (AFC) versus marginal factor cost).

Incorporating both aspects of market power has been the focus of meat packing industry studies such as Azzam and Pagoulatos [1990] and Azzam and Anderson [1996], which have an NEIO perspective, and Morrison [1997, 1998b,c,d] which emphasizes the cost structure. A similar approach for the coffee industry was utilized by Roberts [1984].

The papers by Azzam and coauthors are based on an expanded version of (6.1) with an equality between the representative firm's perceived marginal revenue and and marginal cost:

6.8) $p_Y(1+\theta/\eta) = p_l(1+\theta/\phi) + \partial TC/\partial Y$,

where θ and η are defined as in (6.1) and ϕ is the elasticity of market supply for input x_l (note that Lerner's index becomes $-\theta/\eta$ in this case with conjectural variation). In our notation, the output demand and input supply elasticities can be written as $\eta=-1/\varepsilon_{pY}$ and $\phi=-1/\varepsilon_{pll}$. If $\theta = \partial \ln Y/\partial \ln y_i=1$, as has been assumed for the monopoly-oriented model discussed above, this therefore becomes $p_Y(1+\varepsilon_{pY}) = p_l(1+\varepsilon_{pll}) + \partial TC/\partial Y$.

This equation can be shown to be directly connected to the production theory model, through the expressions for MR and MC, where MC is defined with input x_l adjustment built in (denoted MC^I, as for the ε^I_{TCY} elasticity; see Morrison [1998b,c,e] for further details). The production theory model, however, facilitates further elaboration and interpretation of the individual terms, as well as emphasizing the dependence of this type of expression on a combination of elasticity measures.

To specify this production theory relationship using our combined elasticity expressions, first note that the optimization problem with x_l adjustment built in may be written as: $MR = p_Y + Y \bullet \partial p_Y/\partial Y = MC^I$. Also note that MC^I can explicitly be expressed as: $\partial TC^I/\partial Y = \partial VC/\partial Y + \partial TC/\partial x_l \bullet \partial x_l/\partial Y$, where $\partial TC/\partial x_l = \partial VC/\partial x_l + p_l + x_l \bullet \partial p_l/\partial x_l$, since TC is defined as $TC = VC(p,Y,x,t) + p_l(x_l) \bullet x_l + p_k \bullet x_k$ (where $x_k=K$ is the only fixed input). Thus, given also that $\partial VC/\partial x_l = Z_l$, we get:

6.9) $p_Y + Y \bullet \partial p_Y/\partial Y = (p_l - Z_l + x_l \bullet \partial p_l/\partial x_l) \bullet \partial x_l/\partial Y + \partial VC/\partial Y$,

which is equivalent to (6.8) without the conjectural elasticity, with substitution of x_l with the v inputs incorporated via Z_l (if such substitution is ignored as for 6.8, this term obviously disappears), and the x_l-Y relationship accommodated by $\partial x_l/\partial Y$ (with fixed 1-1 proportions, this also falls out of the equation).

3.2   A nonparametric model

Although we have primarily focused on parametric representation of production and market structure in this text, there is an expanding literature using nonparametric techniques to represent such structure. These models are statistically limited, but also do not require assumptions about functional forms or other structural aspects that may cause issues of specification error.

The nonparametric approach creates an index analogous to a Lerner index of monopoly power by comparing observed data in prices, outputs and inputs, and inferring their optimality in terms of behavioral (cost minimzation or profit maximization) conditions. The simulations typically carried out do not allow for randomness or "white noise" in the data generation process, as is the case for any nonparametric technique. These techniques therefore preclude considering the statistical significance of any measured deviations from perfect competition.

The example of nonparametric measurement of input market power I will rely on here is Love and Shumway [1994], which is similar to the treatment in Ashenfelter and Sullivan [1987] for monopoly power. This methodology is also firmly embedded in earlier literature using nonparametric analysis to identify production structure, technical change, and the impact of R&D, such as Chavas and Cox [1988, 1992], and Fawson and Shumway [1988], as initially motivated in Hanoch and Rothschild [1972] and Varian [1984].

More specifically, in Love and Shumway [1994], they "develop a nonparametric deterministic test for observational consistency of market data with a hypothesized market structure" (p. 1156). They assume profit maximization behavior should be observed, and allow for potential monopsony market power and neutral technical change. This results in a set of linear inequalities that must be satisfied, and that can be evaluated using linear programming (LP) techniques. The optimal LP solution results in indexes of market power and technical change.

This model is initially motivated using a standard profit maximization model, based on the profit expression $\pi = p_Y Y_i - TC(Y_i, \mathbf{p}; x_{li}) - p_l(x_{li} + \bar{x}_l)x_{li}$, for firm i, when market power enters on the input side. Note that the input price vector $\mathbf{p}$ in this expression does not include the price of the input subject to monopsony power, x_{li}. The dependence of the input price on the quantity of the input demanded is represented by $p_l(x_{li} + \bar{x}_l)$, while $\bar{x}_l$ represents the quantity of input l demanded by all other firms. This last adaptation allows consideration of market structures such as Cournot and Bertrand, which depend on the conjectural variations characterized by $\partial \bar{x}_l / \partial x_{li}$; in the monopsony case this term drops out. Similarly, for monopoly power, this could read $\pi = p_Y(Y_i)Y_i - TC(Y_i, \mathbf{p}; x_{li})$, where $\mathbf{p}$ now represents all input prices.

This expression for monopsony profits is used to generate first order conditions for the inputs according to Shephard's lemma (or $VMP_l = MFC_l$ for input l, where MFC is the marginal factor cost of input l, if input-side market power exists)[129]. The first order condition for output is based on a p_Y=MC equation (MR=MC for the case of output market power).

For input-side market power, for example, the first order conditions are p_l = $-x_l \cdot \partial p_l / \partial x_l$ - $\partial VC / \partial x_l$ for the monopsony case, and p_l = $-x_l \cdot \partial p_l / \partial x_l$ • $[1+\partial \, x_l / \partial x_{li}] \cdot x_{li}$ - $\partial VC / \partial x_l$ for the oligopsonistic case with conjectural variations included. The corresponding Lerner index therefore is $-(p_l + \partial VC / \partial x_l)/p_l$ = $(x_l \cdot \partial p_l / \partial x_l)/p_l$ for the monopsonist (the oligopsonist case follows analogously, as does the case of market power in the output market). This base scenario is obviously similar to that for the parametric model in the last sub-section.

The nonparametric treatment, however, deviates from the parametric model at this point. The nonparametric test for market power using the profit maximizing model and culminating in a measure of the Lerner index "explores the implications of profit maximization in recovering the firm's perceived impact on price in a particular factor market", rather than using the model to set up structural equations and estimate the Lerner index. That is, the profit maximizing equation is used as the basis for constructing a "Weak Axiom of Profit Maximization" (WAPM). This behavioral axiom is used to check the data for consistency with the postulated behavior.

This requires rewriting the profit maximizing problem for firm i as

$$6.10) \; \pi_i = p_Y Y_i - \Sigma_j \, p_j v_{ji} - p_l(x_{li} + \overline{x}_l)x_{li} \, ,$$

subject to $F(v_j, x_{li}) \geq Y_i$, where j indexes all inputs except l. For a discrete change in input and output levels, maximization of profits as in (6.10) requires $\Delta \pi_i = p_Y \Delta Y_i - \Sigma_j p_j \Delta v_{ji} - p_l \Delta x_{li} - \Delta p_l x_{li} \leq 0$. To check with the consistency of observations with profit maximization, one would exclude observation s (the input/output combination at time s) relative to observation t (the combination at time t) if it results in a decrease in profits.

More specifically, for the input-output combination chosen at period t to represent a profit maximizing solution, no feasible output/input combination chosen at another observation such as s can generate higher profits with period t prices. This is formalized as the requirement for observed behavior to be consistent with profit maximization:

$$6.11) \; p_Y{}^t(Y_i{}^s - Y_i{}^t) - \Sigma_j p_{ji}(v_{ji}{}^s - v_{ji}{}^t) - p_l{}^t(x_{li}{}^s - x_{li}{}^t) - x_{li}{}^s(p_l{}^s - p_l{}^t) \leq 0 \, .$$

---

[129] The expression I have termed the MFC is called the marginal output (MO) by Love and Shumway. Note also that what they call the "marginal value in production", and motivate along the lines of a VMP term, is essentially the cost-side shadow value. See the next section for further discussion of these types of conditions.

The last term of (6.11) would fall out of the expression if the firm were competitive in all input markets, since the firm can change quantities of x_l purchased without affecting its price (p_l is exogenous). This is therefore the usual WAPM (see Varian [1984]) adapted for market power in the x_l market.

This equation assumes that the x_l input supply curve and the technology are constant between periods s and t, so all changes in demand for x_{li} are due to changes in output and input prices. If these assumptions are appropriate, a nonparametric test for profit maximization with market power can be carried out by checking for consistency of the observed data with equation (6.11). If technical change is possible this becomes more complex. It involves determining whether sets of market power and technical change parameters can be found that solve a LP model, as in Cox and Chavas [1990].

Although this brief overview is only sufficient to familiarize the reader with basic notions underlying nonparametric representations and analyses of production processes and market power, it allows us to see the differences in orientation and justification underlying parametric as compared to nonparametric methods. A parametric treatment requires assumptions about functional forms and explicit specification of how technical change, market structure, and other variables enter the analysis. Nonparametric models do not require these types of specification assumptions, but also do not facilitate, either theoretically or statistically, doing the kind of controlled experiment that is possible using parametric production theory models.

The nonparametric models typically postulate a behavioral assumption such as profit maximization, and develop axioms identifying the characteristics the data should embody to be consistent with this. If other exogenous (or unspecified endogenous) factors are affecting the model, the results of such a comparison are invalid. In some instances the model can be reformulated as a LP problem which allows additional "shift parameters" to be accommodated. As for the parametric models, however, adaptations to the framework to allow for market characteristics such as input or output market power, or (neutral) technical change, allow a more complete representation of what is driving observed behavioral patterns.

4.   MARKET POWER MEASURES AND WELFARE

The measures of production and market structure we have been developing in this text have typically been based on elasticities with respect to output and input levels. When such measures are associated with market power, the elasticities that provide the basis for representation of the market structure characteristics, and the use and interpretation of the associated indicators, are based on the output demand and input supply functions facing the firm.

In this context we therefore move our attention from the cost function to functions representing markets within which the firm operates. The interaction of these measures with those based on the cost function remains important, however, because both marginal and average costs are involved in the analysis of the extent of market power.

For example, we have seen that the elasticity of an (inverse) demand function with respect to output indicates the extent of market power in the product market, while that of an (inverse) supply function with respect to the associated input identifies market power in the input market. As developed above, this is because such elasticities indicate the deviation between the marginal cost (marginal benefit or value) of the output (input) and its observed market (average) price. Since behavior and therefore responses of firms have to do with these *marginal* valuations, they must be distinguished from their average counterparts in order to ascertain the degree of market power.

The first issue that arises for interpreting these measures and evaluating their welfare implications is how MC should be measured and interpreted. This was alluded to above in the context of identifying a cost measure that properly reflects true economic (long run) resource costs for producing an additional unit of output. For example, if short run marginal costs provide the basis for indicators of market power, this may be a very poor indicator of the price that must be received by the firm to maintain the feasibility of long run production, particularly in a capital-intensive environment.

This feasibility ultimately has to do with the profitability of the firm. Thus, even if marginal costs are measured appropriately, it is actually the profitability of the firm, represented by a comparison of average or total rather than marginal values, that determines the "abuse" of market power.

This brings us back again to the lack of a distinction between market power and cost economy measure in some of the macro literature on this topic. If, for example, cost (such as scale) economies exist, MC<AC. If even zero profits are to be maintained, p_Y must be equal to AC, and by definition exceed MC. This emphasizes that markup (or markdown) measures are not interpretable without additional information on the cost structure, and thus on the connection between marginal valuations of output (input) and profitability.

This also again raises issues of what "harm" market power might cause. In particular, if markups, concentration, or (vertical or horizontal) integration are due to the existence of cost economies, it may be beneficial to society to have the larger operations in production. This is particularly likely to be true as high-tech but often very large "chunks" of equipment, that may produce at lowest unit costs, increasingly proliferate. This returns us to arguments in the earlier literature by Demsetz [1973, 1974] and even Schumpeter [1942] that "market power" could be evidence of efficiency rather than inefficiency. That is, it could allow the firm to take advantage of cost economies or make it feasible and profitable to carry out R&D, rather than providing an indication that something is "wrong" in the market.[130]

This is not to say that market power is inherently beneficial; certainly inefficiencies allowed by a lack of competitiveness, or the ability to maintain high prices even though costs are low for large operations, can cause problems. However, in our second-best world it should be kept in mind that there are numerous pieces of the market-power "puzzle" that ideally should be taken into account in order to clearly interpret indicators of market power and determine whether they imply that a problem exists.

Again, this brief discussion emphasizes the importance of representing various cost and market structure characteristics, and their interactions, for appropriate modeling, measurement, and interpretation of economic performance. To pursue more explicitly the interactions among many associated measures we have been developing, it is first worth expanding on the notion of total market power, implied by the potential coexistence of monopoly and monopsony behavior, overviewed in the previous section.

First, note again that the output price markup expression $\text{Prat}_Y = p_Y/MC$ is clearly dependent on the specification of marginal costs. Which marginal cost measure appropriately reflects only market power in the output market, and which might more justifiably represent market power overall, must therefore be addressed. Only if the distinctions among these measures are appropriately made can identification of the separate components be accomplished.

Recall from above that we identified an "intermediate run" cost economy measure taking adjustment of inputs (and thus their prices if monopsony power exists) as $\varepsilon^I_{TCY} = [\partial TC/\partial Y + \partial TC/\partial x_l \, \partial x_l/\partial Y] \cdot (Y/TC)$. This was in turn decomposed into a marginal cost ratio reflecting the impact of monopsony power on marginal costs, and a cost economy measure without the pecuniary effects as $\varepsilon^I_{TCY} = \text{MCrat} \cdot \varepsilon^C_{TCY} \approx (1/\text{Prat}_I) \cdot \varepsilon^C_{TCY}$.

This suggests that the distinction between the technological and pecuniary components of marginal costs reflected in the MCrat measure may be used to write a total market power measure as the product of two components – Prat_Y measured at the given x_l level (based on MC^S or $\partial VC/\partial Y$) and MCrat. That is, we can construct an overall market power measure as a combination of the output-oriented markup measure and the component of marginal costs stemming from monopsony power; $\text{Prat}_Y \cdot \text{MCrat} = \text{Prat}_T$ (where T indicates "total"). Thus, for Prat_Y to capture only the impacts of output market power, it should be based on $MC^S - \text{Prat}_Y = p_Y/MC^S$ – since MCrat is defined as

---

MC^S/MC^I, or MC^C/MC (either notation could be used depending on which the reader finds more transparent)[131]

This can be pursued further to see more explicitly what this implies for profitability as distinguished from "market power". To move in this direction, let us begin by looking at the most common case of just monopoly power (and one output), so that market power is represented by $\text{Prat}_Y = p_Y/MC$. If $p_Y>MC$ it is said that inefficiencies exist in the market because too little output is produced at too high a price, and the firm is generating monopolist profits.

Drawing these conclusions requires an implicit assumption that marginal costs are representative of average costs, since profitability depends on the comparison of average revenue and costs. We have, however, seen a number of reasons marginal and average cost could differ, and thus $\varepsilon_{TCY}=MC/AC$ would deviate from one. The full combined impact of pricing behavior that may cause p_Y/MC to exceed one, and cost economies that allow additional output to be produced more cheaply, may thus be obtained by multiplying these two numbers together

$$6.12)\ P^M\text{rat}_Y \bullet \varepsilon_{TCY} = p_Y/MC \bullet MC/AC = p_Y/AC = P^A\text{rat}_Y\ ,$$

(where A denotes "average", and M "marginal"). With multiple outputs an analogous computation can be carried out; multiplying $P^M\text{rat}_Y$ by ε^I_{TCY} results in $P^A\text{rat}_Y = \Sigma_m\ p_{Ym}\bullet Y_m/TC$ (where $\Sigma_m\ p_{Ym}\bullet Y_m$ is total revenue), or AR/AC (where AR is average revenue).

Price margins are in this sense "supported" by cost economies – such economies allow lower prices on *average* than would be possible at smaller output levels, and thus measured markups do not *necessarily* imply inefficiencies or an abuse of market power. Again, the issue is not whether "big business" is good or bad, but what must be taken into account to analyze what is going on most effectively.

The impact of market power in the input markets may be included by bringing in the MCrat adjustment discussed above. This is somewhat different than the treatment for monopoly power, however, since it is not independent from cost economies, as is the output market. Input costs and thus economies incorporate the impact of input price changes from supply conditions. Thus, as noted above, this pecuniary impact may be decomposed from technological economies using the relationship $\varepsilon^I_{TCY} = MCrat\bullet\varepsilon^C_{TCY} \approx (1/\text{Prat}_I)\bullet\varepsilon^C_{TCY}$.

---

[131] The notation begins to get somewhat confusing here since so many things are happening. Recall that "S" indicates "Short run" without x_l adjustment, and "I" denotes "Intermediate run" including x_l adjustment. The "C" notation emphasizes that this is a cost-based measure only, without incorporating input market adjustment, whereas MC alone suggests full marginal costs including firms' (and resulting market) responses in the x_l market.

In sum, the profitability measure capturing the impacts of market power in the output and input markets and technological cost economies becomes:

$$6.13) \ PROF = P^M rat_Y \cdot \varepsilon^I_{TCY} = Prat_Y \cdot MCrat \cdot \varepsilon^C_{TCY} \approx Prat_Y \cdot (1/Prat_I) \cdot \varepsilon^C_{TCY}.$$

Each of the components of the PROF measure, and their decompositions (into individual output markets or scale versus scope economies, for example) has a specific interpretation. Only if PROF>1, however, is the combination of market power in the output and input markets sufficient for excessive profitability. Again, the individual pieces of the measure contain more interpretable information for specific questions about output and input markets, but the combination also provides an indication of the balance of overall market power compared to cost economies.

Finally, note that cost effects not appearing in the MC measure, such as fixed effects from multi-plant economies will still show up in the denominator of the cost economy measure. Such economies would increase ε_{TCY}, implying less cost economies, so lower markups would imply excess profitability.

5.   FURTHER COMMENTS

In this chapter we have incorporated the impacts of deviations in output and input markets from perfect competition into our models and measures of economic performance that have primarily focused on the cost structure. This extension of our cost-based model again requires recognizing that some assumptions in standard models of productivity and economic performance, in particular that the marginal cost of an input or marginal valuation (benefit) of an input is represented by its market price, no longer holds when market power prevails. Thus, Hotelling's and Shephard's lemma are invalid and cannot be used to represent output supply and input demand behavior.

In the next chapter we discuss another production characteristic that may cause Shephard's lemma to break down for some types of inputs. We will focus on how this may result from market failures, and from regulation that may be in place to accommodate such failures.

In particular, we will assess the impacts of environmental concern and resulting regulation, and how this might affect analysis of economic performance. As has been true for other production characteristics we have explored, these issues may be addressed from various angles. In our context, however, they raise intriguing questions about the required adaptation of standard cost structure and economic performance measures, if these types of market characteristics are important for the firm, sector or economy we wish to represent by such measures.

Chapter 7

Regulatory Structure and Costs

In this chapter we address the issue of regulatory constraints, and their possible market failure motivations and inefficiency outcomes. Regulatory constraints have impacts on firms' behavior similar to capital fixities; they are a rigidity that the firm has no control over even in the long run, so if the constraint is binding there will be a cost associated with it. They can also be thought of as environmental variables; they determine the regulatory environment the firm faces, and thus the constraints within which the firm must operate. In a sense, therefore, they are similar to external effects except that they typically impose costs on rather than generate benefits for producers, and do not imply spillovers.

Regulatory constraints generally take the form of quantity (output rationing, capital use requirements, or damaging-input limits) or price (tax, subsidy, rate of return or output price) restrictions that keep the firm from operating at what would have been its optimal behavior. Such regulations will have costs (or sometimes, as in the case of a subsidy, benefits) that need to be taken into account for appropriate representation of firm behavior and responsiveness. Accommodating these impacts in a model of the productive structure and productivity growth may require consideration of reduced choice and thus quantity changes, or adaptation of the weight (value) on output and inputs and their associated growth rates.

For example, if firms are required to purchase capital to reduce pollution or to increase safety in a plant, this increases capital costs without a corresponding increase in marketed output. This extra cost will reduce the measured productivity of the firm. Alternatively, pollution abatement may involve restrictions that limit the use of environmental "inputs" the firm may be using in production (water, for example), or enhancing workplace safety may require limits on the speed of production, thus reducing observed input productivity. Direct input restrictions may also be imposed by regulation, such as pesticide or chemical limitations. Assuming such inputs are demanded because they increase effective output, this will diminish the efficiency of the remaining inputs.

On the flip side, the regulations and their associated increased costs of production are typically motivated by some type of market failure that keeps market forces from internalizing benefits. In the case of pollution abatement capital regulations, the benefits of reduced pollution are a social benefit that the firm itself may not recognize. That is, pollution can be thought of as a "bad output" that needs to be reduced, or pollution abatement as a "good" output that should be enhanced. But since the firm does not internalize the costs of the bad output or the benefits of the abatement, there are no market forces to motivate behavior. Regulation is therefore necessary to move toward a social optimum. Ideally, regulations are imposed to the point where their incremental costs in terms of reduced productivity are balanced at the margin by the benefits accruing to society at large.

At least two issues emerge from this brief discussion. First, it may be difficult to craft regulations that are able to achieve such a balance, even if the costs and benefits are measurable. Second, almost by definition of a market failure, the benefits generated by regulation are typically not easily observed and thus measurable. Quantifying the "value" of environmental cleanliness is, for example, notoriously difficult to accomplish.

Ultimately, therefore, if the goal is for regulations to create a marginal cost/benefit balance, it is often important to attempt to quantify the two "sides" of the balancing act. In the context of production theory models, the direct link is to the impacts on the firm, which typically means the costs of regulation. As noted above, these costs take the form of restrictions on the quantities or prices of outputs or inputs that keep the firm's unit costs higher than they would otherwise be. This also, of course, inhibits *responses* to economic forces to keep the firms from reaching their optimal cost-output level. Modeling and measuring these constraints and their technological and behavioral impacts is the focus of our discussion in this chapter.

The structure of the problem is very similar to those considered in previous chapters. We wish to determine the impacts of constraints from regulations on production and costs, and the resulting effects on productivity and economic performance. The costs of regulations may therefore be represented either by the direct output or input constraints, or by a suitably constructed regulatory variable, from which we can identify a shadow value. This shadow value (or cost) provides some indication of the marginal benefits the regulation must achieve in order to be justified.

For example, it might be recognized that capital used to enhance safety or protect the environment has different productive attributes than other equipment and structures, and therefore should be separately identified for production and productivity analysis. It might also be important to explicitly capture the distinction between, say, pesticide use and its impact on effective output in terms of abatement levels to characterize productive processes.

In this chapter we consider various nonparametric and parametric approaches to modeling and measuring regulatory effects. The overall issue is to measure the costs imposed, or the impact on the cost-output relationship, from regulatory constraints or distortions.

If our concern is to identify the impacts of investment requirements for pollution abatement capital as in Section 1, for example, the appropriate approach seems to be to separately identify this component of the capital stock and its costs to evaluate its impact on productivity. This involves representing capital input characteristics or composition, where different types of capital have different productive attributes. If we wish to analyze the effects of pesticide regulation (Section 2), we want to identify both the productivity of pesticide use in terms of effective output, and the characteristics of the input in terms of effective abatement. If we address the problem of environmental degradation from an output perspective (Section 3), modeling the impacts on productive processes requires consideration of both the "good" and "bad" outputs. Such environmental questions are of current topical interest in various lay-, academic-, and policy circles.

In addition to raising these issues of output and input characteristics and composition, and resulting questions of their shadow valuation, we consider cost-side regulation in the form of rate of return and output price (profitability) restrictions and questions in Section 4. These issues have a market structure instead of market failure motivation, but are also of current interest in the context of enhanced competitiveness in markets that have exhibited high levels of concentration and possible abuse of market power. In some cases, as alluded to in the previous chapter, regulations to counteract market power and control profitability may incur costs in terms of reduced cost efficiency. Appropriate representation of the production and cost structure, and the impacts of regulatory forces, are therefore very important to capture to analyze such industries and their economic performance.

1. CAPITAL REGULATIONS AND COSTS

For firms in many industries, regulations concerning capital investment may be a significant determinant of costs, and therefore be important to incorporate in models of production processes and productivity. In some industries, for example, the most consequential regulatory constraints may be those targeted toward the safety of employees (often involving the use of heavy equipment) or consumers of products (say, associated with food safety). In others, requirements to limit environmental degradation by purchasing certain types of pollution abatement capital may significantly affect costs of production.

These types of regulatory constraints suggest an increasing role of government in the economy, which has often been cited as a contributing factor to stagnation in (traditionally measured) productivity growth. Such regulations require purchases of capital equipment to produce something other than observed output, with associated benefits that presumably would take the form of production of some other unmeasured output such as safety or environmental protection.   Incorporating these regulations into the analysis of firm production and productivity requires determining how they will change the assumptions on which the model is based, and thus affect the implications for the production structure and measured costs of production.

In some cases regulations may be defined directly in terms of a level of costs the firm must incur in order to satisfy the regulations. In such a case, nonparametric methods may sometimes be used to adapt productivity growth measures, since the costs attributed to production of unmeasured output may simply be eliminated from the measure of productive input costs.

In other situations specific constraints must be directly imposed on the optimization model to identify their impact on production processes. Since this typically involves adaptation of the production theory framework we use to represent production choices, parametric estimates are generally necessary to represent their impacts.

Government regulations regarding safety and pollution standards provide one example where the impact of regulation is often manifested in a particular level of capital costs that must be incurred for production to take place. Investments required to satisfy safety or environmental regulations, such as investment in pollution abatement capital, are unproductive in terms of measured output. Thus, conventional productivity growth measures will be biased downward as the impacts of such regulation increase.

Researchers such as Denison [1979] have explored this hypothesis. He attempted to determine the effects of environmental regulation by estimating the incremental costs of production due to environmental regulations, and using these estimates to impute the percentage reduction in output per unit of input attributable to regulation. Related nonparametric approaches to modeling the impacts of the costs of such regulations have been pursued by, among others, Gray [1984] and Conrad and Morrison [1989].[132]

Gray [1984] considered the impacts of OSHA (The Occupational Safety and Health Administration) and the EPA (Environmental Protection Agency) in the U.S. in an accounting framework. He assumes that compliance costs involve only to pollution abatement capital (PAK) investment, thus affecting capital composition. Standard capital measures should therefore be divided

---

[132] Also see Crandall [1981].

into two components; K=K'+R where R is the amount of "regulatory" or PAK capital, for the impacts of PAK investment to be represented.

Although measures of K are generally used for construction of productivity growth indexes, since the R component of K is not "productive" capital it should not be included. K' should be used rather than K. If the fraction of K used for regulation is δ, so δ=R/K, true productivity growth may then be expressed (using our notation) as $\epsilon'_{TCt} = \epsilon_{TCt} - S_K \delta$, where S_K is the cost share of K and ϵ_{TCt}' is the (negative) cost-side productivity growth measure based on the productive capital stock K'. If, instead compliance costs cannot be represented in terms of input composition, but other measures of regulation applied to different industries such as enforcement effort (EE) can be found, Gray adapts this to $\epsilon'_{TCt} = \epsilon_{TCt} - EE$.

These simple measures of δ and EE, adapted to sum across different industries as outlined by Gray, can be used to adjust standard productivity growth measures as long as δ can be measured for any input affected by compliance. Applying this approach to a number of industries, Gray finds that introducing additional safety and environmental regulations does have a large depressing effect on productivity growth, at least in the short run.

Conrad and Morrison [1989] also consider pollution abatement capital regulations in a nonparametric framework, but the theoretical structure is developed in more detail, and the resulting implementation thus differs somewhat from Gray's treatment. The firm's production decision, assumed to be based on profit maximization, is specified as depending on investment in both productive capital (K) and pollution abatement or regulatory capital (R). This resulting optimization decision can be written as:

$$7.1) \quad \max_{x, IKt, IRt, Y} \Sigma_t e^{-rt} [p_{Yt} Yt - VC(Y_t, K_t, p_t) - PI(IK_t + IR_t)]$$

subject to $IK_t = K_{t+1} - K_t + \delta_t K_t$ and $IR_t = R_{t+1} - R_t + \delta_t R_t$, where IK_t and IR_t are gross investment in K and R, and PI is the common asset price of investment goods, so PI•(IK$_t$+IR$_t$) is expenditure on investment in both types of capital.

In addition, this maximization problem is constrained by two less standard conditions: $TE_t = \xi \cdot Y_t$, and $\overline{NE} - f_t(R) \cdot TE \geq 0$, where TE is total emissions; NE is non-abated emissions; $\overline{NE}$ is the standard set for allowable emissions; ξ is an emission to output parameter which represents the constant proportional relationship between pollutant discharge and production when no standards and therefore no pollution abatement capital exist; and f(R) is the reduction of emissions, reflecting the dependence on the level of pollution abatement capital, where $\partial f/\partial R < 0$ and $\partial^2 f/\partial R^2 > 0$. The first of these conditions therefore represents the flow of pollution from the production process without regulation, and the second characterizes the resulting level of emissions.

The variable cost function is assumed to depend on K but not R, since R is not productive; R is not in the production function for output and thus not in the dual cost function. R is, however, included in total costs as a fixed cost, because if output changes, even if this causes higher fixed costs from greater required R, these costs are take the form of "rental" costs. This is similar to the distinction between adjustment costs that are external rather than internal to the production process.

The first order conditions for this model are adapted only slightly from those for the general production theory model we have been developing in this text. Output is determined by the equality $p_Y - \tau f(R)\xi = \partial VC/\partial Y = MC$ (assuming perfect competition), where $\tau = \tau(1+r)^t$ is the current (undiscounted) shadow value of non-abated emissions. This reflects the fact that additional revenue with a change in output must cover both the increase in production costs and the required extra costs of abatement on the margin.

Optimal K is determined as the capital stock satisfying the equality $-\partial VC/\partial K = Z_K = p_K$, as before. The condition for optimal R is also represented by a shadow value-type equation, but in this case $p_R = p_K = -\tau f(R)\xi x$ (where the rental price of all capital goods is assumed the same).

These adaptations to the model allow the regulatory "distortion" to be recognized in productivity growth computations, and its input-specific impact to be determined by bias measures, as we have developed in earlier chapters. Specifically, some straightforward manipulations of the adapted optimization conditions and interpretation of the shadow value condition on R results in an adjusted productivity growth equation:

7.2) $\varepsilon'_{TCt} = \partial \ln TC/\partial t = (-p_Y Y + p_K \cdot R/TC) \cdot d\ln Y/dt$

$$+ \Sigma_j \, q_j v_j/TC \cdot d\ln v_j/dt + p_K K/TC \cdot d\ln K/dt \, .$$

The final adjustment of the productivity measure ε_{TCt} to reflect the impact of R, therefore, even with this rather complex theoretical framework, is thus very simple. It is based on purging the influence of pollution abatement capital from the output value measure to capture marginal costs correctly, and removing the R component from the total capital stock.

An important insight stemming from this development is that the value of output as well as the input value or quantity should be adapted. This is similar to the case of public capital overviewed in Chapter 5. This adjustment can be written in terms of an error bias as:

7.3) $\varepsilon'_{TCt} = \varepsilon_{TCt} - p_K \cdot R/C \, (d\ln R/dt - d\ln Y/dt)$, where the second term reflects the error in traditional computations from assuming R is used to produce output instead of a cleaner environment. Conrad and Morrison [1989] provide interpretation of this bias term and develop some others that reflect, for example, what productivity might have been in the absence of pollution abatement capital regulation.

Using this framework, they compute nonparametric measures of productivity growth and biases for U.S., Canadian, and German manufacturing that suggest treating R incorrectly in productivity computations biased traditional productivity measures downward, particularly for the late 1970s and for poor productivity growth years in general. Investment in pollution abatement capital also depressed productivity growth measures for these countries on average, with the greatest (but still quite small) impact in the North American countries.

Although the more complete theoretical model underlying the Conrad-Morrison model provides a somewhat richer basis for interpretation of the adjustments and results of PAK regulation than a simple accounting approach, a more detailed consideration of the impact of regulation requires a more complete model.

One way to accomplish this is through adaptation of our parametric production theory-based model along the lines of the extension to environmental or external factors incorporated in Chapter 5. As alluded to there, the r_b variables added as arguments of the cost function can include various environmental factors as determinants of costs, including regulatory variables. Illustrations of this approach are provided in Morrison [1987a, 1988b].[133]

In these studies pollution abatement or regulatory capital, R was included directly in the cost function as an r_b variable, so that increases in R cause higher costs for any given output level. This implies that R should be included separately in the capacity utilization expression from Chapter 3, ($CU_c = 1 - \varepsilon_{TCK} - \varepsilon_{TCR}$) and in resulting productivity growth computations.

The focus of the studies, however, is on the bias of technical change that stems from regulation. In this context, the short run Hicksian regulatory bias becomes:

$$7.4) \quad B_{jb} = \partial S_j / \partial \ln r_b = p_j v_j / TC \cdot (\partial \ln v_j / \partial \ln r_b - \partial \ln TC / \partial \ln r_b) = S_j \cdot (\varepsilon_{jb} - \varepsilon_{TCb})$$

where ε_{jb} and ε_{TCb} are defined as the input-specific and overall cost elasticities with respect to a change in r_b, and $r_b = R$, analogous to the utilization and scale biases outlined in Chapters 3 and 4.

---

[133] This was also the focus of Norsworthy *et al* [1979].

This bias reflects a regulatory distortion. If, for example, $B_{jb}<0$, additional regulation (increased amounts of pollution abatement capital required) will cause the firm to use input j proportionately less; regulation increases are relatively input j saving. The symmetry condition of biases, $B_{jb}=B_{bj}$, is also useful for analysis of the impact of regulation; the interpretation of $B_{bj}<0$ is that an increase in p_j reduces the existing cost impact of regulation. In reverse, if regulatory changes are input j-using (say energy-using), increases in p_j (p_E) will cause regulatory measures to cost more, and therefore be more disruptive, than would be the case if they were input j-saving (energy-saving).

Assessment of these regulation biases therefore provides significant interpretive power about the impacts of PAK regulation on the production process. The bias measures presented in Morrison [1988b] show that pollution abatement regulation has tended to be relatively labor and materials saving and energy using for the primary metals industry.

Recall, however, that this does not imply an absolute decrease in labor and materials use, or increase in energy use, with additional regulation. The estimated components of the labor bias measure presented by Morrison indicate that increases in R augment employment, at existing output levels ($\varepsilon_{LR}>0$, where L denotes labor). But the small positive ε_{LR} value is swamped by a larger overall cost increase with a regulatory change, primarily driven by greater energy requirements, resulting in a negative relative bias.

It is also possible to determine the impacts of regulation on technical change, capacity utilization, and capital valuation from the bias measures if they are defined in terms of the cost elasticities with respect to these variables rather than with respect to p_j. The B_{tR} bias $\partial\varepsilon_{TCt}/\partial\ln R$, for example, represents the impact on technical change of pollution abatement capital increases. The converse bias interpretation is that B_{Rt} reflects a change in the costs of regulation relative to other inputs due to technical progress. Similarly, B_{KR} captures a change in capacity utilization due to changes in required pollution abatement capital. Including regulation in a parametric production theory framework thus leaves significant scope for assessing the impacts of regulation on the production structure.

2.   RESTRICTIONS ON INPUT USE: PESTICIDES

Pesticide and other chemicals used in agriculture have clear benefits to farmers in terms of augmented effective output. Pesticides allow farmers to increase their output by reducing damage from insects and disease. They also permit them to grow a wider variety of crops in places where pests are prevalent, and thus to compete with those not suffering from pest infestation.

Pesticide use also increases the value of harvests by improving the quality and appearance of foods, so less must be discarded. Thus, by increasing the effective harvest (realized output), pesticides lead to a greater supply of quality goods and lower prices in the marketplace, in turn benefiting both farmers and consumers.

However, as with other market failures, these private benefits have their associated social costs that are not internalized by the firm (farm). Pesticide runoff can contaminate water supplies and lead to many environmental repercussions. When there is no accountability for these types of "external costs", that is, costs that do not directly affect the private farmer, the farmer will generally not take these costs into consideration. Farmers instead have an incentive to use pesticides until their marginal benefits equal their private cost, which involves the direct but not indirect social costs of pesticides.

Health and environmental repercussions of pesticide and chemical use have motivated regulatory concerns about their use in agricultural production, and provided incentives to limit their use. The crucial economic question is whether the (marginal social) benefits of pesticides are commensurate with the associated (marginal social) costs. However, as in the related case of pollution abatement capital, it is not straightforward to measure even the marginal benefits, much less costs, of pesticide inputs.

Identifying the true benefits, or marginal productivity, of pesticides involves determining the actual contribution of pesticide use to effective output. The estimation of the marginal pesticide benefits, and thus the associated costs of restrictions on their use, is easier to address than the resulting damage, since the inputs used and outputs produced are at least to some extent observed and marketed.

However, pesticides have a somewhat different role in production than more "standard" inputs. Their true measured impact on effective output has to do with purchased abatement rather than the quantity of pesticides or chemicals used. Thus, benefit estimates presented in the literature are often too large to be plausible. Problems with the implied shape of estimated pesticide demand functions also emerge.

The overriding issue here is how to identify actual abatement, and thus augmentation of effective output, from measured quantities of pesticide use. This involves again the composition or characteristics of an input (pesticides or other chemicals) and output, since abatement "services" will depend on various factors including the chemical composition of pesticides, their historical use, the types of agricultural products produced, and other characteristics of the production structure.

2.1 The Literature

Studies of pesticide benefits have typically attempted to examine whether pesticides are used up to the point where their value marginal product (VMP) equals their marginal cost (private input price), by measuring the marginal product from a production function. One of the first such studies was by Headley [1968], who found the VMP of one dollar's worth of pesticide input to be approximately $4.00. He concluded that the pesticide market is out of equilibrium; pesticides are "underused." A similar study by Fischer [1970] estimated the marginal product of pesticides at between $2.34 and $5.17 per dollar expended (for the three regions examined). Campbell [1976] reaches the even more dramatic conclusion that a marginal dollar's worth of pesticide input yields around $12.00 worth of output. These econometric results contradict anecdotal evidence that pesticides are *overused*, as emphasized by Lichtenberg and Zilberman (LZ) [1986].

LZ suggest that VMP estimates from these types of studies are subject to serious problems associated with mischaracterization of the role of pesticide inputs. They claim that pesticides have a "unique" input role since they serve as "damage control agents."[134] The LZ specification thus directly represents the contribution of pesticides in terms of abatement, which is a function of observed quantities of pesticide use.

The resulting model yields conclusions that are more consistent with observed behavior. For example it predicts an increase in pesticide use when its productivity decreases (from increased pest resistance) to maintain a certain level of abatement, whereas this behavior may generate perverse shapes of demand functions if they are specified in terms of measured quantity levels. This results because if pesticides are treated as a conventional input, VMP measures based on a Cobb-Douglas representation of the technology (like those reported by Headley, Fischer, and Campbell) will be biased upward (as elaborated further below).

Two subsequent studies (Carrasco-Tauber [1988], and Carrasco-Tauber and Moffitt [1992]) also use the methodology suggested by LZ to differentiate abatement through a damage function rather than to include pesticides directly as a standard input. They find, however, that pesticide benefit estimates based on this specification yield results that are not substantively different from conventional models (especially when using aggregate data).

---

[134] A later study by Blackwell and Pagoulatos incorporates biological and physical processes of agricultural ecosystems into the LZ framework, but their model is not applicable to aggregate data.

Chambers and Lichtenberg (CL) [1994] develop a more complete model of pesticide use that further accommodates biases or violations of curvature conditions from possible misspecification of the role of pesticide inputs. Through a dual representation of the LZ damage control model, CL allow for multiple outputs and incorporate input and output prices into a profit function framework. However, the authors recognize remaining limitations in their treatment, stating that the estimates of production elasticities "are somewhat conjectural." Thus, there has yet to be a consensus about the most appropriate way to generate the marginal benefit estimates.

It appears clear, however, that representing pesticides in terms of effective rather than measured quantity levels is an important key. The issues raised also suggest the importance of a model that characterizes the production technology in as flexible a form as possible, to accommodate the multiple interactions among outputs and inputs underlying agricultural production and pesticide productivity.

The basic problem emphasized in the literature is that the Cobb-Douglas (CD) production function framework often used for such analysis is too limited a specification for empirical implementation. Even if only the technology (rather than behavior, as in dual models) is of interest, such a function imposes strict *a priori* assumptions about curvature of the function. It is also based on the assumption of one aggregate output, whereas output composition may be an important issue in the context of pesticide productivity analysis.

The curvature issue has particularly been focused on in the literature. As noted above, LZ discuss in detail how the VMP of pesticides will be overestimated in such a framework because the CD production function imposes curvature that is contrary to what one would expect. In particular, diminishing pesticide effectiveness over time would be expected to cause a reduction in the slope of the VMP and therefore demand function that cannot be picked up with the CD function with its constant logarithmic first derivatives (no cross- or interaction- terms).

These issues have a similar structure to those addressed in previous chapters' discussions of input biases, and quality or characteristics of inputs and outputs. Changing characteristics of pesticides and induced changes in effectiveness with the use of pesticides suggest that abatement should be measured as a function of not only purchased pesticides but also of factors such as interactions with other inputs and outputs, time, and environmental variables (like cumulative pesticide use). Separation of different types of preventative or augmenting chemical inputs such as pesticides and fertilizers may also be important for appropriate analysis of pesticides' impacts on effective output production.

Insights about how the distinction between pesticide quantities and abatement levels can be made have been provided by the treatments in LZ, CL and others referred to above. In these studies abatement is defined as an intermediate input produced by pesticides (combined with other preventative inputs, that we will call P), that provides abatement. This functional relationship is expressed as $g=G(P)$.

In LZ it is assumed also that the production function takes the CD form: $Y=e^{\alpha}V^{\beta}[G(P)]^{\gamma}$, where V represents all productive inputs other than pesticides. In log form this is $\ln Y = \alpha + \beta \ln V + \gamma \ln G(P)$ ($+u$ if the disturbance term is included for estimation purposes as in equation 9 of LZ).

As stated in LZ, the curvature that one would expect for the G(P) function is "quite naturally" represented by a cumulative distribution. They incorporate this insight from the existing literature by assuming alternative functional forms for G(P) that may be substituted into the CD production function to respecify the productive relationship (and the resulting damage control agent demand function) in terms of P and the parameters of the distribution function. The distributions tried were the Pareto, exponential, logistic and Weibull forms, resulting in the production function expressions:

7.5a) $\ln Y = \alpha + \beta \ln V + \gamma \ln \{1-K^{\lambda}P^{-\lambda}\}$

b) $\ln Y = \alpha + \beta \ln V + \gamma \ln \{1-e^{-\lambda P}\}$

c) $\ln Y = \alpha + \beta \ln V + \gamma \ln \{1+\exp(\mu-\sigma P)^{-1}\}$

d) $\ln Y = \alpha + \beta \ln V + \gamma \ln \{1-\exp(-P)^{C}\}$

CL relate this primal side representation of the treatment of abatement to a cost of abatement function $c(p_P,g)$, where p_P is the market price of P. So true costs of abatement are a function of the observed price and the abatement quantity, which we could call $g=G(P)=P'$ for the "effective" amount of pesticide use.

In their dual treatment they construct a profit function defined in terms of the prices of outputs (p_m), inputs (p_j), and P (p_P). But the transformation function underlying it is defined in terms of g, so they get a restricted profit function R defined for a given abatement level. R is nondecreasing in g, and $\partial R/\partial g=R_g$ is the shadow value of abatement activities to the farmer. Thus, the optimization problem for the farmer is to equate the marginal returns and costs of abatement, or $R_g(p_m,p_j;g)=c_g(p_P,g)=\partial c/\partial g$.

Various potential approaches to dealing with the problem of unmeasured abatement (g) are raised in CL. The version pursued in the paper specifies a parametric representation of G(P) that facilitates estimating the parameters of the technology, output supply and input demand functions. The resulting model is similar to LZ in that cumulative distributions for the G(P) function are used, CRS in all inputs but time is imposed, and a multiplicative structure between the production and abatement functions is assumed.

They also identify the $c(p_P, g)$ functions dual to the exponential and logistic G(P) functions. For empirical implementation they append this information to the $R_g(\mathbf{p_m}, \mathbf{p_j}; g) = c_g(p_P, g)$ equality to solve for optimal abatement g, and use the first-order condition for P to solve for pesticide demand. In addition, they note that since P appears on both sides of the first order conditions, it is essentially endogenous to the technological and abatement structural model, which must be recognized for estimation purposes by using, say, instrumental variables estimation.

Another perspective mentioned is based on observed pesticide quantities, similarly to that discussed further below in the context of an abatement cost function A(P). CL indicate that the pesticide demand relationship $P(\mathbf{p_m}, \mathbf{p_j}, p_P)$ (or with some quasi-fixed inputs $P(\mathbf{x}, \mathbf{p_m}, \mathbf{p_j}, p_P)$) will be equal to $\partial c / \partial p_P = c_{pP}(p_P, g(\mathbf{p_m}, \mathbf{p_j}, p_P))$, given the separability inherent in their model.

Since $c(p_P, g)$ represents the costs of abatement, this derivative will involve the measured pesticide cost p_P plus some adaptation for the deviation of abatement from pesticide quantity that may depend on all arguments of the profit function. Consistent estimates of the resulting model could be obtained through instrumental variables estimation in terms of observed pesticide quantities, incorporating a deviation of true (marginal) pesticide cost from its market value.

The focus in this literature on the distinction between pesticide use and abatement, and thus observed and effective costs of abatement, is similar to that for "mismeasured" inputs in the macro literature. In the macro literature this arises in the context of utilization or effort of capital and labor inputs (as discussed in Chapters 3 and 5). These connections suggest at least three ways that we can address these issues within a production theory framework.

We might proxy the "true" levels as in the macro literature, which relies on making some rather *ad-hoc* linkages with other inputs, and using instruments to capture the associated measurement errors. We could attempt to directly measure the abatement function, and include it instead of the quantity of pesticides in the cost or profit function. Alternatively, we could recognize the distinction between optimality in terms of pesticide quantity and abatement as a "wedge" between the measured economic and market valuation of the input, similarly to the adjustment for utilized capital or effective labor input in previous chapters.

The first possibility seems to have little promise, since it is not clear what types of proxies might be used to represent abatement appropriately (although the idea that instrumental variables might be used to accommodate the endogeneity of abatement to some extent should be recognized in the estimation procedures). The second possibility might be carried out along the lines of the existing literature, by setting up a cumulative distribution function G(P) (or a hedonic function of the form P'=P'(P, •)), and including this instead of the quantity of pesticides P in a restricted cost or profit function framework, as is explicitly or implicitly done in LZ and CL.

The g=G(P)=P'(P, •) function could be substituted in directly and nonlinear estimation techniques used for estimation, or a separate equation might be included in the estimating system similarly to the hedonic methods for capital utilization measurement discussed in Chapter 3. The analysis may then be carried out in terms of P' (or g) instead of P even though it cannot be directly measured. A gap between the shadow valuation in terms of P' and the market price p_P may, however, still exist, since the price is not expressed through $c_g(p_P,g)$, as is discussed further below.

More specifically, the crucial characteristic for representing pesticide use and its optimality is the possibility that optimal (private or public) use of pesticides, as well as the difference between the effective and measured or perceived impact of pesticides, sever the usual optimality condition of VMP equal to input price. This deviation or gap may be modeled from either the price or quantity side. And the implied interactions among pesticide use and other inputs, as well as the determinants of the gap between the market and effective quantity or value of pesticides, must be generally specified for appropriate representation of pesticide demand and productivity.

2.2   An Alternative Perspective

Our cost function framework has potential for considering such interactions in the productive process, with appropriate adaptations made to accommodate the characteristics of importance in this situation. In a cost or profit function model the VMP gap implies a deviation from Shephard's or Hotelling's lemma and a possible violation of the associated curvature conditions on the function. The pesticide demand curve derived from a standard cost or profit function may slope up in terms of the observed market quantity of pesticides, as noted by CL and Chambers and Pope [1994].

Including measured pesticide levels (P) rather than the observed price (p_P) in the cost or profit function may facilitate interpretation of this deviation. This somewhat changes the optimization problem for pesticide demand, but allows for the endogeneity of the shadow value of this input, which will differ from the observed market price

Chambers and Pope, for example, find that the Shephard's lemma result $P=\partial TC/\partial p_P$ (or $P=\partial VC/\partial p_P$), generates a pesticide demand curve with the wrong curvature. Actual demand and effective demand exhibit different characteristics. Using the inverse Shephard's/Hotelling's lemma expression for the shadow value $Z_P = -\partial VC/\partial P$, while not imposing this to be equal to p_P, may instead generate shadow value expressions that may be used to identify the difference between effective and market valuation.

This adaptation of the cost-based model, along the lines of the adaptations for fixities and market power in previous chapters, provides only a partial solution to the current problem. It is instead desirable more explicitly to model and measure the "gap" between effective and measured demand, or shadow and market price.

Before moving in this direction, note that to facilitate interpretation of the shadow value the functional form for the cost (or profit) function must be generalized to provide more information about the appropriate underlying curvature of the function, rather than imposing it *a priori*.

That is, since a restricted first order function such as the CD puts too many limits on the shape of the marginal product function, a second order flexible function should be used to represent the technology and behavior. This allows for interrelationships with other inputs, outputs, time, and possibly other measurable environmental factors to be represented, providing greater scope for the data to identify multi-dimensional curvature patterns.

Multiple outputs may also be particularly important to recognize in this context, as in CL, since pesticide use is likely affected by output composition. This can be accommodated within either a cost or profit function framework (or by a distance function if technological relationships are of particular interest or if relevant prices are not defined, as discussed further in the next section). Since output choice may be important for analysis of agricultural production processes and pesticide use, however, a profit function in which output supply decisions are embodied might be a particularly useful tool to accommodate and represent substitution patterns across inputs and outputs.

Keeping these considerations in mind, we can pursue the suggested adaptation of our model to incorporate an abatement gap more formally. Let us begin by asserting that the appropriate function to represent technology and choices, in the multiple output framework where output supply decisions and thus composition is important, is via a profit function. In addition, to model pesticide use we must recognize the potential fixities of some agricultural factors of production. In this case quasi-fixed factors may include land and some labor as well as capital inputs, which implies using a restricted or variable version of the profit function.

The restricted profit function, as alluded to in the previous chapter, is similar to the restricted cost function except that it includes the prices of outputs as arguments rather than the levels, and thus allows Hotelling's lemma (with perfect competition assumed) to be used to generate output supply functions as $Y_m = \partial\pi(\mathbf{p_j},\mathbf{p_m},\mathbf{x},t)/\partial p_m$ (where $\mathbf{p_j}$ is again a vector of input prices, $\mathbf{p_m}$ of output prices, and $\mathbf{x}$ denotes fixed factors). Demand for variable inputs can similarly be obtained as $-v_j = \partial\pi(\mathbf{p_j},\mathbf{p_m},\mathbf{x},t)/\partial p_j$.

If the focus is primarily on input choices and substitution, the Y_m output levels can of course be substituted for p_m. This reproduces the restricted cost function of the form we have been working with, where input demand is modeled as a function of the existing output levels and thus composition.

Again, as we have explored for other refinements of the production theory model, there are various reasons why Shephard's (or in this case Hotelling's) lemma may not hold in the profit function framework. This is by definition true for the quasi-fixed inputs x_k. As we have seen, we may write the optimization equations for these inputs (with adjustment costs incorporated) as Euler equations, which in general form are $p_k = Z_k + A(\Delta x_k)$, where $Z_k = -\partial VC/\partial x_k$, and the "wedge" or gap between the shadow and market price, $A(\Delta x_k)$, depends on costs of adjustment.

Similarly, gaps between the effective or shadow and market prices of other inputs may be incorporated into this type of structure. This may be particularly illuminating if one can conceptualize how the distinction between market and "true" cost (or benefit) of an input emerges, and thus specify the determinants of the gap.

E.g., if the quantity of pesticides (P) is included in the function, the profit-oriented shadow value of P may be computed as $Z^\pi_P = \partial\pi/\partial P$. This represents the potential profitability of having an additional unit of pesticides, through reductions in the use (and thus costs) of other inputs, or augmentation of effective output. If P were a "standard" input, it would be expected that demand for P would ultimately take place where this shadow value (marginal benefit or productivity) is equal to the marginal cost of P, p_P.

Since this cannot be assumed to hold in terms of measured pesticide quantities, the inverse Hotelling's lemma relationship may instead be written as $p_P = Z^\pi_P + A(\bullet)$, or $p_P' = p_P - A(\bullet) = Z^\pi_P$. In this case the $A(\bullet)$ function represents the wedge between abatement and pesticide levels, and thus between the market and true marginal valuation of pesticides, which depends on some as-yet-to-be-determined arguments represented by "$\bullet$".

In particular, if one instead substituted an expression for the abatement function $P'=g=G(P)$ into the profit function, the shadow value expressed in terms of P' rather than P, $Z^\pi_{P'}=\partial\pi/\partial P'$, would be expected to equal the marginal price of abatement. To the farmer in the short run this could be assumed consistently to be equal to p_P.

This is similar to the idea that if utilized capital instead of capital levels were substituted into a short run cost expression, the resulting shadow value would appropriately reflect the optimization condition adapted for adjustment costs. Alternatively this can be written as $p_P = Z^\pi_P = \partial\pi/\partial P = (\partial\pi/\partial P')/(\partial G/\partial P)$ in this case, (since $\partial\pi/\partial P = \partial\pi/\partial G \cdot \partial G/\partial P$). This brings in the density function $\partial G/\partial P$ multiplicatively, although no separability or CRS assumptions are required for implementation of the model (as in LZ and CL). This is the sense in which $A(\cdot)$ function represents the distinction between abatement and P.

The $A(\cdot)$ function may be undefined, be a simple parameter, or be a more complex functional relationship. It should, however, represent the fact that the marginal productivity of the input decreases faster for pesticides than for a typical input; diminishing effectiveness of this factor implies decreasing marginal productivity and thus reductions in its optimal use. This characteristic must somehow be incorporated into the model to obtain appropriate measures of productivity and optimal input use, or marginal product (shadow value) estimates will tend to be biased.

Specification of the $A(\cdot)$ function is thus not straightforward, since the distinction between abatement and pesticide use could potentially depend on a number of (measurable and unmeasurable) factors. For a first approximation to the specification of $A(\cdot)$ the determinants of the gap between Z^π_P and p_P may be unspecified; the shadow value may simply be estimated from parameters based on optimization over other inputs (and outputs) and the deviation between it and the market value computed.

Further insight may be provided by assuming that the true marginal (factor) cost, as contrasted to the marginal price, depends in an unspecified way on the amount of product, which is similar in spirit to the idea of expressing g as a function of P in LZ and CL. This approach is analogous to the adaptation of the equality of price and marginal cost (in an output market) or price and shadow value (in an input market) for market (monopoly or monopsony) power, that we saw in Chapter 6.

For example, recall that if there was monopsony power in the labor market so that $p_L = p_L(L)$, price setting behavior in this market could be modeled by including L as a level instead of price in the cost function, and using the $MFC_L = $ shadow value $= Z_L$ optimization equation (where MFC is marginal factor cost) $p_L + \partial p_L/\partial L \cdot L = Z_L = -\partial VC/\partial L$, or $p_L = -\partial p_L/\partial L \cdot L - \partial VC/\partial L$. This represents the cause of the gap between the input's price and shadow value as the slope of the $p_L(L)$ function that differentiates marginal and average factor price. We saw that this gap or wedge could simply be represented as a parameter, so that $p_L = -\lambda_L \cdot L + Z_L$, or an explicit input supply equation may be postulated that allows for a more complex relationship between labor use and the wage rate.

Similarly, if the price of pesticides was represented directly as effective price per unit, which may increase (via declining effectiveness) as P increases, this could motivate a pesticide price relationship $p_P(P)$, with the associated optimization equation $p_P = -\partial p_P/\partial P \cdot P + Z^{\pi}_P = -\lambda_P \cdot P + Z^{\pi}_P$. This formalizes the determinants of the gap between p_P and Z^{π}_P, albeit in a very simplistic fashion.

Alternatively, other determinants of this gap could be included in a more general $A(\cdot)$ equation. Using similar reasoning to that motivating the $-\lambda_P \cdot P$ gap above, the arguments of $A(\cdot)$ could include any variables that might lead to disequilibrium in pesticide use. For example, if a combination of current and cumulative pesticide use $\Sigma_t P$ were the issue rather than just the current level of P, this might be written as $p_P = -(\lambda_P + \lambda_{\Sigma P} \cdot \Sigma P) \cdot P + Z^{\pi}_P$, which implies a "true price" equation of the form $p_P = \lambda_P \cdot P + \lambda_{\Sigma P} \cdot \Sigma P \cdot P$.

This could more generally be written as $p_P(P, \Sigma P, t)$, where only cross-terms appear in the specification of the wedge between p_P and Z^{π}_P if $A(P)$ is derived from this. The abatement wedge could be even more broadly be specified as $p_p = A(P, \Sigma P, t) + Z^{\pi}_p$ to take the implied time trends into account.

Further refinement of such a model might recognize that "such factors as the potential growth of resistance, common stock externalities, information and human capital problems and the like..." (LZ) potentially underlie the difference between marginal pesticide productivity and marginal cost at common usage levels. LZ also comment that pest prevalence, fire danger, and weather conditions will affect pesticides' ultimate effectiveness.

If such environmental factors are quantifiable (such as degree days or rainfall as weather indicators), it may well be illuminating to include them directly in the model. Characteristics of pesticides that distinguish abatement from quantity of pesticides, such as an index of pesticide "effectiveness" derived from chemical composition of pesticide inputs, might also be incorporated in the model if such characteristics are measurable.

In addition, including regulatory variables in this function could be useful. For example, a regulatory "environmental" variable could be built in to analysis based on U.S. agricultural data to capture possible effects of the 1972 Federal Environmental Pesticide Control Act. This Act required EPA to review all previously registered pesticides under newly established standards for acute and chronic toxicity. Such legislation may have affected the cost of obtaining the same level of abatement, and thus the demand for pesticides. Dummy variables representing the different regulatory climate post-1972 might therefore facilitate obtaining appropriate estimates of pesticide benefits and productivity.

Such additional generalizations would suggest that the true abatement cost function takes the form $c(p_P, P, t, \Sigma P, \Lambda) = p_P(P, t, \Sigma P, \Lambda) \cdot P$, where Λ represents a vector of determinants of the difference between P and $G(P) = P'$ other than those already in the function, such as weather indicators, chemical composition indexes, or direct regulatory factors (dummies for the imposition of regulation, say). Again, if $p_P(\bullet)$ is approximated by a sufficiently flexible functional form, the marginal cost of pesticide use in terms of abatement would be $\partial c(P,t,\Sigma P,\Lambda)/\partial P = p_P + \partial p_P(P,t,\Sigma P,\Lambda)/\partial P \bullet P$.

Such an optimization equation for p_P could be included in the estimation system, similar to the Euler investment or adjustment cost equation for x_k. Inversion of the pricing equation would also facilitate solving explicitly for P to retrieve the demand equation for pesticides (and subsequently, its price elasticity and determinants on other factors).

Note also that some of these factors might instead appear in the profit function itself rather than the $p_P(P, \bullet)$ and thus $A(\bullet)$ function. For example, if t is included in the profit function in a flexible manner, so that technical change or time-related biases may be identified (as in Chapter 2), a t term will appear in the $Z^\pi{}_P$ shadow value expression. In this case it may not be appropriate to include it also in the specification of $A(\bullet)$.

Similarly, external or environmental factors that one might think have a more general impact on production processes than would be reflected just by including them in the $p_P(\bullet)$ or $A(\bullet)$ function might instead be included as arguments of $\pi(\bullet)$, and thus of $Z^\pi{}_P$ for a flexible function. Interactions of P with more "standard" inputs such as labor will also appear in the $Z^\pi{}_P$ measure, which may facilitate interpretation if, say, increases in hired labor lead to under-utilization of pesticides due to strict pesticide safety laws.

A quantity rather than price approach to this problem may also alternatively be pursued by constructing a specific hedonic (quantity) function for abatement to represent pesticide characteristics and thus effectiveness, as suggested above in the context of the $P'=g=G(P)$ relationship. A model along these lines would again focus on the arguments suggested for the $A(\bullet)$ function, but in this case would directly represent the distinction between P' and P; $g = G(P, \bullet) = P' = G(P,t,\Sigma P,\Lambda)$.

This is similar to the notion of incorporating a G(P) expression approximated by a cumulative distribution into the function, but in this case is motivated as a hedonic function identifying input effectiveness via "characteristics" variables. Such functions are often assumed to be log-linear for estimation purposes.[135] But other tyes of functional forms could be used to be more symmetric with the cost/profit and input demand/output supply structure if, say, a generalized Leontief function used for the overall analysis.

---

[135] See Berndt [1989] Chapter 4 for more discussion of hedonic modeling. This can be motivated from either the quantity or price perspective. The price-side models are more prevalent in the literature, but the treatment in this chapter maintains more symmetry with the treatment with other adaptations for utilization and market power in earlier chapters.

In this case, as for the hedonic model incorporating utilized capital into the framework outlined in Chapter 3, P' could be used as an argument of the function, and the P' equation included as a separate estimating equation or simply substituted into the profit function for empirical implementation.

Finally, it is worth noting that model adaptations to build a "gap" into the optimization equation representing pesticide demand, due to the deviation between pesticide quantity and effective use or abatement, could potentially instead be approached from a profit function with pesticide price as an argument. We then again end up implicitly focusing on revaluation or respecification of P rather than its shadow value.

If p_P is used as an argument of the π function, the usual Hotellings lemma result $-\partial\pi/\partial p_P = P$ again will not hold. There will instead be a wedge between the implied expression for optimal pesticide use and true abatement demand. In this case $-\partial\pi/\partial p_P = P + A'(\bullet) = P'$, or $P = \partial\pi/\partial p_P + A'(\bullet)$ (where ' indicates that this is a quantity-side version of the $A(\bullet)$ function above).

The right hand side of the second expression can be interpreted similarly to the $P(\mathbf{p_m},\mathbf{p_j},p_P) = c_{pP}(p_P,g(\mathbf{p_m},\mathbf{p_j},p_P))$ equality in CL. Since $c(p_P,g)$ is the costs of abatement, the associated marginal measure will involve the actual abatement g or P', plus some adaptation for the deviation between P and true abatement. One way to motivate this is through the hedonic price relationship $P'(\bullet)$, although to derive the $A'(\bullet)$ formally $P'(\bullet)$ must also depend on p_P (similarly to $p_P(P)$ above)

An adapted price p_P' could also instead be substituted into the profit function to represent the true shadow value of pesticides, in which case the derivative $\partial\pi/\partial p_{P'}$ should be equal to P by construction. This would be similar to substituting in the shadow value for capital Z_K (representing the utilized capital value) into the TC$(\bullet)$ function in Chapter 3 to force Shephard's lemma in terms of Z_K to hold; then $\partial TC/\partial Z_K = K$.

That is, this approach substitutes in the true shadow or virtual value of an input, when markets are not working according to measured prices and quantities, in the spirit of Lau and Yotoupolous [1971], Toda [1976], Perrin and Fulginiti [1996] and Atkinson and Cornwell [1998]. If, for example, we substitute the marginal price $p_P'= p_P+\lambda_P\bullet P$ for p_P in the cost function, then derivatives with respect to p_P' should behave according to Shephard's lemma. This alternative is unlikely to be a fruitful option, however, since p_P' is not observed and substitution of the p_P' expression for estimation tends to generate difficulties identifying the λ_P parameters.

The types of models overviewed in this sub-section have potential for measuring the shadow value or quantity of pesticide use, and to model the determinants of the deviation of these from their observed market values. These measures may in turn be used to determine the optimality of pesticide use in terms of its true abatement valuation as compared to the associated potential for environmental damage. The potential impact of restrictions on pesticide use may be determined by evaluating the optimality of current use, and determining the loss in productivity, or increase in costs and substitution effects, that would arise from constrained levels of use.

Further, estimates of price responsiveness through elasticity computations can help to determine whether a pesticide tax or use restrictions would be a more effective tool. Price elasticity estimates provide an indication of producers' ability to substitute other inputs for pesticides, and how responsive such substitution may be to price changes induced by taxation. The effect a pesticide tax would have on the costs of production may thus be computed, and compared to impact estimates of pesticide bans.

Finally, we need to address the issue of productivity measurement when there is a discrepancy between measured pesticide quantity and abatement, or measured pesticide price and true abatement cost. If the differences between abatement and observed pesticide prices and quantities are measurable, clearly appropriate productivity growth measures should incorporate this price and quantity information. If, however, they are not directly observable, but instead must be imputed by measurement of the shadow value (or imputed quantity) of pesticide abatement services, this implies an adjustment to the price (or quantity) weight in the standard MFP measure analogous to those for utilization in Chapter 3.

This model therefore provides a rich basis for evaluation of pesticide demand and productivity. Some preliminary results based on the estimating models suggested above are in Felthoven and Morrison [1998]. These initial attempts to model pesticide productivity use aggregate agricultural data on input and output prices and quantities for California and the U.S. from 1959-1989 constructed by Eldon Ball at the USDA/ERS. Panel data for all U.S. states may also be used for such estimation, but the immense heterogeneity of products produced across states causes comparability problems.

Using data on two outputs (animal and crop aggregates), and five inputs including a distinction between pesticides and fertilizers (labor, capital, pesticides, fertilizer, and a materials aggregate) the preliminary results suggest that the shadow value of P may be even lower than its market price. Allowing for a gap between the shadow and market valuation of pesticides, particularly when the dependence of this gap on current and cumulative pesticide use is taken into account, minimizes curvature problems.

Important extensions to this preliminary work will involve using more explicit data on pesticide composition and "bad outputs" from pesticide use, developed at the ERS by Ball and Richard Nehring. These data may be used to measure effective pesticide use and agricultural output production, since they embody information on damage from pesticides that more directly addresses issues of pesticide quantity as compared to abatement.

Results from these aggregate data may also be augmented, as data allow, by estimating such models using more microeconomic data. Such data would be more readily applicable to the types of models developed above, particularly when the focus is on modeling potential characteristics and determinants of effective pesticide use directly (as in a detailed hedonic model focusing on production characteristics).

3.   LACK OF MARKETS: "BAD" OUTPUTS

The converse of the environmental degradation and regulation question involves the output side of the problem. In the previous sections we focused on the measurement of regulatory impacts in the context of the productivity of inputs subject to quantity regulations imposed to counteract their associated environmental damage (or augment their ability to abate such damage). The measurement of the regulatory impacts from the input side has a counterpart in the measurement of the environmental damage inflicted by the production of outputs that use potentially damaging inputs.

That is, in the previous section we saw that pesticides have productivity impacts that take the form of increased effective output, in turn generating revenues for farmers and benefits for consumers (greater quantities and reduced prices of agricultural products). However, they also have associated costs in terms of environmental damage.

The focus there was on the marginal benefit side of pesticide use, and the resulting costs of regulation reducing their use. Such regulations are justified, however, in terms of social optimality or efficiency, if regulatory costs are balanced on the margin by the benefits of reducing environmental damage. This can be expressed in terms of reductions in "bad outputs".

Recognition of bad outputs may be conceptualized similarly to representing effective inputs in the previous section. Essentially, measures of "good" or marketed output production should be "deflated" or reduced by the negative non-marketed outputs in order to measure true social output or beneficial production.

This could potentially be accomplished by the usual aggregation techniques for adding (or, in this case, subtracting) outputs or inputs if direct measures of quantity and prices of bad outputs were obtainable. However, this is thwarted by the lack of appropriate information associated with these non-marketed commodities, such as for prices, which also precludes more direct measurement of the marginal damage. Shadow rather than market prices must be used to impute the true economic valuation (or costs) of the bad outputs.

Using recently constructed data by Eldon Ball and Richard Nehring at the USDA/ERS, some preliminary studies have been carried out to assess the productivity costs of "bad" or negative outputs in U.S. agriculture. At least two threads of thought may be identified in this endeavor – distinguishing between production and welfare impacts of production as in Perrin and Fulginiti [1996] and Gollop and Swinand [1998], and identifying the efficiency implications of bad outputs as in Färe, Grosskopf, Lovell and Yaisawarng [1993] and Ball, Nehring, Färe and Grosskopf [1998]. The theoretical implications of the distance function-based nonparametric activity analysis approach used in Ball *et al* may also be adapted to provide implications about how a parametric distance-, cost-, or profit- function may be used to analyze the impacts of bad outputs.

The distinction between productivity and welfare change was developed in the context of "poorly priced" goods in Perrin and Fulginiti [1996]. This treatment is in the spirit of the utilization and market power adjustments discussed in previous chapters, as noted in their study. However, they extend these notions within a general equilibrium model to evaluate the determination of equilibrium quantities when distortions exist.

In particular, they measure equivalent variation "defined in this context as the consumer-price weighted counterpart of TFP", which differs from TFP due to differences between production and welfare-oriented versions of optimal production (where TFP, or total factor productivity, is analogous to our multifactor productivity concept, MFP, from Chapter 2).

Gollop and Swinand also use this notion to provide a basis for adapting TFP (MFP) measures to represent what they call "TRP" or "total resource productivity" including environmental resources. As they note, the fundamental issue in studies incorporating "bad outputs", or environmental damage from output production, is that measuring productivity based on all resources involves choosing between production and welfare-based paradigms, since welfare measures must recognize jointly-produced externalities and market failures. This distinction involves valuing products according to producers' marginal abatement costs, as compared to shadow prices "consistent with a model of consumer welfare". The model therefore is based on a model of welfare maximization, rather than maximization of profits or minimization of production costs.

In this treatment the bad output is denoted "S", and S/Y (where Y is conventionally measured output) is included in the production set $\Phi = F(Y, S/Y, v, t)$ (where v is a vector of "resources"). S/Y enters in ratio form since environmental regulations typically affect rates rather than levels. For example, pesticide regulation is imposed in the form of application rates per acre. Also note that the function F is decreasing in Y, but increasing in S/Y, v and t, so S/Y acts essentially as an input rather than as an output.

If F is set to one, growth is reflected in the Y variable; the function becomes similar to a distance function assuming technical efficiency, as developed more below. Gollop and Swinand use this specification, taking the total derivative of the function and manipulating it similarly to the standard production function in Chapter 2, to derive an adjusted measure of TFP growth taking environmental damage from "bad outputs" into account:

$$7.6)\ TRP^P = d\ln Y/dt + \rho S/p_Y Y \bullet [d\ln Y/dt - d\ln S/dt] - \Sigma_j\, p_j v_j/p_Y Y\ d\ln v_j/dt$$

where the P superscript denotes "producer equilibrium", and ρ is the marginal abatement cost of S. Thus, as output grows, if S/Y stays constant or $\rho=0$ TRP=TFP. If these conditions do not hold, productivity growth depends on both Y and S/Y.[136]

The impact on welfare compared to production-side productivity, as developed in Gollop and Swinand, involves the definitions of output and weights on the output growth rates in (7.6). S is viewed differently from the production (private) or society perspective, and evaluating benefits to society requires valuing outputs in terms of marginal rates of substitution from the welfare function rather than marginal rates of transformation.

A model of utility or welfare is thus constructed where the marginal utilization of Y is positive and that for S is negative. This is manipulated to generate the "welfare-based productivity growth" measure TRP^W:

$$7.7)\ TRP^W = p_Y Y/p_G G\ d\ln Y/dt - \chi S/p_G G\ d\ln S/dt - \Sigma_j\, p_j v_j/p_G G\ d\ln v_j/dt,$$

where $p_G G$ is output as valued by society, or "through the eyes of a representative consumer", and χ is the absolute value of the shadow price of S (the marginal disutility of an additional unit of S).

The treatment in Gollop and Swinand therefore emphasizes two things. First, even production-side productivity growth measures should be adapted if bad outputs are produced (here more than proportionately to output given the assumption that S/Y enters the production set) or if the marginal cost of abatement is positive. Second, production- and welfare-based measures of productivity will differ according to society's view of the production of S relative to producers', and valuation of S and Y according to the marginal rate of substitution (as in Perrin and Fulginiti).

---

[136] Note that this adaptation of productivity measures is the flip-side of the adaptation for PAK purchases in Section 1. For appropriate productivity measurement, either only productive inputs in terms of measured outputs should be represented in the model, or the unmeasured outputs should be recognized.

Both these measures are, however, difficult to construct empirically since marginal valuations of S are not straightforward to generate. This is especially true for the "welfare" measure based on imputation of society's view of the value of output and the marginal disutility of S. Therefore the production side often again provides the focus for analysis, and shadow values derived from a production-oriented specification may be used to infer what the bias for the welfare-oriented measure might be.

Such a production-side perspective is the basis for Färe *et al* [1993] and Ball *et al* [1998]. The latter study provides a preliminary empirical investigation of the theoretical framework largely developed in Färe *et al* and Färe and Grosskopf [1996]. As might be expected, the results suggest that productivity growth measures adapted for bad outputs indicate lower productivity growth in U.S. agriculture than when "bads" or negative outputs are not accounted for, given patterns of increasing trends in the pesticide and fertilizer variables.

This study is based on nonparametric activity analysis, which precludes asking the types of questions one might address with a parametric model of the technology. However, it provides important insights about how one might think of including bad outputs in productivity analysis.

In particular, these studies frame their analysis in terms of a distance function, which is essentially a multiple output production function allowing for a deviation from technical efficiency, as developed further in the next chapter. A Malmquist productivity index, which is similar to a Törnquist index but from the distance function perspective (also discussed in the next chapter) is constructed to accommodate the bad output information in the distance function specification. The model thus "seeks the greatest feasible expansion of all outputs, both good and bad".

The use of a distance function for analysis is important here since it represents just the technology rather than behavior, as well as allowing for multiple outputs. Although in many cases it is important to model responsiveness, and thus behavior such as cost-mimization or profit maximization, if price data is unavailable it is not a desirable approach. Shadow values may be measured in the distance function context without explicit behavioral assumptions, and without the necessity of price information. These measures are difficult to motivate intuitively, however, in this multi-dimensional framework.

An important contribution of these papers is the duality treatment for bad output production. Although we are not pursuing rigorous derivations in these applications chapters, we can summarize the important results here that may guide the use of a parametric treatment of this problem.

Färe *et al* and Ball *et al* define the technology set by (using our notation):

7.8) T={(**v**,Y,S): **v** can produce (Y,S)} ,

which represents all good and bad outputs Y and S that can be produced with the given input vector **v**. The associated multiple-output production set is then written as

7.9) F(**v**) = {(Y,S): (**v**,Y,S) ∈ T}.

They model the costliness of reducing bad outputs by "weak disposability of outputs", which implies that reductions of bads requires decreases in good outputs, given **v** (or increases in **v** given Y). This imposes a type of jointness on the model termed "null-jointness". By contrast, good outputs are assumed freely disposable. This facilitates analysis in terms of positive prices of good outputs but lack of observable market prices for bad outputs. That is, it allows bad outputs to have nonpositive rather than nonnegative shadow prices.

From this basis, Färe *et al* discuss the curvature of the function when negative outputs are produced (weak disposability exists) and develop the required duality relationships through the duality of the distance and revenue functions. In particular, they note that a distance function may be defined from (7.9) as: $D_O(\mathbf{v},Y,S) \leq 1$ if and only if (Y,S) ∈ F(**v**). If technical efficiency exists, the distance function will equal one, reproducing the frontier of the production set.

For a one-output production function, D_O may be written as: $D_O(\mathbf{v},Y)$ = $\overline{Y}/Y(\mathbf{v})$ where Y(**v**) is the production function, so if observed output production $\overline{Y}$ is technically efficient this is equal to one. If technical efficiency is not reached, this output-oriented distance function (based on the output set and thus analogous to a production function rather than input requirement set) will fall short of one. The output level possible with input vector **v** exceeds the actual output level. In order to accommodate changes in Y and S that go in opposite directions, however, a "directional distance function" is introduced, resulting in a more complicated Malmquist index than for the standard distance function.

This model allows a more rigorous treatment of the issue of bad outputs, in a nonparametric framework based on a directional distance function and Malmquist productivity indexes, than is provided by Gollop and Swinand. Unfortunately, however, in the context of bad outputs the Malmquist index may not have a well-defined solution, and "effectively registers increases in the bads (like the goods), *ceteris paribus* as improvements in productivity".

Nevertheless, this study provides important insights about how bad outputs might be represented in a parametric treatment. For example, as in Färe *et al*, a parametric function for the distance function may be assumed.

Such a function could also be estimated econometrically (by maximum likelihood estimation) rather than by linear programming techniques, as outlined in the next chapter. From this, shadow values can be measured similarly to the measurement of VMPs for inputs in the production function framework, as discussed further in Chapters 8 and 9.

Although this methodology may yield important information about the technology, potential (technical) inefficiency, and shadow prices, it does not reflect behavior and thus price responsiveness. When technical inefficiency is incorporated it also complicates the estimation of a system of equations that could potentially be developed from the distance function similarly to the $p_j=VMP_j$ equations often used to estimate production functions (but with the same problems, such as endogeneity of right hand variables).

Finally, it is possible, as in Pittman [1971], to instead construct a profit function with bad output quantity information incorporated. Such a model may fall prey to problems similar to those encountered by studies representing pesticide demand, as discussed in the previous section. Such a model may tend to have perverse estimated shadow values due to differences in measured and effective levels of unobserved inputs (outputs). A full model of profit maximizing behavior, however, especially when adapted to accommodate issues of fixities and other important characteristics of agricultural production, has potential for addressing these types of issues.

4.   REGULATION AND MARKET POWER

A final type of regulatory issue to raise involves regulations designed to counteract market power that may emerge from some form of "natural monopoly". If market power is deemed to be a problem in terms of profitability – excess profits are being generated that constitute an "abuse of market power" – regulatory responses have often involved regulating the rate of return to capital or price of output. Another response, in particular in the past couple of decades, has been to "deregulate" such industries and force "competitiveness" in different ways.

The former type of regulation – restricting rates of return – has its costs in terms of efficiency (since market forces do not stimulate greatest efficiency if returns to the producer are not forthcoming), as well as direct costs of the regulation. The latter – promoting competitiveness – may also cause efficiency problems if cost economies are the basis for high concentration or market power in an industry, and thus may be lost by dividing or "unbundling" the industry into smaller pieces.

In either case, two issues arise. One is to determine the deviation from optimal market workings caused by the market power, and the second is to evaluate the impact of the regulation itself. Neither is straightforward.

One major industry that has been under scrutiny and the subject of forced "competitiveness" in many developed countries is the electric utility industry. The literature has not approached a consensus about the justifiability or consequences of restructuring the industry. This is at least in part due to problems obtaining a definitive short term assessment of the impacts of structural change in an industry that exhibits complex joint output processes, and which has been regulated and thus distorted for a long time (see Shepherd [1997]).

A fundamental underlying issue for analysis of such an industry is, as highlighted in the previous chapter, what "competitiveness" and "abuse of market power" imply. One would think, for example, that in an industry in which utilization, scale and scope (coordination) economies are important characteristics of the production structure, testing whether $p_Y=MC$ as an indication of market power is fraught with serious difficulties.

First, in a capital-intensive industry, industry "competitiveness" does not imply that firms will only be charging enough to cover variable costs. Feasibility of the industry in the long run clearly implies that firms must be able to cover their capital costs even if they could currently be called "sunk costs". In this case, the standard microeconomic principles argument that a "competitive" firm will produce where price is equated to (short run) marginal costs must be thought through more carefully.

If the price in a competitive industry drops low enough firms will produce output such that $p_Y=MC$, even if the price drops to the minimum of the AVC curve, this does not imply that prices "should" just cover short run marginal costs. For long-term feasibility of the industry long run average total costs must be covered. In a very capital-intensive industry, SMC may be exceedingly low, so even zero profitability will imply pricing above SMC. Unfortunately, however, some suggestions for reform have based their analysis on just such a limited view of "competitiveness".

Similarly, if scale and coordination (scope or jointness) economies prevail, one may not expect output price to equal marginal cost, unless infra-marginal consumers pay higher prices. Again, long run costs of production may not be covered in this case. That is, if MC<AC due to cost economies, price must cover AC for the industry to be feasible, similarly to the case of utilization where SMC may be far less than LMC *or* average costs.

Thus the notion of competitiveness must be carefully defined, and indications of market power "abuse" provided by measures of economic profitability and possibly technical efficiency. The first is somewhat easier to assess than the latter. But it is still not easy to identify what the cost structure might look like, and what the true economic costs of the existing capital stock might be, particularly in an industry that has typically been subject to heavy regulation for most of the documented past. It is even more difficult to determine whether costs may be high because of technical inefficiency, likely combined with regulatory incentives that do not encourage cost efficiency but focus on profitability. A tangled web.

Based on these brief comments about fundamental conceptual and definitional questions, it is useful to overview some issues in the literature about this industry's cost and market structure, and the potential for industry restructuring to generate a more competitive environment.

First, let us consider rate of return regulation and how this might be built into a model in order to identify its impact on the estimated cost structure. This is important for measuring the productivity of an industry that is subject to regulatory constraints, as is emphasized in a number of important papers in in Cowing and Stevenson [1981] (CS).

One treatment of the regulated rate of return issue in the CS volume, which provides insights about how to build rate of return regulation into a production theory framework similar to those we have been working with in this text, is Diewert [1981b]. This framework is useful for evaluation of the impact of rate of return legislation, and of regulations that impose average cost pricing.[137] It provides a context for assessing the impact of these regulations on the deviation of price (or marginal revenue) from marginal (or average) cost, and of the shadow value and market price of capital. This framework, based on the Averch-Johnson [1962] model of the regulated firm, can be adapted to allow consideration of various kinds of pricing policies, like Ramsey strategies, on the shadow value of capital to the firm.

The main extension in this model is to impose, on the profit-maximizing problem of a firm with market power (outlined in Chapter 9), the requirement that profits cannot exceed a certain rate of return. This results in an additional constraint, along with production being technologically feasible, and output supply being consistent with demand, that the optimization process must satisfy.

Formally, the profit maximizing model of Chapter 6, subject to the inverse demand function $D^{-1}(Y,\rho)=p_Y(Y,\rho)$ and the restricted cost function $VC=VC(Y,\cdot)$ (see 9.6), must now also be subject to the condition:

7.6) $p_Y Y - \Sigma_j p_j v_j - \Sigma_k p_k x_k \leq \Sigma_k e_k x_k$,

---

[137] See also the other papers in this volume for additional important contributions about the impact of regulation on economic performance.

where e_k are the K "excess" profit rates that the regulated firm is allowed to earn on its use of each of K stocks of capital, x_k. This is based on the assumption that rate of return regulation allows expensing of the kth type of capital services at a rental price $p_k + e_k = s_k$, where s_k is the "fair rate of return" set by the regulators.

This condition adds a third type of first-order condition to the Shephard's lemma conditions $v_j = \partial VC/\partial p_j$, and $p_Y + Y \cdot \partial p_Y/\partial Y = \partial VC/\partial Y$, which motivate substitution for $\partial VC/\partial p_j$ and $\partial VC/\partial Y$ in the expression used for productivity growth measurement. The third condition becomes $p_k = -\partial VC/\partial x_k + \beta_t e$ rather than $p_K = -\partial VC/\partial x_k = Z_k$ as for the subequilibrium model we encountered earlier, where β_t is a function of the Lagrange multiplier from the optimization problem (which may be estimated for each period t).

Only if capital is being used efficiently so $\beta_t = 0$ will the usual shadow value equation be valid. Thus, the adapted valuation of x_k must be substituted into the productivity growth measurement expression (6.3) (as in equation (4.2) of Chapter 4). This requires, of course, a measure of the allowed "excess profit rates" e set by the regulator.

This is a straightfoward adaptation of the shadow value of fixed inputs for correct representation of the impact of these inputs on productivity growth. Since this extension is based on a structure consistent with the adaptations already accomplished, it has considerable appeal for application to productivity growth in industries subject to rate of return regulation.

It implies further indirect adaptations, however, since productivity growth adjustments to accommodate capacity utilization and scale will also be affected; they depend on the elasticity of costs with respect to the quasi-fixed inputs. In addition, although the markup will not change for any particular value of output since it is entirely dependent on the elasticity of demand, the adapted first order conditions for fixed inputs will affect marginal costs and thus the level of output at which the markup is evaluated. Appropriate productivity growth measurement should therefore consider all these effects for constructing weights on measured output and input growth.

The second type of regulatory response to market power highlighted above has to do with promoting "competitiveness" in an industry. Again, a fundamental issue for evaluating the existence of competitiveness, and the impact of regulation to restructure an industry such as the electric utility industry, involves its production and cost structure. In particular, utilization and cost economy issues are critically important for evaluation of the potential for increased or decreased cost efficiency after restructuring.

Many different approaches have been used to analyze the cost structure of electric utility industries. As discussed in Stokes [1998], some studies (especially for Britain) have used nonparametric cost benefit methodology to do social welfare analysis (see Newberry and Politt [1997] for example).

Others such as Joskow [1989,1996,1997,1998] have been of a more descriptive and institutional nature. These studies have identified various factors that will limit efficiency gains from restructuring in the short term, such as lost economies of coordinating the generation and transmission segments of the electric utility industry. They also have emphasized utilization issues that are particularly problematic since electricity cannot be stored. Electricity supply must therefore nearly match demand to maintain a stable transmission network.

These facets of the cost structure have motivated the vertically integrated market structure of the industry, which has allowed utilization and cost economies to be internalized. In particular, it appears that electric utilities have inseparable cost functions; coordination or jointness of generation, transmission and distribution generates significant economies (see Thompson [1997]. Little quantitative evidence is available, however, about cost economies such as scale economies in this industry.

Econometric studies of the utilities industry include those addressing the determinants of pricing in regulated as compared to competitive environments (see Emmons [1997, Walker and Lough [1997]). Others have focused more specifically on quantifying aspects of the cost structure using parametric models. Thompson [1997], for example, analyzed the cost structure and jointness of three segments of the industry – generation, transmission and distribution – which are often thought to embody different market structures as well as a lack of separability.

Such a study allows analysis of the three critical aspects of cost economies in this industry: utilization, scale economies, and scope or coordination economies (jointness). Thompson asks both how one might characterize cost economies in this industry, and how these cost efficiencies might have changed over time. The latter question is particularly important since some studies finding incentives for restructuring are based on historical data (Emmons [1997]) that may not be applicable for current technologies.

Thompson uses a total cost function for distribution of the form $TC_D(p_E, p_{LT}, p_{LD}, p_{KT}, p_{KD}, Y_H, Y_L, SA, N, t)$, where p_E is the price of power supplied, p_{LT} and p_{LD} are the prices of transmission and distribution labor, p_{KT} and p_{KD} are the prices of transmission and distribution capital, Y_H and Y_L are high- and low-voltage sales volumes, SA is the size of the service area (in square miles), N is the number of customers, and t is a time trend. Some potentially problematic assumptions are imposed, such as linear homogeneity in the overall production process and average generation cost as a proxy for the power supply price. However, a flexible functional form (translog) is used for the model so interactions among the variables, and therefore jointness in the production process, may be tested.

Thompson finds that economies of vertical integration and size were not realized when production and services increased to a growing service area or number of customers. The focus of the analysis is, however, on separability of different services provided by electric utilities, which he rejects. The bundled services provided by utilities appear to be a result of cost economies, including scope economies. Like Joskow [1997], these results suggest that deregulators must consider the efficiency losses of competition in efforts to restructure or "unbundle" this vertically integrated industry.

There is also evidence that more competitiveness in electric utilities industries is associated with lower prices (Emmons [1997], White [1996]). This may imply long run potential for increased efficiency gains in competitive generation (Joskow 1989, 1996, 1997). Much of this evidence again is, however, from historical data, and over time the differential has tended to decline. It is also not clear whether price declines are stimulated by reductions in the potential for monopoly pricing, or increased cost efficiency. The former could arise if firms were indeed taking advantage of their market power to obtain excessive profitability.[138] The latter could emerge if regulatory practices (such as rate-of-return regulation) are such that cost efficiency is not stimulated by market forces.

Many complicating issues convolute analysis of regulatory constraints and reform in industries like electric utilities. But there is clear potential for production models to provide information about the cost structure, and therefore underlying motivations for the existing market structure.

5.   FURTHER COMMENTS

This chapter has raised a variety of regulation issues, with a view toward thinking about insights potentially available from production theory models about regulatory costs and justification, rather than providing a comprehensive overview of regulation economics. In this discussion we have touched on issues about input restrictions (requirements for capital investment, limits on damaging inputs such as pesticides), effective inputs and outputs (abatement rather than quantities of pesticides, bad unmeasured outputs), and linkages between regulation and market structure.

---

[138] Shepherd [1997] thinks this will continue to be possible since it is unlikely that "effective competition" will be sufficient to reduce market power price distortions in the industry. However, industrial organization studies of various industries have found that competitive prices may emerge even with high concentration, if the players in the industry are able to compete effectively. The meat packing industry may be one example. This issue has rich potential for future research given the increased concentration observed, and attributed to information and other types of high-technology, in many industries.

We have ignored many other regulatory issues that may be of interest, including those related to taxes or subsidies, and trade, which one might also want to build into this type of framework. We have also largely side-stepped the notion of regulation and "efficiency". However, any kind of regulatory distortion is typically thought to reduce productive efficiency from its potential competitive level, even if it is designed to counteract other types of distortions like those arising from lack of markets or market power.

Efficiency issues are often addressed in general equilibrium models that assess the appropriate allocation of resources across commodities, and how the "invisible hand" link breaks down when distortions are present. We have not pursued this type of analysis here since our framework in this text is of a partial equilibrium nature. Such analysis however, highlights important problems of evaluating "second best" outcomes.

Another efficiency issue involves the existence of technological and allocative efficiency for particular firms. This type of problem, and its link with regulatory distortions, was raised briefly in this chapter in the context of bad outputs and the use of a distance function that facilitates modeling deviations from technical efficiency. Technical efficiency (being off the production function frontier or within the production set) may be affected, for example, by imposing quantity regulations on inputs, and allocative efficiency (a deviation from the cost minimization point or above the cost frontier) from price impacts of regulation.

Such inefficiencies, as discussed in this chapter, may be directly modeled and their impacts evaluated as "environmental" variables that affect the effective or available technological or cost frontier. This is a similar notion to fixities that cause output to be lower (for given input costs) or costs to be higher (for a given output level) than is possible in the long run.

If not modeled directly, however, these kinds of constraints or distortions may appear as technological or allocative inefficiency. Other unobserved impacts, especially if measured across individual firms, may also cause efficiency to differ from what may be thought of as "best practice" methods. This focus on the existence of technical and allocative efficiency, which are simply assumed to prevail in the types of studies we have been discussing so far in this text, has generated its own literature on the measurement of efficient frontiers. This is the focus of the next chapter.

Chapter 8

Technical Efficiency

The models we have worked with in previous chapters are largely based on evaluating the causes and consequences of shifts in and movements along isoquants (and thus implicitly production functions representing technology) and cost curves (cost functions based on cost minimizing behavior). For analysis of productive processes and performance we have assumed the firm is on the function's frontier or boundary; technical and/or behavioral optimization has been attained. However, there may be inefficiencies in the production system. Something unrecognized in the model, such as management ability, may cause firms to be off the frontier, and our technical and/or allocative efficiency assumptions to be invalid.

That is, as we have seen, if we can incorporate and measure potential causes of observed deviations from full optimization in our model such as fixities, regulations, characteristics of capital, and quality or environmental attributes, this facilitates analysis of productive processes and performance. The resulting model structure provides a rich basis for evaluation of both average and individual production processes across time, space or firms. If, however, some firms are just inherently less efficient, due to some unobservable differentials, we cannot necessarily interpret differences in outputs and inputs as shifts in functions, but instead need to accommodate the possibility of movements within the frontiers.

Obtaining insights about differential efficiencies across individual productive units (decision-making units or DMUs) requires explicitly recognizing that the functions we work with in production theory models are actually bounding functions, so no firm should fall outside (or inside) the associated frontiers. For example, cost curves represent minimum possible costs (given the production function and input prices) for producing any given output level. Firms producing according to "best practice" methods will reach this cost level, and any inefficient firms will incur higher costs than this minimum, and thus be within the frontier.

This deviation from the frontier may stem from either technical or allocative inefficiency. Technical inefficiency implies being inside or below the production function or production possibility frontier, and thus outside or above the relevant isoquant for the particular output level. Allocative inefficiency arises from not achieving the lowest costs for that output level; the firm is on the correct isoquant but not at the cost minimization point and thus on the scale expansion path.

Frontier estimation techniques represent the technology via such a bounding function. This representation may be based on various types of functions, including production-, cost-, or distance-functions. Production rather than cost functions are often used as the basis for analysis, at least in part due to problems identifying an additional component of the stochastic structure (the inefficiency, or one-sided error from the frontier) when also trying to separately represent the full cost structure (and thus allocative inefficiency).

In turn, distance functions may provide a particularly useful technological representation, since their multi-output nature allows consideration of output composition. This is especially important since frontier methods evaluate firms' efficiency relative to "best practice" as exhibited by other comparable units. This implies estimation across a cross-section (or panel) data set, by contrast to the analyses of technical change emphasized in previous chapters, which are typically based on evaluation of time series data. Comparison across microeconomic units often requires careful consideration of differential input and output composition so that this is not confused with inefficiency.

The technological structure and productivity as well as efficiency may be measured based on estimated parameters of, and residuals from, a frontier distance function model. Determinants of measured inefficiency may also be distinguished in a full econometric model of the distance function. In addition the distance function provides the basis for the construction of Malmquist indexes, which are used in frontier studies to decompose multifactor productivity measures into their technical efficiency change and technical change components. Such a distance function model will therefore be the focal point for our overview of frontier concepts and models.

Also, estimation of frontier models may be accomplished by either deterministic or stochastic (econometric) methods. As in the rest of this text, our focus in this chapter will be on the parametric or econometric frontier models, typically called "stochastic production frontier" models. Since technical inefficiency of an individual firm is measured as its deviation from the bounding function, both this function and the associated distance of the observed output/input combination from its potential needs to be estimated. The resulting model therefore has two error terms, one to account for technical inefficiency and another to accommodate other factors that might generate irrelevant noise in the results, such as measurement error and unobserved inputs.

Estimating frontier models thus implies empirically "fitting" a production or cost curve above or below the observed data points rather than through them. This provides a picture of the best practice rather than average firm. The focus on the stochastic structure (two error terms) often makes it difficult to represent a full structural model of production processes. Frontier models, however, have an increasingly important place in empirical analysis of production and productivity, since they answer different types of questions than more traditional econometric modeling where the focus is typically on identifying overall patterns of responsiveness in a sector.

In this chapter, we will first (Section 1) briefly overview some of the fundamental issues that arise when technical inefficiency is allowed for in a model of production processes. In Section 2 we address issues associated with empirical implementation of frontier models, with particular focus on the stochastic specification, and on the use of a distance function as a representation of technology and the basis for computation of efficiency, shadow value, and ultimately productivity measures. The potential for using dual production models when technical and allocative inefficiencies are allowed for is considered in Section 3. Finally, in Section 4 we will discuss productivity index numbers associated with frontier models.[139]

1. FRONTIER MODELING

Following the work of Farrell [1957], researchers applying frontier estimation techniques represent the technology by a bounding function rather than fitting an average function through observed data. Such a function may be based on a production, input requirement or other more general function (depending on whether the focus is on output production or input use), and may be estimated using nonparametric or econometric (stochastic) methods.

As elaborated by Farrell, this methodology represents the "best practice technology" production of a product, defined in terms of the maximum real output producible given available (real) inputs. Technical inefficiency of an individual firm is measured by its deviation from the function (generally measured on a ray from the origin through the actual production point to the frontier, as in the diagrams below).[140]

---

[139] This brief overview simply identifies some of the primary issues involved in efficiency measurement. For an excellent "beginner's guide" to these issues that provides more detail than is possible here as well as empirical illustrations, see Coelli, Rao and Battese [1998]. More detailed and rigorous treatments may be found in Forsund, Lovell and Schmidt [1980], Schmidt [1986], Bauer [1990], Lovell [1993] and Greene [1993].

[140] See Lovell [1993] for a detailed discussion of this theoretical framework and the underlying intuition).

Technical change is therefore characterized by a movement of the technological frontier, stemming from innovation of some form, which may be disembodied or embodied in inputs used for production. Increasing efficiency *given* the technology instead involves moving *toward* the frontier.

How this is accomplished depends on why the deviation from the technological boundary exists. For example, if regulatory distortions keep firms from reaching the existing frontier, removing or adapting these distortions would result in increased efficiency. If instead "inefficiency" arises from short run constraints, one would expect firms facing the least binding constraints would appear the most efficient, and as the constraints are relaxed – the firm moves toward the long run – efficiency will increase .

Appropriate characterization and interpretation of the function representing the technology requires considering what factors facing the firm are determinants of the *technology*, and which might be causes of *inefficiency*. For example, if t (time) or R (a regulatory variable) appear in the technological specification, the implication is that it is a shift variable for the function. For t, this would suggest technical change is exhibited over time, that we would want to distinguish separately from movement toward the frontier. For R, this would indicate that regulations have determined the shape of the frontier by directly affecting the marginal products of inputs, say, rather than causing a deviation from an existing frontier.

A typical approach to representing and measuring technological inefficiency is to base efficiency analysis on one output and multiple inputs (a production function). The associated output oriented efficiency question given the technology becomes: "Given a certain quantity of inputs, what is the most output that can be produced?" Equivalently, from the input side such a question may be expressed in terms of the lowest input level (given observed input composition) that can be used to produce the existing output level. In the polar extreme case from the production function, with one aggregate input and multiple outputs (an input requirement function) this can be stated as: "For production of a certain quantity of outputs, what is the lowest possible input use?"

The latter notion provides the basis for the typical isoquant diagram motivating the idea of a frontier or bounding function in this literature. For example, in Figure 9 (as in Coelli [1995a]), the technology is represented by a piecewise linear convex isoquant. The data points plotted in this diagram, indicating observed output and input levels, are assumed to come from individual firms with a sufficiently similar technological structure that they can be directly compared in terms of their (one) output and (two) input use. This snapshot of the sector under consideration (in this case represented by 5 firms) emphasizes that frontier analysis is based on a cross-section comparison of production processes.

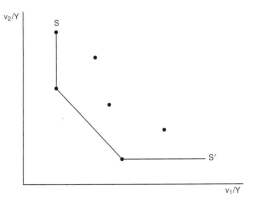

Figure 9. A Piecewise Linear Isoquant

Firms within the frontier are using too many (an inefficient amount of) inputs to generate the output level represented by the SS' isoquant. To identify the appropriate level of input use given the existing input composition (ratio of v_js) a ray can be drawn from the origin to any data point. The place this line crosses an isoquant identifies the point on the isoquant at which the associated firm "should" be able to produce.

The issue addressed in frontier analysis is, if we wish to estimate the implied frontier from the existing data, how do we do it? This is a different perspective than the usual parametric or econometric techniques that fit a line *through* the data points.

Although estimation methods are pursued more in the next section it is worth noting here that various approaches can be used for empirical implementation of frontier models. In particular, nonparametric analysis may be used to trace out a piece-wise isoquant as in Figure 9; this is the basis for "data envelopment analysis" or DEA. Alternatively, if a functional form is assumed for the production function, and thus the isoquant map, the parameters of the function may be estimated parametrically.

Models used for parametric frontier studies are often based on a Cobb-Douglas (CD) production function, similar to those we have seen in previous chapters. This specification may be advantageous for frontier models, since it is difficult to identify both technical and allocative efficiency when the stochastic structure (inefficiency "errors") provides the focus of the analysis. The simple CD form facilitates identifying these stochastic aspects.

The CD form, however, remains very limited for a full analysis of the production structure. In particular, it does not allow biases or substitution effects to be identified, which may cause such production characteristics to be forced into the error terms and thus to appear as inefficiency.

The CD function with the addition of a one-sided (non-negative) inefficiency term to make the production function a bounding rather than average function may be written as:

8.1) $\ln Y_i = f(\ln v_i; \beta) - u_i = \ln A_0 + \Sigma_j \beta_j \ln v_{ij} - u_i$,

where the i's denote individual firms or decision-making units (DMUs) and the j's represent the J inputs. t-subscripts may also be included to represent time if panel rather than cross-section data were used for analysis. Technical efficiency can thus be expressed as $TE_i = Y_i/\exp[f(\ln v_i; \beta)] = \exp(-u_i)$.

Such a model is often represented and estimated using linear programming techniques, so $\Sigma_i u_i$ is minimized subject to the constraints that $u_i \geq 0$, i=1,s...M.[141] However, as noted above, it is also possible to estimate it using more standard econometric methods (often maximum likelihood procedures, as overviewed in more detail in the next section).

Econometric estimates of this function reproduce a smooth isoquant, that takes the form of a rectangular hyperbola (elasticities of substitution between all inputs are equal to one), which is of course a major limiting factor for CD estimation. The data cannot distinguish the curvature of the function so any deviation from the substitution patterns assumed a priori may appear as "inefficiency". Returns to scale are also restricted to be the same across all firms for the CD. In addition, any deviation from the isoquant due to, say, fixities that are not modeled, will appear as unidentified inefficiency.

Note also that the production function model is an output-oriented model by constrast to the isoquant diagram motivation, which has an input orientation. The production function indicates how much output can be expanded given input use, rather than how much inputs can be contracted and still produce the observed output level. This may be motivated more intuitively in a diagram in Y-v_j space (or Y-**v** space, where **v** indicates aggregate input, indicating total output increases given input composition).[142]

The production function representation of the technological structure is not only limited in terms of the functional form and its restrictive substitution and scale economy assumptions, but also by the assumption of a single aggregate output. This is particularly an issue in the context of the micro cross-section data typically used for implementation of frontier

---

[141] See Aigner and Chu [1968] who also discussed the use of quadratic programming techniques.

[142] The output- and input-oriented measures are equivalent if constant returns to scale (CRS) prevails, but are different if non-constant returns to scale exist. This is similar to the duality of the technical change measures discussed in Chapter 2 if CRS exists, although this specification is in terms of the deviation from an isoquant or production function, whereas the previous discussion was in the context of shifts in the curves.

models, since output composition may be an important production characteristic distinguishing otherwise comparable production units.

With multiple outputs as well as inputs, representation of the production technology becomes a multidimensional problem, which takes all typical two-dimensional (output-output, output-input and input-input) diagrams from intermediate microeconomic theory as special cases or two-dimensional "slices" of the full multidimensional function. These various perspectives or "spaces" are captured in standard diagrams of production possibility curves (Y_1/Y_2 space), production functions (Y_1/v_1 space), and isoquants (v_1/v_2 space), where the Y_m are components of the output vector **Y** and v_j are components of the input vector **v**.

Figures (10a,b,c) represent these cases.[143] The production possibility frontier (PPF) in Figure 10a represents the actual real output produced with given input levels as A, and the most output possible with these inputs (and, of course, the observed output composition so we are on a ray from the origin) as B. The technical efficiency measure therefore, in geometric terms, is 0A/0B (which will lie between zero and one).

Similarly, in terms of the familiar one-output/one-input production function (P.F.), the same notion can be represented by DA/DB in Figure 10b. In reverse, the question of how little input can be used to produce the given output level is answered by finding point E given the level of Y, so the technical efficiency is FA/FE in this diagram (which will exceed one).

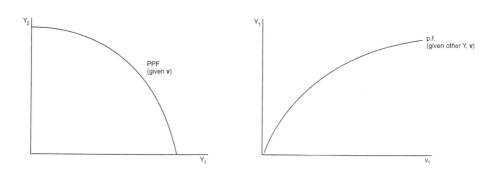

Figure 10a,b. "Spaces" for output-output (PPF) and output-input (P.F.) relationships

---

[143] This treatment follows Coelli and Perelman [1996]. Similar diagrams and more formal discussion in terms of Euclidean distances, etc., are contained in the many more technical surveys of this literature, including Lovell [1993] and Greene [1993].

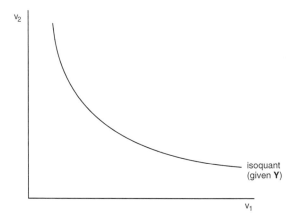

Figure 10c . Input-input (isoquant) space

This input-perspective is more naturally expressed by the isoquant diagram in Figure 10c, where point A shows the least input (given input composition) that could be used to produce the given output level Y_1 (where B is the actual input use). This is the basis for the input-side technical efficiency measure 0B/0A (which will by construction be bounded by one and infinity). The output-oriented question can also implicitly be represented by this diagram (given the production function that implicitly underlies the isoquant map in this diagram) as 0A/0B, where B shows the maximum output from use of the observed inputs, Y_2.

As already noted, in a multi-output/multi-input case all of these diagrams can be thought of as slices along a particular two dimensions of the multidimensional relationship. The full relationship can be represented by the transformation function T, where $0=T(\mathbf{v},\mathbf{Y})$ reflects the production frontier or boundary in terms of the input vector $\mathbf{v}$ and output vector $\mathbf{Y}$ (which becomes $0 = \overline{Y}\text{-}Y(\mathbf{v})$ for a one-output production function).

Alternatively, this information can be represented in terms of the output set of the technology, $F(\mathbf{v})$ – the set of all output vectors $\mathbf{Y}$ which can be produced using the input vector $\mathbf{v}$. This set is the basis for the distance function used in Lovell *et al* [1994], Grosskopf *et al* [1997], and Coelli and Perelman [1996]. The output-oriented distance function $D_O(\mathbf{v},\mathbf{Y})$ is defined as the proportion of actual output to its maximum level according to $F(\mathbf{v})$.

The underlying notion is that $F(\mathbf{v})$ is like a multidimensional production function, and the distance function represents the distance from its frontier. If the firm's output $\mathbf{Y}$ is on the production set or transformation boundary the distance function is equal to one (there is no "distance" from the frontier).

If **Y** is instead within the function (by definition it is impossible to transcend the boundary) the distance of the functional value from one indicates the extent of the firm falls short of the technological "ideal" or best practice use of technology. This distance therefore represents the technical inefficiency of the firm – which, for an output perspective is a summary version of the 0A/0B measures developed diagrammatically above.

If defined in terms of only one output, and with $D_O=1$, the distance function collapses to a standard production function. Thus, all the developments in this chapter also apply to this more restricted model. Also, interpretations of the parameters of the function, in terms of marginal products for example, are largely retained from more standard microeconomic models based on one aggregate output.

That is, in previous chapters we have said that $Z_k=p_k$ in equilibrium, where Z_k is the cost-side shadow value of input x_k ($\partial VC/\partial x_k$), so any deviation between the implicit (economic or shadow) and market valuation of x_k indicates the extent of input fixity or other constraints. From the primal side a similar optimality condition implies that $VMP_j=MP_j \bullet p_Y = p_j$ for any input v_j (where MP_j is the marginal product of input j, $\partial Y/\partial v_j$, and VMP_j is the value of the marginal product). Thus, if the marginal product can be estimated and the price of output is known, the deviation between $MP_j \bullet p_Y$ and p_j may also be used to determine the deviation from optimum use of v_j.

Note, however, that with multiple outputs the definition of the marginal product, as well as that of the relevant output price, must be addressed carefully. Also, since the technology-based distance function does not assume any type of behavioral optimization, the interpretation of this deviation is not obvious. The deviation could arise from many types of technological or behavioral factors affecting the ability to optimize in a profit maximizing (or cost minimizing) manner.

Similarly, if inefficiency appears to exist in the overall model (D_O differs significantly from one) the model structure is insufficient to determine whether identifiable characteristics of the production process, such as short run fixities, might be driving this evidence of inefficiency. Only with as complete a structural model of the technology (and behavior) as possible might one be able to determine whether some identifiable production characteristic underlies the evidence of inefficiency. Recognizing differential and observable environmental factors that may affect firms' relative behavior would also facilitate interpretation of measured inefficiency.

Empirical implementation of this model in a stochastic framework, which is our focus here, allows noise from errors in data to be accommodated, as well as inference to be made from standard errors. Even without the addition of a white noise error to the model in (8.1), however, various methods may be used to approximate u_i for empirical implementation.

As noted in Coelli [1995a] and discussed more in Coelli, Rao and Battese [1998], Afriat [1972] for example assumed that the u_i "errors" had a gamma distribution and used maximum likelihood estimation to estimate the technical efficiency term. Schmidt [1976] expanded on this by considering exponential and half-normal distributions as alternative assumptions for the distribution of the u_i variables. The possibility that "corrected ordinary least squares" (COLS) may be used for such a model was raised by Richmond [1974]. This technique, which essentially pushes an ordinary least squares (OLS) estimated model up so that the intercept allows the curve to become a bounding function rather than being fitted through the data, provides unbiased estimates of the slope coefficients. Maximum likelihood techniques may also be used to estimate a stochastic version of the model, as discussed in more detail in the next section.

Accommodating the possibility of technical inefficiency by additional stochastic structure (error terms) in frontier models precludes a complete structural deterministic specification of the technology and behavior, since too many production components need to be identified. However, *determinants* of the technological base (arguments of the function representing the technology) and also of the apparent inefficiency may be built into these models, as developed below. Thus, with care, quite a bit of explanatory power may be incorporated into the frontier models.

Note also, however, that additional explanatory power from increased complexity of the model of the technology may reduce the measured inefficiency, since more factors are allowed to provide "explanations" of the patterns. Expanding the potential of the model to represent substitutability by using a flexible functional form, for example, allows the estimated frontiers to be more malleable and thus explain some potential evidence of inefficiency through differential substitution patterns.

Thus, although functional form assumptions must be imposed for parametric estimation of the technological and production structure, the restrictiveness of these assumptions is minimized when using a flexible functional form (particularly for a distance function model that allows the specification of multiple outputs and thus output composition changes). Similarly, including technical change or other environmental factors as arguments allows the data to distinguish movements toward (or away from) the function from shifts in the function, thus increasing the possibility that firms in a certain "state of nature" will be seen to be on the frontier.[144]

---

[144] Morrison, Johnston and Frengley [1998] for example found that deregulation in New Zealand did not seem to affect inefficiency, but instead changed the economic climate facing farmers sufficiently that the entire technological frontier shifted. The farmers appear to have been operating at close to optimal technical efficiently both before and after

Inefficiency determinants may also be incorporated into econometric models to allow explanations of measured deviations from the technological frontier.

Careful consideration of the different factors affecting efficiency, and how they might be determinants of the technology as compared to efficiency, is therefore important not only for explanatory power but also appropriate interpretation of the model and resulting measures. In particular, one would think that in most cases when markets are working technological efficiency would be encouraged by economic factors. If not, we would ideally like to identify what "failure" of market forces is causing observed inefficiency.

2.   EMPIRICAL SPECIFICATION

The first questions that arise for empirical implementation of frontier production models, as for most types of parametric economic analysis, are what type of function to use for representation of the technology (and possibly behavior), and what kind of functional form to assume. Then, since frontier analysis fundamentally focuses on the error structure, the stochastic specification of the model and required distributional assumptions become important to consider in more depth than we have for other models which are typically estimated using standard single- or systems- estimation techniques.

We have addressed the first question to some extent above. First, primal representations of the technology, rather than dual models of the technology and behavior, are typically used for frontier analysis. This is largely due to difficulties of identifying the additional stochastic or error structure underlying allocative inefficiency, within a full model of the production structure and technical inefficiency, as discussed more in the next section.

If a primal perspective is used, however, in many cases multiple outputs are important to represent, which suggests that a distance rather than production function is preferred for analysis. The use of a distance function to represent inefficiency may most clearly be elaborated by assuming a particular functional form and working through the manipulations required to generate an empirically implementable model.

As noted above, many researchers in this area (such as Battese and Coelli [1992, 1995]) use the Cobb-Douglas (CD) functional form for estimation of production frontiers. However, it is particularly important in a multi-output, multi-input context (if sufficient degrees of freedom are available) not to put a priori restrictions on the relationships between inputs or outputs, since such restrictions constrain the representation of substitutability.

---

the shift, given the differing incentives in the two different states of nature. Deregulation thus affected output (and to some extent input) composition, but not technical efficiency.

That is, flexibility is needed to capture the various possible curvatures of functional relationships in the different output and input "spaces" or dimensions, rather than imposing restrictions such as the rectangular hyperbola isoquants of the CD form.[145] Thus, a flexible representation of the technology that allows for input and output substitution and the impacts of environmental variables (such as regulation) within the function, and embodies theoretically required (monotonicity, homogeneity and curvature) conditions on the function, is desirable as a basis for empirical implementation of the model.

One functional form that has become quite popular in this literature is the Zellner-Revankar generalized production function (see Forsund and Hjalmarson [1979] and Kumbhakar, Ghosh and McGukin [1991]), that allows for differing returns to scale across firms. The more common translog (TL) functional form has also been used for a number of studies (Lovell *et al* [1994], Grosskopf *et al* [1997], Coelli and Perelman [1996], and Morrison, Johnston and Frengley [1998] in the distance function context, and Greene [1980] and others for production functions).

The TL function has desirable flexibility properties since it is a second-order expansion of the CD. The incorporation of second-order (interaction- or cross-) terms across arguments of the function accommodates differential substitution across inputs (and outputs for the distance function) and allows for scale and potentially technical change (with panel data) and regulatory biases, without restrictive assumptions about the shape of the technological relationships. The log-linear form also permits the distance, and thus the one-sided inefficiency error, to be separated from the function additively.

The disadvantage of this higher level of parameterization is that degrees of freedom and possibly multicollinearity problems may arise with small data sets, especially when the cross-section is limited. These problems are reduced when behavioral optimization is assumed which allows for specification of a system of equations representing profit maximizing choices (as discussed for the production function case in Chapter 11). However, stochastic production frontier techniques are typically most readily applicable to single equation models, due to problems allocating the inefficiency "error" across input and output choices, as discussed further in the next section in the context of dual models.

In addition, the intuition of the distance function model is not simple to motivate even without further complications from a flexible functional form.

---

[145] As discussed in Klein [1953] and noted in Coelli and Perelman [1996], this is also implied for outputs, which violates curvature assumptions since production possibility frontiers such as those in figure 10a will by construction have the same shape as the isoquants in Figure 10c.

Thus, for this chapter we will for simplicity develop the representation of the distance function in terms of the CD functional form.[146]

The CD distance function with M outputs and J inputs and for I firms is:

$$8.2) \ \ln D_{Oi} = \alpha_0 + \Sigma_m \ \alpha_m \ \ln Y_{mi} + \Sigma_j \ \beta_j \ \ln v_{ji} + \Sigma_b \ \gamma_b \ r_{bi}$$

where "O" indicates an output-oriented distance function, and **r** is a vector of B exogenous variables (potentially including a technical change or trend term t, and any other environmental variables which may affect the production technology rather than provide evidence of inefficiency).

Economic theory requires certain regularity conditions to hold for this function (as discussed in more detail in Chapter 11), including homogeneity of degree one in outputs (since we are specifying this function with an output orientation rather than an input requirement frontier perspective, which would imply homogeneity of degree one in inputs). This condition requires the constraint $\Sigma_m \ \alpha_m = 1$.[147]

As in Lovell *et al* [1994], we impose this constraint by normalizing the function by one of the outputs. This procedure is justified by the the the fact that homogeneity implies:

$$8.3a) \ \ D_O(\mathbf{v}, \omega \mathbf{Y}) = \omega D_O(\mathbf{v}, \mathbf{Y}) \text{ for any } \omega > 0 \ ,$$

so, if ω is set arbitrarily at $1/Y_1$,

$$8.3b) \ D_O(\mathbf{v}, \mathbf{Y}/Y_1) = D_O(\mathbf{v}, \mathbf{Y})/Y_1 \ .$$

Thus, (8.2) becomes:

$$8.2') \ \ln D_{Oi}/Y_{1i} = \alpha_0 + \Sigma_m \ \alpha_m \ \ln Y'_{mi} + \Sigma_j \ \beta_j \ \ln v_{ji} + \Sigma_b \ \gamma_b \ r_{bi}$$

where now the summation sign over m implies summing only the M-1 outputs not used for normalization, since $Y'_{mi} = Y_{mi}/Y_{1i}$ and thus $Y'_{1i} = 1$ ($\ln Y'_{1i} = 0$). Note also that if M=1, as suggested above, this function reduces to the standard one-output CD function.

---

[146] Since the CD may be generalized to a translog function by including cross-terms for all arguments of the function the following treatment follows through analogously for the TL, although the first (logarithmic) derivatives underlying the "marginal products" are functions of the data and parameters rather than just parameters.

[147] For the translog form these restrictions are: $\Sigma_m \ \beta_m = 1$, $\Sigma_n \ \beta_{mn} = 0$, $\Sigma_b \ \gamma_{mb} = 0$, $\Sigma_m \ \beta_{km} = 0$ for homogeneity and $\beta_{mn} = \beta_{nm}$ and $\beta_{kl} = \beta_{lk}$ for symmetry, where m,n denote the outputs, k,l the inputs, and b the environmental variables.

The next question involves the stochastic nature of the problem. As briefly discussed in the previous section, this is a more complex issue than in more typical econometric implementation where adding a normal error term allows the function to be fitted through the data. Frontier estimation by definition implies a one-sided technical inefficiency "error"; one cannot exceed the maximum possible output level. This draws more attention to the stochastic or econometric specification for these models than we have addressed for our models in previous chapters.

In the deterministic (technical) efficiency literature the one-sided error term u_i, is generally assumed to have a half-normal or gamma distribution (although some studies have assumed an exponential distribution). As noted in the previous section, if such a model is estimated parametrically it is often implemented by corrected ordinary least squares (COLS), which essentially shifts the estimated frontier up from the ordinary least squares (OLS) case until it is a bounding instead of fitted function. Lovell *et al* [1994] and Grosskopf *et al* [1997] use variants on this method to estimate the distance function; this is discussed as an alternative in Coelli and Perelman [1996].[148]

However, deterministic specifications are limiting in a very important sense; problems in the data from errors in data generation or different reporting practices across DMUs, or other "white noise" from various sources, will have an impact on the estimation of the frontier. Such noise in the data can generate very misleading results, particularly if it causes outliers which could tend to position and shape the frontier in perverse ways, since in deterministic models (of production and distance functions) all deviations from the frontier are assumed to be due to technical efficiency.

Some relief from this problem may be obtained by "screening" the data beforehand to identify and adapt or purge outliers. For example, Timmer [1971] suggested dropping a particular percentage of firms closest to the frontier and re-estimating to determine the sensitivity to outliers. Others researchers simply delete observations that appear uninterpretable. Such arbitrary methods, however, seem "second-best" to allowing for white noise within the estimating procedure by using stochastic methods. Using stochastic techniques also permits the estimation of standard errors and tests of hypotheses that are precluded by the deterministic methods because certain maximum likelihood regularity conditions are violated (See Schmidt [1976] and Coelli *et al* [1998]).

---

[148] As noted above, a number of alternative estimation techniques may be used. Nonparametric piece-wise linear frontiers may be estimated by linear programming methods, which is the focus of many of the Färe references provided in this chapter. Their parametric equivalents are used in Forsund and Hjalmarson [1979]. Nonparametric frontiers may be estimation using FDH (see Deprins *et al* [1984]).

Stochastic production frontier models are typically attributed to Aigner, Lovell and Schmidt [1977] and Meeusen and van den Broeck [1977]. These models have two error terms – one to account for technical inefficiency ($-u_i$) and another (v_i) to accommodate other factors that might generate irrelevant noise in the results such as measurement error (including that involved for individual firms from mistakes in or inattention to record-keeping) and unobserved inputs. The v_i are usually assumed to be well approximated by a normal distribution, as is standard in econometric studies ignoring the u_i error term such as those we have alluded to in previous chapters.

Estimation of these models is often by maximum likelihood (ML) techniques.[149] These methods may be preferable to other possibilities such as the variant of the COLS method suggested by Richmond [1974], since ML estimates are asymptotically more efficient. This is evident empirically when sample sizes are large or measured inefficiencies substantive.[150] Although numerical solutions for the likelihood are required, so ML is more computationally demanding than COLS, this problem has become less of a binding constraint with the availability of econometric packages such as FRONTIER (Coelli [1994]), and LIMDEP (Greene [1992]).

A common criticism of the parametric models is that there is no clear justification for specification of any particular distributional form for the u_i. In particular, functional forms such as the half-normal have a mode at zero, and therefore *a priori* imply inefficiency impacts have the highest probability of falling in the neighborhood of zero. However, it may well be that there are a few efficient firms and many inefficient firms. In any case, as for any other functional form assumption, one would want the data to instead dictate what the shape of the relevant inefficiency distribution would be.

The half-normal and gamma distributions used extensively in the early literature have been extended to more general distributional forms such as the truncated-normal (Stevenson [1980]) and two-parameter gamma (Greene [1990]). These functional forms allow for a wider range of distributional shapes, and permit non-zero modes, but are computationally more complex.

Another problem with this treatment is that there is no direct specification of what underlies the technical inefficiency. A common procedure to identify determinants of inefficiency in this literature is to compute inefficiency "scores" for the DMU's and then to regress these in a second-stage on potential firm-specific environmental variables that may be possible determinants (see, for example, Pitt and Lee [1981]).

---

[149] See Coelli and Perelman [1996] and Hetemaki [1996a,b] for the distance function case, and Coelli [1995a] for a brief but comprehensive discussion of the underlying literature.

[150] This is indicated by, for example, the Monte Carlo experiments done in Olsen, Schmidt and Waldman [1980] and Coelli [1995b].

This is, however, not consistent in terms of stochastic specification. If in the first stage inefficiency effects are assumed independently and identically distributed, whereas in the second stage they are assumed to be a function of firm-specific characteristics, the two assumptions are contradictory. This type of inconsistency was recognized, and adaptations provided, in Kumbhakar *et al* [1991], and Reifschneider and Stevenson [1991].

It is thus preferable to generalize the distribution assumptions on the u_i error, as well as to build determinants of technical inefficiency directly into the model rather than doing a two-stage procedure. Stochastic models incorporating determinants of technical inefficiency directly have been developed by Kumbhakar, Ghosh and McGukin [1991], Reifschneider and Stevenson [1991] and Huang and Liu [1994], and have been extended to accommodate panel data by Battese and Coelli [1995].[151] These models make specific assumptions about both the form and arguments of the u_i error term. It becomes a function of environmental variables and thus has a more general shape than allowed by a simple distributional assumption.

Incorporating both the symmetric error (noise) term and the asymmetric (inefficiency) term with its determinants, first involves rewriting the distance or technical inefficiency measure ln (D_{Oi}) as $-u_i$, and adding the combined error term $w_i = v_i - u_i$ to the CD function defined in terms of $-\ln Y_{1i}$:

$$8.4)\ -\ln Y_{1i} = \alpha_0 + \Sigma_m\, \alpha_m\, \ln Y'_{mi} + \Sigma_j\, \beta_j\, \ln v_{ji} + \Sigma_b\, \gamma_b\, r_{bi} + v_i + u_i$$

as in Coelli and Perelman [1996] for the translog case.

The resulting stochastic CD distance function can then be estimated by maximum likelihood (ML) assuming standard distributional assumptions for the v_i and u_i terms are appropriate. The v_i are random variables assumed to be i.i.d. (independently and identically distributed) $N(0,\sigma_v^2)$.[152] The u_i are nonnegative random variables independently distributed as truncations at zero of the $N(m_i,\sigma_U^2)$ distribution, where $m_i = z_{it}\delta$, z_{it} is a px1 vector of determinants of an individual firms's efficiency (firm-specific characteristics), and δ is a 1xp vector of parameters to be estimated (as in Battese and Coelli [1995]).[153] Thus, for example, both technical change and

---

[151] These procedures have been automated in the FRONTIER package available from Tim Coelli. Coelli also has developed a package to do nonparametric DEA estimation.

[152] There is some potential for confusion here when distinguishing between v_i or v_{ji} and v_i. Since I have used the notation v_j for variable input j in previous sections, I have maintained that convention in this chapter. However, the white noise error in a stochastic frontier model is typically denoted v_i. I have instead used the notation v_i for this two-sided error to be similar to the standard notation and yet limit notational problems.

[153] Another potential notational difficulty arises for the z-variables. Since these firm-specific environmental variables are typically denoted z_i, I have used this notation here. These

time-varying technical inefficiency effects may be incorporated in the model by including a time trend in both the CD and m(•) functions.

Although the predicted value of the distance function (inefficiency) is not directly observable since it is contained in the combined error term w_i, estimates may be obtained using a modification of the conditional expectations formulas in Battese and Coelli [1988] and Coelli and Perelman [1996]. These methods also permit the use of unbalanced panels for estimation of (8.4), as developed by Battese, Coelli and Colby [1989].

Various tests for different forms of both the technological and stochastic specifications may be carried out in this framework. If, for example, the more complex TL functional specification is used to approximate the technological relationship, the importance of including the second order terms may be evaluated by determining their joint significance. If only the first order terms are significant, the CD seems a justifiable assumption (although this criteria is rarely met in practice). Also, constant returns to scale may be tested by imposing homogeneity of degree -1 in inputs and determining whether this is a justifiable constraint.[154] Either of these tests may be carried out using the log-likelihood value from the estimated models.

The stochastic model specification also nests some more restrictive earlier models as special cases. If z_i is simply a constant term, the model becomes equivalent to the truncated normal specification in Stevenson [1980], and Battese and Coelli [1988]. If instead all parameters in the inefficiency function (the δs) are equal to zero, the model collapses to the half-normal specification in Aigner *et al* [1977]. In reverse, additional z-variables are added to the m(•) function to reflect interactions between the farm characteristics and input variables, the model becomes a non-neutral stochastic frontier model similar to that in Huang and Liu [1994].

One more stochastic issue that should be raised briefly has to do with the use of cross-section as compared to panel data. By construction, frontier models involve consideration of micro units, or at least a cross-section of different (but assumed technologically similar) sub-sectors that can be compared to determine their efficiency given a particular technology. Using cross-section time-series (panel) data raises some econometric issues. But it also has advantages in terms of facilitating the consistency of estimators, reducing the importance of distributional assumptions on the u_i, eliminating the requirement that inefficiencies are independent of the regressors, and allowing separate identification of technical change and efficiency.

---

variables should not be confused with the shadow value notation Z_k. Note also that these variables are in some sense similar to our r_b variables, since they represent environmental factors. However, in this case they are firm-specific factors that are assumed to directly impact measured inefficiency, rather than the technological patterns.

[154] This results in a model of the form $-\ln Y_{1it} + \ln v_{1it} = f(\mathbf{Y'}, \mathbf{v'}, \mathbf{r})$

As alluded to above, writing the model in terms of a panel simply involves adding t subscripts representing time periods to the i subscripts representing the firm. Such a model is conceptually similar to the cross-sectional specification. The econometric extension to allow for panel data is developed in Pitt and Lee [1981].

As summarized in Coelli *et al* [1998], consistent estimation of the u_i terms is facilitated as the number of time periods in the sample increase. With panel data, however, it should also be recognized that technical inefficiency may be time-dependent, particularly if learning takes place, which was often ignored in early panel data applications.

Kumbhakar [1990] refined the model to allow such time dependencies, such that $u_{it} = [1 + \exp(bt + ct^2)]^{-1}u_i$, u_i is assumed to have a half-normal distribution and b and c are estimable parameters. An alternative to this, where $u_{it}=[\exp\{-\eta(t-T)\}]u_i$, where u_i is assumed to have a truncated normal distribution and η is a parameter, was provided in Battese and Coelli [1992].

Finally, since the distance function specification is somewhat different than traditional production or input requirement functions, it is useful to overview how the resulting parameter estimates may be interpreted. As noted above, measures similar to (proportional or logarithmic) marginal products from a CD production function may be computed for a distance function model. Although we will postpone more rigorous discussion of the duality underlying the distance function and thus the formal interpretation of output shadow values to Chapter 9, we can briefly elaborate this here.

First let us consider the input coefficients, since they are the most closely analogous to those from estimation of a production function. For the CD function, the input v_j coefficient (β_{vj}) generally represents (in proportionate or share terms) the shape of a production function in v_j-aggregate Y space via the derivative $\partial\ln Y/\partial\ln v_j = \partial Y/\partial v_j \bullet (v_j/Y)$ (holding all other arguments of the function fixed). In the distance function context this may be written as $\partial\ln Y_1/\partial\ln v_j = \partial Y_1/\partial v_j \bullet (v_j/Y_1)$. Since the right-hand-side output variables Y'_m are expressed in relative terms, this implies increasing Y_1 with Y_m/Y_1 fixed, and thus increasing overall output. Note, however, that since the left-hand variable is typically written as $-\ln Y_1$, the sign should be the opposite in the distance function framework; a negative β_{vj} estimate would be expected.

The resulting implications are similar to those resulting from coefficient estimates of a CD production function; a (negative) estimated coefficient β_{vj} may be interpreted as the "returns" to input v_j, or as its impact on, or contribution to, production. Similarly, if squared terms $(\ln v_j)^2$ are included in the function, the associated coefficients β_{vjvj} provide information about the curvature of the production function in v_j-Y space – whether returns are positive and increasing, or decreasing. The latter would be expected, although with a multi-output and multi-input function, this is not obvious.

Cross-terms with other inputs or outputs might also be included if more flexibility of the function seemed appropriate. Such parameters would indicate interactions or substitutability or complementarity (jointness). For example if a cross term between inputs v_1 and v_2, β_{v1v2}, had a positive estimate, this would imply that the (negative) return to v_1 increases with increases, in v_2, or the absolute value of the proportional marginal product drops, suggesting the v_1 and v_2 are technological substitutes. The reverse would indicate a complementary relationship or jointness.

Interpretation of the Y_m-terms is somewhat more complex, since these arguments of the function are specified in relative terms. However, as suggested by Figure 10a, the first order coefficients β_{ym} reflect the trade-off of Y_1 and Y_m as embodied in a PPF (given all input levels).[155] That is, these terms directly measure the impact of a change in Y_m/Y_1 on Y_1; α_{ym} $= \partial \ln Y_1 / \partial \ln Y'_m = \partial \ln Y_1 / \partial \ln (Y_m/Y_1)$. This can be rewritten to more clearly capture the Y_m-Y_1 relationship represented by the PPF..

Say we have a PPF with Y_m/Y_1 and Y_1 on the axes. Using the quotient rule, this implies that the slope of the function in this "space" would be: $\partial(Y_m/Y_1)/\partial Y_1 = 1/Y_1 \cdot (\partial Y_m/\partial Y_1 - Y_m/Y_1)$.[156] Multiplying this by $Y_1/(Y_m/Y_1)$ $= Y_1^2/Y_m$ to characterize this in proportionate terms, we obtain: $\partial \ln (Y_m/Y_1)/\partial \ln Y_1 = \partial \ln Y_m/\partial \ln Y_1 - 1$. However, this is still in inverse form; we want instead to provide an interpretation for the estimated coefficient $\alpha_{Ym} = \partial \ln Y_1 / \partial \ln (Y_m/Y_1)$. To accomplish this, we use the relationship $\partial \ln(Y_m/Y_1)/\partial \ln Y_1 = 1/[\partial \ln Y_1/\partial \ln (Y_m/Y_1)]$. This suggests we can obtain the inverse and then construct the expression for $\partial \ln Y_m/\partial \ln Y_1 = 1 + \partial \ln(Y_m/Y_1)/\partial \ln Y_1 = 1 + 1/[\partial \ln Y_1/\partial \ln(Y_m/Y_1)] = 1 + 1/\alpha_{Ym}$, or $\partial \ln Y_1/\partial \ln Y_m = 1/(\partial \ln Y_m/\partial \ln Y_1) = [1/(1+1/\alpha_{Ym})]$.

These somewhat complex manipulations indicate that the logarithmic first derivative (parameter for the CD) for an output provides information about the (absolute value of the) slope of the PPF, and therefore the "contribution" of Y_m to overall production. The interpretation in terms of the slope of the PPF is not direct, however. The coefficient representing the slope of the PPF in Y_m-Y_1 space is somewhat smaller than in Y'_m-Y_1 space, but maintains the same sign, relative coefficient values and statistical significance as those directly obtained from the α_{Ym} values (if they are in the appropriate range of 0 to 1). They are therefore *representative* of the slope of the PPF (in absolute value).

---

[155] Note again that the $-\ln Y_1$ term on the left hand side of (8.4) causes these terms to be positive rather than negative as would be suggested by the slope of the PPF. If $\ln Y_1$ is used instead of $-\ln Y_1$ as the dependent variable, therefore, both the input "marginal product" and output "contribution" or PPF slope will have more intuitive signs.

[156] From the quotient rule for differentiation we can derive $\partial(Y_m/Y_1)/\partial Y_1 = ((\partial Y_m/\partial Y_1) \cdot Y_1 - Y_m)/Y_1^2 = (1/Y_1) \cdot (\partial Y_m/\partial Y_1 - Y_m/Y_1)$.

Thus, the larger the α_{Ym} estimate, the more Y_1 must be reduced to accommodate an increase in Y_m at given input levels. A smaller value may imply more "jointness" – less tradeoff required, or a "flatter" PPF overall. However, it also may be interpreted as being close to the Y_1 axis, so the contribution to output of Y_1 is large relative to Y_m.

Cross-terms with respect to the Y_m variables, such as those with other outputs, inputs, or r_b-variables may be interpreted as the effect these variables have on the trade-off between Y_1 and Y_m; they indicate how the contribution of Y_m to total output changes. An impact that increases the "marginal product" of Y_m ($\partial \ln Y_1 / \partial \ln Y'_m$) suggests increasing the share, or contribution to output, of Y_m. This emphasizes that the "returns to" or "contributions of" the inputs and outputs provided by the first order CD term may be adapted in a more flexible model to include these cross effects for a full evaluation of these returns and their determinants.

Note again that these "marginal products" may be used similarly to shadow values of inputs and outputs. They may be compared with price data to determine optimality if such market price data is available. That is, if optimization is correct we will observe $VMP_j = p_j$, where $VMP_j = \partial Y / \partial v_j \bullet p_Y$. Since, for example, the CD parameter β_{vj} represents $\partial \ln Y / \partial \ln v_j = \partial Y / \partial v_j \bullet (v_j / Y)$, so $\partial Y / \partial v_j = \beta_{vj} \bullet (Y / v_j)$, the "test" of optimality becomes whether the "shadow value" $\beta_{vj} \bullet (Y / v_j) \bullet p_Y$ is equal to p_j. Similar (but clearly more complex) manipulations may be carried out to determine the shadow values of the outputs, as discussed further in the next chapter.

3.   DUAL MODELS

Dual models have provided the focus for most of this text, since they allow direct modeling of input choice behavior and thus responsiveness. In this chapter we have instead primarily discussed the specification and estimation of models of the technological structure, via production or distance function models.

Most models in the frontier literature follow this route since it is difficult to put structure on the behavioral relationships, and therefore identify allocative as well as technical efficiency, when at the same time focusing on the stochastic or econometric structure – to measure a second error term u_i. Also, in cross-sectional data appropriate (and varying) prices across DMUs may not be possible to measure, which makes a specification focusing on input and output quantity levels, rather than prices, more attractive.

In addition, in many cases when stochastic frontier methods are used, the application is to DMUs in sectors where market forces may not operate effectively, and therefore identifiable inefficiencies might well appear.

For example, frontier methods have been applied to service industries such as education (see Grosskopf *et al* 1997 for one example), banking (Ferrier and Lovell [1990]), and hospitals (Morrison [1998f]), regulated industries such as airlines (Kumbhakar [1992]), and agriculture in developing countries (Battese and Coelli [1992]). In such cases the behavioral assumption of cost minimization (or profit maximiation for a profit function specification or systems of equations based on a production function) may be invalid.

The use of technology-based models for such applications is sometimes rationalized by appealing to the idea that firms optimize in terms of expected future costs or profits, which will not necessarily be reflected in actual realized values. That is, although direct estimation of the production function will result in biased and inconsistent estimates of the parameters if the usual behavioral assumption of cost minimization (or profit maximization) apply, if firms are instead optimizing in terms of *expected* costs (profits) such estimation has been shown to be justifiable.[157]

In many cases, however, representation of behavior, responsiveness, and allocative (in)efficiency may be an important part of the production process to directly characterize. It is then desirable to return to our cost function specification, which may be generally expressed with the stochastic frontier error terms (for cost inefficiency) and a time trend (for panel data) as $TC(Y_i, p_i, t) + v_i + u_I$ (or with multiple outputs as $TC(\mathbf{Y}_i, \mathbf{p}_i, t) + v_i + u_i.$)[158]

Such a function is, for example, used in Schmidt and Lovell [1979] for steam-electric generating plants, using a CD representation of the cost function and both ML and COLS as alternatives estimating techniques. They also suggest estimation of a system of equations to increase the efficiency of estimation and facilitate identifying allocative inefficiency, which will appear as error terms in the input demand equations (violations of the cost minimization assumptions).

---

[157] If firms are cost minimizing, input levels are correlated with the error term. (See Zellner Kmenta and Dreze [1966].) If this aspect of production is important, however, systems estimation is necessary and identification of technical and allocative efficiency become more problematic since the link between allocative inefficiency in the cost function and input demand equations must be recognized. The technology also typically must be represented by a self-dual form, which is limiting. Input price data must be available, and variations in the prices across DMU's must be evident, which is often a problem with the cross-section data sets that often provide the basis for this type of analysis. Estimation is therefore generally accomplished via a production (or distance) instead of cost (or profit) function. See Coelli [1995a] and the references provided for more details.

[158] Note that the existence of fixed factors is not incorporated in this specification. Typically the impacts of fixed factors is picked up as "inefficiency" in these models, although recent work by Kumbhakar, and by Atkinson, as elaborated further below, generalizes models to take scale economies and utilization also into account.

This last extension is similar to our discussion of Shephard's or Hotelling's lemma discrepancies or violations, that drive deviations between the observed demand for inputs and the derivatives of the cost (profit) function with respect to their prices, or between the shadow values and market prices of inputs. In frontier models, however, typically no structure is placed on such deviations. They are simply assumed to represent "wrong" input (output) choices, or higher costs than necessary since the firm is not on its scale expansion path.

We have highlighted throughout this text the potential advantages of representing technology and behavior within a rich model of the production and cost structure. But in frontier models limitations are imposed by the necessity of identifying the technical and allocative inefficiency terms with no more information about forces underlying these deviations from the technical and cost frontiers.

Self-dual functional forms must be used for estimation, or problems may arise from the linkage between the allocative error terms and the cost function from which the input demand expressions are derived.[159] Also, numerical solutions for the complicated likelihood functions emerging from the resulting systems models may prove difficult to obtain, and no packaged program yet exists to carry out such computations.

One "fix" for this may be to estimate the cost function using single equation methods (although with a flexible functional form this is likely to cause degrees of freedom or multicollinearity problems for limited data sets). From this a cost efficiency measure $CE = \overline{TC}_i/TC_i(Y_i, \mathbf{p}_i)$ (where $\overline{TC}_i$ is actual costs and $TC_i(\bullet)$ is minimum costs) may be constructed.

If the function estimated is self-dual (like the CD), dividing this measure into its technical and allocative efficiency components involves reproducing the production function implied by the cost function parameters and calculating the technical efficiency measure $TE = \overline{Y}_i/Y(\mathbf{v}_i)$ (where the denominator reflects potential output). Allocative efficiencies are then estimated as the remaining cost inefficiency not explained by technical inefficiency, $AE = CE/TE$.

If a more complex functional form is estimated, the decomposition may still in most cases be accomplished using duality results, as suggested by Kopp and Diewert [1982] and refined by Zieschang [1983]. This involves computing a numerical solution of J-1 non-linear relations (where J is the number of inputs), which is not trivial.

---

[159] See Greene [1980], Bauer [190], Greene [1993], Ferrier and Lovell [1990] and Coelli *et al* [1998] for further discussion of these problems.

The problems of frontier estimation using dual models are difficult to side-step effectively. However, some authors have approached this problem from a more similar perspective to that used in previous chapters of this text.

In particular, in a useful set of papers, Atkinson and two co-authors (Atkinson and Halvorsen [Atkinson and Halvorsen [1990], Atkinson and Cornwell [1994, 1998] estimated systems of equations representing the cost structure. Their model represents the "inefficiencies" captured by the types of deviations from Shephard's or Hotelling's lemma we have discussed in the preceding chapters in this text, as well as representing technical and allocative inefficiency.[160]

Atkinson and Cornwell [1998] (AC) is a particularly useful example to elaborate, since it is quite comprehensive. AC use panel data to identify deviations from allocative efficiency (shadow prices differing from market prices) and from scale efficiency (marginal cost deviating from output price) in a cost function model of the U.S. airline industry. The measured inefficiencies are interpreted as arising from regulatory distortions (and monopoly power), as is often the underlying motivation in such analyses.

Although the reasons for the deviations between market and true economic internal or shadow prices are not explicitly specified, the specification and implementation of the model has clear connections with both the types of models we have been overviewing and the frontier literature. In particular, we have seen that deviations of shadow from market prices may arise from private input fixities due to adjustment costs, other spillovers or constraints arising from external or regulatory factors, and market power in both input and output markets.

In some cases we have put a specific form on the deviation, such as with an Euler adjustment cost equation for fixities, or an output demand (input supply or pricing) equation for market power. But in other cases we have left the gap or wedge unspecified. This is essentially the treatment in the Atkinson papers – the deviations are interpreted as error terms indicating allocative or scale inefficiency, and technical inefficiency is allowed for.

The Atkinson models deal with the deviation between shadow and market price by incorporating the internal instead of market price directly in the cost (or profit) function, as mentioned as a possibility in the previous chapter to represent poorly priced goods. This is based on Lau and Yotopoulos [1971], where shadow prices are specified as parametric functions of market prices. These functions are, however, nested in a cost or profit function model so if internal or shadow and observed market prices are equivalent this becomes a special case.

---

[160] Additional insights about this type of decomposition into various production/cost characteristics is provided in Kumbhakar [1992, 1997].

In the Atkinson and Cornwell [1998] study the price deviations from allocative (for inputs) and scale (for outputs) inefficiency, and potential output deviations from technical inefficiency, are parametrically estimated. The panel data used allows price inefficiency parameters to be estimated without incorporating functions of other explanatory variables, which reduces the potential for specification error but limits the interpretive power of the allocative, scale and technical efficiency measures. Although the model attempts to identify a lot of information from the data, which may be why some fairly extreme estimates of technical and scale inefficiency (interpreted as monopoly power) emerge, the framework is a rich basis for evaluation of productive and market structure.

More specifically, in this treatment the production function for firm i is assumed to be either of the form:

$$8.5a) \quad Y_i = a_i f(v_i; x_i),$$

if it is written as an output-based technical efficiency measure, or

$$8.5b) \quad Y_i = f(b_i v_{1i}, \ldots b_i v_{ji}; x_i),$$

if specified as an input-based measure, where the a_i and b_i are firm-i-specific parameters indicating the amount maximum output falls short of its potential for a given set of inputs, or the amount actual use of input j exceeds minimal use for a given output level. That is, for the output-side measure technical efficiency is represented by $Y_i/f(v_i; x_i) = a_i$, where $0 < a_i \leq 1$. Alternatively, this may be expressed in terms of all inputs (given input composition) as $v_i/b_i v_i = 1/b_i$, where again $0 < b_i \leq 1$.

The J components of the **v** vector are assumed to be variable inputs, and the K components of **x** are quasi-fixed. Fixity is incorporated here since "a long-run profit function is indeterminate except under decreasing returns to scale", so "some output must be considered quasi-fixed in the short run".[161]

Ultimately the model is estimated in terms of variable shadow costs, but since the shadow profit system encounters computational difficulties, initially it is developed in terms of shadow profits. As we have seen, adapting this to a cost function simply requires substituting the output level(s) for the output price in the profit function.

---

[161] Note that this implicitly assumes that nonconstant returns to scale do not make sense in the long run, which is consistent with the interpretation often given for a U-shaped average long run cost curve arising from "some kind of " long run fixity. Since this may not be "attached" to any particular measurable input, however – it may have to do with, say, managerial inputs that are not independently measured – the incorporation of fixities is not strictly necessary in this context.

Although the cost model implies that output is given, as we discussed in Chapter 6 one can construct a pricing equation based on the $p_Y=MC$ equality in order to build output supply (and pricing) decisions into the cost model. This is essentially the reasoning process used by AC.

Defining variable profits in terms of short run restricted profits evaluated at the marginal price of output (p_{Yi}') and variable shadow input prices $(\mathbf{p}_j')$, and using (8.5a), AC specify the general restricted shadow-profit frontier as:

8.6a) $G(p_{Yi}',\mathbf{p}_i'; \mathbf{x}_i)$

The distinction between p_{Yi}' and p_{Yi} is explicitly made in terms of market power; they state that $p_{Yi}' = \partial p/\partial Y_i \cdot Y_i + p_{Yi}$ (following Diewert [1982]). The VMP equalities are written as $a_i p_{Yi}' MP_j = p_{ji}'$, with MP_j denoting the marginal product of input j, $\partial f/\partial v_j$, from (8.5).

For estimation purposes actual observed profits must be expressed in terms of shadow prices, which requires also defining $\mathbf{p}_i'=\mathbf{K}_i\mathbf{p}_i$, where $\mathbf{K}_i$ is a JxJ diagonal matrix with elements $k_{ji}\geq 0$, and $p_{Yi}'=\delta_{Yi}p_{Yi}$. The parameters k_{ji} and δ_{Yi} therefore measure the gaps or wedges between market and shadow prices, so if they are equal to one Hotelling's lemma implications are valid and actual profits are maximized. A problem arises, however, because these parameters are not separately identifiable from the technical efficiency parameter a_i unless some additional *a priori* restrictions are imposed.

If instead (8.5b) is used to specify the shadow profit frontier, we obtain:

8.6b) $G(p_{Yi}',\mathbf{p}_i'/b_i; \mathbf{x}_i)$,

which incurs less identification problems than (8.6a) when the goal is to estimate price and technical efficiency jointly. For estimation purposes this is further adapted to a normalized shadow-profit frontier $\pi^*_i = G(q_i'/b_i;\mathbf{x}_i)$, where $q_i'=\mathbf{p}_i'/p_{Yi}'$ since one of the price inefficiency parameters is redundant. Also, b_i must be normalized to 1 for the most efficient firm, since without further restrictions some parameters are unidentified.

Estimating equations are generated by assuming a functional form for (8.6b), and using Hotelling's lemma in terms of shadow prices to construct input demand equations. A price equation similar to our shadow value equation for the quasi-fixed input(s) is also appended to the system, which allows for a test of the efficient utilization of this input(s).

For empirical tractability, this model was adapted to a cost framework as in Atkinson and Cornwell [1994]. Output choice is then represented by a $p_{Yi}'=\partial p_{Yi}/\partial Y_i \cdot Y_i + p_{Yi}$ equation (with p_{Yi}' approximated by $p_{Yi}-\delta_{Yi}$ added to the model, so δ_{Yi} becomes another parameter to be estimated), rather than a Hotelling's lemma expression with respect to the output price p_{Yi}.

This stems from defining the output-based shadow-cost equation:

8.7) $TC^*(Y_i/a_i, \mathbf{p}_i') = \min_{v_i} [\mathbf{p}_i'\mathbf{v}_i \mid f(\mathbf{v}_i) = Y_i/a_i]$,

with the associated profit-maximization problem:

8.8) $\max_{v_i} [p_{Yi}(a_i f(\mathbf{v}_i)) \bullet a_i f(\mathbf{v}_i) - \mathbf{p}_i'\mathbf{v}_i] = \max_{Y_i/ai} [p_{Yi}(Y_i) \bullet Y_i - TC^*(Y_i/a_i, \mathbf{p}_i')]$.

(or similarly for Y_i and $\mathbf{p}_i'/b_i$ with an input perspective)

In spirit this model is quite similar to the kind of specifications we have been developing, although it stems from a frontier or efficiency perspective, so "errors" assumed to arise from allocative inefficiency for inputs, and scale inefficiency for output. Also, some normalizations, and adaptation to the cost framework are necessary for identification of the different "inefficiency" measures. However, this approach provides a clear link between the duality-based "standard" econometric and efficiency specifications to evaluating production structure, productivity and efficiency.

4.   PRODUCTIVITY AND EFFICIENCY

Our index number computations of productivity growth in Chapter 2 relied on assumptions of perfect competition and correct optimization in output and input markets. That is, observed input and output prices were assumed to well approximate the associated marginal benefits and costs of an additional unit of input or output.

In previous chapters we have developed adaptations for productivity growth measures if these assumptions do not hold – if Shephard's or Hotelling's lemma is violated due to, say, fixities, external impacts without market prices, or market power. We have seen in this chapter that efficiency measurement may be interpreted similarly in the sense that there may be deviations between the true economic value of an input or output and its market price. In the efficiency literature, however, this is generally motivated in the context of deviations from true revenue maximization (or output maximization given inputs, and thus technical efficiency)[162] or cost minimization (or input minimization given outputs and input prices, and thus technical and allocative efficiency).

---

[162] Note that if this is for multiple outputs, it also assumes scale efficiency in the sense that the firm is choosing the appropriate output mix based on observed output prices as well as maximum overall output.

Index number methods have been developed in the efficiency literature that differ from standard Törnquist productivity growth measurement techniques (the traditional productivity measures we have developed with aggregate input growth as a share-weighted average of individual growth) in two important ways. The resulting measures have been called Malmquist productivity growth indexes.

These measures are based only on quantity data since information on prices is not necessary for representation of productivity growth if only technical inefficiency is assumed. Also, Malmquist indexes allow decomposition between technical change (shifts in the technological frontier) and technical efficiency change (firms getting closer to the frontier).

The indexes are based on distance functions that may be computed using either parametric or nonparametric frontier estimation methods. Panel data are, however, required to carry out such computations, whereas time series data are sufficient to compute index numbers representing the standard Solow productivity growth residual.

This is a different approach from the type of productivity growth index adaptations developed in previous chapters, where the focus was on constructing appropriate valuation (or quantity) measures for inputs and outputs to identify technical change separately from factors that cause markets to be "imperfect" or "inefficient". Such a cost perspective requires, in most cases, parametric estimation of the deviations of market prices from their true economic values, whereas the Malmquist index procedures instead veer away from pricing issues and instead deal only with quantities and technical relationships.

The Malmquist multifactor productivity (MFP) index was defined in Caves, Christensen and Diewert [1982], and used by Nishimizu and Page [1982] and Färe, Grosskopf, Norris and Zhang [1994] among others. The Nishimizu and Page study used linear programming methods to compute parametric production frontiers and measure MFP change as a combination of technical change and technical efficiency change. The Färe et al paper instead used nonparametric data envelopment analysis (DEA) techniques to construct the distance function estimates that allow identification of the two components of the index.[163]

---

[163] "Data envelopment analysis" or DEA is a popular nonparametric alternative to the stochastic frontier approach overviewed in this chapter. This technique uses linear programming techniques to trace out the frontier. Although we do not address issues pertaining to DEA analysis in this overview of inefficiency estimation methods, a number of discussions of DEA appear in the literature on efficiency and productivity. An excellent textbook treatment of both this and stochastic methods is in Coelli, Rao and Perelman [1998], where both a summary and application of these techniques is provided. More

Malmquist indexes are theoretically based on distance functions. They may be computed from either an input- or output- perspective, although we will focus here on the output approach, as in earlier sections of this chapter.

First, we can use the definition of the production set defined in the previous chapter (equation 7.9), adapted here to accommodate the more general underlying transformation function for the $\mathbf{Y}$ and $\mathbf{v}$ vectors:

8.9) $F(\mathbf{v}) = \{\mathbf{Y}: \mathbf{v} \text{ can produce } \mathbf{Y}\}$.

The distance function can formally be defined from this output set as:

8.10) $D_O(\mathbf{v},\mathbf{Y}) = \min_Y \{\Theta: (\mathbf{Y}/\Theta) \in F(\mathbf{v})\}$,

where the value of this function, as discussed above, will be equal to one if observed output $\mathbf{Y}$ is on the production frontier, and fall short of one if technical efficiency is not obtained.

As developed by Färe *et al* [1994], and overviewed in depth but less rigorously in Coelli *et al* [1998], The Malmquist MFP index calculates the ratio of the distances of each data point relative to a common technology. The Malmquist index between period 0 (the base period) and period 1 can be written as (where the M and D are output-oriented functions; the O subscript is omitted for simplicity):

8.11) $M(\mathbf{Y}_0,\mathbf{v}_0,\mathbf{Y}_1,\mathbf{v}_1) = [D^0(\mathbf{Y}_1,\mathbf{v}_1)/D^0(\mathbf{Y}_0,\mathbf{v}_0) \cdot D^1(\mathbf{Y}_1,\mathbf{v}_1)/D^1(\mathbf{Y}_0,\mathbf{v}_0)]^{1/2}$.

M is therefore a geometric mean of two MFP indexes, one with respect to the base year technology and one for the period 1 technology, where $D^0(\mathbf{Y}_1,\mathbf{v}_1)$, for example, reflects the distance from the period 1 observed output-input point to the technological frontier in the base period.

This measure can be rewritten, as discussed in Coelli *et al* [1998], to emphasize its potential decomposition into technical efficiency and technology changes, as:

8.12) $M(\mathbf{Y}_0,\mathbf{v}_0,\mathbf{Y}_1,\mathbf{v}_1)$

$$= D^1(\mathbf{Y}_1,\mathbf{v}_1)/D^0(\mathbf{Y}_0,\mathbf{v}_0) [D^0(\mathbf{Y}_1,\mathbf{v}_1)/D^1(\mathbf{Y}_1,\mathbf{v}_1) \cdot D^0(\mathbf{Y}_0,\mathbf{v}_0)/D^1(\mathbf{Y}_0,\mathbf{v}_0)]^{1/2}$$

---

rigorous and detailed treatments may be found in Grosskopf [1993] and Färe, Grosskopf and Roos [1997].

where the first term outside the square brackets (EC for "efficiency change") measures the ratio of the distance functions in the two periods measured in terms of their own observed output/input combinations and associated current technology. Thus if this measure exceeds one the firm has moved closer to the frontier; $D^1(Y_1,v_1)$ is closer to one than is $D^0(Y_0,v_0)$. This indicates an increase in MFP due to increased technical efficiency given a particular frontier. The term in the square brackets (TC for "technical change") instead measures technical change or a shift in the frontier; it is the geometric mean of the shift in technology between the two periods, evaluated at v_1 and v_0.

That is, the first expression within the brackets indicates, for the output/input combination from period 1, what the distance from the frontier would have been in the base year as compared to year 1. The denominator will always be less than or equal to one. If technical change is occurring, so the frontier is shifting out, the numerator will be greater than one if the output/input combination in period 1 were infeasible given the technology in period 0, or will be less than but closer to one than the denominator. In either case this component will exceed one.

A similar interpretation holds for the second expression within the brackets, in terms of the period 0 reference output/input combination. Thus, if M>1 overall productivity growth has been positive, combining both technical efficiency and change components.

This has been illustrated in a very useful diagrammatic form in Coelli *et al* [1998], as in Figure 11 below.[164] As they show, for a constant returns to scale (CRS) technology with a single output where the firm produces at points D and E in periods 0 and 1, the components of (8.12) may be written as $EC=(Y_1/Y_c)/(Y_0/Y_a)$ and $TC=[\{(Y_1/Y_b)/(Y_1/Y_c)\}\cdot\{(Y_0/Y_a)/Y_0/Y_b)\}]$.

The difficulty in specifying a Malmquist productivity index is therefore identifying the different component distance functions. The four distance function measures must be computed for each firm in each pair of adjacent time periods. This may be accomplished with either mathematical programming or econometric/stochastic frontier techniques.

Also, assumptions about returns to scale and the neutrality of technical change are very important for specification of these indexes. Grifell-Tatje and Lovell [1995] show, for example, that if NCRS is assumed the Malmquist index may not correctly measure MFP. The period 0 and 1 indexes are also only equivalent for neutral technical change, so, $D^1(v,Y) = A(t)\cdot D(v,Y)$ for all t (see Färe, Grosskopf and Roos [1997]).[165]

---

[164] Another very clear discussion of these models is in Gouyette and Perelman [1997].

[165] It is also worth commenting that Diewert [1992] has suggested an alternative Malmquist (Hicks-Moorsteen) MFP index that is a ratio of a Malmquist output to Malmquist input

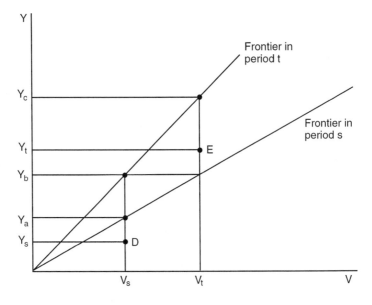

Figure 11. Malmquist Productivity Index

5.   FURTHER COMMENTS

In this chapter we have discussed the last topic related to the traditional productivity growth literature that we will address in this text. In the efficiency or frontier literature it is recognized that typical assumptions of technical and allocative efficiency may not be valid in some instances. This may particularly be the case when constraints keep firms from optimizing effectively, although if possible it would seem best to attempt to characterize these constraints more directly, rather than lumping the resulting inconsistencies from full optimization together as "inefficiency".

This literature, however, provide a very useful framework for analysis, particularly of situations where comparisons across units (firms especially, but sometimes sectors, states or regions) with similar technological processes may be made (cross-section or panel data is available). It is also especially appropriate in instances where one might not think the usual optimization assumptions are valid (such as in developing economies, sectors subject to

---

index, and thus is more similar in terms of motivation to a standard MFP index that is based on a ratio of an output to input index. Färe, Grosskopf and Roos [1997] show that this will equal the Malmquist index defined here if certain restrictions (an input-homothetic and CRS technology) prevail. Other illuminating characteristics of this index are also developed in this survey paper.

regulatory constraints, and service or public industries), or when restrictions such as regulatory constraints are not directly observable or measurable.

Discussion of these models has also highlighted the usefulness in some instances of functions that are not standard fare for most students in microeconomic theory classes, such as distance functions. The distance function is particularly useful for situations in which the technological framework is the focus of analysis, price information may be unavailable, and multiple outputs are important.[166]

As for any of the modeling and measuring methods we have discussed in this text, this framework has its advantages and disadvantages; it can do some things and cannot do others. Although great strides have been made in the recent literature, for example, to address issues of distributional and functional form assumptions, limitations of inefficiency models remain an issue. Identification of efficiency separately from other production structure characteristics is also at times difficult, particular when allocative efficiency is the focus of analysis, due to the emphasis on the stochastic structure.

Finally, it should be emphasized that anything that is not modeled in the technological representation may appear as inefficiency. For example, short run fixities or regulatory constraints may affect input or output composition directly. Quality differences across firms might also cause measured output and input levels to differ across firms.

Quality or compositional problems are therefore particularly critical for this type of analysis. However, it is unclear whether one would want to treat the resulting measures, stemming from these types of production characteristics, as evidence of "inefficiency". The empirical results of such analysis should therefore be interpreted with care.

We now move on to the second section of this text. Until now we have looked at various inter-twined literatures focusing on the measurement of economic performance of economic entities – from firms to countries. We have discussed issues raised in the traditional productivity, hedonics, duality, externalities/macro, market power/IO, regulation, and efficiency literatures.

In the following chapters we will step back to overview the foundations of these models in more depth. We will discuss the duality theory underlying the models we have been outlining, and the econometric implications, data construction questions, and other issues that are necessary to "get a handle on" in order to understand how to construct, implement and interpret models of production processes and performance.

---

[166] Other variants on this functional relationship and a more rigorous treatment of both the output and input distance functions, is contained in Färe, and Primont [1995].

Chapter 9

Underlying Theory and Implementation Issues

In previous chapters we developed a production theory framework for the analysis of production and productivity growth and linked it to a number of related literatures, including not only the traditional productivity, but also the macro, IO, and efficiency literatures. This framework highlights the linkages between different aspects of productivity that must be unraveled to present a detailed and interpretable picture of the impacts and responses that determine economic performance.

Moving toward empirical identification of these various performance aspects involves, however, a number of issues that we have so far largely swept under the rug. The first of these we need to address is the underlying theoretical justification for development and use of such a model. Problems involved in constructing appropriate data also need to be considered. Further specification questions involve determining the relevant function to represent the characteristics of the productive unit to be analyzed, making assumptions about functional forms, and confronting issues of stochastic structure and econometric estimation. The remainder of this text is devoted to addressing these issues in turn.

More specifically, our cost-based production theory model, founded on the neoclassical framework represented by typical intermediate microeconomics diagrams but generalized to represent additional dimensions of technological and market structure, summarizes many production characteristics underlying economic performance. However, the multi-dimensional nature of such a model, plus the multitude of changes occurring at any one time in observed real-word data, stresses the need to directly implement the full model in order to quantify the different "pieces of the puzzle" we have been targeting. Only then can we impute, or draw out independently, the impacts of any one change from the overall trends, which is the type of comparative statics experiment we typically wish to conduct.

For example, distinguishing technical change (a shift in the production function) from scale economies (embodied in the shape of the production and thus cost structure) and markups (from output and input market structure) is not possible to accomplish through direct data manipulation.

Similarly, input-specific impacts of technical change, which depend on the "twist" of an isoquant as it shifts (biases), are not discernible from direct observation. Instead, dealing with these issues requires more complete analysis of the structure of costs and production, which is possible to do only with additional information on the form of the cost and production functions, as provided by formal theoretical model construction, and empirical application by econometric, or parametric, methods.

Developing such a parametric framework, and generating numerical evidence of different performance aspects, requires detailed consideration of the underlying economic theory relating these functions to facilitate the use and interpretation of computed measures. Only then should estimation of the functional relationships, and manipulation of the results to compute economic indicators addressing the questions of interest, proceed.

This chapter begins to outline the building blocks required for empirical implementation of our production theory structure. It takes the first step, emphasizing the theoretical foundations from production theory. Section 1 overviews the important theoretical concepts necessary to generate justifiable and consistent parametric measures of production structure and economic performance. The next sections summarize the duality theory underlying a number of functional relationships used in this text, from the most fundamental production and cost function specifications (Section 2) to profit maximization (Section 3), dynamic (the value function, Section 4), and multiple-output (distance and revenue functions, Section 5) frameworks. Section 6 then gathers together the performance measures we have alluded to in previous chapters, motivated in terms of 1st and 2nd order cost-elasticities. This provides a basis for elaboration of data construction and econometric specification for empirical implementation in the following chapters.

1.   THE BASIC PRODUCTION THEORY MODEL

Implementable production theory-based models of production processes and economic performance specifically portray the technological structure through various types of functional relationships. As discussed in previous chapters, this is in some cases accomplished by relying on a production function, but if behavioral responses are the focus of analysis it instead requires a framework based on, say, a dual cost or profit function. This structure is possible to estimate via econometric methods, to quantify the technological or production and market structure of a firm, industry, or economy, once the underlying theoretical basis is established, data constructed, and stochastic structure specified.

To pursue the first of these steps – the specification of a theoretically justifiable model structure – additional production and especially duality theory must be formalized. Duality relationships and properties are typically developed from the primary production theory models of our economic theory classes, for example the standard cost function $TC(\mathbf{p},Y,t)$. But natural extensions such as those we have overviewed in previous chapters may then be carried out using the same conceptual base. In this section we will sketch out the conceptual reasoning sequence underlying the formal duality relationships supporting such an exercise.

The foundation for production theory models is the production function, which summarizes the technological base underlying decisions of the firm. When behavioral assumptions such as cost minimization or profit maximization are added to this, we can construct an explicit optimization problem for the firm using these behavioral assumptions as the goal of optimization, and the production function as the constraint.

Solving the first order conditions of such a model allows us to define a function directly representing the optimal choices of the firm. The resulting cost or profit function is "dual" to the production function in the sense that it is explicitly based on the technological structure underlying the production function relationship, so the technology itself may implicitly be reproduced by a reverse optimization process.

For example, in graphical terms, cost minimization requires identifying the scale expansion path (SEP) as a set of tangencies of isocost curves, defined by the given relative input prices, and the isoquants. The shape of this path obviously depends fundamentally on the shape of the isoquants, which in turn is determined by the form of the production function.[167]

Therefore, information on scale expansion paths supported by different input price combinations could, in reverse, allow us to "back out" or trace out the form of the isoquants. Since the SEP provides the basis for the dual cost function (the TC-Y relationship), this means the cost function could in principle be used to trace out the shape of the production function.

Consider the basic cost function of standard microeconomic theory referred to above, the long run function $TC(\mathbf{p},Y,t)$. Since it is founded on the SEP, the optimized (cost minimizing) levels of all inputs are incorporated in the function. Constructing a model based on this function therefore allows us to reproduce and assess such behavior. In turn, it allows us to explore the dependence of input demand and therefore costs on any exogenous variable included as an argument of the function.

In particular, *demand equations* for factors of production are derived from this function using Shephard's lemma (a duality result used before and

---

[167] The reasoning in this section can be traced through using the diagrams in Chapter 1.

motivated more formally in the next section) to obtain the long run optimal demand for input j; $\partial TC(p_j,\mathbf{p},Y,t)/\partial p_j = v_j(p_j;\mathbf{p},Y,t)$, where $\mathbf{p}$ here excludes the price of input j. For just K and L inputs (from a two-dimensional diagram in K-L space) this would be, for example, $\partial TC(p_L,p_K,Y,t)/\partial p_L = L(p_L;p_K,Y,t)$. This procedure graphically implies identifying a point on the TC function (implying L demand), by finding for a particular p_L, say, given p_K, Y, and t, what the associated point on the SEP would be. The resulting input demand function includes all arguments other than p_j (p_L) as shift variables.[168]

That is, the function may be drawn in L-p_L space for any given Y, p_K and t, and changes in these last three arguments of the cost and therefore labor demand function explicitly become shift factors. This allows us to carry out conceptual, and ultimately empirical, experiments about the response of (labor) input demand to changes in the economic climate facing the firm. That is, for the basic cost function the possible changes to address involve p_K, Y or t, which would imply changes in the isocost line, movements between isoquants, or adaptations to the isoquant map, respectively. Observed data would be expected to capture a combination of such changes.

Similarly, the (long run) total cost function may be represented as $TC(Y;\mathbf{p},t)$, which implies a marginal cost function $MC(Y;\mathbf{p},t) = \partial TC(Y;\mathbf{p},t)/\partial Y$ and average cost function $AC(Y;\mathbf{p},t)=TC(Y;\mathbf{p},t)/Y$ in TC-Y space, both of which are explicitly dependent on the levels of the input prices and the technology. These arguments of the function are thus shift factors. This in turn allows us to construct estimates of $\varepsilon_{TCY}(Y;\mathbf{p},t)= [\partial TC(\bullet)/\partial Y]\bullet(Y/TC)$, which in this context represents long run scale economies or the shape of the long run cost function, and to identify its underlying determinants.

The cost function framework therefore provides a rich basis for the analysis of shifts in, movements along and shapes of input demand and long run cost functions. It is a multi-dimensional picture of various 2-dimensional diagrams from intermediate microeconomics classes. We can therefore use it to impute various aspects of technology and choices, and thus performance. As we have seen, however, this particular framework is limited in its interpretability since it does not include other characteristics that may be important for appropriate representation of firm behavior.

---

[168] Note that this full specification of the arguments of the function is usually simplified by writing $v_j(p_j,\mathbf{p},Y,t)$ as just v_j, as we have done in previous chapters, leaving the functional nature of the demand expression from the optimization process implicit. This simplifies the exposition at the cost of perhaps not emphasizing or keeping in mind that these demand functions (as well as other values solved for from the cost function such as shadow values) will be functions of all the arguments of the cost function.

If short run constraints from fixity of certain inputs are important characteristics for the application at hand, for example, we have seen that this may be accommodated by including the levels rather than the prices of the fixed factors as arguments, resulting in $VC(\mathbf{p},Y,t,\mathbf{x})$ (or $VC(p_L,Y,t,K)$).

Such restricted or variable cost functions represent subequilibrium in the sense that they explicitly reflect short run constraints that keep the firm from reaching a steady state, and therefore capture the difference between short and long run behavior. This results in a different picture (the "SEP" becomes a horizontal line at the given K, with K on the vertical axis), and shift variables (changes in K allow movement toward equilibrium cost levels if in subequilibrium, but p_K changes do not alter K use), of the cost relationship.

Short-run cost curves are thus instead directly measured by these functions. These curves represent substitution among variable inputs when fixed factors cannot be substituted, and utilization of the fixed factor(s).

In most cases one can also capture the long run "desired" levels of fixed inputs by imputing the long run envelope of the short run curves, which provides additional information about input substitution patterns, although it is not observed directly from the data. This is accomplished by combining knowledge about the observed point on the horizontal "expansion path" with information about the difference between the capital price that would support that point as an equilibrium value (that would define an isocost line tangent at the point), and the existing market price. This deviation thus implies adjustment toward the long run by rotating the imputed isocost line around the isoquant toward the tangency point defined by the observed market price.

More explicit adjustment processes might be built in if the model embodies partial adjustment. If costs of adjustment are incorporated, for example, this implies that the true cost of adding more capital is higher than the observed market price. Then movement may proceed part-way toward equilibrium based on the given p_K, but will stop short before reaching that point when the extra costs become a binding constraint.

The "true" p_K including adjustment costs, $p_K'=p_K+A(\bullet)$, thus identifies the observed optimal short run capital level, which will differ from that corresponding to the market price ignoring the amortized adjustment costs by an amount specifically determined by the "wedge" $A(\bullet)$. The adjustment costs will be reflected by the appearance of another "exogenous" variable in the production and thus cost equation; if investment ΔK is taking place less output may be produced from a given amount of inputs, so costs of a given amount of output are higher. The endogeneity involved makes graphing such a relationship difficult; behavior will depend on optimization over a time horizon given the extent of adjustment costs ($VC(\Delta K; \bullet)$). The adjustment process is thus determined by all arguments of the cost function.

Another possible dimension affecting responses and adjustment involves the choice of output level. In the isoquant diagram summarizing the cost structure, if an exogenous variable such as p_L changes, responses are assumed to be based on a given output demand level, implying a movement around an isoquant (if possible given fixity constraints). If the exogenous change instead involves an adaptation in output production, Y, there is no specific reason stating how this comes about; the diagram simply reflects optimal cost minimizing responses on the new isoquant.

If profit maximization is incorporated, however, this generates an additional "layer" of the adjustment process. This is represented, as emphasized in Chapter 6, in a cost curve diagram in TC-Y space by the addition of an output price or demand function, according to which the firm makes output choices. If any exogenous change in the isoquant diagram occurs, therefore, responses involve not only movement around a particular isoquant, but movements *between* isoquants motivated by the change.

If p_L changes, for example, it will affect marginal costs, and thus the choice of Y (the relevant isoquant), as well as adapt the isocost line and generate associated movements around an isoquant. This additional choice dimension therefore increases the richness of the structural model, but complicates the reasoning sequence underlying the analysis and thus the representation of the full range of firm behavior.

Finally, it is important, as we have seen, to recognize multiple outputs (output composition) for many problems. This implies that multiple inter-connected isoquant and therefore cost diagrams now are required to represent the optimization process.

If, for example, increases in output Y_1 occur, this will affect the diagrams representing behavior in the output Y_m market. If scope economies (jointness or complementarity) exist, for example, additional production of Y_1 will augment the potential for (reduce the overall cost of) producing Y_m. The marginal products of the inputs in terms of Y_m will then increase, so isoquants in the Y_m diagram will shift in as for a technical change. Similarly, the cost curves in TC_m-Y_m space will drop. This will clearly affect overall choice patterns, which will be even more complicated if profit-maximizing choices for a combination of outputs is accommodated.

Specification of models that allow us to represent multiple dimensions of behavior and responses, and thus to carry out these types of conceptual experiments and ultimately to quantify them, requires developing a more rigorous theoretical base in which to explicitly document the relationships. This is the role of duality theory.

2.   PRODUCTION AND COST STRUCTURE

The methodology provided by duality theory, effectively summarized in Diewert [1984], facilitates explicitly representing the structure of the production process and therefore productivity growth. This section provides a somewhat simplified overview of Diewert's treatment, which gathers together and formalizes a number of results that have been alluded to in previous sections of this text. This treatment highlights the theoretical concepts necessary to support empirical implementation of models used for extension and refinement of productivity growth measurement and interpretation in other chapters of this text.

The fundamental idea of duality theory is that the technology represented by the production function $Y(\mathbf{v},t)$ (where, as before, t is a time counter or other technology indicator, Y is output and $\mathbf{v}$ is a vector of variable inputs) can be described equivalently in other forms, most of which also incorporate optimizing behavior. One of these forms is the cost function which reflects the minimum total cost of producing a particular output level, Y, given the production technology and input prices. Since the production function is by definition a constraint on this minimization problem, the cost function $TC(\mathbf{p},Y,t)$ (where $\mathbf{p}$ is the vector of input prices corresponding to $\mathbf{v}$) not only reflects cost minimization but also completely describes the technology of the firm. In reverse, this implies that in certain circumstances $TC(\cdot)$ can be used to reproduce the original production function.

Similarly, in the short run with, say, capital fixed, this duality can be developed in terms of a production function distinguishing variable from fixed inputs, $Y(\mathbf{v},\mathbf{x},t)$, and the corresponding restricted or variable cost function $VC(\mathbf{p},t,Y,\mathbf{x})$ (where $\mathbf{x}$ is a vector of K fixed inputs). Incorporating adjustment costs makes this $VC(\mathbf{p},t,Y,\mathbf{x},\Delta\mathbf{x})$, where dynamic adjustment toward long run desired levels of the quasi-fixed jnputs is implicitly captured. Again, since this cost function includes all information on the production technology, behavior and constraints facing the firm, it is a very useful basis for empirical analysis of the behavior of firms.

Other dual functions also can provide a useful structure for analysis. Profit maximization, for example, not only involves all the information contained in the cost function, but also implies output choice. These choices are reflected in the profit function $\pi(\mathbf{p},p_Y,t)$ or restricted profit function $\pi(\mathbf{p},p_Y,t,x)$, where p_Y instead of Y is exogenous.[169]

---

[169] Functions such as indirect production or distance functions also can be used for analysis, but are not as often used because they are less intuitive representations.

Finally, multiple outputs can be brought into the analysis via the cost or profit function. Alternatively, a general multi-output transformation or production set can be used to develop the distance function.

In this and the following sections of this chapter we will explore this sequence of models more formally.

First, to formalize the cost function and motivate its uses we start by defining the total cost function as

$$9.1)\ TC(Y,\mathbf{p},t) = \min_v \{\mathbf{p}^T\mathbf{v} : Y(\mathbf{v},t) \geq \overline{Y}\}$$

where $(p_1,p_2,...p_J)=\mathbf{p}>>0_J$ is a vector of J positive input prices, $>>$ means strictly positive (every element is greater than zero), $\overline{Y}$ is a particular output level, no monopsony exists (input prices are exogenous), and the "T" superscript indicates a transposed vector (so $\mathbf{p}^T\mathbf{v}$ could alternatively be written as $\Sigma_j p_j v_j$).[170]

If a solution to the cost minimization problem (which involves solving first order conditions for all inputs in the v vector as well as satisfying the $Y(\mathbf{v},t) \geq \overline{Y}$ constraint) exists, we can state a number of regularity conditions that the resulting function must satisfy:

(a) $TC(\bullet)$ is a nonnegative function ($TC(Y,t,\mathbf{p})\geq 0$);

(b) $TC(\bullet)$ is (positively) linearly homogeneous in input prices for any fixed output level $(TC(Y,t,\lambda\mathbf{p})\equiv \lambda TC(Y,t,\mathbf{p})$ for $\lambda>0$);[171]

(c) $TC(\bullet)$ is increasing in input prices ($TC(Y,t,\mathbf{p}_1)>TC(Y,t,\mathbf{p}_0)$ if $\mathbf{p}_1>\mathbf{p}_0$, or $\partial TC/\partial p_j>0$;

(d) $TC(\bullet)$ is a concave function of $\mathbf{p}$ (informally, $\partial^2 TC/\partial p_j^2\leq 0$);[172]

(e) $TC(\bullet)$ is continuous in $\mathbf{p}$ and continuous from below in Y; and

(f) $TC(\bullet)$ is nondecreasing in Y for fixed $\mathbf{p}$ $(TC(Y^0,t,\mathbf{p})\leq TC(Y^1,t,\mathbf{p})$ for $Y^0\leq Y^1$, or $\partial TC/\partial Y\geq 0$).

Another required theoretical relationship, sometimes presented as a regularity condition, is symmetry. By the symmetry of the Hessian matrix

---

[170] An important point to emphasize here, which is fundamental but sometimes forgotten in application, is that $TC(Y,\mathbf{p},t)$ is the *minimum* cost, so it represents points on the (long run in this case) cost curve, whereas $\Sigma_j p_j v_j$ is simply a *definition* of costs.

[171] The terms linear homogeneous and homogeneous of degree one are used interchangeably. Note also that homogeneity of degree one of this function implies homogeneity of degree zero of the derivative functions, so, once Shephard's lemma is invoked, the input demand equations become homogeneous of degree zero, as elaborated further below. This indicates that proportionate changes in all input prices don't change demand; they do not change the shape (just the value) of the isocost line tangent to any particular isoquant.

[172] More formally, if $TC(Y,\mathbf{p}^0,t)=\min_x\{\mathbf{p}^{0T}\mathbf{v} : Y(\mathbf{v},t) \geq \overline{Y}\} = \mathbf{p}^{0T}\mathbf{v}^0$, and $TC(Y,\mathbf{p}^1,t) = \min_x\{\mathbf{p}^{1T}\mathbf{v} : Y(\mathbf{v},t) \geq \overline{Y}\} = \mathbf{p}^{1T}\mathbf{v}^1$, then $TC(Y,t,\lambda\mathbf{p}_0 + (1-\lambda)\mathbf{p}^1) \geq \lambda\mathbf{p}^{0T}\mathbf{v}^0 + (1-\lambda)\mathbf{p}^{1T}\mathbf{v}^1 = \lambda TC(Y,t,\mathbf{p}^0) + (1-\lambda)TC(Y,t,\mathbf{p}^1)$.

(or set of 2nd derivatives, as stated by Young's theorem)[173] it must be that $\partial^2 TC/\partial p_i p_j = \partial^2 TC/\partial p_j p_i$, and similarly for the cross-derivatives with respect to any two arguments of the function.[174]

Most of these conditions are quite intuitive, even though they look messy. (a), for example, simply reflects the fact that costs are positive for productive firms. If not, production would be infinite if output price were positive. (b) indicates that the units of measurement for costs do not matter; if all prices increase by a particular factor, minimum possible total costs of production for a given output level must change by the same proportion (this is a "required" homogeneity condition that must be embodied in any assumed functional form). (c) implies that if a price increases costs must also increase. If this is not the case costs could not have been minimized in the first place (this is a monotonicity condition because it "signs" the first derivative). (d) is less obvious but still has some interpretation potential. As an input price rises minimum costs also go up, but this increase will not be proportional because substitution occurs. The marginal product of input j drops with increased use, so the demand curve for this input slopes down. A proportionate increase in costs is therefore an upper bound on the increase (this is termed a curvature condition).[175] (e) in effect says that inputs must be divisible. This is required for derivatives to be defined for analysis, although discontinuities could result if indivisibilities exist. (f) ensures that marginal cost as well as total cost is positive, which is necessary for optimization to make sense. If this does not hold and marginal revenue is positive, optimal production will not be defined.

Only if a function satisfies all of these (quite reasonable) properties will it be a valid cost function for theoretical and empirical work. This implies that many types of functions that have been assumed for empirical analysis cannot be justified theoretically. For example, a linear cost function $TC(Y, \mathbf{p}, t) = \alpha + \Sigma_j \delta_j p_j + \gamma t + \beta Y$, where α, δ_j, γ and β are parameters, violates property (b) (linear homogeneity in input prices).

---

[173] Somewhat more formally, Young's theorem states that the second partial derivative should be invariant to the order of differentiation. Note also that all these properties, and our treatment of functions representing the production structure in general, assumes that continuous first and second partial derivatives exist for all arguments of the function.

[174] This implies some restrictions on the functional form, since it indicates that the parameter for any cross relationship will be the same no matter what order the arguments are in.

[175] Since this result is relatively nonintuitive and is important for many duality theory results Diewert [1984] provides a useful geometric illustration of why it occurs. In brief, this shows that if two cost minimizing situations are considered with two different price vectors but the same isoquant, the average of these minimum costs at the average price between the two periods will be lower than can be reached at the average price level between the two periods. This implies the intuition mentioned here. For further details, see Diewert [1984].

Once a valid functional form for the cost function is specified (as elaborated in Chapter 11), the conceptual process underlying this duality theory result can be reversed to reconstruct the firm's underlying production function by setting up the optimization problem

$$9.2) \; Y'(\mathbf{v},t) = \max_Y \{ Y : \mathbf{p}^T\mathbf{v} \geq TC(Y,\mathbf{p},t) \text{ for every } \mathbf{p} >> 0 \} \; .$$

This will reproduce the convex hull of the isoquants reflecting the production technology, so if the production function, and therefore the isoquants, fulfill standard regulatory conditions,[176] $Y'(\mathbf{v},t)=Y(\mathbf{v},t)$. This follows because cost minimization will never reflect nonconvexities or incorrect slopes in isoquants because they are irrelevant for behavior.[177] This suggests that for empirical application it does not really matter whether the technology truly is represented by $Y'(\bullet)$ or $Y(\bullet)$, because observable market data will never allow us to identify the difference. The nonconvex areas will be ignored by rational economic agents.

The cost function therefore completely represents the information on the technology contained in the production function, and reflects optimization behavior since its construction is based on the solution to an optimization problem. Working with a cost function is thus a particularly useful way to proceed to develop an empirically implementable model; all the information on factor or input demand patterns can be inferred from the cost function.

As suggested by the conceptual discussion in the previous section, this implication stems from the result called Shephard's lemma, employed in the previous chapters, which is formally based on the envelope theorem. This lemma states that if $TC(Y,\mathbf{p},t)$ satisfies all regularity properties mentioned above, it will be the case that $v_j(Y,\mathbf{p},t) = \partial TC(Y,\mathbf{p},t)/\partial p_j$, for all j, where $v_j(Y,\mathbf{p},t)$ is the cost minimizing input quantity of input j needed to produce Y units of output given input prices $\mathbf{p}$ and the level of technology t. This can be motivated very loosely by noting that since $TC(Y,\mathbf{p},t)$ represents minimum costs, and therefore $TC(Y,\mathbf{p},t)=\Sigma p_j v_j^*$ where $v_j^*=v_j(\bullet)$ is the optimal demand for input v_j, it must be true that $\partial TC/\partial p_j = v_j^* = v_j(\bullet)$.

Using the duality theory foundation we can also illustrate that some theoretically required properties of demand functions are met by the $v_j(\bullet)$ functions. For example, as long as $TC(\bullet)$ is twice differentiable, property (d) implies that these demand curves are downward sloping, so the requirement that (compensated) input demand curves be downward sloping is satisfied.

---

[176] See Diewert [1984] for a rigorous treatment of regulatory conditions for different types of functions.

[177] But these will not exist anyway if regularity conditions on the original function are globally satisfied.

In addition, homogeneity of degree zero in prices is satisfied by construction; a standard duality result asserts that if a function like TC(Y,$\mathbf{p}$,t) is homogeneous of degree n in an argument, say $\mathbf{p}$, then the derivative function $\partial TC/\partial p_j$ is homogeneous of degree n-1. Since property (b) requires TC($\cdot$) to be linearly homogeneous in prices, $\partial TC/\partial p_j$ is homogeneous of degree zero.

It can also be shown from this that not all inputs can be inferior. This is somewhat more complex to illustrate, but can be derived in three steps. First note that linear homogeneity in prices property of TC($\cdot$) from (b) will also hold for a derivative of this function with respect to another argument of the function, and thus will be true for $\partial TC/\partial Y$.[178] Using this, Euler's theorem implies that summing up the derivatives of $\partial TC/\partial Y$ with respect to the different components of $\mathbf{p}$, multiplied by the corresponding price, and adding, reproduces the function: $\Sigma_j p_j \partial^2 TC/\partial Y \partial p_j = \partial TC/\partial Y$. Since $\partial^2 TC/\partial Y \partial p_j = \partial^2 TC/\partial p_j \partial Y = \partial v_j/\partial Y$ by the symmetry of the Hessian matrix and Shephard's lemma, this implies $\Sigma_j p_j \partial v_j/\partial Y = \partial TC/\partial Y > 0$ from (f). Therefore not all the $\partial v_j/\partial Y$ derivatives can be negative.

Once input fixity is recognized in this function, the levels of these factors appear in the cost function because the cost minimization expression becomes (for one fixed input, K):

9.3) $TC(Y,\mathbf{p},t,K) = \min_v \{\mathbf{p}^T\mathbf{v} + p_K K : Y(\mathbf{v},t,K) \geq \overline{Y} \}$,

where the $\mathbf{p}$ and $\mathbf{v}$ vectors no longer include the price and quantity of K and $\overline{Y}$ is a particular output level. In this case optimization is only possible over the variable inputs in $\mathbf{p}^T\mathbf{v}$, which is defined as variable costs or VC. The first order condition for K is deleted, and all resulting input demand equations end up depending on the level rather than the price of K.

Lau [1978] has shown that standard cost function properties are maintained for variable costs when fixed inputs exist. In particular, Shephard's lemma still holds (for the variable inputs), so $v_j(Y,\mathbf{p},t,K) = \partial VC(Y,\mathbf{p},t,K)/\partial p_j$, with appropriate properties. This must be interpreted as a short-run input demand function since it depends on K. More generally, this will be $v_j(Y,\mathbf{p},t,\mathbf{x}) = \partial VC(Y,\mathbf{p},t,\mathbf{x})/\partial p_j$, for a vector of K fixed inputs $\mathbf{x}$.

In addition, Lau [1978] showed that what I have called an inverse Shephard's lemma (since it is in terms of factor levels rather than prices), $\partial VC(Y,\mathbf{p},t,x_k)/\partial x_k = -Z_k$, exists for x_k. Z_k is interpreted as a (positive) shadow value for the factor that will equal its market price p_K if in equilibrium. That is, the derivative with respect to x_k shows how variable costs can be reduced with a relaxation in the fixity constraint on x_k, which provides a marginal measure of the value of a unit of the x_k stock.

---

[178] This is also a standard duality theory result. See Diewert [1984].

Associated regularity conditions require VC to be decreasing ($\partial VC/\partial x_k < 0$) and convex ($\partial^2 VC/\partial^2 x_k > 0$) in x_k; the shadow value is positive and declines with changes in the stock of x_k. Using these properties along with the Shephard's lemma property of optimal variable input demands allows for a rich specification of the firm's behavior in the short and long run which is useful for empirical analysis of firm behavior.

Due to the construction of the cost function, therefore, theoretically consistent and valid input demands may directly be represented, whether in a short or long run context. Once these demand functions are derived from a specific functional form for the underlying cost function, the demand functions themselves and changes in input demand resulting from changes in any arguments of the function can be specified and assessed.

In addition, adding other arguments into the function does not in general cause these overall properties to be violated, although the appropriate properties with respect to these prices may not be well specified. For example, "environmental" variables may not have homogeneity properties such as those for the productive inputs.

More specifically, we can add a vector **r**, which denotes B other arguments of the function that may be choice or fixed variables but do not necessarily have an impact on internal scale economies. That is, they may not define the choices of the firm but instead its operating environment. In this case, the technology can be summarized by a restricted cost function of the form VC(**p**,t,Y,**x**,**r**).[179] The r_b variables, defined as "environmental or behavioral parameters" by McFadden [1978], may be any determinants of costs (and therefore firm behavior) other than commodity levels.

These factors therefore represent one version of McFadden's [1978] "z" variables that may not be subject to curvature restrictions or other regularity conditions. This is the sense in which we incorporated, for example, adjustment costs, regulation, and other external variables into the cost function in Chapters 3, 5 and 6.

Finally, the cost function naturally accommodates multiple outputs as individual arguments of the function. In this case, however, the production function constraint must be rewritten in terms of a transformation function or production set that is more general. Also, this complicates the ability to reproduce the production technology from the cost function – to directly establish its duality. This duality, however, as well as the definition and connection of many multiple-output representations of the technology, may be developed as in Färe and Primont [1995].

---

[179] Note that this can also be extended to the case of multiple outputs, although representation of capacity utilization is problematic in this case, as shown by Berndt and Fuss [1989].

Although many other duality theory results have been generated for dual cost models, these provide the foundation for constructing empirically implementable models of firm behavior that are often used for analysis of production and thus cost structure.

3.   PROFIT MAXIMIZATION

The detailed overview of the cost function and its duality properties in the previous section provides the theoretical "underpinnings" for most of the model development in this text, since our focus has been on the cost structure and thus the cost function is the natural basis for analysis. However, we have also mentioned other functions that we might use for specifications in which, say, output supply decisions are important (the profit function), or the technological relationship (like a production function) with multiple outputs and technical inefficiency provide the focus of the analysis.

We will discuss the choice of function for empirical analysis in the next chapter, but for now will briefly overview some of the duality relationships that connect these different specifications of the technology and behavior to the production function and to each other.

First, the extension to the profit function is quite straightforward since it simply endogenizes output supply choices. For example, for one output (the multiple output case follows analogously), the profit function is of the form $\pi(p_Y, \mathbf{p}, t)$, which follows from the optimization problem:

$$9.4) \quad \pi(p_Y, \mathbf{p}, t) = \max_{Y, v} \{ p_Y Y - \mathbf{p}^T \mathbf{v} : Y(\mathbf{v}, t) \geq \overline{Y} \},$$

where the elements of the $\mathbf{p}$ vector, $Y(\cdot)$, and $\overline{Y}$ are defined as above, and p_Y is output price.

The regularity conditions corresponding to this problem are very similar to those for the cost function, although some are reversed in sign since costs appear here with a minus sign:

(a) $\pi(\cdot)$ is a nonnegative function ($\pi(p_Y, t, \mathbf{p}) \geq 0$);

(b) $\pi(\cdot)$ is (positively) linearly homogeneous in all prices ($\pi(t, \lambda p_Y, \lambda \mathbf{p}) \equiv \lambda \pi(t, p_Y, \mathbf{p})$ for $\lambda > 0$);

(c) $\pi(\cdot)$ is non-decreasing in output price ($\pi(p_{Y1}, t, \mathbf{p}) \geq \pi(p_{Y0}, t, \mathbf{p})$ if $p_{Y1} > p_{Y0}$, or $\partial \pi / \partial p_Y \geq 0$);

(c) $\pi(\cdot)$ is non-increasing in input prices ($\pi(p_Y, t, \mathbf{p}_1) \leq \pi(p_Y, t, \mathbf{p}_0)$ if $\mathbf{p}_1 > \mathbf{p}_0$, or $\partial \pi / \partial p_j \leq 0$);

(d) $\pi(\cdot)$ is a convex function of all prices (informally, $\partial^2 \pi / \partial p_j^2 \geq 0$ and similarly for p_Y); and

(e) $\pi(\cdot)$ is continuous in $\mathbf{p}$.

The interpretation of these conditions is directly analogous to those for the cost function. Profits must be positive when all inputs and outputs are variable – otherwise the firm would not produce. The homogeneity property says if all prices change by a certain proportion, so do profits. The monotonicity (1st derivative) conditions (c) and (d) state that if output price gets higher profits will increase, and if input prices go up profits will fall. Finally, the curvature (2nd derivative) condition essentially indicates that profits will somewhere have a maximum (the firm will eventually encounter decreasing scale economies) or else profit maximization would not be well defined (the scale of operations would be expanded forever).

It can also be shown that the profit function is directly dual to the production function; it represents the same technology, while adding profit maximizing behavioral responses (Diewert [1984]). Essentially the profit function carries out the standard intermediate microeconomics exercise of adding a given output price and the p_Y=MC condition to the cost structure implied by the cost curves.

Output supply as well as input demand conditions may thus be represented directly using Hotelling's lemma (a somewhat generalized version of Shephard's lemma); $Y = \partial\pi/\partial p_Y$ and $v_j = -\partial\pi/\partial p_j$. Note that the input demand curves in this case incorporate output supply behavior; they are profit-maximizing levels of input demands rather than reflecting the SEP of an isoquant diagram.

Similarly, an "inverse" Hotelling's lemma may used to solve for shadow values of anything that appears in the function in quantity levels. For example, for a restricted profit function with K as an argument, the shadow value of K in terms of its marginal enhancement of profitability (allowing for output supply responses) is $Z^\pi_K = \partial\pi/\partial K$ (see Lau [1978]), where the "π" superscript emphasizes that this is a profit-oriented measure.

The profit function is therefore another useful basis for analysis of production decisions if output supply is important to represent and the profit maximization assumption appears valid.[180] Also, all extensions to the cost function model, such as quasi-fixed inputs (dynamics), multiple outputs, and external effects, may analogously be built into the framework.

In addition, if output markets may be characterized as somehow "imperfect", this breaks down the Hotelling's lemma condition as discussed as length in Chapter 6. We can support the development in Chapter 6 here

---

[180] Note, however, that the standard assumption of CRS may not be imposed here, since a profit maximizing solution is not defined with perfect competition and CRS. In fact, the notion of scale economies is not directly represented within this framework, since they involve the cost-output relationship embodied in the cost structure. Thus, if cost economies are the focus of the analysis, this may not be a preferable model base.

by more explicit theoretical representation of the optimization condition appended to the cost framework if imperfect competition prevails.

As in Chapter 6, an output demand equation $Y=D(p_Y,\rho)$, where ρ is a vector of demand curve shift variables, implying an inverse demand equation $p_Y=D^{-1}(Y, \rho)$, can be used to derive the optimizing relationship

$$9.5)\ D^{-1}(Y, \rho) = p_Y = -\partial D^{-1}(Y, \rho)/\partial Y \cdot Y + \partial VC/\partial Y$$

from the expression $MR = Y \cdot \partial D^{-1}(Y, \rho)/\partial Y + D^{-1}(Y, \rho) = \partial VC/\partial Y = MC$, so $p_Y = -\partial p_Y(Y,\rho)/\partial Y \cdot Y - \partial VC/\partial Y$ (where MR denotes marginal revenue).

Formally, this extension to a model with market imperfections can be motivated by the maximization problem

$$9.6)\ \text{Max}_{v,\Delta x,Y}\ R(0) = \int_0^\infty e^{-rt}\ (p_{Yt}Y_t - \Sigma_j\ p_{jt}v_{jt} - \Sigma_k\ a_{kt}z_{kt})\ dt\ ,$$

subject to the constraints represented by the demand function $D(p_Y,\rho)$, the restricted cost function $VC=VC(Y,\mathbf{p},\mathbf{x},t)$, the definition of gross investment $z_k= \Delta x_k+ \delta_k x_k$, the vector of depreciation rates δ, and the asset purchase prices of the factors in the $\mathbf{x}$ vector, $\mathbf{a}$.

Regularity conditions, Shephard's lemma and the Euler equations representing optimal variable input demand and investment levels for this model of profit maximization with imperfect competition are based on the cost specification from above. However, the additional first order condition (9.5) endogenizes both output price and quantity, and the optimal input levels now depend on these profit maximizing values.

4.   DYNAMIC ADJUSTMENT

In Chapter 3 as well as in the previous section, the potential importance of fixity of factors, and thus implicitly a dynamic framework if adjustment of these factors is to be considered, was emphasized. We have primarily discussed this in the context of a static cost (or profit) function incorporating the levels of the fixed factors. In this case observed data are assumed to be based on short run optimization, so parameter estimates represent short run behavior, and the long run can be imputed from this using an equilibrium expression representing the long run "desired" value(s) of the fixed factor(s).

We have also raised the possibility of including adjustment costs in the function more directly by recognizing that investment in stock inputs is costly in terms of the use of other variable inputs. We are then able to represent investment behavior by an Euler equation.

The Euler equation from calculus of variations, or the Hamiltonian from optimal control theory (both of which are used for such models) are the dynamic equivalents of using a Lagrangian equation (and resulting first order conditions) to represent constrained optimization for a static problem. For such models a *path* of optimization decisions is generated, depending on a present value profit maximization problem and the linkage between periods implied by the stock nature of the quasi-fixed input and the associated "equations of motion" representing the connection between its stock and flow (such as the perpetual inventory equation for K in Chapter 10).

More formally, if Δx is in the **r** vector, as discussed briefly in Chapter 3, investment equations are implied. The optimization problem facing the firm in this case is to choose the path of x_k, or Δx_k, in addition to the vector of variable inputs at each time period, to minimize the present value of the stream of costs from producing output Y at each future period:

$$9.7) \quad \text{Min}_{x,\Delta x} \; TC(0) = \int_o^\infty e^{-it}[VC(\mathbf{p},\mathbf{x},\Delta\mathbf{x},\mathbf{r},t,Y) + \Sigma_k p_k x_k] \; dt + \Sigma_k q_k x_k(0),$$

where $p_k = q_k(r+\delta_k) = $ the rental price of x_k, q_k are the asset prices of new quasi-fixed inputs, $\mathbf{x}(0)$ are the initial stocks of quasi-fixed inputs, **r** contains all r_b components except $\Delta\mathbf{x}$, i is the long run discount rate, and VC captures minimization at each point in time over all variable inputs given any $\mathbf{x},Y$ levels.[181] Minimization of this yields the Euler first order conditions:

$$9.8) \quad p_k = -\partial VC/\partial x_k - i\partial VC/\partial\Delta x_k + \Delta x_k \partial^2 VC/\partial x_k \partial\Delta x_k + \Delta\Delta x_k \partial^2 VC/\partial(\Delta x_k)^2$$

for each x_k variable, where $\Delta\Delta x_k$ denotes the second derivative of x_k with respect to time, $\Delta(\Delta x_k)$ (as in Berndt, Fuss and Waverman [1980], where the equation is in continuous form which is more rigorously justified).[182]

This set of equations implicitly represents investment, and therefore adjustment toward long run equilibrium, of the firm. In this form they can be used as estimating equations representing the flow into the stock input as in Pindyck and Rotemberg [1983] and Morrison [1988c,1992a].

---

[181] See Berndt-Fuss-Waverman [1980] or Morrison and Berndt [1981] for clarification of the underlying steps.

[182] Note that any factor that is in the form of a stock, and thus has inherent connections across time periods that make static analysis inappropriate for representation of its optimal use, requires using dynamic optimization methods. For example, although not focused on in this text, characterizing the use of scarce natural resource stocks requires recognizing the connection between periods. In this case there is no flow into the stock (unless exploration is taking place to increase proven reserves, or biological growth occurs as for a fish or tree stock), but there is a flow out. Resources used this period are removed from the stock, restricting the available stock in the next period.

Depending on the functional form it may also be possible analytically to solve for the Δx_k levels, to represent investment choices more directly. For example, in Berndt *et al* [1980] this is accomplished by using a quadratic form for VC($\cdot$), so that second derivatives do not depend on the data. Their development results in a partial adjustment framework where the adjustment parameter depends on the discount rate and parameters of the model. These investment equations, however, become intractable to solve for with multiple quasi-fixed inputs unless some independence is assumed, as discussed in Morrison and Berndt [1981].

As touched on in Chapter 3, it should be noted that for any investment specification expectations become an issue, since the firm is making current decisions about a path of behavior toward a long run horizon, which depends on future expected exogenous variables. This can be dealt with in a number of ways, none of which are completely satisfactory.

For example, Berndt, Fuss and Waverman [1980] simply assume static expectations so only current variables are relevant for the decision making process. Pindyck and Rotemberg [1983] rely instead on the analytical equivalence of rational expectations and the "cleansing of errors" resulting from using Three Stage Least Squares as an estimating technique. Morrison [1986b] outlines the use of "partial" rational expectations or adaptive expectations frameworks based on constructing time series analysis ARIMA specifications of price paths. These approaches to modeling expectations formation processes are discussed further in Chapter 11.

Another way to deal with dynamic adjustment, which is somewhat more rigorous and opaque but allows multiple quasi-fixed inputs to be incorporated more readily, is to use the value function of the dynamic duality literature. As noted in Chapter 3, this literature is typically attributed to Epstein [1981] or Epstein and Denny [1983] and has been applied by, for example, Howard and Shumway [1988] (HS).[183]

As Howard and Shumway outline, the basic structure of this model revolves around the notion of the value function $J(p_Y,\mathbf{p}_j,\mathbf{p}_k,i,\mathbf{x})$, where, as before, we define p_Y as the price of output,[184] $\mathbf{p}_j$ as a vector of J variable input prices, $\mathbf{p}_k$ as a vector of prices for the K quasi-fixed inputs represented by $\mathbf{x}$, and i as the real discount rate. This very general function is based on the profit-maximizing problem

$$9.9) \ J(\cdot) = \max\nolimits_{Y,v,dx} V(\cdot) = \int_0^\infty e^{-it}[p_Y Y(\mathbf{v},\mathbf{x},\mathbf{dx}) - \Sigma_j p_j v_j - \Sigma_k p_k x_k] \, dt \, ,$$

---

[183] Another commonly-cited application, where the theoretical development is based on a transformation rather than production function, with regularity properties more rigorously defined, is Luh and Stefanou [1991].

[184] This could also be a vector of output prices, but for now we will retain the assumption of one output for simplicity. The extension is analogous.

subject to $\mathbf{v},\mathbf{x} >> 0$, $d\mathbf{x}_t = \mathbf{I}_t - \delta\mathbf{x}_{t-1}$, $\mathbf{x}(0) = \mathbf{x}_0 >> 0$, and where the net change in $\mathbf{x}$, written $d\mathbf{x}$, should be interpreted as $d\mathbf{x}/dt$ (investment in $\mathbf{x}$ representing adjustment costs), $\mathbf{I}$ is gross investment in $\mathbf{x}$, $\mathbf{x}_0$ is the initial endowment of $\mathbf{x}$, and all variables are implicitly a function of time (although the t subscripts have been left out for notational simplicity).

This value function has regularity conditions similar to those for the simpler cost and profit functions discussed in the previous section. It is considered dual to the static profit maximization problem (for each time period for given $\mathbf{x}$ levels). It is assumed that $\partial Y/\partial \mathbf{dx} << 0$ (positive adjustment costs exist), that in the limit $\mathbf{dx}(t)=0$ (a steady state equilibrium exists), and that $J(\bullet)$ is twice continuously differentiable, convex in prices, and concave in quasi-fixed inputs. The last three assumptions ensure that short and long run solutions exist for the optimization problem, and thus provide a basis for using the envelope condition to establish duality between $J(\bullet)$ and the production function $Y(\bullet)$.[185]

Again this problem, like any dynamic problem, requires some assumption about future expected prices. Empirical implementation of these models typically is based on the assumption that expectations are static. Thus decisions made at any time period are based on the assumption that all information on future prices is embodied in currently observed prices.

As noted by HS, the value function defined in (9.9) is a static approximation to the full dynamic optimization problem. This function satisfies the Hamilton-Jacobi equation for an optimal control problem similar to the Euler equation reproduced above. In this case the condition can be written as $iJ(p_Y, \mathbf{p}_j, \mathbf{p}_k, \mathbf{x}) = \max_{Y,\mathbf{v},\mathbf{dx}} [p_Y Y(\mathbf{v},\mathbf{x},\mathbf{dx}) - \Sigma_j p_j v_j - \Sigma_k p_k x_k + J_\mathbf{x}\mathbf{dx}]$, where $J_\mathbf{x}$ represents the shadow price(s) for the quasi-fixed input(s).

This equation facilitates the evaluation of dynamic processes, since it implicitly represents investment decisions. The correspondence says that the value function is equal to the discounted present value of current profit plus the marginal value of optimal change in net investment. Thus, using this relationship, demand paths for the variable and quasi-fixed input can be derived by differentiation similarly to Hotelling's lemma. For one quasi-fixed input x_k these equations become: $Y = iJ_{pY} - J_{xkpY}dx$, $v_j = -iJ_{pj} + J_{xkpj}dx$, and $dx = J_{xkpk}^{-1}(iJ_{pk} + x_k)$, where the subscipts represent derivatives with respect to p_Y, x_k, p_k and p_j.

Note that this function, as often derived, does not embody technical change. As discussed by HS, incorporating a general disembodied technical relationship $A(t)$ changes the value function such that the output supply and input demand relationships are adapted to: $Y = iJ_{pY} - J_{xkpY}dx - J_{HpY}dA$, $v_j = -iJ_{pj} + J_{xkpj}dx - J_{Hpj}dA$, and $dx = J_{xkpk}^{-1}(iJ_{pk} + x_k - J_{Hpk}dA)$, where dA is dA/dt.

---

[185] See Epstein [1981].

This function therefore allows a highly generalized and thus detailed picture of production processes to be captured, adapting optimal output supply, variable input demand, and investment equations to reflect dynamic adjustment paths.[186] It is, however, based on the same principles as representation of output supply and input demand from more standard production theory functions. The increased richness of the function also means that estimation becomes more complex.

5. DISTANCE AND REVENUE FUNCTIONS

The last type of function we will consider in some detail is the distance function. This function is typically motivated as dual to the revenue rather than the production function; it is, in fact more *equivalent* to the production function (in a multi-dimensional sense), and thus implies technical maximization of output, and, in turn, revenue for given output prices.

Note, however, that with multiple outputs this also involves choosing the "right" combination of outputs. That is, not only finding a point on the production possibility frontier discussed in Chapter 8, but a point on this frontier where an "iso-revenue" line, with its slope determined by the ratio of output prices, is tangent to the curve. This is the output-output-space equivalent of finding the cost minimizing input demand level, given the iso-cost line representing relative input prices, in an isoquant diagram (which is instead in input-input-space – inputs on both axes – as in Figure 1, Ch. 1).

The distance function is typically defined according to the production set $F(v)$, defined in (8.9) as $F(v) = \{Y: v$ can produce $Y\}$. This function has properties that ensure that the function logically represents productive possibilities,[187] such as: positive production must involve positive input levels, $F(v)$ satisfies strong disposability of outputs and inputs (if an output level Y is in $F(v)$ and $Y' \leq Y$ then Y' must be in $F(v)$, and conversely for inputs), and $F(v)$ is closed, bounded and convex. The last (combined) property contains a curvature condition; it says that if two combinations of outputs can be produced with any v vector, any average of these output levels could also be produced (or be within the function, implying also continuous divisibility).

---

[186] Note also that if the value function has a particular form, as discussed by Epstein and Denny [1983], the investment equation can be expressed as a multivariate flexible accelerator similarly to the Berndt, *et al* [1980] expression alluded to above.

[187] See Färe and Primont [1995] for a much more rigorous description of these types of properties.

From this function, as outlined in Chapter 8, the output-oriented distance function (which is the type of distance function most closely interpretable to a production function since it implies maximimum output given inputs) is defined as in (8.10): $D_O(v,Y) = \min_Y \{\Theta: (Y/\Theta) \in F(v)\}$. The properties of this function follow directly from those on the technology or production set. More formally, they are:

(a) if $Y \in F(v)$, then $D_O(\bullet) \le 1$;

(b) $D_O(\bullet) = 1$ if Y is on the frontier of $F(v)$;[188]

(c) $D_O(\bullet)$ is (positively) linearly homogeneous in Y ($D_O(v,\lambda Y) \equiv \lambda D_O(v,Y)$ for $\lambda > 0$);

(d) $D_O(\bullet)$ is increasing in v ($D_O(v_1,Y) > D_O(v_0,Y)$ if $v_1 > v_0$, or $\partial D_O/\partial v > 0$);

(e) $D_O(\bullet)$ is non-decreasing in Y ($D_O(v,Y_1) \ge D_O(v,Y_0)$ if $Y_1 > Y_0$, or $\partial D_O/\partial Y \ge 0$); and

e) $D_O(\bullet)$ is convex in Y.

As discussed to some extent in Chapters 7 and 8, this function is a useful foundation for applications in which relative technical efficiency is a focus, when there are multiple outputs, and also potentially when price data are not available. The function also provides a basis for constructing shadow values, which reflect the "contribution" of an output to overall production, or a "marginal product" version of the value of a particular input, as alluded to in the earlier chapters.

More specifically, the output shadow values can be developed using the duality of the revenue and distance functions.[189] The revenue function can be formally defined as:

$$9.10)\quad R(v,p_Y) = \max_Y \{p_Y^T Y: Y \in F(v)\},$$

where p_Y denotes the vector of output prices. This function directly describes the maximum revenue possible given the technology and output prices for a given vector v. It therefore reproduces the technology. The duality between the revenue and distance function can be derived by showing their mutual dependence:

---

[188] Input distance functions are defined symmetrically in terms of an isoquant diagram as, in essense, how few inputs may be used (the input requirement) for producing a given output vector. In this case if there is a "distance" from the frontier it is within the isoquant, and therefore the distance will exceed one rather than fall short of it. A distance of one still implies being on the frontier, but in this case the frontier is defined according to the isoquant. This treatment is more similar to a technologically-oriented *cost* function, but will not be emphasized here to limit the extensions made. See Färe and Primont [1995] for a more rigorous overview of these functions, and Coelli *et al* [1998] and Hetemaki [1996] for more introductory treatments.

[189] For the input distance function, which typically is used to derive input shadow values, this would involve the duality with the cost function.

9.11a) $R(\mathbf{v},\mathbf{p_Y}) = \max_Y \{\mathbf{p_Y}^T\mathbf{Y}: D_O(\mathbf{v},\mathbf{Y}) \leq 1\}$,

9.11b) $D_O(\mathbf{v},\mathbf{Y}) = \max_{pY} \{\mathbf{p_Y}^T\mathbf{Y}: R(\mathbf{v},\mathbf{p_Y}) \leq 1\}$.

This relationship can be used to motivate the idea of shadow values in the output-oriented framework. The underlying conceptual issue is that, since the distance function is not specified directly in terms of output production like the production function, the contributions of outputs (or marginal products of inputs) cannot be computed simply as derivatives. They involve the *combination* of outputs that determine revenue.

More formally, we first need to explicitly specify the Lagrangian for the optimization problem (9.11a) as max $\Lambda(\mathbf{Y}, \Theta) = \mathbf{p_Y}^T\mathbf{Y} + \Theta(1-D_O(\mathbf{v},\mathbf{Y}))$, which results in the first order condition $\mathbf{p_Y} - \Theta\nabla_Y D_O(\mathbf{v},\mathbf{Y}) = 0$, where ∇_Y is a vector of first derivatives of $D_O(\mathbf{v},\mathbf{Y})$ with respect to the outputs, so one such equation exists for each component of total output.

Färe and Primont [1995] show that $\Theta(\mathbf{v},\mathbf{p_Y}) = R(\mathbf{v},\mathbf{p_Y})$; the optimal value of the Lagrangian multiplier equals maximum revenue for each $\mathbf{v}$, $\mathbf{p_Y}$ combination. Further, if we define

9.12) $z(\mathbf{v},\mathbf{Y}) = \nabla_Y D_O(\mathbf{v},\mathbf{Y})$,

substitute $z(\mathbf{v},\mathbf{Y})$ into the first order conditions, and use the definition of the Lagrangian function, we can derive:

9.13) $z = R(\mathbf{v},\mathbf{p_Y}) \cdot z(\mathbf{v},\mathbf{Y}) = R(\mathbf{v},\mathbf{p_Y})\nabla_Y D_O(\mathbf{v},\mathbf{Y})$

which can be interpreted as the (relative) output shadow price vector for the outputs, given $\mathbf{v}$.

Färe *et al* [1993] show from this that the derivatives of the distance function with respect to $\mathbf{Y}$ can be interpreted as revenue-deflated relative output shadow prices:

9.14) $z_m(\mathbf{v},\mathbf{Y}) = \partial D_O(\mathbf{v},\mathbf{Y})/\partial Y_m = Z^D_m(\mathbf{v},\mathbf{Y})/R^*(\mathbf{v},\mathbf{Z}^D)$

where the D superscript indicates that this is defined according to the distance function, the m indicates that this expression is for output Y_m, the Z notation suggests that this will be the basis for a shadow value definition based on the derivative of the distance function, and $R^*(\mathbf{v},\mathbf{Z}^D)$ denotes shadow revenue (revenue evaluated at shadow instead of market values of the outputs).

The problem with this is that $R^*(\mathbf{v},\mathbf{Z}^D)$ depends on the shadow prices that we are trying to define. In order to define the absolute instead of relative shadow prices, therefore, one shadow value must be assumed to equal the market price. If, say, $Z^D_1 = p_{Y1}$, then $R^*(\mathbf{v},\mathbf{Z}^D)$ becomes $p_{Y1}/\partial D_O(\mathbf{v},\mathbf{Y})/\partial Y_1$, so

$$9.15)\ Z^D_m = R^*(\mathbf{v},\mathbf{Z}^D) \cdot \partial D_O(\mathbf{v},\mathbf{Y})/\partial Y_m$$

$$= p_{Y1} \cdot [(\partial D_O(\mathbf{v},\mathbf{Y})/\partial Y_m)/(\partial D_O(\mathbf{v},\mathbf{Y})/\partial Y_1)] \ .$$

or $Z^D_m / p_{Y1} = [\partial D_O(\mathbf{v},\mathbf{Y})/\partial Y_m]/[\partial D_O(\mathbf{v},\mathbf{Y})/\partial Y_1]$. This equivalence expresses the ratio of derivatives of the distance functions as the relative price ratio, where one of these may be imputed as a shadow value given knowledge of the other's market price.

This ratio may thus also be interpreted as the marginal rate of transformation between these two outputs, or the slope of the production possibility frontier. This is analogous to computing the marginal rate of substitution between inputs, or the slope of the isoquant, as the ratio of the marginal products of the inputs.

If equilibrium prevails this will equal the ratio of the market prices, but if not, one shadow price may be computed to equate the price ratio to the slope of the isoquant. This is closely related to the conceptual basis provided for the shadow value Z_K as the price that would make the current capital level optimal for a given labor input price and output level, in Chapter 3.

Input shadow values may also be computed in this framework. Although typically their construction is motivated from the input-based distance function (analogously to the output shadow values from D_O here), it is also possible to compute them more similarly to those based on a production function directly from D_O.

That is, since the output-oriented distance function is essentially a multiple-output production function, one can construct "marginal product" estimates as overviewed in Chapter 8 to use similarly to a primal-side version of our cost-side Z_K measure. More specifically, $VMP_j = MP_j \cdot p_Y$ which would equal p_j in equilibrium, can be thought of as an technologically-based shadow value for input j. The required MP_j may be computed from the logarithmic version of the marginal product $\partial \ln Y_1/\partial \ln v_j = \partial Y_1/\partial v_j \cdot (v_j/Y_1)$ from Chapter 8 (where $-\ln Y_1$ is the dependent variable of the transformed distance function, as in 8.4, and this derivative holds all relative output levels constant which implies a general increase in output levels), as $MP_j = \partial \ln Y_1/\partial \ln v_j \cdot (Y_1/v_j)$.

6.   MEASURES REPRESENTING FIRM BEHAVIOR

The development of the cost-based production theory framework for evaluation of production structure and performance in previous chapters, plus the theoretical foundation provided in the foregoing sections of this chapter, suggest numerous measures that may be computed to represent the different production structure characteristics we have been focusing on.

Most of these measures involve either first or second order derivatives, and thus elasticities, of the cost function. Others may be computed from derivatives (and thus elasticities – their proportional or logarithmic counterparts) of profit, output demand, input supply, distance or revenue functions. In this section we will summarize some of this information to highlight the potential for empirical computation of these measures.

The input demand, output supply, investment and other behavioral equations implied by the theoretical development above completely represent the production structure. For empirical implementation, these decisions may be given explicit form by assuming a functional form for the function used for analysis, and estimating a system of equations comprised of these expressions (as discussed further in Chapter 11), to quantify the parameters defining the shapes of the functions and their derivatives.

In particular, in the cost based framework we have developed in this text (which suggests the cost function may be preferred for analysis, which will be maintained for this section), once the parameters of the model are estimated, the elasticities discussed in previous chapters can directly be computed. These elasticities represent various aspects of the production process we have focused on, such as technical change, capacity utilization, and cost economies (and their components and determinants). We can also measure input demand elasticities and biases.

If based on a restricted cost framework, these measures represent only short run behavior, although long run or steady state responses may also be imputed. Movement to a long run point may be implicit or explicit depending on whether investment equations are actually derived and used.

For example, a cost-side technical change measure has been motivated in terms of a first derivative of the cost function (1st order). That is, it is based on the cost elasticity $\varepsilon_{TCt} = \partial \ln TC(\bullet)/\partial t$ where $TC(\bullet)$ is the total cost function.

If this (logarithmic or proportionate) derivative is constructed, the resulting index of technical change will depend on the exogenous variables facing the firm; these variables are arguments of the cost function itself and therefore of its derivative. Therefore, determining how technical change is affected by exogenous variables simply requires computing the elasticity of ε_{TCt} with respect to one of these variables, which in turn involves taking the second derivative of the cost function.

We have seen that we can intepret such indicators as bias measures in some contexts. For example, $\partial\varepsilon_{TCt}/\partial\ln p_j = \partial^2\ln TC/\partial t\partial\ln p_j$ indicates how technical change is affected by change in the price of input j. As mentioned in Chapter 2, this is equivalent to computing the bias B_{jt}, which is the symmetric second derivative $\partial^2\ln TC/\partial\ln p_j\partial t$, since $\partial\ln TC/\partial\ln p_j=S_j$ (where S_j is the input j cost share). These expressions can easily be computed from estimated parameters of an implementable cost equation system.

Another first order cost elasticity, if the cost function used as a base is a variable or restricted function, has been shown to be $\varepsilon_{TCk}= \partial\ln TC(\bullet)/\partial x_k$, which is the (negative) cost-side net shadow value $-(Z_k-p_k)\bullet x_k/TC$. This expression stems from the first derivative property of the VC function, $\partial VC(\bullet)/\partial x_k = -Z_k$. Associated second derivatives – elasticities of this elasticity – have been shown to be interpretable as utilization biases.

Second order elasticities based on Z_k rather than ε_{TCk} may also be computed to show, for example, what the impact of an increase in demand for output would imply for the shadow value of capital (Z_K), and thus for investment behavior. Similarly, elasticities with respect to an input price provide indications of substitutability with the (quasi-)fixed factor. A positive value of the elasticity with respect to the price of labor or wage indicates that potential for substitution exists; resulting declines in labor use would be accommodated by increased capital investment. These shadow value elasticities may be written as $\varepsilon_{ZKY}= \partial\ln Z_K/\partial\ln Y$, and $\varepsilon_{ZKj}= \partial\ln Z_K/\partial\ln p_j$.

The ε_{TCk} measure is closely related to (or a component of) the overall cost economy measure, represented again by a first-order proportional derivative or elasticity: $\varepsilon_{TCY}=\partial\ln TC/\partial\ln Y$.[190] Its second derivatives, motivated as scale biases in Chapter 4, can be used to identify the determinants of scale economies. For example, $\partial^2\ln TC/\partial\ln Y\partial\ln p_j = \partial\varepsilon_{TCY}/\partial p_j$ shows how returns to scale are affected by changes in the price of input j. Similar derivatives can be constructed to assess the impacts of any other exogenous variable.[191]

As discussed in Chapter 3, the ε_{TCY} measure is a combination of capacity utilization and returns to scale. If constant returns to scale exist, but fixities also prevail, the ε_{TCY} elasticities are equivalent to the ε_{TCK} elasticities. They can be used to reflect capacity utilization and its variations with changes in exogenous variable (utilization biases), as discussed in Chapter 3.

If both fixity and returns to scale are evident, however, distinguishing the two becomes somewhat more difficult. As we have seen, in this case the expression $CU_c = TC^*/TC = (VC + \Sigma_k Z_k x_k)/(VC + \Sigma_k p_k x_k) = 1-\Sigma_k\varepsilon_{TCk}$ must directly be constructed and its derivative taken to determine CU and its changes. To separately identify scale economies $\eta=\varepsilon^L_{TCY}$ must be computed.

---

[190] Recall that primal returns to scale are measured by the inverse of this measure.
[191] See Morrison [1988b] for further details.

The long run $\eta=\varepsilon^L_{TCY}$ measure can be computed as a full long run elasticity, as outlined in Chapter 4. Alternatively it can be represented using the equality developed in Morrison [1992b], $\varepsilon_{TCY} = \varepsilon^L_{TCY}CU_c = (MC \cdot Y/TC^*)$ $\cdot(TC^*/TC)$, where $MC = \partial TC/\partial Y = \partial VC/\partial Y$ in the short run. This results in the expression $\varepsilon^L_{TCY}=MC \cdot Y/TC^*$, which can be used to construct measures of returns to scale and its derivatives.

With multiple outputs, scope economies are reflected in the ε_{TCYm} measures, which reflect the marginal-to-average cost ratio for the particular output (and are components of the ε_{TCY} measure), and the associated 2nd order derivatives with respect to other outputs. That is, ε_{TCYm} is based on the first derivative of the cost function, $\partial TC/\partial Y_m$ (or $\partial VC/\partial Y_m$ with fixities). If the derivative of this (2nd derivative of TC or VC) with respect to Y_1 is negative, this implies that some jointness, or scope economies, exists. If it is negative, scope diseconomies, or economies of specialization, are evident.

Note also that, as we saw earlier in this chapter, additional shadow value-type computations may be carried out for other functions such as profit or distance functions, or for other arguments of the functions such as external factors. These values again reflect true economic or "effective" contributions of the factors. This is a rich basis, therefore, for analysis of a full set of performance indicators, such as technical change, and cost economies.

A last first order derivative or elasticity that we have not devoted as much attention to as an indicator of productive structure or performance has to do with input prices. In derivative form this is Shephard's or Hotelling's lemma, which we have seen reproduces input demand for the associated input for markets which are "working". That is, $v_j=\partial TC/\partial p_j$. In logarithmic or elasticity form this measures the cost shares: $S_j=\partial \ln TC/\partial \ln p_j$.

These derivatives or elasticities are not directly indicative of economic performance (although they typically provide the basis for the system of estimating equations, as emphasized more in Chapter 11). But second order derivatives from these expressions may be used to summarize not only (technical change and other) biases, as we have seen, but also a full pattern of substitution responses of firms.

That is, this provides the basis for measuring input demand elasticities. For example, the own-demand elasticity (responsiveness of labor demand, say, to wage increases) is $\varepsilon_{jpj} = \partial \ln v_j/\partial \ln p_j$. Similarly, substitutability or complementarity among the variable inputs may be represented by the cross-demand elasticities $\varepsilon_{jpi} = \partial \ln v_j/\partial \ln p_i$.

Output, utilization, and other types of elasticities can be specified if Y, fixed inputs or other associated variables are included as arguments of the cost function and thus the demand equation $v_j(\cdot)=\partial TC(\cdot)/\partial p_j$. For example, the elasticity of demand for input j with respect to a change in output is $\partial \ln v_j/\partial \ln Y=\varepsilon_{jY}$. Substitution of the variable with the fixed input may be similarly represented by $\partial \ln v_j / \partial \ln x_k = \varepsilon_{jk}$, and of the (internal) variable input with an externally provided factor by $\partial \ln v_j / \partial \ln r_b = \varepsilon_{jb}$.

For multiple outputs the input- and output- specific "scale" (cost) effects may be computed as elasticities with respect to components of the $\mathbf{Y}$ vector; $\varepsilon_{jYm} = \partial \ln v_j / \partial \ln Y_m$.[192] If $\varepsilon_{jYm} < \varepsilon_{TCY}$, for example, this suggests a smaller increase in input j is necessary than on average over all inputs to support an output m increase – output Y_m expansion is input v_j-saving.

In logarithmic form elasticities provide the basis for bias expressions, since the resulting measures become *relative* measures of responsiveness. As we have seen, for example, the short run scale or output bias may be written as $\partial S_j / \partial \ln Y = B_{Yt} = S_j(\varepsilon_{jY} - \varepsilon_{TCY})$.

Input demand elasticities are sometimes presented instead as Allen partial elasticities of substitution (AES), which are combinations of (total) cost derivatives and are symmetric ($\sigma_{ij} = \sigma_{ji}$). They can be written in terms of input shares, and therefore are primarily used when a translog model is specified since shares are a natural unit for such a model.[193]

Short run Allen elasticities are specified as:

9.16) $\sigma_{jn} = TC \cdot TC_{jn} / TC_j \cdot TC_n \big|_{x = \bar{x}}$

where n can denote variable input prices (p_i), x_k, t or Y. Thus, for the translog functional form presented in Chapter 11, for example, Allen elasticities for variable input price changes become

9.17) $\sigma_{ji} = [(VC/TC)\gamma_{ji} + S_j S_i \cdot (TC/VC)]/S_j S_i, \ j \neq i$ and

$$\sigma_{jj} = [(VC/TC)\gamma_{jj} + (S_j^2 - S_j) \cdot (TC/VC)]/S_j^2$$

for the own-elasticity of input j. Similarly, short run output elasticities are:

9.18) $\sigma_{jY} = [(VC/TC)\gamma_{jY} + S_j \cdot \varepsilon_{TCY} \cdot (TC/VC)]/S_j \cdot \varepsilon_{TCY}$,

and elasticities with respect to t are analogous with t substituted for Y. Quasi-fixed input elasticities are slightly different because the x_k appear both in VC and in the remainder of the TC expression:

9.19) $\sigma_{jk} = [(VC/TC)\gamma_{jk} + S_j \cdot (\varepsilon_{TCk}(TC/VC) - p_k(x_k/VC))]/S_j \cdot \varepsilon_{TCk}$.

---

[192] Note that there will be no input-specific scope elasticities since this would require a third-order approximation.

[193] See Berndt [1990] Chapter 9 for further discussion of the translog model.

The relationships between these AES expressions and the input demand elasticities derived above are straightforward. For example, the short run cross price elasticities are $\partial\ln v_j/\partial\ln p_i \equiv \varepsilon_{ji} = S_i\sigma_{ji}$. Similarly, the demand elasticity with respect to technical change is $\partial\ln v_j/\partial t \equiv \varepsilon_{jt} = \varepsilon_{TCt}\sigma_{jt}$. Elasticities with respect to output and fixed inputs follow analogously.

Another form in which elasticities are sometimes expressed is Morishima elasticities. These are "relative" elasticity representations, but this time in terms of other inputs. They therefore approximate the notion of changes in a marginal rate of substitution from a change in the price ratio. For example, the Morishima elasticity, MES_{ji}, can be expressed as: $MES_{ji} = \varepsilon_{ji}-\varepsilon_{jj}$.[194] All information necessary for computation of Morishima elasticities is thus contained in the demand elasticities ε_{ji} .

Cost-based first and second order elasticities therefore summarize detailed input and output patterns underlying the cost structure. They also allow assessment of market power questions, although they do not directly permit consideration of what might affect output demand or input supply functions.

For example, the cost function may be used to compute a marginal cost value to compare to output price to determine whether a "wedge" exists between the market and true economic (shadow) marginal valuation of output (marginal cost). This is similar to comparing market and shadow values of inputs that might violate Shephard's lemma due to fixities or market failures.

However, evaluation of the cause of the wedge is not possible without information on the output demand structure, since it depends on the deviation of marginal revenue from price; $MR=p_Y+\partial p_Y(Y)/\partial Y \cdot Y$, so $\partial p_Y/\partial Y \cdot Y$ reflects the wedge. Assessing this further requires evaluation of the $p_Y(Y)$ relationship. In particular, it was shown in Chapter 6 that the markup is based on an elasticity of this (inverse) output demand function with respect to output, $\varepsilon_{PY} = \partial\ln p_Y(Y)/\partial\ln Y$.

Similarly, for an input supply relationship $p_l(x_l)$, the deviation of the shadow from the market price for this input will depend on the difference between the marginal and average factor costs, $MFC= p_l + \partial p_l(x_l)/\partial x_l \cdot x_l$ and p_l. This will in turn depend on, and thus could be represented by, the elasticity of the input supply or pricing equation with respect to the input level; $\varepsilon_{pll} = \partial\ln p_l(x_l)/\partial\ln x_l$. If this (or the output demand) relationship is fully specified, and the assumed functional form sufficiently flexible (containing cross- or second order terms), we can also determine the dependence of these relationships on the arguments of the input supply (output demand) function via elasticities of these first order elasticity expressions.

Finally, two additional points should be noted about the elasticities overviewed in this section.

---

[194] See Huang [1991] for further discussion of this.

First, since the elasticities depend on the data as well as on the parameters, they will vary by observation. Changes over time in technical change, returns to scale, and capacity utilization measures are important for analysis so they are generally reported as indexes (with values for each time period). However, for input demand elasticities, some "average" value is more often of interest. So these measures are often reported for the observation where the deflators used for estimation are normalized to one, for some "representative" observation, or as averages over particular time periods.

Second, since the parameters each have associated distributions, the elasticities constructed from them also have a stochastic specification, so it is possible to compute standard errors. Depending on the complexity of the functional form and the nature of the data, however, these standard errors may be difficult to compute, since they typically involve a combination of parameters (and data), each with its own standard error. One procedure to accomplish this is to specify the equations directly as functions of the parameters and compute the estimated covariance matrix for this set of functions by linearizing the functions around the estimated parameter values. This permits the use of standard formulas for the variance and covariance of linear functions of random variables.[195]

7.   FURTHER COMMENTS

This chapter has overviewed the theoretical foundations of the production theory models discussed in previous chapters. Empirical implementation of these quite complex models is, however, not as straightforward.

For all models of production structure and productivity growth, including those based on accounting or simple parametric methods, when moving toward empirical implementation a crucial question is how to construct relevant data. Problems that emerge may be especially critical for capital, since its durability poses measurement questions and the economic theory underlying the notion of capital has no direct counterpart in standard balance sheet or income statement entries for firms. This is a particularly important obstacle in the restricted cost function context since capital is a primary emphasis for capacity utilization measurement. Such questions must be dealt with before econometric estimation may proceed, in order ultimately to generate meaningful results. This is the focus of the following chapter.

---

[195] This can be done with econometric packages such as TSP by the ANALYZ command. Bootstrapping methods can also be used.

Chapter 10

Data Construction for Estimation and Measurement

Data used for estimating production theory models, or generating accounting measures of productivity growth, are typically time series of prices and quantities of output, and labor, capital, and materials inputs, for a firm, industry, or economy. Although it is useful to include information on as many outputs and inputs as possible in order to reflect all production and costs, and thus detailed production structure patterns, many data issues complicate the construction of such data.

For example, output is usually measured as an aggregate of all types of production. However, in many cases it may be important to identify output categories separately, especially if product quality and composition differ across time or productive unit under consideration. Quality and composition issues and related aggregation questions are pervasive for construction of data to be used for analysis of production processes and performance.

For inputs, the categories often distinguished are capital (K), labor (L), energy (E), non-energy intermediate materials (M), and sometimes purchased services (PS). Inputs such as land and inventories are often included in the measure of capital. Others, like pollution abatement capital, may be implicitly included, and some, such as R&D or advertising expenses, are the focus of some studies but often otherwise ignored.

The construction of data on any of these output and input components raises questions and complications, but representation of capital services is perhaps the most problematic. Some issues about the distinction between capital stock and services were raised in Chapter 3. However, even more fundamental issues, involving its durable or stock nature, lurk under the development of the base measures of capital quantity and price. The stock issue also creates difficulties for measurement of other capital-related inputs such as labor (human capital) and R&D.

Capital data construction requires representing the current flow of input use. The *services* from the available stock of capital, and the *rental* or *user* prices of these services, are the relevant values for construction of productivity growth measures, neither of which are readily observable.

Aggregation problems also raise serious questions, since none of the data categories, except possibly labor, can be represented in terms of one unit of measurement. And even for labor, which has a natural measurement in terms of workers (or better yet, hours) the "effective" input from a given worker-hour will differ depending on a number of quality issues. Possibly the most important of these is the amount of human capital (education and training) embodied in the person, but spatial (regional or country) and demographic characteristics are also likely to have an impact.

Therefore, quantity indexes aggregating (or adding up) "apples and oranges" (like tons of iron ore and yards of cloth in the M category, or managers and assembly-line workers for L) must be constructed. This is difficult to accomplish in a justifiable and thus interpretable manner.

Other questions arise about aggregation across firms, regions, or industries to obtain production data for analysis of patterns and trends in industries or countries. These questions involve whether a "representative producer" may be invoked for analysis, or whether reallocations within, say, industries, are critical for representing the aggregate.

In this chapter such questions, particularly those related to composition, capital measurement and aggregation, are addressed to facilitate appropriate data construction for representation of production processes and productivity growth. Section 1 overviews problems arising for construction of non-capital output and input data, and Section 2 focuses conceptual and then analytical questions underlying capital measurement procedures. Finally, Section 3 elaborates some of the aggregation issues that arise in data construction.

1.   NON-CAPITAL OUTPUT AND INPUT DATA

Many issues arise when attempting to construct appropriate price and quantity measures of non-capital inputs and outputs. These issues are wide-ranging but often involve aggregating across heterogeneous commodities. Problems arising from quality or compositional differentials across time or productive unit are raised here primarily in the context of output measurement, but are pervasive across all outputs and inputs. Identifying such differentials may involve careful specification of the disaggregated components and appropriate adding based on index numbers, or construction of a model or index explicitly representing the underlying characteristics. In any case, they raise important issues to take into account in either or both the data construction and modeling process.[196]

---

[196] A comprehensive overview of data for productivity measurement developed by the by the U.S. BLS, with a focus on compositional issues, is provided in Dean and Harper [1998].

1.1   Output production

Output (Y) measurement for a single-output firm is fairly straightforward, since there is only one type of unit involved – say bushels of apples, pairs of shoes or tons of steel. Therefore, an (average) price per bushel, pair or ton can generally be specified in dollars (or other monetary units) as total value of the product divided by the quantity of the commodity; quantity and price indexes can directly be measured.

Even in this simple case, however, questions begin to emerge. In particular, it is not immediately clear how quality differences, or product heterogeneity, can be handled. In a few cases (tons of steel might be an example) this is not a critical issue since the product is quite homogeneous. But in most cases (e.g. computers produced) quality or characteristics of a particular unit might differ dramatically over time or across companies.

If the product is very heterogeneous, capturing characteristics of the product becomes an important issue. These problems are not well dealt with using conventional data gathering procedures, but some researchers have attempted to accommodate them using careful and detailed index number or hedonic measurement techniques.

For example, Triplett [1989] and Gordon [1989] applied such reasoning to the measurement of computer price (and thus implicitly quantity) indexes. As elaborated further below, the computer problem is one that has generated much attention, both in terms of its measurement as an output produced, and as an input into production of other commodities. Another topical application has been to pharmaceuticals (see Berndt *et al* [1993, 1996]).

Inventories also pose difficulties for output measurement because sales and production differ from change in output inventories. For productivity measurement, sales data must be adjusted by inventory change to determine the true production for given inputs used during a particular period.

Other questions might arise for data at the firm level about how to deal with promotional "giveaways" or other sales promotions that affect the value of the output produced, and purchases of final goods for resale. Again, while these problems are often finessed, they should not be forgotten.

Additional dilemmas arise if the firm produces multiple products. The issue of how to combine goods that are measured in different units is a standard index-number problem that is difficult to deal with. While determining the total value of production is quite straightforward, dividing this value into its aggregate quantity and price (deflator) components is not.

Index number theories are generally relied on to provide the best guide to the type of index to compute, but even theoretically founded measures are not truly justifiable unless relative price or quantity changes across commodities are "very" similar, or marginal products do not change with changes in prices.[197] These problems, of course, become more severe when aggregation to an industry or country is attempted. These aggregation and index number issues will be elaborated further in Section 4.

Another issue that has gained increasing attention in the recent literature is "new products".[198] This is in a sense a special case of the characteristics or quality problem, since it is not always clear when something might be called a new product or is instead a derivation (in terms of characteristics) from an old product.[199]

This is sometimes dealt with simply as an aggregation question. For example, Gordon and Griliches [1997] say it involves "taking individual categories of consumer expenditure, assessing quality-change bias for each category, and then aggregating using appropriate weights".

As we have seen, such an issue can also motivate explicitly modeling the characteristics of products (or factors) through, say, hedonic models, or directly dealing with composition by disaggregating different types of products with varying characteristics. In this sense the case of multiple outputs is similar to distinguishing labor educational categories, or differentiating structures and/or high tech equipment from other capital, as referred to in previous chapters.

This problem has often been addressed in the context of biases in consumer price index (CPI) measurement arising from changing quality or types of consumer products over time, where the CPI is a price index for overall production from the consumption side.

Some researchers have focused on bias estimates derived from research on characteristics of particular product categories, and assumed the remainder of the CPI has been measured appropriately (Lebow *et al* [1994], Shapiro and Wilcox [1996]). However, a component by component evaluation by Boskin *et al* [1996], and reported on briefly in Gordon and Griliches [1997], indicates that quality increases of about 0.6 percent per year are being generated overall. These changes differ by category, with the largest changes associated with high-tech equipment.

---

[197] The sufficient conditions of proportionate (constant relative) prices and quantities are due to Hicks and Leontief, respectively, and are discussed by Parks [1971]. Even if these conditions do not hold, however, separability allows aggregation. One of the simplest separability requirements is that the relationship between two commodities, represented by the ratio of their marginal products, does not change with alterations in relative prices of other commodities.

[198] See not only the references cited below but also the many interesting studies in Bresnahan and Gordon [1996] for further details about this important question.

[199] See in particular Gordon and Griliches [1997], and the many related studies in the edited volume by Bresnahan and Gordon [1996].

The quality changes arise from varying characteristics such as variety of fruits and vegetables, size of residential units, length of life of automobiles and increasingly high-tech electronics and appliances. If not taken into account, they will appear as price instead of quantity increases that will bias estimates of productivity growth by understating output quantity increases.

The discussion in Gordon and Griliches [1997] highlights the role of the CPI as an index designed to compare over time "the minimum expenditure required to achieve the same level of well being". Questions immediately arise about how one might determine the "same level of well being", since this involves welfare comparisons which cannot easily be measured. Abstracting from this question, however, raises another one that is more relevant here. If we assume that "well being" can be inferred by comparing bundles of commodities consumed, how do we impute this between two periods if the products have different characteristics or are even different commodities altogether?

In terms of construction of price index numbers (and therefore implicitly quantity measures) the "product cycle" becomes of importance when new good or characteristics of goods is in question. The product cycle suggests that new goods are typically priced high initially, with prices subsequently falling and then possibly beginning to rise again as the product "matures".

It has been shown for both the computer and pharmaceuticals industries (see Berndt et al [1993,1996] and Dulberger [1993], respectively) that this pattern, plus lags in bringing commodities into CPI computations, causes upward biases in price indexes and thus downward biases in the growth of quality-adjusted product quantity. Even more dramatic indicators of biases in the computer industry have been implied by more specific analysis of their characteristics in hedonic analyses such as Triplett [1989].[200] Another bias results from product or market definitions as noted by Gordon and Griliches:

> "When a new product is finally introduced into the CPI, no comparison is made of the price and quality of the new product with the price and quality of an old product that performed the same function. For instance, people flock to rent videos, but the declining price of seeing a movie at home... is not taken into account in the CPI". (p. 85)

In addition, some new products have no really close counterparts, such as E-mail and cellular phones which have such different characteristics than their pre-cursors that it is difficult to link them with previously existing markets, and thus to identify their impact on well-being.

---

[200] This study also provides an extensive overview of the literature on and techniques for hedonic analysis. See also Berndt [1990] Chapter 4 for a general overview of the hedonic literature.

Some recent literature, however, attempts to recognize increases in product variety and their potential impact on consumer welfare by looking at market shares of different types of products.[201] In this case if new models gain market share, one can infer that they embody characteristics preferred by consumers even at possibly higher prices.

As noted also by Griliches and Gordon (and discussed in more detail in Chapter 7), when output measurement is focused on determining the "effective product" or welfare enhancement from new or better products, we might also want to recognize the associated "bads".

One type of bad output appears, for example, in the context of air travel, where the number of travellers has increased dramatically, but at a great cost in terms of congestion and service. The effective quantity of product in standard units such as air-miles has declined since negative products are being created simultaneously.

Possibly even more importantly, if consumers are becoming better off by increased quality and variety of products, but this is associated with reduced environmental quality, crime, or other "bads", this should also be recognized in a more macro context focusing on welfare implications. Output growth should be "deflated" by recognition of these associated negative products.

For the purposes we are primarily raising these issues here – that is, representation of economic performance of a firm or sector – the quality and characteristics of the produced products are the primary issue. When assessing productivity growth for an entire economy, however, these broader questions become important to take into consideration.

1.2   Labor

Labor input (L) is relatively easy to measure compared to most inputs, since labor statistics are generally presented in terms of wage bill paid (total expenditure) and number of workers or worker-hours (quantity). This allows a direct division of the expenditure into quantity and price. Problems still arise, however, for identifying "effective" labor input.

First, although hours worked would be a better measure of true labor input than number of workers, many firms do not collect the data necessary to provide such information. In addition, as alluded to above, there may be important differences by type of worker. For example, it may be useful to distinguish between salaried (non-production) and wage (production) employees. Also, entrepreneurial input is not typically included in data on laborers. A similar problem arises from contract or temporary labor demand. This component of labor is often reported differently than standard labor

---

[201] See, for example, Berry [1994], Trajtenberg [1990], and Hausman [1996].

expenses on income statements of firms, provoking questions about whether this input should be considered part of labor or of purchased services.

The quality of labor might also change over time, which has caused some researchers to make adaptations to account for education, training and other quality components that might affect the average efficiency of workers independently of overall technical change.[202] All these issues need to be addressed to construct relevant measures of labor input quantities and price.

The issue of labor composition and its impact on the appropriate measurement of effective labor inputs, addressed in detail by Jorgenson *et al* [1987], is particularly important. A somewhat more recent and even more comprehensive discussion of labor composition in the U.S., as well as estimates generated using U.S. BLS data is contained in U.S. BLS [1993].

In the latter study a number of reasons workers might differ in their level of skill are discussed, with a particular empirical focus on adjusting for educational attainment and work experience, as well as decomposing the data by gender. A theoretical model connects this with the human capital and hedonic wage literatures, which recognize the stock nature of skill characteristics that are accumulated through time. Since the amount of time invested in education or gaining experience may be measured, this provides a reasonable step toward adapting existing data for the most easily observed contributors to the deviation between labor hours and effective units.

Adapting labor data to represent effective units may be accomplished by careful weighting of the inputs in the aggregation process (such as a Törnqvist index with wages used as weights to represent the "productivity" of the type of worker; see Section 4 below). It can alternatively be carrried out by constructing an index of "effectiveness" or "efficiency" to multiply by the hours measure (as in Jorgenson *et al* [1987]).

The BLS procedures rely on a detailed creation of appropriate weights for aggregating labor inputs, based on wage equations with characteristics of workers as explanatory variables.[203] This is similar in spirit to constructing a hedonic price index to distinguish price from quantity growth more appropriately. This process is discussed in some detail in U.S. BLS [1993], as is the contribution of composition (separated from hours to indicate their independent sources of growth) to MFP measures independently from the L and K measures discussed in Chapter 2 (following U.S. BLS [1983]).

---

[202] See Jorgenson, *et al* [1987] for a discussion of how such labor data might be constructed. This reference also provides important information on measurement of other inputs. Again, adjustment of labor data for quality changes might also take the form of hedonic measurement.

[203] See Dean, Harper and Sherwood [1996] for a detailed and broader overview of the issues involves in constructing changing-weight output and input indexes to represent compositional changers.

Note also again that labor compositional issues may alternatively be dealt with by including an index of human capital as a separate input into the production theory model to identify its independent impact, or it could be accommodated by including separate categories for labor types that might be expected to have a different marginal products. One more possible approach, elaborated further in Chapter 11, is to explicitly represent the distinction between measured and effective input as measurement error. This is particularly appropriate if it appears important unmeasured characteristics have impacts on marginal products.

This discussion, although brief, touches on some important issues affecting the measurement of labor inputs. As shown in U.S. BLS [1993], the quality/composition issue is not only conceptually but also empirically very important, as documented in a number of tables indicating changes in labor characteristics from 1949 to 1990.

1.3   Materials inputs

Three different "materials" inputs are often distinguished in productivity studies – intermediate materials, purchased services, and energy. Although energy has a very small cost share it is often thought to have important indirect effects, such as its impact on the obsolescence of energy-inefficient capital in the 1970s. In reverse, intermediate materials typically has a very large cost-share – often exceeding 70% and in many industries increasing relative to capital and labor inputs – and yet rarely is a focus of analysis.

Service inputs are also important to distinguish, particularly given their swelling cost share, although they are often "lumped in" with materials. There is an increasing tendency of firms to hire firms to carry out tasks historically often accomplished within the firm (cleaning, accounting, and legal services, for example). This "outsourcing" allows increased flexibility of responsiveness to economic forces, since it reduces the problem of labor hoarding (services are typically paid for as a flow). However, if this labor input is not recognized, misleading interpretation of measures such as labor productivity will result.

These patterns suggest that an important focus of data construction, which has not been targeted in much of the existing literature, is to further analyze the composition of the materials input.[204] Even though this has not

---

[204] One place where this may have particularly important implications is for agricultural products. In food industries, which comprise about 20% of U.S. manufacturing, the materials input component has embodied a falling share of agricultural products, which in turn impacts on agricultural producers. Current research by Catherine Morrison and Jim MacDonald at the USDA/ERS is focused on using micro data to untangle the different components of materials costs in food processing industries.

yet generated much interest, at least the changing overall materials share, and the resulting inappropriateness of value added specifications for analysis of most productive processes, is now generally accepted.

More specific issues of materials measurement involve, again, thinking carefully about the units of measurement and potential composition/quality issues within each of the standard categories.

Energy input (E), for example, is sometimes measured in units which facilitate direct summation of different types of energy use – either BTUs or megawatt hours, for example. In this case simple summation of BTUs (MWHs) generates a quantity measure, and summation of the expenditures on these energy sources and division of this value by the quantity of BTUs (MWHs) results in a direct average price per BTU (MWH) measure.

Some issues arise here, however, about whether input- or output-BTUs are a more valid measure for the quantity of energy demanded, since conversion efficiency differs, affecting the validity of such a simple aggregation process.[205] Also, it is sometimes not completely clear whether a particular input is an energy or non-energy material input. For example, is crude petroleum in the refining sector an energy or material input? Finally, if energy sources are measured in different units, a quantity index must instead be developed based on index number theory, since substitution between energy sources is not perfect. Ultimately, therefore, individual judgment and assumptions are still built into the data by the researcher.

Non-energy intermediate materials (M) and purchased services (PS) tend to be "catch-all" categories which include data on numerous inputs with widely varying units of measurement. Quality changes over time are, of course, generally difficult to deal with in such a context. Another problem is distinguishing what belongs in these categories rather than others. Justification of aggregation procedures also remains an issue, as for measurement of any output or input category, particular with such a potentially broad range of heterogeneous components.

In particular, an important obstacle for construction of these data is that many inputs in these categories appear on firms' income statements only in terms of the value of the input, with no measure of quantity or price. Since it is fundamentally important to determine how much of the value change can justifiably be considered a result of changes in unit price over time rather than in the quantity units themselves, relevant price indexes or deflators must be found to use for aggregation purposes. Only then can meaningful quantity and price indexes be distinguished.

---

[205] See Berndt [1978] for further discussion of this problem.

Accomplishing this is sometimes difficult. Some researchers have argued that an overall GDP deflator is useful for many purposes,[206] or that if an input might be thought of as labor-intensive an overall labor cost deflator might be better. It is, however, also often possible to find output deflators for specific industries,[207] and these might in many cases be preferable. For example, if a certain type of chemical is used for production, it might be most justifiable to use a chemical-industry-product deflator than an overall GDP deflator. Obtaining appropriate deflators for service inputs is even more problematic.

Note also that many of these quality issues are symmetric to those raised in the context of output production and "new goods". In particular, new electronic goods may be intermediate products for, say, production of an automobile or an appliance, so issues raised in terms of their output price biases have direct relevance here. If appropriate disaggregated data are available, it may be that the associated price weights on specific categories can be used for more appropriate aggregation using index number approaches (as discussed below) rather than simply using some aggregate deflator, but in many cases such data are simply not available

Finally, it should be emphasized that when using microeconomic data it may be particularly difficult to determine what category an input might fall into. For example, is repairs and maintenance (R&M) a materials or capital cost? One might think such information should qualify a capital expenditure measure, but this is often thrown into the M component. Sometimes it is even difficult to determine whether a factor is an output or input, such as doctors-in-training in hospital settings. Constructing and using micro data should therefore be pursued with care and thought since the interpretation of resulting measures is dependent on these types of choices, and variations in treatment do not have the potential to "cancel out" in the aggregate.

Overall, although much of the necessary information for non-capital data construction is obtainable from balance sheets and income statements of firms, or from aggregate data in government publications, many issues arise concerning interpreation and use of the data. These issues should be kept in mind when using the data, and ultimately interpreting the empirical results.

---

[206] Schankerman and Nadiri [1986] have used this for R&D expenditures, for example.

[207] These correspond to the output prices constructed for particular industries that might end up being intermediate goods to another industry. U.S. government statistics provide information up to a 7-digit level of disaggregation (where 2-digit industries comprise, for example, the 20 manufacturing industries in the manufacturing sector, moving to 3-digit, for example, divides the 2-digit food processing industry into 10 categories, and to 4-digit divides the meat products industry into four categories. 4-digit U.S. manufacturing data identifies 450 different; such data are available in NBER (National Bureau of Economic Research) productivity database, outlined in Bartlesman and Gray [1996].

1.4   R&D

Two more data issues may be raised here. First, an input often not taken into account in studies of productive behavior, but which may provide an explicit reason for technical progress to occur, is R&D. There is an extensive literature focusing on the issue of R&D, but when it is not the direct target of analysis it is often ignored. This seems largely because there are so many problems measuring both the stock and services of R&D, determining potential lags, and representing the probability distribution of expected returns, that may be important to link it to measured performance.

The stock-flow issue raises similar problems to other types of capital discussed below in the context of capital measurement, such as depreciation (which is often assumed to be about 10%/year) and user cost (which is often assumed to be well approximated by a GDP deflator).[208] Other issues are more unique to this particular input.

An excellent overview of the issues involved in R&D measurement, data availability, historical and current views, findings and estimates of the contribution of R&D to productivity growth, may be found in U.S. BLS [1989]. We will therefore just briefly touch on some fundamental issues.

The data on R&D expenditures primarily used to construct measures of R&D stocks for productivity computations are published by the National Science Foundation. When using these data, however, a number of problems are encountered. In particular, R&D is often carried out by large companies that produce many products, so dividing R&D expenditures into the different industries that the associated product might fit into is problematic. In addition, much R&D data available by "product field" refer only to applied research, whereas basic research is also important to take into account in order to identify the extent of and returns to R&D expenditures.

Also, measures of R&D expenditures reflect all labor and materials purchased for research. This raises two issues. One involves the capital contribution (like pollution abatement expenditures, capital purchased to "produce" R&D would be expected to have a different impact than that explicitly designated to output product), which is imputed from the implied depreciation measures for these assets rather than from expenditure data. These inputs will also typically already be embodied in the L and M measures, which implies that they need to be removed from those data.[209]

---

[208] See Mansfield [1987] for a more complete assessment of this issue.

[209] This very brief overview of some the issues encountered when attempting to construct R&D measures for productivity computations is obviously at best only indicative. For further information see US BLS [1989] and the many references provided, as well as useful surveys by Griliches [1991, 1994].

1.5   Service industries

Finally, it is worth noting the importance – and difficulty – of defining and measuring outputs and inputs for service industries. In this chapter (and in this text overall), we have implicitly been discussing the measurement of outputs, inputs, and thus production structure in the context of a sector or a firm that produces readily measurable products – for example a manufacturing or agricultural industry. However, a greater (and increasing proportion) of GNP in developed countries is devoted to service industries.

Service industries, that span a broad range including financial, communications, education, medical and many other types of services, often produce outputs that are not easily measurable. This is particularly true for, say, educational or medical services, where the quality issues we have been discussing are notoriously difficult to deal with. But it is also true of services such as banking, where clear markets exist but exactly what the "output" produced might be is not easily defined, much less measured.

An increasing amount of effort is now being devoted to such questions by both government agencies and academics. This is of interest both conceptually and also practically. New BLS and BEA (Bureau of Economic Analysis) measures have suggested that output per hour growth in the nonfarm business sector have been understated by about 1.3 percent per year. This suggests the mismeasurement of service output may be one significant "cause" of measured productivity growth declines, particularly given its ever-increasing share of the "pie" of U.S. GNP.[210] Some of these issues are overviewed in Baily and Zitzewitz [1998].[211] Others are discussed in Kendrick [1985], Englander [1989], Lebow and Sichel [1992], Gordon [1996], Fixler and Siegel [1998], and the many studies devoted to output measurement in service industries in Griliches [1992].

The difficulties of service sector output and input measurement complicate analysis of performance in these industries, due to not only quality but also definitional questions. However, conceptually, analysis of such industries may proceed analogously to those industries in which more standard "goods" rather than "services" are produced. Although I will not pursue this in any greater depth here, it is a rich area for future research.

---

[210] See the *Economic Report of the President*, February 1998 and Baumol [1967].

[211] Since this study is based on cross-sectional comparisons it can side-step issues of quality change over time, but still need to address questions of quality differences across industries and countries.

2. CAPITAL DATA CONSTRUCTION

Construction of capital data series poses even more difficulties than for most other inputs and outputs.

First, the categories are not clearly defined. Although capital plant (structures or buildings) and equipment typically provide the basis of the capital measure, other categories might also be thought to be important. As mentioned previously, inputs such as R&D have stock and therefore capital aspects, and therefore might comprise one component of the productive capital stock base available to the firm. Maintenance could also be considered part of capital holdings, since it may add to the stock (or at least the durability) of capital equipment.[212]

Other capital inputs which do not produce measurable output, such as pollution abatement capital, might by contrast be irrelevant for productivity measurement, and therefore should *not* be included in capital stock measures. Inventories also are often specified as an element of the capital stock, but arguably do not provide productive services, and therefore might be left out for productivity computations.

More standard components of the capital stock might also generate troublesome questions. Land, for example, may bestow widely ranging capital gains on its owner, which causes problems valuing it as a component of capital (its rental price could be negative if land values are improving, which is virtually meaningless in terms of its productive input).[213]

In addition, once data on these different components of the capital stock are developed and the relevant components determined, aggregation of these into an overall capital measure is required. The aggregation difficulties mentioned for the non-capital inputs are thus also again pervasive.

A primary difficulty that distinguishes the measurement of capital inputs, however, involves how to deal with measurement of a durable good that is not considered a "cost" to the firm by standard accounting practices. Expenditures on non-capital inputs (L, E, M and PS), in an accounting framework, are thought to encompass virtually all "valid" production costs.

---

[212] It might be useful here to mention here that if working with firm data, only some of the components of the balance sheet are consistent with an economist's notion of capital stock. Categories that might be included, for example, include both tangible and intangible fixed assets, "investments", inventories, and accounts receivable. The point is, however, to measure productive assets rather than financial assets, so "investments" in bonds or accounts receivables would not be considered part of the capital stock. Sometimes some categories of financial capital, however, are included under the heading of "working capital".

[213] Land is obviously particularly important for agricultural applications. Although I will not pursue this here, see Ball [1985] for an excellent discussion of data construction for productivity analysis of U.S. agriculture.

Categories on standard balance sheets representing capital outlays include depreciation (the amount allowed by the tax authorities, which may have no "economic" basis), taxes, R&D, equipment and structure rentals, R&M, and possibly current investment expenditures. Any revenue over and above these yearly expenditures on capital, and non-capital costs, are considered accounting "profits". However, additional expenses accrue to existing capital (and entrepreneurial) inputs that have a true economic opportunity cost.

Economists often go to the other extreme in computing the "expenditure" on (or returns to) capital. From the economist's perspective, if perfect competition and constant returns to scale prevail, all the "profits" measured by accountants are really returns to capital. They are necessary payments to the capital base; they represent its opportunity costs. If this is valid, a residual method of constructing the price of capital may be used, that imputes an internal rate of return to capital and assumes this *ex-post* rate of return is the capital stock's legitimate cost.[214]

For most productivity growth computations, neither of these concepts of capital's quantity, price and value are really valid.

The accountant's definition ignores the fact that there is a real cost of putting funds into a durable capital stock. This cost, often called the "user" cost of capital, includes not only the (economic) rate of depreciation, but also the loss of the return one could obtain on the money elsewhere, given the risk incurred. The firm (or the investor who provided the necessary funds) therefore *should* receive a certain amount of return to compensate for these costs. To an economist these are costs, not part of profits for the firm.

The economist's residual conception of capital also, however, has shortcomings. Some returns picked up in a measure of the *ex-post* or internal rate of return generated by a residual method may be due to technological and market characteristics like returns to scale and market power (imperfect competition in output or input markets). Some of the estimated returns could also be attributable to omitted inputs such as inventories, purchased services, selling expenses, or land.

For scale economies, it may be justifiable for the firm to absorb this as a return to K, since if larger firms incur lower average cost due to their technological base, increasing size is efficient. However, separate measurement of these returns is required for appropriate evaluation of capital value. For imperfect competition, returns or profits generated from market power should be distinguished to determine possible associated welfare loss.

---

[214] This is computed by taking the dollar value of sales (revenues), subtracting expenditures on variable inputs (non-capital costs) to obtain the value of or "returns to" capital, and then computing the capital price by dividing these returns by a measure of the quantity of capital. This procedure is also discussed in Chapter 11.

If other inputs are important for production and generating returns, this also should be independently represented rather than lumped into overall capital.

These residual quantity and price measures are *ex-post* indicators in the sense that all returns observed in retrospect are included, rather than those expected *a priori*. One would thus instead want to construct *ex-ante* measure independent of the impacts of these additional characteristics of the production and market structures to appropriately value the capital stock.

That is, determining what portion of revenues should be considered "pure" profits, and what part is truly a return to capital, is crucial for correctly imputing the contribution of capital to production and assessing productivity or efficiency fluctuations. Methods used to measure capital quantity and price must therefore carefully deal with these issues.

Ideally the capital stock can be measured by adding up investment in capital goods over time for each component of the stock, allowing for inflation in investment prices, depreciation, maintenance, obsolescence and anything else that alters the usefulness of a dollar's worth of capital investment over time. This generates a constant dollar (or other monetary unit) level of capital for each asset, that can be considered the effective stock available for production. The flow of capital services (quantity of capital used each year) is then generally assumed to be a constant proportion of the corresponding capital stock.

The associated price of capital services for each capital input may be measured as the price of investment goods (the "asset" price), adjusted for taxes, discount rates, depreciation and capital gains to generate a "rental price" or "user price" for each component of the capital stock. These procedures result in *ex-ante* measures of the service quantity and rental price of each type of capital, which can then be aggregated using index number methods such as Törnqvist or Divisia aggregation (see Section 3 below), to compute measures of the quantity and price of the overall capital input.

Unfortunately, however, the necessary data are often not available in a convenient form for constructing these types of measures. For example, quality differentials and aggregation problems abound, and appropriate measures of price deflators, obsolescence, and other crucial determinants of the effective available stock and user cost of capital, may not be available.

Keeping in mind this summary of the issues involved in constructing capital stock measures, let us proceed to formalize the ideas raised above, first focusing on the computation of capital stock measures.

As mentioned already briefly, a relevant measure of the available capital stock is derived as "what is left" of the investment in past time periods for the firm. This is generally written for each capital asset x_k as

$$10.1)\ x_{k,t} = \Sigma_\tau^T\ x_{k,t,t-\tau} = \Sigma_\tau^T\ s_{k,t,\tau}\ z_{k,t-\tau}\ ,$$

(from equation (6.2) in Berndt [1990], and motivated in Christensen and Jorgenson [1969]), where T is the life of the durable good, $x_{k,t,t-\tau}$ is the stock of x_k in time period t still remaining from investment in period t-τ, $s_{k,t,\tau}$ is defined as the physical survival rate for age τ investment in time period t for asset k, and $z_{k,t-\tau}$ is gross investment in asset k at time t-τ. This summation must be done for each asset individually, and then the assets aggregated based on their user costs, computed as discussed below.

Determining the level of $x_{k,t}$ for each asset therefore requires finding a "benchmark" level of the stock in period 0 (if only one firm is being considered and the startup period is included in the data this could be zero, otherwise another basis must be found). The investment values must then be divided by relevant deflators representing price changes over time due to inflation, to make the units comparable over time (get the numbers into constant dollars). Finally, investment from period 0 is cumulated (added up) based on some assumption about survival rates (or depreciation).[215]

Finding a benchmark is often difficult (requiring some judgement, past data, numbers from other studies, or hand-waving, particularly for aggregate data). Obtaining deflators for the different assets also can pose problems, although, as noted for the materials quantity deflators, sometimes output price series for the supplying industries involved (office equipment, for example) are available and may be justifiable to use.[216] In addition, for output and materials inventories (if included) it may be legitimate to use the output and materials deflators generated for the non-capital inputs.

The survival rate problem is perhaps the trickiest of all; we must determine how to characterize $s_{k,t,\tau}$, which is often theoretically motivated in terms of physical deterioration, but generally referred to as a depreciation rate. There are a number of standard assumptions regarding $s_{k,t,\tau}$, including:

(a) one-hoss shay (the machine runs at full tilt until it dies, and the dying time often is based on a Winfrey distribution of observed service lives);

(b) constant exponential decay (δ %/time period, implying $s_\tau = (1-\delta)^\tau$);

(c) straight line or linear depreciation (say, 5% of the original investment each period); and

---

[215] This can often be done using standard available programs. For example, the econometric software package PC TSP (Time Series Processor) has a CAPITL command that cumulates a series of investment values when given a benchmark and a depreciation rate.

[216] This is somewhat questionable, however, since sales or exise taxes are generally omitted in such data. It also may be useful to note here that the capital gains computation will depend on these deflators since capital gains is measured as the increase in price (value) of the stock one already has, which is the change in the deflator between time periods.

(d) decelerated depreciation (any method where the age-price profile declines slower than concave – one hoss shay may be included here due to the shape of the mortality distribution).[217]

None of these measures is consistent with accounting methods generally used to compute depreciation, which are based primarily on statutory taxation provisions concerning write-offs for investments. The depreciation numbers found on most company's balance sheets are, therefore, not very useful for construction of economic theory-based capital measures.

The assumption most commonly used to compute economic depreciation is a form of exponential decay called the perpetual inventory method, based on geometric deterioration. This assumption implies services never actually reach zero so every unit of investment is perpetually part of the capital stock or inventory.

The perpetual inventory method essentially assumes that $K_t = (1-\delta_t)K_{t-1} + I_{t-1}$, where K_t is the capital stock at the beginning of time t and I_{t-1} is investment in period t-1. Often a constant exponential rate is assumed for δ_t, as implied by (b) above. A somewhat extended version of this is the method used by the U.S. BLS, which is based on an hyperbolic function. Other assumptions may also be imposed on the time pattern of δ_t to generate different shapes of depreciation functions.[218]

Hulten and Wykoff [1981a,b] tested which assumptions about depreciation patterns appeared justifiable. They set up a general representation for the survival function called the Box-Cox form, which can take on different depreciation assumptions as special cases. Data on second-hand asset prices were then employed to assess which pattern seems best to approximate observed data trends.

They concluded that geometric decline appears justifiable, and that constant exponential depreciation (perpetual inventory or geometric with $\delta_t=\delta$) is a valid assumption. Straight-line methods also seem to approximate exhibited data patterns reasonably well. Even though special cases of geometric functions were sometimes statistically rejected, sensitivity analyses suggested that the stock levels computed with different assumptions about the time path of δ_t were virtually identical.

Many researchers have interpreted these results as a justification for computing depreciation using a constant exponential method. Common

---

[217] See Berndt [1990], Hulten and Wykoff [1980,1981a,b], or Hansson [1988] for more information. Also see Hulten [1990] for a comprehensive overview of these and other capital measurement issues.

[218] For a very useful set of papers overviewing both the historical literature and recent debates about the measurement of depreciation, see the papers on this issue in the January 1996 *Economic Inquiry*, including an excellent overview of standard confusions about the specification of depreciation by Hulten and Wykoff.

assumptions for δ are 12-15% for equipment and 6-7% for structures, although the OECD tends to use 10% and 5% respectively.[219]

Alternatively, it is sometimes possible to obtain supplementary information on use and scrapping of machinery and the assumed life of structures and make some assumptions. This approach is sometimes used for aggregate data (such as for Sweden, as elaborated in Blades [1983]), although it would seem more appropriate for less aggregated data.

This discussion of capital stock data construction has implications about development of the capital price measure. Since the underlying theory specifies the service flow from capital as the relevant input, it is necessary to construct corresponding data series measuring the service flow price.

This concept is the basis for the notion of a user cost of capital that not only includes the investment price, but adjusts it by interest and depreciation rates, capital gains and taxes. The idea is that the only portion of capital costs the firm truly incurs is an implicit rental price each year, which is the interest rate on the investment price, plus the deterioration involved, less capital gains, adjusted by taxes (corporate income taxes, depreciation deductions, etc.). This is represented by the equation

10.2) $p_{Kt} = TX_t \cdot (i_t\, q_{Kt\text{-}1} + \delta q_{Kt} - \Delta q_{Kt}) + b_t$

(from Berndt [1990]), where b_t represents the effective property tax rate, q_{Kt} is the asset price of capital input x_K in time t, Δq_{Kt} is $(q_{Kt}\text{-}q_{Kt\text{-}1})$, representing capital gains, i_t is the interest rate, δ is the depreciation rate, and TX_t is the effective" rate of taxation on capital income given by $TX_t = (1 - T_t\theta_t - \kappa_t)/(1 - T_t)$, where T_t is the effective corporate income tax rate, θ_t is the present value of depreciation deductions for tax purposes on a dollar's investment over the lifetime of the good, and κ_t is the effective rate of the investment tax credit.[220]

There are a number of immediate qualifications about this formula, although most are minor. First, it is important whether available deflators are based on end-of-the-year or beginning-of-the-year prices, because of the time dimension and lags implied in this formula. This formula implicitly assumes that "t" refers to the end of the current time period, while other variables are measured as current year totals. In some cases the distinction between q_{Kt} and $q_{Kt\text{-}1}$ is not made, so (10.2) reduces to $p_{Kt} = TX_t \cdot [(i_t+\delta)q_{Kt} - \Delta q_{Kt}] + b_t$, or $p_{Kt} = TX_t \cdot (i_t+\delta)q_{Kt} + b_t$ if capital gains are also ignored.

---

[219] Recently, statistical agencies such as the BLS have generated more specific depreciation measures for different components of the capital stock. One important adaptation of this has been to recognize higher depreciation rates, often specified at about 15% or even higher, for more high-tech capital equipment that experiences rapid obsolescence.

[220] As in Berndt [1990], p. 6.39. See Hall and Jorgenson [1967] and Christensen and Jorgenson [1969] for further elaboration of this.

The latter assumption is imposed especially for explicitly *ex-ante* measures, although in the U.S. the official BLS figures include a modified version of them in their *ex-post* measure. They compute a three-year moving average of capital gains ($\bar{q}_{Kt}$ becomes $(q_{Kt}+q_{Kt-1}+q_{Kt-2})/3$ and $q_{Kt}=(q_{Ktc}- q_{Kt-1}))$ instead of the standard first difference, due to large historical fluctuations in capital gains (especially for land). This procedure smooths these great variations.

Another issue is whether i_t is computed as an internal rate of return (*ex-post*), as discussed above, or a market rate (*ex-ante*). Computing the internal rate of return essentially involves taking the capital stock data, data on all other variables such as depreciation, and the total value of capital from the residual calculation and working backwards to solve for the implied i_t. In a sense, therefore, this is again a residual measure.

In other words, take the expression for the user cost of capital from the last section multiplied by K_t to obtain net value:

$$10.3) \quad NR_t = x_{kt}p_{kt} = x_{kt}\{TX_t \bullet [i_t \, q_{kt-1} + \delta q_{kt} - \Delta q_{kt}] + b_t\}$$

where NR_t is net revenues (revenues less variable costs)s. For more than one asset, this becomes the summation $\Sigma_k x_{k,t} p_{k,t}$, as outlined in Harper *et al* [1989]. Once x_{kt} or $\Sigma_k x_{kt}$ is computed, data on all other variables including NR_t from the residual calculation are used to solve for i_t, resulting in an internal rate of return assumed the same for all assets.[221]

By contrast, for the market or *ex-ante* rate, instead of assuming the value of capital is known and i_t should be solved for, i_t is assumed and the price of capital p_k (and therefore its value $x_k p_k$) is calculated. In the U.S. a Moody's bond yield (for Baa bonds) is often used for i_t in construction of manufacturing data.

A further issue to be addressed here is whether this measure of i_t should be considered an after- or before- tax return, since the former is relevant when the taxation adjustments in (10.2) are made. Another problem is that when representing an individual firm, risk should be taken into account.

Data on taxes and their use must be carefully constructed for appropriate user cost measurement. Computing b_t is straightforward; it is available on income statements in the form of land and asset tax information. Identifying how to measure TX_t is, however, more complicated.

---

[221] This rate of return may only be computed for the entire capital stock, not individual assets, since net revenue cannot be allocated across assets. If a number of assets exist, as is generally the case, different depreciation and rates of return must be substituted in and a more complex equation results. See Harper *et al* [1989].

It would be desirable to employ statutory marginal tax rates to approximate T_t, and assume this is the appropriate rate facing the firm for returns to any capital asset, but the marginal tax rates may not be observed, particular if taxes are paid in different jurisdictions.

In addition, once T_t is determined, data on depreciation deductions and investment tax credits (that may not be readily available) are also required. A useful alternative, therefore, is to rely on the notion of an "effective tax rate" – call this T'_t – used by Christensen and Jorgenson [1969], which is simply measured as taxes paid divided by property income before taxes. Although this is an average rate, there is much precedent in the literature for using this value to summarize all the tax parameters as $TX_t = 1/(1-T'_t)$.

The problem of risk can be dealt with either by imputing the average risk of related companies, or by inferring firm-specific risk. More specifically, risk is often incorporated into the rate of return by simply assuming a larger discount rate than that for bond yields (generally imposed in an *ad-hoc* mannner). Alternatively one could rely on using a rate of return for some more risky assets – possibly a weighted average of rates of return for the industry in which the firm produces.[222]   One way these data may be used to accomodate risk is by using the Capital Asset Pricing Model from finance theory, as suggested by Auerbach [1983].[223]

This adjustment for risk may deal in part with the problem of expectations, an issue that arises because of the capital gains term in the rental price formula. Harper *et al* [1989], for example, note that ideally Δq_{kt} should reflect *expected* capital gains, particularly for *ex-ante* measures. However, it is difficult to identify this expected level of returns. Thus many researchers use realized levels or drop this component entirely.

Note also that other adaptations to user cost computations may be useful to deal with the types of quality changes discussed for outputs and non-capital inputs in Section 1. Hulten [1996], for example, recognizes that increasing the capital quality causes an associated resource cost, that he measures as a "cost elasticity of producing capital with respect to the rate of technical change". This may cause an increase in embodied technical change

---

[222] This information is often available through standard data banks or websites like CitiBank's in the U.S.

[223] One approach to this is to use a CAPM model, which isolates firm-specific risk. Essentially, the "beta" (β) from a CAPM model identifies the riskiness of an asset compared to the market, since it is based on the equation: $r_H - r_f = \alpha + \beta(r_M - r_f)$, where r_H is the rate of return to the individual firm, r_f is the risk-free return, β is the firm-specific "beta", and r_M is the market rate of return. Clearly, if the return to the firm is exactly the market rate, $\beta=1$ and $\alpha=0$. If the asset is less risky than the market as a whole $\beta<1$ and if it is more risky $\beta>1$. This can be used to adjust the rate of return information to more closely approximate that faced by the firm.

to appear as a decrease in the Solow residual, and is shown to be "latent" in user cost of capital computations, since the investment good price deflator is a function of the cost elasticity.[224]

Finally, it is worth emphasizing once again that inputs in addition to those typically measured as "capital" may have capital characteristics such as R&D and human capital. The capital connection depends both on their stock nature (for example, depreciation becomes an issue) and their implications for "knowledge generation" or synergies.

This discussion has summarized many issues to be recognized when constructing capital data measures. A remaining problem, pervasive in any type of data construction, is how to aggregate the different types of capital once individual measures for assets have been developed.

3.   AGGREGATION ISSUES

Aggregation of heterogeneous outputs and inputs is a very difficult issue for empirical implementation. Although the theory is quite well developed (albeit somewhat complex), problems arise because in practice methodologies used for aggregation, if not data aggregation itself, often cannot be theoretically rationalized. The question of aggregation therefore is often broken down into two parts. It must be determined whether aggregation is justifiable (separability theory), and also what methods or procedures are valid to carry out the aggregation (index number theory).[225]

The first question has to do with the rationale for aggregating various goods into a "Hicksian Composite" that summarizes the quantity changes of all the underlying goods consistently – as if it were a single commodity. The necessary conditions are complicated, but a sufficient property of the data is that relative prices of the goods to be aggregated do not change over time, as shown by Hicks [1946]. Fixed proportions (constant relative quantities) of goods is also sufficient to justify aggregation, as discussed by Parks [1971].

A simple test of whether these conditions are satisfied is to compare price and quantity indexes of different commodities. Although such a procedure rarely provides strong evidence justifying aggregation, it may generate information on what commodities come close to satisfying the conditions.[226]

---

[224] This turns out also to be related to the knowledge capital ideas raised in Chapter 5, since endogenous growth with R&D externalities imply a larger value for this cost elasticity.

[225] See Caves, Christensen and Diewert [1982], Diewert [1976,1980,1984,1986], and Blackorby, Primont and Russell [1978] for further elaboration of index number and separability theory. Another classic study to peruse is Green [1964].

[226] Parks [1971] uses this method to evaluate aggregation and outlines other studies that have also considered these conditions empirically.

Alternatively, separability of two goods from another is satisfied if the relative marginal products of the two goods in question do not change with a change in the price of another good. Assessing the appropriateness of this condition for any particular set of data requires more structure than simple data analysis. If the separability requirements are satisfied, however, aggregation of the two goods is justified; the aggregated goods "move together" as a combined substitute (or complement) for others.[227]

If the assumptions are not justified, or the technology is not appropriately represented by the aggregation procedures, the aggregate index (aggregator function) will not be consistent. The question of consistency involves separability considerations, but also has to do with how to represent the aggregate, which requires index number theory. Problems with either of these aspects of the aggregation problem can cause errors. Before elaborating possible methodologies for construction of aggregator functions, therefore, it is useful to consider what it means for an index not to be consistent.

Denny [1980] provides a useful and simple way of showing the loss of information that arises with errors in aggregation.[228] His approach is to consider an example illustrated by an isoquant diagram, where two types of capital, K_1 and K_2, are used along with labor for production. The resulting production function is $Y(K_1, K_2, L)$. If an aggregator function for total capital $K=g(K_1, K_2)$ is valid, this function can be written as $Y(K, L)$.

Problems arise, however, if the correct representation of the K_1, K_2 combination depend on L and Y, in which case the aggregator function cannot consistently be defined. In addition, to minimize aggregation errors, the aggregator must correctly represent the technology; it must reproduce the correct amount of effective capital input to combine with L to produce Y.

To illustrate this, say that one level of aggregate capital can be represented by the line AB, a larger value is reflected in the line CD, and the isoquant tangent to AB (defined for given quantities of output and labor) can be drawn as (Y_0, L_0) in Figure 12. This assumes a simple linear version of the aggregator function $g(K_1, K_2)$. The loss of information from this version of the aggregator function results because any point on line AB, say Z, is indistinguishable from another point, say X, on the same line once aggregation is accomplished. However, it may not be the case that these points all have the same implications for technical efficiency.

---

[227] Berndt and Christensen [1973] discuss ways to determine whether aggregation is justified in a parametric framework. See Blackorby, Primont and Russell [1978] for a more elaborate discussion of separability conditions. Since these conditions may be complex, and are difficult to check and to satisfy, further consideration of them will not be pursued here.

[228] For further details of the following discussion, see Denny [1980].

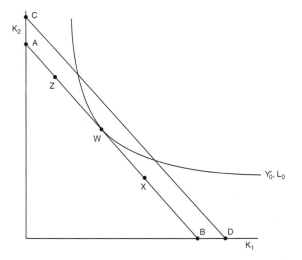

Figure 12. Aggregation and Loss of Information

Further consideration of the (Y_0, L_0) isoquant motivates a useful interpretation of this. The only point at which the aggregator correctly represents the input combination producing Y_0 is at the tangency point W. The only case in which aggregation is valid is therefore when the aggregator function is consistent with the production function – if the line AB can be "bent" so that it coincides with the (Y_0, L_0) isoquant. The aggregator function must correctly represent the relationship between K_1 and K_2 embodied in the given technology. In addition, for this consistency to hold in general, this aggregator function must be appropriate for any (Y, L) combination.

For the latter condition to hold, it must be the case that the AB curve may justifiably be drawn in K_1-K_2 space without any dependence on the levels of Y and L. This implies that the production function can actually be written as $Y(K, L) = Y(g(K_1, K_2), L)$, so that the marginal rate of substitution between K_1 and K_2 does not depend on L.[229] Even when the rental prices of K_1 and K_2 do not vary proportionally, therefore, this "weak separability" condition[230] and

---

[229] To see this, recall that the marginal rate of substitution in this case is $(\partial Y/\partial K_1)/(\partial Y/\partial K_2)$, which can be rewritten using the chain rule as $(\partial Y/\partial g \cdot \partial g/\partial K_1)/(\partial Y/\partial g \cdot \partial g/\partial K_2) = (\partial g/\partial K_1)/(\partial g/\partial K_2)$. Since the g function does not depend on L, therefore, neither does this ratio, and the tradeoffs between K_1 and K_2 are not affected by changes in labor. In this sense they are independent of L.

[230] Variants on these separability conditions such as "strong separability" and "recursive separability" are defined and used in more rigorous developments of this aggregation problem. For a formal treatment of separability conditions, see Blackorby, Primont and Russell [1978].

homotheticity[231] of $g(K_1,K_2)$ allow a capital aggregator function to exist. In addition, to aggregate across production sectors, it must also be the case that these conditions hold for each production sector, and the sectors must have "almost" identical isoquants.

Although errors will exist any time these conditions do not hold in practice, there are special circumstances in which the index number procedure used for aggregation will cause less errors than otherwise. In particular, we can specify conditions that should be true for an aggregator function and see which types of index numbers satisfy these conditions and therefore are more acceptable. This is the basis for what is called the *test* or *axiomatic* approach to index number theory, as elaborated in Diewert [1980].

Further, if the index number procedure were consistent with the existing production function (the relationship between K_1 and K_2, for example, were appropriately represented for the given technology) the aggregation procedure would be reasonably defensible. This is the idea underlying the theory of exact and superlative index numbers in Diewert [1976, 1984], where an index number is exact to a particular functional form if it exactly replicates the ratio of the relevant functions at the two sets of prices.

For example, consider an input price index for capital. After a price change in any capital component, the measure of the change in overall input price should incorporate substitution among the components consistent with that implied by the underlying cost function. If so, the capital price index will reproduce the ratio of the capital-cost functions $(g(\cdot))$ at the two price combinations.[232] In addition, the change in the cost of inputs in general will equal the ratio of the total cost functions for the two price conditions. This is a primary result of the *microeconomic* approach to index numbers.

It is clear that aggregation procedures will substantively affect empirical estimates of inputs and outputs, and therefore any econometric estimation or index number generation such as indexes of productivity growth. It is thus worthwhile pursuing this a bit to see which types of index numbers have been proposed, which seem most justifiable, and what they imply.

The basic index number problem is to take the value of many different commodities and partition their combined value into price and quantity indexes representative of the entire group. Since dollars (or other monetary value units) provide a common measure for commodities, once the total value of (expenditure on or revenue from) the commodities is known, and either a price or quantity index has been found, the corresponding quantity or price index can be determined implicitly. Computing the implicit index simply requires dividing the value by the initially computed index.

---

[231] The index must also be independent of scale for the aggregator to be well defined.
[232] For more formal treatments, see the studies by Diewert cited in this section.

Formally, we can express this problem as in Diewert [1989a],[233] where the prices and quantities of the J commodities we wish to aggregate for each time period t=1,...T (t could also be different economic units instead of time) are represented by the vectors $p_t \equiv (p_{1,t},...,p_{J,t})$ and $v_t \equiv (v_{1,t},...,v_{J,t})$. Based on this, the index number problem can be expressed as the problem of condensing this information to find T values of aggregate prices (P_t) and quantities (V_t) of all J commodities such that $P_t V_t = \Sigma_j \, p_j v_j$. The quantity and price indexes V_t and P_t therefore each summarize all the price and quantity information by one aggregate number for each time period t.

One might think that this could be accomplished quite simply using some type of average. Three alternative versions of this were suggested in the 18th and 19th centuries.[234] One possibility is to compute the arithmetic average of the period t prices divided by the arithmetic average of the period t-1 prices as $P_t/P_{t-1} = (\Sigma_j p_{j,t}/J)/(\Sigma_j p_{j,t-1}/J)$ where P_t/P_{t-1} is interpreted as the ratio of aggregated prices in periods t-1 and t. Similarly, instead of taking a ratio of the averages, one could take the average of the price ratios themselves, using either an arithmetic or geometric mean. However, problems emerge for these formulas. The first is not invariant to changes in the units of measurement, and the other runs into problems because prices are not randomly distributed but instead are systematically related.

This simple beginning to index number theory eventually led to a large literature where different indexes were suggested and then subjected to tests of their consistency with intuitively reasonable axioms and with microeconomic theory. Some of the most commonly recognized indexes, are the Laspeyres, Paasche, Fisher ideal, and Törnqvist (or Divisia, the continuous version of the discrete Törnqvist index).

Laspeyres and Paasche indexes attempt to deal with the relationship between prices by basing their comparison on constant quantities, or a given "market basket" of goods (the reverse can be done to generate a quantity index based on prices, in which case prices are assumed constant). The basic idea of this approach is to weight the prices by a given set of quantities, v_j, generating indexes of the form

$$10.4) \quad P_t/P_{t-1} = \Sigma_j p_{j,t} v_j / \Sigma_j p_{j,t-1} v_j \, ,$$

where the Laspeyres index (P_L) uses the quantities from the base period (period t-1) and the Paasche (P_P) from period t.

---

[233] See this paper for further elaboration of the following index number discussion and proofs of the assertions made.

[234] See Diewert [1989a] for further references and elaboration.

The Fisher ideal index is a geometric mean of the Paasche and Laspeyres indexes,

10.5) $P_t/P_{t-1} = (P_L P_P)^{1/2}$.

Finally, the Törnqvist index is a geometric mean of the price ratios,

10.6) $P_t/P_{t-1} = \Pi_j (p_{j,t}/p_{j,t-1})^{\bar{S}_j}$,

where $\bar{S}_j \equiv (1/2) \cdot (p_{jt-1} v_{j,t-1}/\Sigma_i p_{j,t-1} v_{j,t-1}) + (1/2) \cdot (p_{j,t} v_{j,t}/\Sigma_j p_{j,t} v_{j,t}) = (1/2) \cdot (S_{j,t-1} + S_{j,t})$ is the average expenditure share on good j for j=1,...J, and Π_j represents the product of all the j values.

Perhaps the most popular index currently used by economists is this last index – the Törnqvist index, commonly referred to as a Divisia index even when measured in its discrete form.[235] This is at least in part due to the support provided this index by the microeconomic approach to justifying index number formulas; the Törnqvist index is consistent with the popular translog functional form. Since this is a "flexible" functional form which provides a second order approximation to an arbitrary function (as discussed further in the next section) the Törnqvist formula is quite general.

Specifically, the Törnqvist index allows for substitution among the inputs, which is assumed away in the Laspeyres and Paasche forms. The assumption of no substitution between periods for these indexes implies that the P_L and P_P indexes are upper and lower bounds to the true index, which provides some justification for using the combination of the two contained in the Fisher index.[236]

Theoretical arguments supporting the more complete representation of the technology by the Törnqvist index have been persuasive in the view of many researchers. However, in practice, if changes between years are small, the empirical deviations between the indexes tend to be negligible.

One somewhat minor implication of using the Törnqvist (Divisia) index for aggregation is that if growth rates are computed for the resulting index, consistency requires a different method of computing these rates than is commonly applied. This issue of consistency between formulas used, however, can make a significant difference in practice if output or input changes between years are large, which may be the case if using data for an individual firm.

---

[235] Some standard statistical programs have a command that directly estimates this index. In TSP the DIVIND command will carry out these manipulations, and in SHAZAM the INDEX command can be used.

[236] Theoretical and graphical expositions of this result are outlined in a number of standard intermediate microeconomics texts, including Hirschleifer [1990]

A standard way to think of computing growth rates, for some aggregate input V (or some output Y) between years t and t-1, is the growth rate $(V_t-V_{t-1})/V_{t-1}$. This assumes the base to compute the percentage from is the quantity in the first year. However, when aggregation is done in terms of index numbers, the formula is, instead, $\ln(V_t/V_{t-1})$. This is because the standard command to create a Törnqvist or Divisia quantity index equivalently to the price index above is based on the formula

$$10.7)\ \ln (V_t/V_{t-1}) = \Sigma_j\ \overline{S}_j\ \ln (v_{j,t}/v_{j,t-1}),$$

where v_j is the quantity of the jth factor of the J to be aggregated, and V represents the aggregated quantity vector, as stated above. If this expression is exponentiated (as is often the case), so it appears more similar to (10.6), (10.7) becomes

$$10.8)\ V_t/V_{t-1} = \Pi_j (v_{j,t}/v_{j,t-1})^{\overline{S}_j},\ \text{so}\ V_t = V_{t-1}[\Pi_j (v_{j,t}/v_{j,t-1})^{\overline{S}_j}].$$

Two points from this formula are worth elaborating. First, what this implies for the interpretation of the growth rate compared to that commonly measured, and second, what it suggests is the proper procedure for cumulating the resulting growth rates to obtain a quantity index.

To clarify the first point, we can rely on the definition of logarithms. Without going through the algebra, we can assert that this formula is equivalent to computing the growth rate as $(V_t-V_{t-1})/[(V_t+V_{t-1})/2]$, or evaluating the change in terms of the average of the two quantities instead of the first year only. If the quantity changes are not large (or are miniscule as suggested by the theory underlying the formulas that are based on continuous rather than discrete changes), the difference between the two formulas is small. However, with large changes this formula underestimates the growth rate compared to the more standard measure based on year t-1. The interpretation of the growth rate is, therefore, altered.

This should not matter for computation of the levels (the quantity index), however, if the corresponding formula is used for reconstructing the quantity index.[237] To illustrate this, note that if the standard growth rate formula $(V_t-V_{t-1})/V_{t-1}=GR$ (where GR denotes "Growth Rate") is used, this implies that $V_t-V_{t-1}=GR \cdot V_{t-1}$, so $V_t=GR \cdot V_{t-1}+V_{t-1}=V_{t-1} \cdot (GR+1)$. Therefore, the usual procedures for computing levels from a series of growth rates are valid.

---

[237] For a homogeneous output or input these manipulations are not even necessary, but since in most applications all outputs and inputs are not homogeneous, and even those which are provide the basis for further aggregation, they therefore should be consistent with the other computations.

However, when the $\ln(V_t/V_{t-1})$=GR formula is used, cumulating up the growth rates is somewhat different; V_t/V_{t-1}=exp(GR) (where exp means exponentiated), so V_t=exp(GR)•V_{t-1}. Therefore, instead of adding one to the computed rates and then cumulating them, the growth rate should be exponentiated and then cumulation can proceed.

A last but important note about these indexes is that the Törnqvist index, when written in logarithmic form as in 10.7, looks very similar to the primal productivity growth formula (2.1) (reproduced here as ε_{Yt} = dln Y/dt - Σ_j S_j dln v_j/dt), which can be rewritten more in the style of (6.9) as:

$$10.9)\quad \varepsilon_{Yt} = \ln (Y_t/Y_{t-1}) - \Sigma_j \; \overline{S}_j \; \ln (v_{j,t}/v_{j,t-1}) \; .$$

Thus the share-weighted aggregate input measure generally used for productivity growth computations is simply a Törnqvist index of the various inputs specified. This might be thought of as a further motivation for using such indexes for aggregation of inputs; consistency is maintained between aggregation within each input specification and for overall input aggregation.

In addition to issues of aggregation across outputs and inputs, there are aggregation issues associated with aggregation across firms, sectors and regions. Some similar problems arise to those overviewed for aggregation across commodities, since heterogeneity must once again be taken into account when adding or comparing across units. However, other issues that emerge have a quite different motivation.

Both the theoretical and particularly empirical literatures for aggregation across productive units focus on the impact of the heterogeneity of these underlying units on empirical results for the aggregate. In a sense it is a search for "aggregation bias". As for the literature on aggregate estimation of production characteristics such as scale economies and market power, little clear analytical linkage can be identified. But empirical patterns can be evaluated, and often suggest reallocations across individual heterogeneous units may have a large effect on measured aggregate productivity growth.

A useful overview of issues raised by productivity studies based on micro data is provided by Foster, Krizan and Haltiwanger [1998].[238] Increasing accessibility of (and power of computers to analyze) establishment and firm data, and empirical implications about the violation of "representative firm" assumptions from studies on the heterogeneity of firms in most industries, suggest that this is both an interesting and fruitful forefront of research.

---

[238] Some topical and recent literature in this area, as referenced by Foster *et al*, include Baily, Hulten and Campbell [1992], Baily, Bartlesman and Haltiwanger [1996, 1997], Bartelsman and Dhrymes [1994], Dwyer [1995, 1997], Haltiwanger [1997] and Olley and Pakes [1996] for the U.S., and Tybout [1996], Aw, Chen and Roberts [1997], Liu and Tybout [1996], and Griliches and Regev [1995] for other countries.

Foster *et al* focus on clear patterns of output and input reallocation across producers, that are primarily evident in the U.S. within sectors. Associated with this are large and persistent differentials in productivity levels and growth rates across establishments in the same sector, although low productivity does tend to be associated with exit. In fact, entry and exit play a definitive role in this process. The authors emphasize that this suggests observed reallocations may have much to say about aggregate productivity growth rates that is being missed by firm and industry aggregation.

Foster *et al* find that empirical estimates of reallocation on productivity growth measurement vary significantly across studies. They attribute much of this to differences in the country under consideration, sectoral coverage, time period, frequency and the methodology used. They then provide their own estimates, including those for service sectors (which are typically excluded from such analysis).

The methodology used for this exercise is to apply decomposition formulas to indexes of labor SFP growth and MFP growth for different sectors. These decomposition formulas vary. The two used for comparison in Foster *et al* are based on Baily Hulten and Campbell [1992] and Griliches and Regev [1995] respectively.

In these decompositions the change in productivity for industry i in period t is attributed to plant-level characteristics. These include a within plant-component based on plant-level changes weighted by industry share, a between-plant component that reflects changing shares weighted by the difference between plant and industry productivity, and a cross-term capturing the contribution of exiting plants.

More specifically, the change in productivity is decomposed into:

$$10.10) \quad \Delta P_{it} = \sum_{e \in C} s_{et-1} \Delta p_{et} + \sum_{e \in C} (p_{et-1} - P_{it-1}) \Delta s_{et} + \sum_{e \in C} \Delta p_{et} \Delta s_{et}$$

$$+ \sum_{e \in N} s_{et}(p_{et} - P_{it-1}) - \sum_{e \in X} s_{et-1}(p_{et-1} - P_{it-1}),$$

where P_{it} is the index of industry productivity $P_{it} = \sum_{e \in i} s_{et} p_{et}$, s_{et} is the share of plant e in industry i (output share), p_{et} is an index of plant level productivity, C denotes continuing plants, N represents entering plants, and X indicates exiting plants.

Using such a decomposition, Foster *et al* show that reallocation of outputs and inputs across establishments is significant, with a pace that varies secularly, cyclically and by industry. There are also large productivity differentials across establishments in the same industry, with entering plants tending to have higher productivity levels than exiting plants, which underlies the importance of exit and entry to aggregate productivity.

However the evidence varies not only by industry and time period but also by methodology, suggesting measurement error problems. It could also arise from product differentiation and heterogeneity across producers, which are largely ignored here but are critically important in such a context. The time frame of analysis (short, intermediate and long run) is also important. A longer time horizon tends to generate greater differentials from selection and learning effects, which supports the importance of such effects.

Overall, Foster *el al* conclude that "high-quality micro data on establishments that permit measurement of output, input and productivity growth at the establishment level and aggregation of these growth rates on a consistent basis over time are essential for understanding the determinants of aggregate productivity growth".

Finally, note that our discussion of aggregation across productive units or sectors presupposes that we are dealing with time series data. That is, questions of productivity or performance growth by definition imply that we are analyzing data across time. However, many issues of productivity, economic performance, and efficiency involve comparisons across productive units. This was explicitly the case in our discussion of efficiency measurement in Chapter 8, in which the idea is to establish best-practice methods within a group of "decision making units" (DMUs) and compare each unit to the frontier.

More generally, we may wish to compare patterns across productive units or sectors (firms, regions, industries or countries) to further establish differential productivity patterns. This implies constructing and using panel data, which has a cross-section as well as time series dimension. In some sense, however, heterogeneity issues are even more of an issue in this case, since when comparing across productive units we may not be referring to continuous changes in output and input composition, but possibly very different types of products produced, and inputs or technologies used. Environmental factors may also be particularly important in this scenario, since they may impinge on the demand for a product, supply of factors, or other constraints facing firm or industry behavior.

We will not pursue the idea of comparisons using cross-section or panel data in this text, except to discuss some basic econometric issues that arise for panel data in the next chapter. Note, however, that the richer basis of panel data, even with the comparison difficulties across sub-sectors, may provide important and useful insights about production and cost structure, as well as increase the efficiency of estimation. Fixed (or possibly random) effects can also be used to accommodate, to at least some extent, measurable aspects of environmental characteristics (region, or multi-plant economies, for example) as shift factors affecting firms' or other productive units' relative cost-output relationship.

4. FURTHER COMMENTS

Once output and input data are constructed for representation of economic performance for a firm, region, industry or country, as discussed in this chapter, accounting measures of productivity growth may directly be computed as outlined in Chapter 2. However, as emphasized throughout this text, for analysis of additional production structure patterns buried in the productivity residual but embodied in the cost or production function, econometric methods are necessary.

Estimation of a full model of the production structure allow us to compute 1st and 2nd order cost elasticities representing, for example, marginal shadow values, utilization and other cost economies and biases. This type of analysis raises its own complications, however, since a stochastic structure must also be specified. Such issues of empirical implementation and econometric specification are the subject of the next chapter.

Chapter 11

Issues of Econometric Implementation

The production theory and data construction discussions in the previous two chapters provide a foundation for combining our theoretical structure and available data to quantify the types of measures we have discussed throughout this text. Such an empirical representation of production processes, however, also requires some consideration of measurement methods or procedures, which is the focus of this final chapter.

Throughout this text we have commented on the potential for estimation of the indicators, mainly based theoretically on cost derivatives (and elasticities, their proportional or logarithmic counterpart), that we have developed to represent various aspects of economic performance. We have seen that representation of input demand involves elasticities with respect to input prices; utilization and shadow values have to do with elasticities with respect to factor quantities; scale and other cost economies are associated with elasticities with respect to output levels; and technical change is reflected by elasticities with respect to time, the "state of technology", or more explicitly specified technological determinants such as R&D. The resulting framework allows a rich representation of production processes.

In many cases at least one of these production characteristics may be imputed from the data by nonparametric or simple parametric techniques. However, in most cases identification of a combination of these characteristics requires carrying out simultaneously a number of "controlled experiments", using our neoclassical framework that is theoretically and empirically based on such comparative statics.

This can only be accomplished via a full model of production processes, plus statistical techniques that allow us to "hold other things constant" while identifying the impacts on one particular type of change. Very broadly speaking, this is the role of econometric models and 'methods.

In particular, for the types of models we have developed in this text, systems estimation is the required form of econometric analysis. That is, the set of elasticities summarized above not only represents measures that can be computed from a functional form and estimated parameters of a function, but also captures relationships that can provide the basis for estimation.

Most cost models, for example, are estimated via a set of input demand relationships. Shephard's lemma (or the logarithmic form of this resulting in share equations) is used as the basis for constructing a set of input demand equations with input levels as left-hand-side (choice or endogenous) variables, and the arguments of the cost function as right-hand-side (independent, exogenous or explanatory) variables.

For a sufficiently flexible functional form, cross-equation restrictions will be embodied in such a system since cross-input parameters will appear in more than one input demand equation. In some cases the cost function itself also may (or even should) be estimated as another equation of the system, with obvious consequences in terms of parameters that will appear in more than one equation. Thus, system estimation procedures that recognize these interrelationships among input choices and thus equations in the system must be relied on for estimation and resulting inference of production responses.

Other elasticity expressions may also be used to increase the power of the estimating model, if measurable left-hand side variables can be determined. For example, output and input pricing equations from the market power models of Chapter 6 may be constructed with the observed output (say) price on the left hand side, and expressions for the marginal cost and "wedge" from market power on the right hand side. These equations could also be used, assuming perfect competition, to specify estimable $p_Y=MC$ equations. Euler equations for fixed inputs, with p_k on the left- side and expressions for adjustment costs (that cause $Z_k{\neq}p_k$) on the right- hand-side may also be derived and used for estimation. Again, cross-equation restrictions will result, so systems estimation techniques must be relied on.

In certain cases, some of the right-hand-side variables in such systems may be endogenous. We have seen, for example, that both output (input) price and quantity become endogenous variables when market power exists. Similarly, in a cost function framework it could be that output levels are not truly exogenous. It may also be thought that, in a dynamic model where expectations become an issue, the true "expected" prices that are the basis for firms' decisions are not fully represented by observed prices; the "true" price is in some sense endogenous. Finally, the possibility of measurement errors mentioned in the previous chapter might to some extent "endogenize" observed true or effective "exogenous" variables. In these cases we must utilize systems estimations methods that allow for this, such as those based on instrumental variables methods.

Finally, appropriate estimation methods rely on the type of data used. Although only touched on here, since the models discussed in this text are typically estimated using time series data, panel estimation issues are becoming increasingly important to be familiar with, given the increasing availability and richness of such data.

The brief overview of empirical implementation issues in this chapter just begins to highlight some of these primary considerations one might want to address for econometric estimation of the types of models we have discussed in this text. Further consideration of these issues will require perusal of econometrics texts and manuals for statistical programs.

In this chapter we initially (in Section 1) briefly overview some nonparametric and simple econometric methods for estimating production characteristics. We then begin to raise questions to address for econometric implementation of the structural models we have been developing.

The first issue to consider for econometric implementation is about functional forms and specification. The question of what *type* of function might be most useful to represent the production structure, and what arguments of the function should be included, is addressed in Section 2. How to approximate the true function by a functional *form* that has appropriate characteristics, and is sufficiently "flexible" to represent the many important relationships among decision variables of the firm, is addressed in Section 3.

The second primary issue addressed is endogeneity, or errors in measurement, of independent variables. For empirical implementation, once a structural model is specified, the appropriate econometric framework or stochastic structure must be established. This involves determining what stochastic assumptions are relevant, and thus the statistical procedures that should be used for estimation. A full model of production processes might be subject to various complications, including simultaneity or endogeneity problems, expectations issues, autoregressive or measurement errors and multiple data dimensions. In Section 4 we overview how some of these difficulties encountered in empirical applications might be accommodated.

1. EMPIRICAL SPECIFICATIONS

In this text we have discussed many measures representing production structure characteristics. In some cases one such measure might be imputed from the data without a parametric specification.

In particular, we have already extensively pursued the problems involved in identifying the impacts of technical change using nonparametric techniques. In sum, as overviewed in Chapter 2, a MFP measure may be constructed nonparametrically as a Solow residual. This residual, however, embodies all production characteristics not directly represented by measured output and input prices and quantities, such as fixities and cost economies. If one wishes to interpret the residual measure in terms of technical change, therefore, these characteristics must be separately modeled and measured.

Similarly, other production characteristics we have discussed may be measured by nonparametric methods if they are the primary focus of analysis. Only one such measure can typically be derived, however, from nonparametric analysis; other aspects of the production process must be assumed away for interpretability of the measure. This is also true for some simple parametric treatments.

Berndt and Fuss [1986] and Hulten [1986], for example, generate nonparametric measures of the shadow value of capital (Z_K). Their approaches rely on the notion that the shadow value of the capital stock is captured in the measured "value" of the firm. This is implemented in Berndt and Fuss by using a Tobin's q measure, and in Hulten by computing the *ex-post* value of capital from the value of output. Both of these measures are based on construction of a residual value, so they may include returns to something other than the capital base.

Berndt and Fuss [1986] rely on the Tobin's q idea that the market value of a firm (represented by the stock market valuation), as compared to the actual value of the firm's capital (reflected in the firm's replacement value), captures the difference between the shadow and market prices of capital. However, the resulting measure, constructed as a ratio of these two values, includes many things that might not be thought of as relevant to a true capital shadow value, such as goodwill. This is a problem that arises by construction for Tobin's q-type measures, as noted in Chapter 3.

This approach is also based on the assumption of only one quasi-fixed input, and implicitly on the assumptions of perfect competition and CRS. Unless such simplifying assumptions are made, it is not possible to identify excess returns to one factor independently from other returns. Returns not captured by measured market values cannot be distinguished without a more complete structural model if more than one such "imperfection" exists.

Hulten [1986] instead computes the *ex-post* residual value of capital as $p_Y Y - VC(\bullet) = Z_K K$, which, given a measure of K, can be used to impute Z_K. He then focuses on how difficult a valid *ex-ante* measure of the price of capital (p_K) is to compute relative to the *ex-post* measure.

However, construction of the *ex-post* measure raises additional problems. Again, if NCRS, multiple quasi-fixed inputs, market power, or other aspects of the production structure exist that are not explicitly recognized, returns to these technological and market characteristics are included in addition to the true return to capital in the residual and thus in the Z_K measure. Therefore, restrictive assumptions are necessary to measure Z_K nonparametrically.

Another approach to isolating the impact of subequilibrium and thus the deviation between shadow and market values of capital, suggested by the development of capacity utilization adjustments in Chapter 3, is to use published capacity utilization measures.

More specifically, the error adjustment for fixity (of capital only) can be expressed from (4.4) as $\varepsilon_{TCt} + \varepsilon_{TCK} \cdot (d\ln Y/dt - d\ln K/dt)$ where the second term is the generally ignored error bias. Thus, since $CU_c = (1 - \varepsilon_{TCK})$ implies $\varepsilon_{TCK} = 1 - CU_c$, the error adjustment can be made using only a capacity utilization measure. The adaptation of the cost measure to decompose the primal productivity growth index into its technical change and utilization components is thus also possible, since this simply requires dividing by the capacity utilization measure CU_c, as in (4.5).

This approach again raises potentially severe problems. In addition to requiring the assumption of only one quasi-fixed input (from the error bias correction in (4.3) it is clear that the different ε_{TCk} components cannot be untangled without further information), published capacity utilization measures are not consistent with economic theory.

In particular, as outlined in Chapter 3, these measures disallow overutilization of fixed inputs and therefore always fall short of one. It is clear, though, that in many cases overutilization of an existing amount of fixed stocks will occur. This could result simply from the inability of investment to keep up with demand, in which case economic CU measures would exceed one. Thus, since the physical notion of capacity utilization has little interpretative power in terms of economic values and thus shadow values of fixed inputs, use of these measures does not appear constructive. [239]

It thus seems that although it would be ideal to generate a nonparametric measure of Z_K and use this directly to adjust productivity growth or other measures for fixity, no really justifiable measure for this purpose exists. Parametric methods which use a specific form of the variable cost function and thus imply an explicit functional form for $Z_K = -\partial VC/\partial K$ will in most cases be preferable to identify the bias resulting from subequilibrium.

Measuring scale economies is also problematic. A fundamental difficulty is the lack of any theoretical framework for identification of scale economies from raw data, which of course results in a paucity of published measures. Therefore, although the theory developed in Chapter 4 suggests returns to scale measures may be used directly to adjust for scale economies, the scope for direct application of this theory is extremely limited.

---

[239] If fluctuations rather than the level of productivity growth is the primary issue, using standard measures that are highly correlated with economic measures might be justifiable. Although it is difficult to determine which measures might be suitable for this, Morrison [1985b] showed that FRB measures tend to more closely track economic measures than measures like the Wharton index. Another potentially useful although somewhat *ad-hoc* adaptation to this is to try to identify the level of capacity utilization where investment and inflationary pressures are likely to begin, and normalize the index to one at this value to correct for problems with levels.

Some approaches to this do, however, have potential. First, a number of parametric studies have been carried out which attempt to measure returns to scale for different industries, and these might be used (with some hand-waving) in productivity studies of the same industry.[240] These measures will generally not be fully consistent with the theoretical structure or the data (unless they are based on the same data set) in any particular study, but may at least provide some insights.

For example, a study by Christensen and Greene [1976] on electric utilities plants suggests returns to scale were "used up" by 1970. This in turn implies that η, the inverse of a primal returns to scale measure (or the cost-side equivalent ε^L_{TCY}), exceeded one after 1970, whereas it fell short of one before 1970. For a productivity study on electric utilities this information could be useful for interpreting changes in productivity during this period, even if the theoretical structure and data used were not identical.

Another possible approach relies on parametric methods that impose little (or no) structure on the interactions among different characteristics of the production structure. Such an exercise might be based on a simple approximation to a cost function that allows computation of the cost side scale economy measure $\partial \ln TC / \partial \ln Y = \varepsilon_{TCY}$, perhaps just as a parameter. This could provide basic evidence about the shape of the cost curves even without a full structure to facilitate interpretation, but requires potentially seriously limiting assumptions about this shape due to the underlying *a priori* assumptions about functional form.

For example, this may be implemented by imposing a simple log-linear relationship as an approximation to $TC(\mathbf{p}, Y, t)$:[241]

11.1) $\ln TC = \alpha + \beta \ln Y + \gamma t + \Sigma_j \delta_j \ln p_j$,

where β directly represents the cost elasticity with respect to output, ε_{TCY}. An estimated value for β could thus potentially be used to represent scale economies, and thus to adjust productivity growth measures for the existence of returns to scale using an equation such as (4.2).

This method also has implications for separating (again in an ad-hoc manner) the impacts of scale and fixities, by assuming the alternative approximation:

---

[240] This is the type of procedure used often, for example, in general equilibrium studies where the model is too complex to measure elasticities necessary for the analysis. Measures from other studies or some "average" measure from a set of studies are often simply inserted into the analysis.

[241] This satisfies required properties unlike a linear form for which linear homogeneity is violated.

11.2) $\ln VC = \alpha + \beta \ln Y + \gamma t + \Sigma_j \delta_j \ln p_j + \phi \ln K$,

where the **p** vector now does not include p_K. This is, of course, a simplistic approximation to the short run cost function represented by VC(Y,t,**p**,K). Since here ϕ measures $\partial \ln VC/\partial \ln K = -Z_K \cdot (K/VC) = \varepsilon_{VCK}$, estimated ϕ and β parameters, along with information on $p_K K$ (the difference between TC and VC), may be used to measure and adjust productivity growth indexes for both returns to scale and subequilibrium.

However, the full structure linking ε_{VCK}, ε_{TCK} and ε_{TCY}, as well as recognition of any other cross effects, is ignored in this unsophisticated specification, so it is not theoretically very well justified. It also does not facilitate interpretation since the measures are simply parameters; the underlying determinants of the measures are not specified.

This simplicity, as alluded to above, involves the restrictive shapes on the relationships imposed by the log-linear specification. If, for example, the associated parameter is negative, which would be true for ϕ if monotonicity conditions hold, the graphical relationship in VC-K space would be a rectangular hyperbola (in ln VC-ln K space it would be a straight, downward sloping, line). Similar restrictions are implied for the positive TC-Y or VC-Y relationships. This precludes the data providing information on the shapes of the curves. The basic shape is pre-supposed by the log-linear assumption. This is the sense in which, more generally, restrictive functional form assumptions limit applicability and interpretation of structural estimates.

A final approach to mention to measure a "scale effect" (μ, or ε_{TCY} in our notation if resulting from scale economies) is based on the procedures suggested by Hall [1986], which were targeted toward taking markups into account (as discussed in the theoretical context in Chapters 5 and 6). Since this process is designed particularly to distinguish marginal from average costs or price, it can potentially be used either for measuring markups (the difference between output price and marginal cost), or scale economies (the difference between average and marginal cost).

Since this methodology is based on a quite ingenious but straightforward parametric modeling approach that has had wide-ranging applications in the literature, it is worth digressing a moment to consider the estimation process in more detail than in previous chapters.

The contribution by Hall provided a framework in which to measure marginal cost within the original Solow [1957] tradition. Hall's specification depends on the expression for marginal cost $MC = p_L \Delta L/(\Delta Y - \tau Y)$.[242] This can be manipulated to read:

---

[242] This stems from the idea that capital is fixed, so short run changes in costs ($\Delta p_L L$) from an output change (ΔY) result only from alterations to labor use (ΔL). In

11.3) $\Delta Y/Y = \mu \cdot [(p_L L/p_Y Y) \cdot \Delta L/L] + \tau + u_t$,

where $\mu = p_Y/MC$, and $\tau_t = \tau + u_t$ is analogous to our ε_{Yt} measure.

The assumptions about τ_t are very important for Hall's analysis. One implication of the model is that technical progress can be "viewed as random deviations from an underlying constant rate" (Hall [1986], p. 290). In addition, u_t is assumed uncorrelated with cyclical fluctuations, which is based on the idea that "true" productivity growth should not be correlated with the business cycle. In this scenario, productivity growth measures that indicate procyclical productivity, for example, are picking up some aspects of the production process other than just technical change.

The justification for this is straightforward; technical change should not decline in a cyclical downturn because technology does not just disappear. Instead, other changes firms make during cycles or other characteristics of the technology, such as utilization changes, the ability to take advantage of scale economies, and markups, instead drive the observed productivity fluctuations. Hall attributes all this cyclical variability to markup behavior, and estimates μ assuming τ is an average technical change variable and relying on a lack of correlation between u_t and cyclical behavior.[243]

The Hall specification assumes that Y is value-added output, L is the only input under consideration, and L and p_L are measures of hourly labor input and price. Hall comments on the potential incorporation of additional inputs, retaining the assumption that Y refers to value added output and that the technological relationship between capital and labor is very simple.

As seen in previous chapters, others have used a Solow residual approach as a basis for analysis in gross output specifications, substituting a weighted average of all the inputs rather than just labor into (11.3). This results in:

11.3') $d\ln Y/dt = \mu \cdot [\Sigma j \, (p_j v_j/p_Y Y) \cdot d\ln v_j/dt] + \tau + u_t$.

Estimation using this expression is analogous to Hall [1986] and is quite straightforward. In most cases it involves, as alluded to in Chapter 5, estimation of just the one μ parameter, since the weights on the input growth terms are not estimated; the nonparametric residual is simply computed.

---

addition, this indicates that the change in output should be adjusted for the amount that output would have risen simply from technical change with no change in labor input (τY). See Hall [1986] for further details.

[243] This is the reverse of the approach used by Solow, who assumed MC could be measured by p_Y (perfect competition) and then solved for τ. As we have already seen in detail, Solow's approach results in a residual that includes changes in all aspects of observed productivity, including markups, utilization, etc., as our estimate of "productivity", rather than just technical change.

The estimation method involves constructing measures of $\Delta Y/Y$ or $d\ln Y/dt$ for the dependent variable, and similarly aggregate input growth for the independent variable, calculating the average of the traditional technical change measure for τ, and running a regression to estimate μ. The specification of τ is not critical in this format since it is simply a constant; it is assumed not to embody a time trend so multiplicative scaling does not make any difference. Once the estimate of μ is obtained it can then be used to compute $MC = p_Y/\mu$ from the definition $\mu = p_Y/MC$.

The idea is to choose as an estimator of μ a value just high enough to leave the residual uncorrelated with the business cycle. This suggests, however, one qualification that makes this too complex to be dealt with simply by using an OLS (ordinary least squares) estimation procedure.

To impose the assumption that u is uncorrelated with the business cycle instrumental variables instead of OLS techniques should be used, with a measure of the business cycle as the instrument. Hall uses a measure of the rate of growth of real GNP ($\Delta GNP/GNP$) as an instrument in his initial work. In later studies he constructs a more comprehensive instrumental variable taking changes in defense spending, oil price changes, and other things into account to create a variable that more clearly should exhibit the desired correlation characteristics. The estimation procedures are still quite simple and single equation estimation is sufficient.

Like nonparametric measures, however, single equation models are too limited to represent production processes effectively, especially when all variation is assumed to be embodied in one parameter. The μ parameter has alternatively been interpreted as scale economies, markups, utilization, or some combination of these production characteristics. The measure therefore becomes a "catch-all" similarly to the residual nonparametric measures; only so much can be identified directly from the data using such simple models. Other single equation methods, resulting from postulating a basic cost function relationship, or a demand function for one input, are also limited in their applicability since the assumed interactions among outputs and inputs are so restricted *a priori*.

In sum, a number of nonparametric and simple parametric approaches may be pursued to impute the cost elasticities necessary to adjust productivity growth indexes to reflect production characteristics such as returns to scale and fixity. However, none of them can appropriately identify the structure that is implied by a production process that simultaneously embodies all these characteristics. Therefore, many researchers have turned to more complete structural production theory models to provide a framework in which to measure indicators of economic performance.

2.   FUNCTIONS FOR EMPIRICAL ANALYSIS

The choice of the function to use for analysis is important since it determines what types of equations represent the production technology and behavior, and what economic performance indicators may be generated directly from these equations.

A production function might initially be thought to be the most useful to specify and work with, since it directly represents the production technology, and indicators such as productivity growth indexes are generally motivated in this context. However, as a basis for representing the behavior and thus responses of firms, the production function has shortcomings.

The main problem with the production function specification, which was recognized early in the development of empirically implementable structural production theory models, and provided initiative to move to other specifications, involves the endogeneity versus exogeneity of right-hand side variables. Essentially, if behavioral assumptions are incorporated, the production function framework results in a system of pricing equations for estimation that are implicitly based on the premise that the firm decides what prices to pay for given quantities of inputs.

More specifically, in the production function specification the first-order conditions underlying the system of estimating equations stem from the profit maximization equalities $p_j = p_Y \cdot MP_j \equiv p_Y \cdot \partial Y(\mathbf{v},t)/\partial v_j$, where $p_Y \cdot MP_j = VMP_j$ is the value of the marginal product. Thus, the production function is used to define the marginal products, and the profit maximization assumption is superimposed to generate the estimating system.

However, in this scenario the input price p_j turns up on the left-hand side of the equation for estimation and the marginal product expression (which is a function of the v_js and t through the chosen functional form for the production function) appears on the right hand side. This implies that the v_js are exogenous (independent variables) and the prices endogenous (dependent variables), whereas one would think firms work the other way around – they observe the market price and choose input demand.[244]

It seems more natural to represent firm's behavior in terms of costs. If estimation is based on a cost function, the input demand functions can be derived directly from Shephard's Lemma; $v_j = \partial TC/\partial p_j$. Input demand is therefore by construction the endogenous variable, which facilitates using these expressions as the basis for a system of estimation equations.[245]

---

[244] A classic paper about the stochastic specification of models based on the production function is Zellner, Kmenta and Dreze [1966].

[245] Note that the assumption of input prices being exogenous and demand endogenous is more relevant at the firm level, but for an aggregate economy the opposite might

Further, if one wishes to represent input demand elasticities or biases, this implies specifying the model in terms of input demand.

In addition, the cost focus is intuitively amenable to derivation and interpretation of economic indicators. The primal (output) concept of productivity growth has a natural cost counterpart in terms of the cost of a particular output level (as we have seen), as does capacity utilization since it ultimately depends on discrepancies between the shadow values and markets price of inputs.

Use of a cost function model also avoids messy issues of long run behavior. With constant returns to scale and perfect competition (which in many cases are maintained hypotheses) profit maximization in the long run is not defined although cost minimization for a given output level is. Finally, cost functions are representative of a firm that does not really have a choice over its output supply, like some types of regulated firms.

A cost-based framework therefore may have important advantages for analysis. Specifying and implementing a cost function model may, however, pose some problems. In particular, although many econometricians have found that more robust estimates are generated from estimation of cost than profit functions, the built-in assumption of a given or exogenous output level in a cost function framework is often questionable, particularly when these functions are used to represent an aggregate of firms.

Some researchers have attempted to deal with this problem by "instrumenting" the output level, which in a sense endogenizes it.[246] This might be a somewhat *ad-hoc* solution, however, if the output level is truly endogenous. In this case a profit function might be preferable.

A profit function, specified by $\pi(\mathbf{p}, p_Y, t)$ as constrasted to the cost function $TC(\mathbf{p}, Y, t)$, embodies the assumption of profit maximization subject to a given output price, as overviewed in Chapter 6. The function is therefore dependent on the price instead of quantity of output. This allows the use of an additional Hotelling's lemma result to augment the system of estimating equations; $Y = \partial\pi/\partial p_Y$ becomes the output supply equation, as noted by Lau [1978] among others.

Although the profit maximization framework appears to be a more complete specification of firm behavior, some important restrictions on the assumptions about such behavior remain. For example, the assumption of perfect competition is directly built into the model, whereas one might think market imperfections could cause difficulties with such a specification.[247]

---

be thought to be the case. Therefore, for some applications this could cause a production function approach to be preferable.

[246] This will be discussed further in the Section 4.

[247] This can be dealt with to a certain extent by adding a marginal revenue function to the analysis, as done in Chapter 6.

Also, as mentioned in the context of the production function, some types of indicators appear more naturally to be specified in terms of costs, such as capacity utilization which is based on a cost derivative. Thus the cost function still tends to be a popular basis for analysis of production processes.

Additional issues arise if multiple outputs or quasi-fixed inputs are important for the analysis. First, if multiple outputs are important to represent, either the cost or profit function may be used for analysis. The output or output price levels simply become vectors. This simple theoretical extension, however, sometimes raises estimation issues, since researchers often find it difficult to identify all output and input choices. That is, convergence or curvature problems sometimes emerge in estimation.

One way this is sometimes dealt with is to return to the technological specification rather than to focus on behavior and choices. In a multiple output context, as we saw in Chapter 8, this may be accomplished by using a distance function $D_O(\mathbf{Y},\mathbf{v})$ for analysis, which is essentially a multiple-output production function. If the distance is set equal to one, this reproduces the multiple output production frontier. If $D_O(\bullet)$ is allowed to deviate from one, technical inefficiency may also be represented, as in Chapter 8.

In addition to the advantage of accommodating multiple outputs, this function, if estimated alone rather than as a system, does not require price data, or involve behavioral assumptions. However, degrees of freedom and multicollinearity problems are often an issue if the dimension of the problem (number of outputs and inputs) is large, a reasonably flexible function is assumed, and a single equation estimated. If profit maximizing assumptions are imposed to generate a system of estimating equations (which can be done if the focus is not on technical efficiency), the resulting model also has endogeneity problems analogous to the production function.

If, in turn, multiple quasi-fixed *inputs* are important, the cost and profit function frameworks are both somewhat limited. The combined adjustment of quasi-fixed inputs is problematic to represent if many are involved, as alluded to in Chapter 4. The value function of the dynamic duality literature, $J(\mathbf{p}_m,\mathbf{p}_j)$, is in this case a useful function. Such a function is often difficult to estimate, however, since so much must be identified from the data – not only optimal output and input decisions, but also the underlying dynamics associated with the quasi-fixed factors. Increased generality therefore has its benefits but also generates potential difficulties.

The appropriate function to use for analysis therefore depends on a number of characteristics of the problem to be addressed, and the data available for analysis. It depends on whether behavior and responses are important to represent, or alternatively whether the additional behavioral assumptions would be inappropriate. It depends on the dimensionality of the problem, in terms of outputs, inputs, and the extent of fixity.

Often, however, the structure allowed by the cost function model (with input demand represented but not relying on the assumption of profit maximization in the output market), facilitates empirical analysis. In this case the full cost structure and associated input demand responses, (limited) quasi-fixities, and multiple outputs, may be fully represented. The following discussion of functional forms therefore focuses on cost functions.[248]

A final point to emphasize is that once a function is chosen, the arguments must be carefully specified. That is, basic microeconomic theory indicates that arguments of a cost function should include the output level and input prices. Typically t is also included. However, a number of other arguments might also be incorporated in the cost function, as emphasized throughout this text. The appropriate specification of arguments therefore depends on the application being addressed and data availability.

3. FUNCTIONAL FORMS

Many different functional forms have been used for estimation of factor demand models and subsequent parametric estimation of elasticities representing production processes. Choices between functional forms are based on the questions to be addressed. Some functions simplify computations of elasticity formulas and specification of constraints such as constant returns to scale; some facilitate consideration of dynamic interactions; some allow curvature conditions to be directly imposed; and some enhance the ability to identify the difference between short and long run behavior. Most modern studies of production structure are, however, based on a "flexible" functional form, which allows a general specification of interactions among arguments of the function such as input substitution.[249]

That is, "flexible" functional forms allow the data to identify patterns among the arguments of the function since by definition they impose no *a-priori* restrictions on these interactions. Formally, flexible functional forms "provide a second order (differential) approximation to an arbitrary twice continuously differentiable function" as Diewert [1974] (and others) has shown. Thus, using a flexible functional form for, say, a cost function, allows a close approximation to the true function.[250]

---

[248] Clearly the same types of functional forms may be assumed for the other functions mentioned here; one simply has to specify them in terms of the appropriate arguments of the function, and ensure that the regularity conditions from Chapter 9 are satisfied

[249] A useful (much more detailed and rigorous) reference in this area is Lau [1986].

[250] Although I will not pursue the theory behind flexibility further, the interested reader can find further development of the theory as well as a more detailed discussion of different functional forms in Lau [1978], Diewert [1974], and Diewert and Wales [1987].

One example of a flexible functional form that has been used extensively for analysis of production is a translog form, which is a second-order (including all squared and cross-effects among arguments of the function) log-linear relationship. The translog cost function assuming instantaneous adjustment of all inputs takes the form:

$$11.4) \ \ln TC(Y,\mathbf{p},t) = \alpha_0 + \Sigma_j \, \alpha_j \ln p_j + .5 \, \Sigma_i \, \Sigma_j \, \gamma_{ij} \ln p_i \ln p_j + \delta_Y \ln Y$$

$$+ \Sigma_j \, \delta_{jY} \ln p_j \ln Y + .5 \, \delta_{YY} (\ln Y)^2 + \delta_t \, t + \Sigma_j \, \delta_{jt} \ln p_j \, t + .5 \, \delta_{tt} \, t^2$$

where p_j represents the price of the jth input, and regularity conditions (linear homogeneity in prices and symmetry) require $\Sigma_j \alpha_j = 1$, $\Sigma_i \, \gamma_{ij} = 0$ $\Sigma_j \, \delta_{jt} = 0$, $\Sigma_j \, \delta_{jY} = 0$, and $\gamma_{ij} = \gamma_{ji}$ for all i,j=1,2,...J.

Translog production or profit functions could similarly be defined by constructing a second order Taylor series expansion in logarithms of the general function. Since the translog has no constraints on second order terms it is deemed "flexible".

It is clear from initial observation that this function is an extension of the Cobb-Douglas (CD) functional form; it is a 2nd instead of 1st order log-linear form. The 1st order CD form, as discussed before, is restrictive in terms of the substitution assumptions incorporated. Elasticities of substitution between all inputs are one and shares of the inputs are constant. The shapes of isoquants are therefore imposed by *a-priori* assumption. Extending this to a second order function relaxes these constraints because cross-effects between inputs are recognized. The function can therefore represent more complex substitution patterns.[251]

It can be shown by direct manipulation that the standard cost function regularity condition of linear homogeneity in input prices, as in Chapter 9, is satisfied by this translog function due to its log-linear form. However, whether some other conditions hold depends on the parameter estimates.

In particular, monotonicity conditions depend on the sign of the fitted shares; the $S_j = \partial \ln TC / \partial \ln p_j$ must be positive. The concavity conditions are more complex. They depend on the γ_{ij} parameters and are not globally satisfied; they must be checked at each data point to identify violations.

---

[251] It should be noted that although simple functional forms like the Cobb-Douglas are self-dual, in the sense that a Cobb-Douglas cost function can be derived by cost minimization based on a Cobb-Douglas production function, this is not true for more general forms. The cost minimization problem, in fact, cannot analytically be solved using flexible forms. Therefore, the principles of a particular type of functional form are applied directly to the general function $TC(\mathbf{p},Y,t)$ rather than derived through cost minimization.

Note also that this function, although homogeneous of degree one in prices, as noted, is *not* necessarily linearly homogeneous in output. The latter question has to do with the existence of returns to scale. If $\delta_{jy}=0$ for all j, for example, the translog function is homothetic. If, in addition, $\delta_{YY}=0$, this reduces to homogeneity, and if, further, $\delta_Y=1$, CRS, or linear homogeneity in output, exists. These restrictions may be imposed on the function to check whether the more restricted scale specifications are justified by the data.

The translog function has generally been applied to long run (instantaneous adjustment) factor demand models, such as many developed by Dale Jorgenson[252], although it is possible to construct a short run version of this function as initiated by Brown and Christensen [1981]. The advantage of the translog functional form in the former context is that, since it is defined in terms of logarithms, elasticity computations as well as restrictions on the form (such as those for CRS) depend only on the parameter estimates rather than being a function of the data itself.

When extended to a short run function, however, the logarithmic form causes a problem. Imputing the long run demand for the fixed factor(s), which requires constructing and solving the expression(s) $p_k = Z_k = -\partial VC/\partial x_k$, cannot be accomplished analytically even with only one quasi-fixed input. Instead, algorithms to solve the equations numerically are required.

Other studies, especially those that explicitly incorporate fixities and dynamic adjustment, have used a (normalized) quadratic function. This function is useful for these types of studies because second order derivatives (in levels) do not depend on the data, so adjustment matrixes are much easier to derive than would otherwise be the case. The computation of a flexible accelerator investment equation that depends on the rate of interest and parameters of the model in Berndt, Fuss and Waverman [1980], for example, is possible because they rely on the normalized quadratic function. Such a short run cost function with only capital (K) quasi-fixed can be expressed as

$$11.5)\ VC(Y,\mathbf{p},K,\Delta K,t) = L + \Sigma_j\ p_j v_j = \alpha_0 + \alpha_t t + \Sigma_j\ \alpha_j p_j + \alpha_Y Y + \alpha_K K$$

$$+ \alpha_{\Delta K}\Delta K + .5(\Sigma_i\Sigma_j\ \gamma_{ij}\ p_{ij} + \gamma_{YY}\ Y^2 + \gamma_{KK}\ K^2 + \gamma_{\Delta K\Delta K}(\Delta K)^2 + \gamma_{tt}\ t^2)$$

$$+ \Sigma_j\ \gamma_{jY}\ p_j Y + \Sigma_j\gamma_{jK}\ p_j K + \Sigma_j\ \gamma_{j\Delta K}\ p_j\ \Delta K + \Sigma_j\ \gamma_{jt} p_j t + \gamma_{YK}\ Y{\bullet}K$$

$$+ \gamma_{Y\Delta K}\ Y{\bullet}\Delta K + \gamma_{tK}\ t{\bullet}K + \gamma_{t\Delta K}\ t{\bullet}\Delta K + \gamma_{K\Delta K}\ K{\bullet}\Delta K\ ,$$

[252] See Jorgenson [1988] and the references contained in that study.

where j does not index capital (K) or labor (L), but represents all other inputs. This function is normalized by the price of labor (p_L), and adjustment costs for capital are included since $\Delta K = K_t - K_{t-1}$ is an argument of the function. This is a second-order approximation in terms of levels of the function's arguments, rather than logarithms, but still includes all cross-terms among the arguments, and thus is flexible. Note also that the normalization is necesssary for linear homogeneity in prices to be satisfied.

By contrast to the translog model, for which the estimating equations are naturally expressed as shares, this function facilitates defining input demand equations directly using Shephard's lemma. This is advantageous in the sense that input demand elasticities are more familiar and thus more easily interpretable than elasticities based on shares, such as the Allen-Uzawa elasticities discussed in the previous chapter. In addition, the full set of input demand elasticities may be estimated, rather than dropping one share equation and solving for the parameters of that equations implicitly, which is required because the shares sum to one (as elaborated below).

However, at least two problems are imbedded in this function. One input must be chosen for normalization (and the results are not invariant to which is chosen), and the function does not easily reduce to constant returns to scale; CRS is not a nested specification. Therefore, although CRS versions of (11.5) have been estimated,[253] testing the possible returns to scale specifications is not straightforward.

Another functional form that has desirable properties is the generalized Leontief (GL), which is a second-order expansion in square roots rather than logs or levels of the arguments of the functions. This function reduces to a linear function without the 2nd order terms, so it is a generalized version of a cost function based on a fixed proportions production function.

Like the translog function, such a model does not facilitate modeling a full dynamic adjustment process because the second derivatives are functions of all the arguments of the functions rather than just being parameters. Thus it is less desirable than the quadratic if the investment mechanism is the focus of analysis.[254] It does, however, allow determinants of second order effects such as biases to be identified. The GL form also, unlike the translog, allows analytical imputation of long run quasi-fixed input, x_k^* (or capacity output, Y^*) values, and, in fact, tends empirically to generate less curvature violations in such a model than the translog. Thus, it is particularly useful for approximation of a restricted cost function.

---

[253] See, for example, Morrison and Berndt [1981].

[254] Although a dynamic process can be incorporated in this case using Euler equations as in Morrison [1992a]. The problem arises because these equations cannot be solved to generate an explicit investment equation, but instead investment is implicitly determined via a pricing equation.

A variant of the generalized Leontief variable or restricted cost function was developed in Morrison [1988a] and has been empirically applied by Morrison [1992a], among others. This function, allowing for multiple fixed inputs, can be expressed as:

$$11.6) \; VC = Y \, [\Sigma_k \Sigma_j \, \alpha_{ij} \, p_i^{.5} \, p_j^{.5} + \Sigma_j \, \Sigma_m \, \delta_{jm} \, p_j \, s_m^{.5} + \Sigma_j \, p_j \, \Sigma_m \Sigma_n \, \gamma_{mn} \, s_m^{.5} \, s_n^{.5}]$$

$$+ \, Y^{.5}[\Sigma_j \Sigma_k \, \delta_{jk} \, p_j \, x_k^{.5} + \Sigma_j p_j \, \Sigma_m \Sigma_k \, \gamma_{mk} \, s_m^{.5} \, x_k^{.5}] + \Sigma_j p_j \, \Sigma_k \Sigma_l \, \gamma_{lk} \, x_k^{.5} \, x_l^{.5},$$

where p_i and p_j represent prices of all variable inputs, x_k and x_l denote fixed inputs, and s_m and s_n enumerate output (Y) and other exogenous arguments of VC(•) not included in the returns to scale specification, such as the state of technology (t), investment in quasi-fixed inputs Δx, or external r_b variables. Note that linear homogeneity in prices is embodied in this function through the square root terms for prices, although this also necessitates multiplying any terms not including prices to be multiplied by a $\Sigma_j \, p_j$ term.

Note also, however, that this function is asymmetric in output levels. Although this allows CRS to be nested within the model (see Morrison [1988a] for a discussion of the properties of this functional form), it causes the extension to multiple outputs to be problematic. Construction of a more symmetric form, simply in terms of all cross-effects in square roots, does not allow direct parameter constraints to reproduce different homogeneity specifications. However, whether CRS is a reasonable specification may still be determined by assessing whether the ε^L_{TCY} elasticity statistically differs from one (such a specification is used in Morrison [1998b,d]).

Another issue that is problematic for both the log-linear and GL forms is zero values for arguments of the function. Zero output values for the translog function, for example, will not be possible to accommodate since taking logarithms will not be possible. For the GL form the construction of data for estimation will not cause problems, but if an optimization equation with respect to any zero variable (in levels) is specified a zero value will appear in the denominator, again causing the estimation process to blow up.

Zero values are not an issue for aggregate estimation, but potentially emerge in micro data, particularly for panel data with a variety of outputs (inputs) specified which some firms may not produce (use). The levels-based specification of the quadratic function is then advantageous. However, the disadvantages of targeting one variable for nomalization, thus causing asymmetry of demand equations, remains. Although demand equations for the non-normalized inputs may be specified according to Shephard's lemma, the equation for the other input (here labor) becomes $L = VC(•) - \Sigma_j \, p_j v_j$, so estimation may not be invariant to the choice of the normalizing input.

In this case one might think it would be useful to combine functional forms so that the advantages of each are retained. As long as the form remains flexible, and satisfies required regularity conditions, this should not limit analysis. For example, a generalized Leontief-quadratic (GLQ) form was specified and estimated in Morrison [1998a]. This form embodies linear homogeneity as does the GL, but allows zero values for outputs and inputs (expressed as levels) to be dealt with. One such form (where r_k denotes any arguments of the function other than input prices and (multiple) outputs) is:

$$11.7) \quad VC(\mathbf{Y},\mathbf{p},\mathbf{r}) = \Sigma_i\Sigma_j\, \alpha_{ij}\, p_i^{.5}\, p_j^{.5} + \Sigma_i\Sigma_m\, \delta_{im}\, p_i\, Y_m + \Sigma_i\Sigma_k\, \delta_{ik}\, p_i r_k$$

$$+ \Sigma_i p_i\, (\Sigma_m\Sigma_n\, \gamma_{mn}\, Y_m\, Y_n + \Sigma_m\Sigma_k\, \gamma_{mk}\, Y_m\, r_k + \Sigma_k\Sigma_l\, \gamma_{lk}\, r_k\, r_l)\,,$$

One disadvantage of all the functions discussed so far is that none of them directly impose curvature (2nd order) regularity conditions. As noted for the translog, such conditions must instead be tested for by computing the associated second derivatives, and checking their signs.

These conditions (seen in Chapter 9) imply that input demand curves slope down, and output supply curves (for a profit maximization model) slope up, which is required for logical consistency of our production models. A second order flexible form, however, because it allows the function to represent various shapes depending on the data, precludes imposing curvature without serious limitations on the form that destroy its flexibility.

A final type of functional form to be considered here, therefore (although many more could be specified),[255] is one that constrains curvature conditions to be satisfied. This forces the data to satisfy properties that must hold for our production theory models to be relevant. Since for some applications curvature conditions are violated empirically, these conditions may be binding. This is especially true for models that contain fixed factors, where even the monotonicity condition might fail, as reflected by negative estimated shadow values (in practice this seems especially true for the translog, as noted above). This raises questions about the specification's validity, but if desired may be dealt with by functional form assumptions.

A number of researchers have attempted to accommodate this problem. One approach suggested by Diewert and Wales [1987] (DW) is to specify a flexible functional form that is still sufficiently complex to impose curvature without losing the flexibility property. This complexity increases the

---

[255] Some of these are the generalized Box-Cox and the Fourier functions. For further references and comments see Berndt [1990], Chapter 9. For a comparison of some flexible functional forms, see Guilkey, Lovell and Sickles [1983].

problems involved in estimating the parameters and constructing indicators, but may be preferable to alternative restrictive specifications.

One form suggested by DW is the generalized McFadden:

$$11.8a) \ TC(\mathbf{p},Y,t) = g^1(p)Y + \Sigma_j \ b_{jj} \ p_jY + \Sigma_j \ b_jp_j + \Sigma_j \ b_{jt} \ p_j \ t{\bullet}Y + b_t(\Sigma_j \ \alpha_jp_j) \ t$$

$$+ \ b_{YY} \ (\Sigma_j\beta_jp_j)^2 + b_{tt} \ (\Sigma_j\gamma_jp_j) \ t^2Y, \quad \text{with } g(\bullet) \text{ defined as}$$

$$11.8b) \ g^1(\mathbf{p}) \equiv .5 \ p_1^{-1} \ \Sigma_i \ \Sigma_j \ c_{ij} \ p_i \ p_j \ , \ c_{ij} =c_{ji} \ \text{ for } 2{\leq}i,j{\leq}J,$$

only Y, $\mathbf{p}$ and t as arguments, and the parameters α_j, β_j and γ_j pre-selected by the researcher. Note that this functional form also requires an arbitrary normalization due to the construction of the g^1 expression.

Although numerous issues arise about functional forms, many of them can be accommodated using variations on the forms introduced here. The important characteristics of these forms are that they are flexible and satisfy regularity conditions. They can represent either short- or long- run functions by alternatively using quantities or prices of factors as arguments. They also can allow for adjustment costs or environmental or regulation effects by including x_k or r_b variables as arguments of the function, and interactions between these and other arguments through the form's flexibility. Therefore, although only a limited number of possible functional forms have been presented, they are quite broadly representative, and provide a rich basis for empirical analysis of production processes.

4. SOME ECONOMETRIC ISSUES

For empirical implementation of production models based on the functions and functional forms discussed in the previous sections, systems of equations representing the underlying technology and behavior must be specified, which are typically based on derivatives of the functions. Estimation of these equation systems may then proceed using appropriate econometric techniques. Many issues emerge when pursing this final step. In this section we concentrate on some of the econometric considerations that are most often raised in the literature, using cost functions as an example, although the issues encountered are similar for other functions.[256]

---

[256] I will only be highlighting specific problems that should be considered. Further elaboration of the econometric theory requires perusal of any standard econometrics

4.1 Systems of equations

A system of equations for estimation, which reflects the production structure (technology and behavior), may be constructed using versions of Shephard's and Hotelling's lemmas. The most fundamental equations generally specified for estimation are the (optimal) input demand equations, represented by $v_j = \partial TC/\partial p_j$ for input j. These equations reproduce the familiar isoquant diagram version of the cost minimizing input demand choice. They therefore summarize the full range of input substitution patterns of the firm, and contain all the parameters required for construction of elasticities symbolizing this behavior. For increased efficiency of estimation, however, as well as direct representation of cost levels, researchers often also estimate the cost function itself.

If the function used for analysis is a restricted or variable cost function, these demand equations may only be constructed for variable inputs. In this case, additional information may be provided by shadow value equations from the Hotelling's lemma-based expression $Z_k = -\partial VC/\partial x_k$. These equations are therefore sometimes also used for estimation purposes.

Such an approach raises a problem, however, because Z_k, the shadow or *ex-post* value for fixed input k, is not in general observable. And if the market price p_k is instead used as the dependent variable this is equivalent to imposing (an inverse) Shephard's lemma (equilibrium in the factor market).

If capital is the only quasi-fixed input, some researchers have assumed that a residual or *ex-post* value $Z_K = (p_Y Y - VC)/K$ may be computed and used as the dependent variable of the equation. The motivation for this is analogous to Hulten's [1986] nonparametric method for constructing Z_K. However, as noted above in this context, such a procedure is not justifiable unless restrictive assumptions like CRS and perfect competition are valid.

If the shadow value expression is not used, an alternative equation also based on a perfect competition assumption (and implicitly also endogenizing output price, since p_Y becomes a dependent variable), $p_Y = MC \equiv \partial VC/\partial Y$, is sometimes invoked.[257] Adding this equation to the system of input demand and cost function equations sometimes facilitates "tying down" estimates of the fixed input parameters, since in practice these estimates may not be very robust unless an extra structural equation is included in the system.

---

textbook. For a more focused discussion of factor demand model estimation, and some exercises, see Chapter 9 in Berndt [1990].

[257] See Mork [1978] and Morrison [1988a] for examples of this in the perfect and imperfect competition case, respectively. With imperfect competition this equality becomes MR=MC, so this may involve also incorporating a revenue or output demand function. Note also that in the latter case both output and output price become endogenous, so the price-setting inference is appropriate.

As the specification of the production process becomes more detailed, additional optimization equations may be implied for estimation and analysis. For example, for a dynamic model such as those developed by Berndt, Fuss and Waverman [1980], Nadiri and Prucha [1989], and others, the shadow value equation expands into a complete investment equation based on an Euler equation, as discussed in Chapter 9. Such investment equations can be specified in most cases for all quasi-fixed inputs, although once multiple quasi-fixed inputs are included some difficulties can arise with cross-effects on the adjustment matrix.[258]

Finally, it should be noted that for some specifications it is not valid to estimate the entire system of equations because the errors are dependent on one another. In particular, for the translog functional form share equations are natural to use for analysis because the function is specified in logarithms. But, since the sum of the input shares must equal one, the errors on the share equations sum to zero. Therefore, one of the equations must be dropped. The standard one to delete is a materials (M) equation.

Working backward from the adding up restrictions allows estimation of the parameters of the omitted equation. Although this seems somewhat questionable at first glance, it turns out that the results are numerically invariant to which equation is dropped because of the dependence, as long as a maximum likelihood estimation procedure is employed.[259] This has now become such a standard procedure that most researchers do not elaborate further but simply mention which of the equations was left out of the system.

Once the system of estimation equations is specified, the next issue the empirical researcher encounters is what estimation method to utilize. Single equation ordinary least squares (OLS) is not appropriate due to the cross-equation restrictions in a full estimating system; the same parameter will appear in different equations and must be constrained to be equal everywhere. Interrelatedness is inherent among the equations.

Thus, systems estimation procedures such as Zellner's "seemingly unrelated" (so sometimes called SUR) systems techniques are often used. This implies, however, that there is no simultaneity, or endogeneity of right-hand-side variables, in the system of equations.

---

[258] This is discussed in more detail in Morrison and Berndt [1981]. If the Euler equation is estimated directly rather than solving for the investment level, in most cases this difficulty does not arise.

[259] Since iterative Zellner (seemingly unrelated) methods are equivalent to maximum likelihood estimation, using standard iterative systems estimation methods is sufficient for invariance to which equation is deleted. As discussed in more detail in Berndt [1990, Chapter 9], however, if one-step Zellner efficient techniques are used, care must be taken that the first round estimate of the disturbance covariance matrix does not impose the symmetry restrictions.

In this case an additive disturbance term is appended to each of the equations of the system, and it is assumed that the resulting disturbance vector is independently and identically normally distributed with mean vector zero and constant, non-singular covariance matrix Ω. The estimation procedure uses equation-by-equation ordinary least squares to obtain an estimate of Ω, and then does generalized least squares using this estimated disturbance covariance matrix on the system of equations.

This method is often denoted Zellner-efficient (ZEF).[260] If the ZEF estimator is iterated until changes in the estimate of Ω from one estimation to the next become very small, the iterative Zellner (IZEF) estimator is obtained. This estimator generates results numerically equivalent to maximum likelihood estimates.

In a number of cases, however, it is questionable whether using standard systems estimation techniques is justifiable. For example, if analysis is based on a dynamic adjustment model, the investment levels of quasi-fixed inputs are independent variables for most equations but comprise the dependent variable in the investment equation. For a model with only one quasi-fixed input this is not a problem because the system is recursive; there are no two equations where the independent and dependent variables show up on opposite sides of the equation. However, if more than one quasi-fixed input exists, so that, for example, the x_l equation is a function of the x_k value and vice versa (for any two quasi-fixed factors x_l and x_k), simultaneous equation estimation techniques must be used.

Full Information Maximum Likelihood (FIML) methods are sometimes used to deal with simultaneity if the assumption of normal errors is invoked, as it generally is, and the entire system is fully specified.[261] For a large model with nonlinearities, however, some researchers have found that it is difficult to obtain convergence by FIML. Additional difficulties arise if the vector of disturbance terms on the system of estimating equations cannot be assumed independently and identically multivariate normally distributed with mean vector zero and a constant non-singular covariance matrix.

---

[260] This is sometimes also called the minimum chi-square estimator. Most statistical programs used for econometric estimation have a package that does this type of estimation. In TSP the LSQ command carries out estimation on a system of equations, and has a number of options that may be chosen for different types of algorithms and numbers of iterations on both the parameters and variance-covariance matrix. With only one iteration this reproduces the SUR or ZEF estimator, and when iterated to convergence it becomes the IZEF estimator. This command is also capable of dealing with nonlinear models, which occurs with some functional forms, although some other statistical programs have difficulties with nonlinearities.

[261] By constrast, three stage least squares, as discussed below, may be used for a subset of equations specifying a system, if all the relationships cannot be identified.

For example, the simple assumption of additive disturbance terms is often justified by saying it represents random errors by firms. However, some researchers have questioned whether this is reasonable. McElroy [1987] argues that errors are not due to firms' but to econometrician's errors, and that this implies the entire optimization process should be imbedded in a stochastic framework. The assumed pattern of errors can then be very different, with additive or multiplicative error terms on the estimating equations, which implies that standard systems techniques may not be used. More complex estimation procedures requiring formal specification of the likelihood function may be required.[262]

Another instance in which the usual assumptions about errors are inappropriate is when heteroskedasticity exists. An example where this could occur is when input demand equations are specified over a time series. In this case the variance of the disturbance term may not be constant but instead tend to grow as the scale of operations, and therefore both the levels of demand and output, increases. If one thinks the increase in variance could be proportional to the change in output level – output change in a sense indexes the scale increase – then an adjustment for heteroskedasticity using output might be relevant. A simple correction to reduce this disturbance heteroskedasticity would be to specify the input demand levels in terms of input-output levels (v_j/Y) instead of just v_j.

4.2   Instrumental variables estimation

The systems estimation procedure instead chosen by many researchers is three stage least squares (THSLS, or, if iterative, ITHSLS). This is a common approach to dealing with simultaneity that uses instrumental variables (IV) to "endogenize" the factors that appear as both independent and dependent variables. This technique is also often used to accommodate the possibilities of endogenous input prices or output mentioned above.

In particular, Pindyck and Rotemberg [1983] demonstrated that one way to alleviate the problem of nonstatic expectations of the future path of input prices is to instrument current prices (which represent the relevant stream of expected future prices with error) using THSLS. Unfortunately, however, as Hausman [1975] has shown, THSLS methods are not in general numerically equivalent to FIML, even though their asymptotic properties are the same.[263]

---

[262] This also implies in some circumstances that the cost function should not be estimated along with the demand or share equations because all information from this function is redundant. See Berndt [1990] Chapter 9 for a more complete overview of the problem and McElroy [1987] for more details.

[263] See Berndt [1990] Chapter 9 for a more complete discussion, and Hausman [1975] for more details.

Also, an important question for IV estimation is what variables to use as instruments. A standard approach is to use lagged values of the variables, as was done by Pindyck and Rotemberg [1983]. As they mention, other instruments might be thought to be more independent, but sometimes do not result in very reasonable estimates. Some such possibilities are overall macroeconomic variables like a cost of living index, rate of interest, unemployment rate, and Gross National Product (GNP). When using aggregated data, however (say, for an entire industry), it should be recognized that these variables may be somewhat endogenous; the industry may have a significant effect on the macro measures.

Pindyck and Rotemberg argued for the use of instrumental variables to deal with nonstatic expectations based on the Hansen and Singleton [1982] result that estimates will be consistent with rational expectations about future input prices if the current input prices are considered endogenous in a THSLS estimation. In particular, Hansen and Singleton [1982] show that if one uses an instrumental variable procedure, and chooses instruments that are likely to help determine the expectations of the decision makers in the firms under consideration, consistency with error orthogonality and rational expectations is ensured.

Although the resulting estimates will be *consistent* with rational expectations, the procedure does not explicitly identify how expectations are formed and therefore does not provide any interpretation of the impact of expectations. In some cases the interpretive and explanatory power of the model may thus be augmented by incorporating a more explicit expectations formation specification.

Morrison [1986b] considered two alternative versions of non-static expectations that do not require a full econometric model of the expectations formation process used by firms (which would be required for a true rational expectations model) but do extend the analysis to allow some interpretation of the processes. The approaches developed, based on adaptive and "partially rational" expectations, rely on ARIMA models[264] to calculate the expected variables, which are then inserted into the model for estimation instead of the current measured variables. Empirical estimation of such models suggests that the relatively straightforward adaptive expectations framework, which simply requires modeling an IMA(1,1) moving average process, reflects the important impacts of nonstatic expectations on decision making without causing volatile parameter estimates or necessitating complex ARIMA modeling.

---

[264] See the texts by Nelson [1973] or Pindyck and Rubinfeld [1981] for further relatively simple elaboration of these types of models and their estimation.

More specifically, assume an expected value of the observed exogenous variable π_t, $E(\pi_t)$, in a simple economic structural model can be represented by a rational distributed lag[265]

11.11) $E(\pi_t) = a + b[L(\bullet)/D(\bullet)]\,\pi_t + \upsilon_t$,

where $L(\bullet)$ and $D(\bullet)$ are polynomials in the lag operator. From the properties of a rational distributed lag, the path of expected variables expressed in this manner is a form of general or unrestricted rational expectations, and can be characterized by time series techniques, using a general ARIMA model. The adaptive expectations version of this is a special case of an IMA(1,1) process, as shown by Nelson [1973].

Because the adaptive expectations process is relatively simple, it can be shown that the series of anticipated variables can be substituted directly into the estimating equations to generate structural expectations parameters representing expectations formation consistent with the rest of the model. This results because the entire impact on the change in expected prices is incorporated in the first shock, as is clear from the formalization of the adaptive expectations or IMA(1,1) process as $\pi_{t+1}-\pi_t=(1-\varpi)e_t$. Since the difference in the expected exogenous variables, $\pi_{t+1}-\pi_t$, appears in the investment equations of dynamic models, $(1-\varpi)e_t$ can directly be substituted.

With a more complex ARIMA process, however, the order of the ARIMA process must be determined using Time Series Analysis (TSA) methods, and the resulting "expected values" substituted into the analysis. This is equivalent to incorporating a compound parameter representing expectations errors in the estimating equations.[266]

Another econometric issue that needs to be addressed here, particularly for models including investment equations, is the potential existence of serially correlated errors. One way this can be accommodated in systems estimation is elaborated by Berndt [1990], Chapter 9, who applies a Koyck transformation analogous to that used for single equation systems. In matrix notation the first-order autoregressive stochastic process is specified as:

---

[265] See Nerlove [1972] for one development of this. See also Morrison [1986b] for further details of this procedure and the manipulations outlined below.

[266] Except for this tangential connection, time series methods are ignored in this chapter. Time series models, in particular those dealing with nonstationarity, have become quite popular in the past decade. Since the type of data used for studies of economic performance are time series that often exhibit nonstationarity, this may be an issue. However, most equation systems used for this type of analysis are too complex to be dealt with using currently available techniques. Also, most corrections for nonstationarity have little substantive impact on the estimates, although perhaps increasing efficiency.

11.9) $U_t = RU_{t-1} + \xi_t$.

(11.9) is the systems version of the first order univariate autoregressive scheme $u_t=\rho u_{t-1}+\varepsilon_t$, $t=2,...T$. For the n-equation system of equations $Y_t=V_t\beta+U_t$, where Y_t is an nx1 vector, V_t is an nxJ matrix and β is a Jx1 vector of parameters, this can be used to transform the system to one which is consistent with normality assumptions as

$$11.10) \quad Y_t = RY_{t-1} + (V_t-RV_{t-1})\beta + \xi_t \,,$$

which again has its obvious counterpart in single equation models. The transformed system can then be estimated using system estimation methods incorporating nonlinear parameter restrictions. The special case when R is diagonal can be tested as a restriction on this general specification.

An exception arises for systems with dependencies among the equations such as for the translog, where the shares sum to one, resulting in singular disturbance covariance and residual cross-products matrixes. This implies the very strong restriction that each column of R sums to a given constant. For example, if R is diagonal, all elements of the diagonal matrix must be constant.[267] Care must therefore be taken when applying autoregressive techniques to singular systems and interpreting the results.

Another more popular technique often invoked for doing systems estimation with instrumental variables when serially correlated errors may be an issue is the generalized method of moments (GMM) procedure.[268]

If the error terms on the equations in the system are serially independent, and the same instruments are used for each equation, THSLS coincides with the GMM estimator. If serially correlated errors exist, however, THSLS estimates will be consistent but not asymptotically efficient since they use the "wrong" covariance matrix. The correct weighting matrix may be computed using the GMM approach. The GMM approach is therefore a more general and powerful version of THSLS estimation

In particular, the GMM estimator (available as an option in statistical packages like TSP) can allow for conditional heteroskedasticity of the disturbances (the HET option in TSP), and serial correlation (say, moving average disturbances – the NMA option). In fact, quite general forms of heteroskedasticity and autocorrelation in the errors are permitted, with different forms leading to different weighting matrixes. GMM also "nests" most estimation procedures including maximum likelihood, and is thus a powerful IV estimation procedure for systems of equations.

---

[267] This was shown by Berndt and Savin [1975].
[268] See Hansen [1982] for discussion of the connection between THSLS and GMM models.

A final issue to take into account, that also supports using IV estimation, involves measurement error. This issue is related to questions about both model development and data construction we have previously addressed. In particular, if our production structure model does not reflect all production characteristics, variations in outputs and inputs will embody unexplained components that will appear in the error terms of the estimating equations.

This problem may arise from error in the construction of prices indexes, like biases from incomplete adjustments for changes in quality such as those discussed in Chapter 10 for computers and pharmaceuticals. As discussed (and measured) by Siegel [1995], such errors will appear in price and therefore quantity measures. Therefore, in models for which output and input quantities are dependent variables (and prices explanatory variables), additional error will be incorporated in the error structure of the model.

If one can provide specific structure for this error, as in Siegel [1995], the resulting biases may be explicitly accommodated in the model. More generally, econometric procedures may be used to reflect these errors in variables, as overviewed in Siegel [1997]. He bases his analysis on a reduced-form model "explaining" MFP growth of the form (in our notation)

11.12) $MFP = A + b_1 r_1 + b_2 r_2 + u$,

where A is the rate of disembodied (or "external") technical change, r_1 and r_2 are external factors (the rate of R&D investment and the rate of investment in computers), and u is a classical (white noise) disturbance term.

From the various production structure characteristics embodied in MFP growth measures, as well as potential biases in the data used for estimation (as emphasized in previous chapters), one might expect that MFP is an "error-ridden indicator of MFP growth"; $MFP = MFP^* + \varepsilon$, where ε is a measurement error term. As discussed by Siegel [1997], if the standard errors-in-variables assumptions hold,

11.13) $E(u) = E(\varepsilon) = cov(\varepsilon,u) = cov(\varepsilon,r_1) = cov (\varepsilon,r_2) = 0$,

estimates of b_1 and b_2 will be unbiased but inefficient. For this application, however, the last two assumptions are likely to be violated since changes in computer and R&D are correlated with the measurement error term (changes in output and labor quality that are not incorporated in the price series).

Thus, measurement errors arise from price mis-measurement due to incomplete adjustment for product and labor quality changes, and differences between "true" and reported prices due to economic fluctuations. Other mis-specifications could also cause (11.13) to be invalid, and thus the estimates of b_1 and b_2 to be inefficient and inconsistent.

The "fix" proposed for this problem is, again, instrumental variables. In Siegel [1997], a full-information version of IV, or a "multiple-indicators, multiple-causes" (MIMIC) model is estimated. This requires identifying proxies and determinants of MFP*, as well as analogously corrected specified adaptations to the measurement of L and Y, and a supply shock S. More generally, this may be considered another version of the endogeneity of variables underlying our production structure specification that underlies the desirablity of using IV estimation.

4.3   Time-series/cross-section data

Economic performance studies tend to be based on time series data, since they focus on evaluating changes in the technological and cost structure of a productive unit over time. Comparisons across units (a cross-section) also can be carried out, particularly if differentials in units' efficiency are targeted. If the data have both time-series and cross-sectional dimensions (across years and productive units) they are in the form of panel data.

Adding this dimension to the data generates comparability problems, since unobserved environmental or technological variations may be reflected in differential observed productivity patterns. Difficulties are also created since the disturbance terms will be a combination of time-series and cross-section disturbances, plus some combination of both. However, due to the greater degrees of freedom and additional structure from the broader data set, it also tends to augment efficiency of estimation.

Panel data are increasingly being used for performance analysis, due to the greater recent availability and accessibility of micro data. Unbalanced panels (where the same productive units are not all represented for each time period) also are often utilized for such studies.

Panel data applications are not only across micro units. The Ball *et al* study discussed in Chapter 8, for example, was empirically implemented for a panel of data of 48 U.S. states from the late 1940s to early 1990s. Panel data may also be across industries; Morrison and Siegel [1997], for example, analyzed 450 4-digit U.S. manufacturing industries over the years 1959-89.

The increasing use of panel data has generated great interest in the development of appropriate econometric techniques for such data sets. The basic problem with panel data is that one might expect differences in behavior across productive units simply from their inherent characteristics (environmental factors such as region, or the particular entrepreneur's management practices) which are in some sense "fixed". Such differences may also be correlated with some observable factor driving the analysis. For example, management structure or the feasible technological base may depend on size (amount of output produced).

If such differentials are important for estimation, this has implications for how to organize the data. That is, since the kinds of models discussed in this text tend to focus on the time dimension, the cross-section dimension can be thought of as augmenting the time series with information that is not dependent across units. In this case one might organize the data by unit – "stacking" it by firm. The first 20 observations may be, for example, for a 20 year period for firm 1, and the second 20 observations represent the data for firm two for the same time period. The resulting data set is "pooled".

Traditional methods used for estimation over pooled or panel data are primarily fixed-effects (dummy variables) or error components estimation procedures.[269] More complex models may incorporate random effects. Although we will not pursue these methods in depth here, it is worth overviewing briefly what they involve.[270]

The easiest way to analyze the pooled data set would be to simply estimate it as if the observations were all independent (as a pure panel). However, one would think that there would be interdependencies in both the time and cross-section dimension that would be inappropriately forced into the error term by relying on such a procedure.

The most straightforward way to deal with this is to introduce dummy variables for the time and/or cross-section dimensions. Given our focus on the time dimension, it seems particularly useful to incorporate dummy variables for the cross-sectional units, to adapt for any fixed environmental factors that would shift cost levels. We may then still treat the time dimension as implied by our cost model – delineating the time dimension through the time counter t. For example, if each productive unit has data for 1970-1995, the time counter would call each 1970 data point "1", and count from there. Alternatively we could also bring in dummy variables for each time period. Note, however, that if data are limited adding many dummies may result in a serious loss of degrees of freedom.

The use of dummy variables to deal with cross-section variation is typically called "fixed effects" estimation.[271] Such a model assumes that the only difference across productive units is one of levels; slope terms remain the same. However, if this is imposed on a system of equations, and the input demand equations, say, have fixed effects, this implies unit-specific slope terms in the cost equation. That is, since the input demand equations are based on derivatives of the cost equation, intercepts in the input demand equations imply parameters on a price variable in the cost function.

---

[269] See Griffiths, Hill and Judge [1993] for further discussion of these methods, as well as the studies by Griliches and Chamberlain in the *Handbook of Econometrics*.

[270] Textbooks that address panel data include Judge *et al* [1985], which is a good introduction, and Kmenta [1986]. Baltagi [1995] provides an overview of model complications.

[271] TSP allows estimation of both fixed and random effects models.

The error components model instead explicitly recognizes the three different parts of a combined error term mentioned above. It incorporates the fact that that error terms may be correlated across time and individual units in a combined error of the form $\omega_{it} = \upsilon_i + \nu_t + \varepsilon_{it}$, where the notation appears similar to that for inefficiency models but the interpretation is different. υ_i refers to the cross-section error component, ν_t to the time-series error component, and ε_{it} the combined error component, each of which is assumed normally and independently distributed.

Even without the standard extensions of econometric analysis to serial correlation and other complications, this model runs into problems similar to those encountered for the efficiency models. It is difficult to allocate these different error terms across equations that are derived from each other. If these errors are assumed to be associated with the cost function, this implies something about the input demand functions constructed as derivatives.

This provides another example, therefore, where potentially desirable refinements to the stochastic specification are precluded, or at least greatly complicated, by the richness of the structural production theory model we have been developing. Although some systems estimation procedures have been developed that can help us extend and test our stochastic specification, in most cases these types of models are estimated with fairly simple econometric methodologies, assuming that stochastic structure is adequately reflected in the model through the greater structural content.

5.   FURTHER COMMENTS

This overview of a selected set of empirical implementation issues covers a number of problems one might encounter when proceeding to estimate systems of equations representing production theory models for productivity growth analysis. The discussion here is not meant to be comprehensive but simply to overview some issues that typically are raised in the literature.

Once estimation is carried out, the resulting parameter estimates may be used to construct estimates of the various economic performance indicators, based on 1st and 2nd order derivatives (and thus elasticities) of the cost system, as discussed in Chapter 9. This production theory-based structure for modeling and measuring production processes and performance therefore provides a rich basis for evaluation of the cost structure and various associated questions of technological, production and market structure.

Chapter 12

Pulling It Together

In this text I have explored a number of issues about the conceptualization, representation, measurement and interpretation of economic performance. In this treatment I have attempted to link many threads of thought to identify where models are similar (even if not obvious) and differ (even if there are clear linkages that could be drawn on). I have also posed questions about how to interpret models that must by definition be a limited representation of the myriad technical, economic and other forces at work in markets that determine the observed performance of firms, sectors and economies.

Too many issues and potential applications of these models have been raised to effectively summarize them here. However, it is useful to highlight some of the overall themes that seem particularly important as targets for future work on modeling and measuring economic performance.

First, we have emphasized the distinction between capital stock and service flow, mainly from short run fixities, but also potentially arising from obsolescence and other characteristics of capital related to evolving quality and composition. Many of these issues beg for further attention.

Capital issues are one of the overriding themes of this text. The availability and characteristics of capital are crucial factors determining current and future potential economic performance. However, the numerous associated questions are not easy to address, and many researchers have been hard pressed to definitively link capital investment to productivity patterns.

The ultimate issue is how to represent the characteristics of the capital base. This is at least to some extent a quality issue, since any particular type of capital may have rapidly changing characteristics determining its "effectiveness". It is also raises compositional questions. Composition may involve characteristics, but also has to do with the roles of different types of capital (structures as compared to equipment, output producing as compared to pollution abatement capital) that should be identified to understand the potential productivity of the capital or technological base.

A related but distinct question about capital and its contribution to performance is how to *untangle* the different possible determinants of capital service flow as compared to stock, since many may be operative at once.

For example, as noted in Chapter 3, deviations of shadow from market value have been alternatively interpreted as the impacts of utilization fluctuations or obsolescence/vintage. These have very different implications for both capital data construction and modeling of capital productivity impacts, and so should be independently identified.

Also, capital – particularly those components of capital that may be considered high-tech or information technology capital – may cause an "extra" stimulus for growth. This may appear as excess returns due to synergies such as the creation of spillovers across firms, or augmenting the quality of life in the workplace, that should be independently represented for appropriate consideration of capital's impact on productivity and growth. These issues are of great importance, but it is difficult even to model them in isolation, much less to untangle their differential impacts.

Another broad focus in this text has been the recognition of various kinds of potential cost economies associated with output production. It is not easy to justify such measures as indicative of a firm's, or "representative firm's" cost structure when based on aggregate data. Useful indications about the impacts of increasing scale of operations, joint production, or other aspects of cost economies may however still be measured using the framework developed in this text. This is a promising base for future analysis of cost structure. But it raises additional questions.

For example, the importance of multiple outputs is emphasized in a number of chapters in this text. For many empirical applications it seems that either the composition (within a firm or an industry) or allocation (across firms or industries) of output types may provide important information about economic performance patterns, and this may differ widely across firms.

This is closely related to the issues of capital composition emphasized above. Many changes in technological and market structure appear to be closely connected to the *kinds* of output that are produced, rather than simply their levels. Analyses founded on models representing output production as an aggregate miss this potentially critical dimension. Further research targeted toward the representation and evaluation of output composition patterns, as well as quality, are likely to provide important insights about the economic performance of firms, industries and economies.

Another output-oriented issue has to do with negative or "bad" outputs that are typically ignored, or, more generally, output "jointness". If production externalities or interconnections exist, in many cases we might want to take them into account, but doing so is difficult. For "bad" outputs, for example, physical measures of damage may in some cases be constructed (such as the amount of damaging chemicals remaining in the soil for pesticides) but often their measurement is by construction more subjective (e.g., the aesthetic damage associated with bad air pollution).

Although compositional and quality issues are important for all outputs and inputs, one more factor that is worth particularly highlighting as a potential important contributor to productivity and performance changes is intermediate materials. Questions about the treatment of intermediate materials inputs have wide-ranging implications, at least in part because of its very large cost share for most firms and industries. Also, this input category is made up of a number of wide-ranging identifiable components such as purchased services and natural resources.

For example, the contribution to a particular sector from purchased services (outsourcing) from another sector (possibly generating spillover or agglomeration effects) or another country (implying trade issues) my be important for interpretation of performance trends. The increasing reliance on purchased services and outsourcing is likely, in fact, a critical aspect of the production structure determining observed performance trends.

Primary inputs also may be important to take into account. For example if scarcity of natural resources is a concern, the contribution of resource inputs should be separately analyzed. Other primary inputs such as agricultural products may also experience changing patterns as a materials component (the agricultural sector contribution to the food system has been declining as the demand structure for food products has been changing). Addressing these types of concerns requires recognition of a combination of output and materials compositional patterns.

Many of the compositional and quality problems highlighted above may be addressed by more careful consideration of the sub-components of the aggregate output or input measure. Since a fundamental issue here is aggregation across different types of outputs or inputs, decomposing the measures may uncover illuminating patterns. Further assessment of quality changes, either to adapt the data or to build quality changes directly into the model, may also be useful. Hedonic methods may be a particularly helpful methodology to address these types of questions.

Another aggregation-related issue raised a few times in this text and touched on above has to do with aggregation across firms. Strictly speaking, the models we have been developing here refer to firm behavior; a production function, for example, represents the technology of a firm, and thus an "aggregate production function" may be difficult to justify. This becomes even more critical as we refine our model further in an attempt to represent utilization fluctuations, scale effects or economies, and markups, for example, with aggregate data. In particular, the underlying attempt to measure the marginal cost may be convoluted by heterogeneity across productive units, as well as entry and exit, in an industry aggregate.

No particularly useful theoretical base may be relied on to justify the use of firm-based models to measure the behavior of a "representative firm".

This suggests that there could be a problem of aggregation bias. However, many questions of interest to economists have to do with general trends in an industry (or even an entire economy) rather than the technology and behavior of any one particular plant or firm. Analysis across a broad base of heterogeneous productive units, which simply highlights their differences, may not be of much use to analyze such trends.

Since little theoretical basis exists for interpreting aggregate measures in the presence of heterogeneity, it seems particularly important to generate empirical evidence to determine the impact of aggregation. As noted before, my own research has indicated that trends found using more micro data for estimation are often maintained in aggregated data, at least for substantive implications. Addressing this issue further is crucial, but requires extensive analysis comparing estimates at various aggregation levels using different modeling perspectives. It will also be useful to compare top-down (macro) and bottom-up (micro) approaches and their empirical implications.

Another issue related to aggregation involves the existence and extent of spillovers. If spillovers occur across firms, this will have implications for analysis at the firm as compared to the industry level. Similar discrepancies for estimated results at different levels of aggregation might occur if spillovers occur across industries, or even across countries. A potentially useful contribution to assessment of aggregation bias might, therefore, result from more detailed analysis of spillovers. More generally, in fact, extensive exploration of spillover effects may help to illuminate links between productivity and growth patterns, due to the underlying synergies that affect both productivity growth fluctuations and the potential for ongoing growth.

This brings us back again to compositional issues, since different types of inputs may have varying potential for generating spillovers. For example, investment in information technology has a much greater likelihood of generating spillovers than does, say, construction of office buildings. Similarly, the possibility of interactions or spillovers deriving from highly trained or educated laborers is much greater than that for laborers that provide cleaning services. The private and social returns to other factors such as different types of R&D may also vary (such as public as compared to private, or basic as compared to applied R&D).[272]

Differences between social and private returns to private and public capital stocks, and particularly specific components of these stocks, may thus be an illuminating focus of future research. This was highlighted by the "new" growth theory in terms of a contribution of knowledge capital, but has not been pursued as extensively empirically as seems warranted, even given the obvious complexity of untangling these different impacts.

---

[272] See, for example, Lichtenberg and Siegel [1991].

These aggregation and composition questions in turn raise issues about empirical implementation of production theory models using micro data. As noted before, micro/panel data are useful for many applications, although in many cases they are difficult to obtain. They also may contain much more "noise", that suggests measurement error, than more aggregate data in which such errors may counteract each other to some extent. In addition, in many cases relevant (or at least varying across units) prices are not obtainable, so cost analysis is precluded.

These data do, however, allow questions to be asked that cannot be addressed at more aggregate levels. Clearly micro panel-data sets provide an important base for future research. Attempting to carry out cost studies for such data will be a particularly promising avenue for future research if associated price data are available. Both theoretical and econometric issues for analysis of this kind of data, however, need to be carefully addressed for such an exploration to be fruitful.

Micro data sets also facilitate analysis of the existence of technical and allocative inefficiency. As noted in Chapters 7 and 8, however, in many cases identifying the different types of production characteristics emphasized in this text, such as fixities that might be interpreted separately from general "inefficiency"issues, result in some "explanation" of measured inefficiency.

Also composition and quality issues rear their heads again. These are in fact particularly important in the context of inefficiency measurement, since when micro productivity units are analyzed in terms of their efficiency relative to best practice, differential output and input composition and quality become critical factors to take into account.

The recent literature, however, allows a more full representation of the structural model to be characterized along with the stochastic structure identifying inefficiency and its determinants. So this is a rich base for future research, particularly given the increasing availability of micro panel data.

Economic performance *questions* also differ widely across industries, suggesting provocative applications of production theory crafted according to the particular industry of interest. For example, critical regulatory issues have arisen in industries like telecommunications and electric utilities that highlight the importance of cost economies as an indicator of the potential success of regulatory reform. Analysis using a full cost structure model can provide useful implications for analysis of policy questions.

Similarly, questions of concentration and vertical/horizontal integration in many industries, or the reverse question of the role of and causes for "downsizing", depend heavily on the existence and characteristics of cost economies. That is, scale, scope and multiplant economies, for example, may be a stimulus underlying the existing market structure.

Service industries also are of currently great topical interest. Productivity and efficiency of financial institutions, the medical establishment, educational systems and other crucial industries that comprise an increasingly large proportion of GNP are very important to address. In such industries, a primary initial question involves the appropriate definition and measurement of outputs and inputs, which in many cases poses serious difficulties. Analysis of service industries will be a particularly important goal of future research, however since developed economies are rapidly moving toward an increasing reliance on service institutions.

A final point to emphasize here is the importance of synthesis as well as consensus in the productivity and growth literatures. Economic performance issues are fundamental to many types of economic analysis. In this text we have, for example, linked the insights from our micro-production-theory-based model to closely related questions in the macro and the IO literature. We have also related the traditional productivity approach to the ideas emphasized in the efficiency literature. Along the way, we have touched on theoretical issues such as the construction of price and quantity indexes that are fundamentally connected to performance analysis. Other issues that we have mentioned link our analysis to the labor economics literature (labor demand and productivity) and the international trade literature (supply of exports and demand for imports of final products as well as materials, and the impact of import penetration and thus competitiveness on performance).

However, studies in these literatures typically are carried out in isolation from others in related literatures. Much may be accomplished, for example, from using ideas raised in the macro literature as refinements to micro-based studies to determine their theoretical and empirical impact. In reverse, clearly more direct recognition of the microfoundations of macro studies may be illuminating both for construction of the macro models, and their empirical implementation and interpretation.

More connection between the seemingly diverse, but actually closely interrelated literatures on economic performance in different fields should be drawn on, to provide both stronger underpinnings of the theoretical models, and clearer interpretation and comparison of empirical results.

In sum, many different threads of thought can be followed in an attempt to untangle different pieces of the overall economic performance puzzle for firms, industries and countries. The focus in this text has been on the representation of the cost structure for appropriate evaluation of many questions of economic performance, including productivity, markups, and efficiency. Extensions of the cost-based models in various dimensions will be fruitful. However, some of the most critical but difficult areas of research for our examination of economic performance involve addressing broad issues of composition/quality, aggregation, and spillovers in more depth.

REFERENCES

Ades, Alberta F., and Edward L. Glaeser, [1994], "Evidence of Growth, Increasing Returns and the Extent of the Market", NBER Working Paper #4714, April.

Afriat, S.N. [1972], "Efficiency Esatimation of Production Functions", *International Economic Review*, 13, pp. 568-598.

Aigner, D.J., and S.F. Chu [1968], "On Estimating the Industry Production Function", *American Economic Review*, 58, pp. 826-839.

Aigner, D.J., C.A.K. Lovell and P. Schmidt [1977], "Formulation and Estimation of Stochastic Frontier Production Function Models", *Journal of Econometrics*, 6, pp. 21-37.

Alston, J.M., G.W. Norton, and P.G. Pardey [1995], *Science Under Scarcity*, Cornell University Press.

Appelbaum, Eli [1979], "Testing Price Taking Behavior", *Journal of Econometrics*, 9(3), February, pp. 283-294.

Appelbaum, Elie [1982], "The Estimation of the Degree of Oligopoly Power", *Journal of Econometrics*, 19, pp. 287-299.

Aschauer, D.A. [1988], "Government Spending and the 'Falling Rate of Profit'", *Economic Perspectives*, 12, pp. 11-17.

Aschauer, David [1989], "Is Public Expenditure Productive", *Journal of Monetary Economics*, March, pp. 177-200.

Aschauer, David [1991], *Public Investment and Private Sector Growth: The Economic Benefits of Reducing America's "Third Deficit*, Washington, D.C., Economic Policy Institute.

Ashenfelter, O., and D. Sullivan [1987], "Nonparametric Tests of Market Structure: An Application to the Cigarette Industry", *Journal of Industrial Economics*, 35, June, pp. 483-498.

Atkinson, S.E., and C. Cornwell [1994], "Parametric Estimation of Allocation and Technical Efficiency with Panel Data", *International Economic Review*, 35, pp. 231-44.

Atkinson, S.E., and C. Cornwell [1998], "Profit versus Cost Frontier Estimation of Price and Technical Inefficiency: A Parametric Approach with Panel Data", *Southern Economic Journal*, 64(3), pp. 753-764.

Atkinson, S.E. and R. Halvorsen [1990], "Tests of Allocative Efficiency in Regulated Multi-Product Firms", *Resources and Energy*, 12, pp. 65-77.

Auerbach, Alan J. [1983], "Taxation, Corporate Financial Policy and the Cost of Capital", *Journal of Economic Literature*, 21(3), September, pp. 905-940.

Averch, H., and L. Johnson [1962], "Behavior of the Firm under Regulatory Constraint", *American Economic Review*, 52, December, pp. 1053-1069.

Aw, Bee Yan, Xiaomin Chen and Mark J. Robert [1997], "Firm-Level Evidence on Productivity Differentials, Turnovers and Exports in Taiwanese Manufacturing", NBER Working Paper #6235.

Azzam, Azzeddine M., and Dale G. Anderson [1996], *Assessing Competition in Meatpacking: Economic History, Theory and Evidence*, USDA/GIPSA report GIPSA-RR-96-6.

338

Azzam, Azzeddine M., and Emilio Pagoulatos [1990], "Testing Oligopolistic and Oligopsonistic Behavior: An Application to the U.S. Meat-Packing Industry", *Journal of Agricultural Economics*, 41, pp. 362-70.

Azzam, Azzeddine M., and John R. Schroeter [1995], "The Tradeoff Between Oligopsony Power and Cost Efficiency in Horizontal Consolidation: An Example from Beef Packing", *American Journal of Agricultural Economics*, 77, pp. 825-36.

Baily, Martin .N. [1981], "The Productivity Growth Slowdown and Capital Accumulation", *American Economic Review*, Papers and Proceedings, 71(2), May, pp. 326-331.

Baily, Martin N., Eric J. Bartelsman and John Haltiwanger [1996], "Downsizing and Productivity Growth: Myth or Reality?", *Small Business Economics*, 8, pp. 259-278.

Baily, Martin N. and Alok K. Chakrabarti [1988], *Innovation and the Productivity Crisis*, Washington, D.C.: The Brookings Institution.

Baily, Martin N. and Robert J. Gordon [1988], "Measurement Issues, the Productivity Slowdown, and the Explosion of Computer Power", *Brookings Papers on Economic Activity*, 2, pp. 347-420.

Baily, Martin N., Charles Hulten and David Campbell [1992], "Productivity Dynamics in Manufacturing Plants", *Brookings Papers on Economic Activity: Microeconomics*, pp. 187-249.

Baily, Martin N. and Charles L. Schultze [1990], "The Productivity of Capital in a Period of Slower Growth", *Brookings Papers on Economic Activity*: Microeconomics 1990 (Martin Neil Baily and Clifford Winston, eds.), pp. 369-406.

Baily, Martin N. and Eric Zitzewitz [1998], "Service Sector Productivity Comparisons: Lessons for Measurement", presented at the CRIW/NBER/BLS Conference on *New Directions in Productivity Analysis*, March 1998, and forthcoming in the proceedings of the conference.

Bain, Joe S. [1951], "Relation of Profit Rate to Industry Concentration: American Manufacturing, 1936-1940", *Quarterly Journal of Economics*, 65, pp. 488-500.

Bain, Joe S. [1956], *Barriers to New Competition*, Cambridge, Harvard University Press.

Ball, V. Eldon [1985], "Output, Input and Productivity Measurement in U.S., Agriculture, 1948-79", *American Journal of Agricultural Economics*, August, pp. 475-486.

Ball, Eldon, Richard Nehring, Rolf Fare and Shawna Grosskopf [1998], "Productivity of the U.S. Agricultural Sector: The Case of Undesirable Outputs", presented at the CRIW/NBER/BLS Conference on *New Directions in Productivity Analysis*, March 1998, and forthcoming in the proceedings of that conference.

Baltagi, B. [1995], *Econometric Analysis of Panel Data*, New York: Wiley.

Bartlesman, Eric, Ricardo J. Caballero and Richard K. Lyons [1994], "Customer- and Supplier-Driven Externalities", *American Economic Review*, 84(4), September, pp. 1075-1084.

Bartlesman, Eric J., and Phoebus J. Dhrymes [1994], "Productivity Dynamics: U.S. Manufacturing Plants, 1972-86", Board of Governors of the Federal Research Board, Finance and Economics Discussion Series, 94-1.

Bartlesman, Eric J., and Wayne Gray [1996], "The NBER Manufacturing Productivity Database", NBER Technical Working Paper #205, October.

Barro, Robert J., and Xavier Sala-I-Martin [1994], "Quality Improvements in Models of Growth", NBER Working Paper #4610, January.

Basu, Susanto [1996], "Procyclical Productivity: Increasing Returns or Cyclical Utilization?" *Quarterly Journal of Economics*, August, 111(3), pp. 719-751.

Basu, Susanto and Fernald, John G. [1995], "Are Apparent Productive Spillovers a Figment of Specification Error?" *Journal of Monetary Economics*, August, *36*(1), pp. 165-188.

Basu, Susanto and John Fernald [1998], "Why is Productivity Procyclical? Why do We Care?", presented at the CRIW/NBER/BLS Conference on *New Directions in Productivity Analysis*, March 1998, and forthcoming in the proceedings of that conference.

Basu, Susanto, and Miles Kimball [1997], "Cyclical Productivity with Unobserved Input Variation", NBER Working Paper #5915.

Battese, G.E., and T. J. Coelli [1988], "Prediction of Firm -Level Technical Efficiencies With a Generalised Frontier Production Function and Panel Data", *Journal of Econometrics*, 38, pp. 387-399.

Battese, G.E. and T.J. Coelli [1992], "Frontier Production Functions, Technical Efficiency and Panel Data: With Application to Paddy Farmers in India", *The Journal of Productivity Analysis*, 3, pp. 153-169.

Battese, G.E., and T.J. Coelli [1995], "A Model for Technical Inefficiency Effects in a Stochastic Frontier Production Function for Panel Data", *Empirical Economics*, 20, pp. 325-332.

Battese, G.E., Tim J. Coelli and T. Colby [1989], "Estimation of Frontier Production Functions and the Efficiencies of Indian Farms Using Panel Data from ICRISAT's Village Level Studies", *Journal of Quantitative Economics*, 5(2), pp. 327-348.

Bauer, P. W. [1990], "Recent Developments in the Econometric Estimation of Frontiers", *Journal of Econometrics*, 46, pp. 39-56.

Baumol, W.J. [1967], "Macroeconomics of Unbalanced Growth: The Anatomy of an Urban Crisis", *American Economic Review*, 57, pp. 415-426.

Baumol, W.J., J.C. Panzar, and R.D. Willig [1982], Contestable Markets and the Theory of Industry Structure, New York: Harcourt Brace Jovanovich.

Benhabib, Jess and Boyan Jovanovic [1991], "Externalities and Growth Accounting", *American Economic Review*, 81(1), March, pp. 82-113.

Berndt, Ernst R. [1978], "Aggregate Energy Efficiency, and Productivity Measurement", *Annual Review of Energy*, 3, Palo Alto, California: Annual Reviews Inc., pp. 225-274.

Berndt, Ernst R. [1982], "From Technocracy to Net Energy Analysis: Engineers, Economists and Recurring Energy Theories of Value", Sloan School of Management Working Paper pp. 1353-82, MIT, September.

Berndt, Ernst R., [1983], "Quality Adjustment, Hedonics, and Modern Empirical Demand Analysis", in *Price Level Measurement*, (W. Erwin Diewert and Claude Montmarquette, eds.) Proceedings from a Conference Sponsored by Statistics Canada, Ottawa: Minister of Supply and Services Canada, October, pp. 817-863.

Berndt, Ernst R. [1990], *The Practice of Econometrics: Classic and Contemporary*, Addison-Wesley publishers.

Berndt, Ernst R., and Laurits R. Christensen [1973], "The Translog Function and the Substitution of Equipment, Structures, and Labor in U.S. Manufacturing 1929-68", *Journal of Econometrics*, 1(1), pp. 81-114.

Berndt, Ernst R, Iain Cockburn and Zvi Griliches [1996], "Pharmaceutical Innovations and Market Dynamics: Tracking Effects on Price Indexes for Anti-Depressant Drugs", *Brookings Papers on Economic Activity*, Microeconomics, pp. 133-188.

Berndt, Ernst R., Melvyn Fuss and Leonard Waverman [1980], *Empirical Analysis of Dynamic Adjustment Models of the Demand for Energy in U.S. Manufacturing Industries 1947-74*, Final Research Report, Palo Alto, California, Electric Power Research Institute, November.

Berndt, Ernst R., and Melvyn Fuss [1986], "Productivity Measurement Using Capital Asset Valuation to adjust for Variations in Utilization", *Journal of Econometrics*, 33(1/2), October/November, pp. 7-30.

Berndt, Ernst R., and Melvyn Fuss [1989], "Economic Capacity Utilization and Productivity Measurement for Multiproduct Firms with Multiple Quasi-Fixed Inputs", manuscript, January.

Berndt, Ernst R., Zvi Griliches and Joshua Rosett [1993], "Auditing the Producer Price Index: Micro Evidence from Prescription Pharmaceutical Preparations", *Journal of Business and Economic Statistics*, July, 11(3), pp. 251-64.

Berndt, Ernst R., and Dieter Hesse [1986], "Measuring and Assessing Capacity Utilization in the Manufacturing Sectors of Nine OECD Countries", *European Economic Review*, 30, pp. 961-989.

Berndt, Ernst R., and Mohammed S. Khaled [1979], "Parametric Productivity Measurement and Choice Among Flexible Functional Forms", *Journal of Political Economy*", 87(6), pp. 1220-1245.

Berndt, Ernst R., Charles Kolstad and J.K. Lee [1993], "Measuring the Energy Efficiency and Productivity Impacts of Embodied Technical Change, *Energy Journal*, 14(1), pp. 33-56

Berndt, Ernst R., and Catherine J. Morrison [1995], "High-Tech Capital and Economic Performance in U.S. Manufacturing Industries: An Exploratory Analysis", *Journal of Econometrics*, 65(1), January, pp. 9-43

Berndt, Ernst R., Catherine J. Morrison and David O. Wood [1983], "The Modeling, Interpretation and Measurement of Capacity Utilization", Bureau of the Census Technical Note, May.

Berndt, Ernst R., Catherine J. Morrison and Larry S. Rosenblum [1992], "High-Tech Capital Formation and Labor Composition in U.S. Manufacturing Industries", NBER Working Paper #4010.

Berndt, Ernst R. and N. Eugene Savin [1975], "Estimation and Hypothesis Testing in Singular Equation Systems with Autoregressive Disturbances" *Econometrica*, 43(5/6), September/November, pp. 937-957.

Berndt, Ernst R. and David O. Wood [1982], "The Specification and Measurement of Technical Change in U.S. Manufacturing", in *Advances in the Economics of Energy and Resources*, (John R. Moroney, ed.), 4, Greenwich, CT: JAI Press, pp. 199-221.

Berndt, Ernst R., and David O. Wood [1984], "Energy Price Changes and the Induced Revaluation of Durable Capital in U.S. Manufacturing During the OPEC Decade, MIT Energy Laboratory Report 84-003, March.

Berndt, Ernst R., and David O. Wood [1987], "Energy Price Shocks and Productivity Growth: A Survey", in *Energy: Markets and Regulation*, (Richard L. Gordon, Henry D. Jacoby and Martin B. Zimmerman, eds.), Cambridge: MIT Press.

Bernstein, J.I., and P. Mohnen [1994], "International R&D Spillovers Between U.S. and Japanese R&D Intensive Sectors", CVS Research Report #94-20.

Bernstein, J.I. and M.I. Nadiri [1988a], "Interindustry R&D Spillovers, Rates of Return and Production in High-Tech Industires", *American Economic Review*, 78, pp. 429-434.

Bernstein, Jeffrey I., and M. I. Nadiri [1988b], "Rates of Return on Physical and R&D Capital and Structure of Production Process: Cross Section and Time Series Evidence", (B. Raj, ed.), *Advances in Econometrics and Modeling*, Kluwer Academic Publishers.

Bernstein, Jeffrey I., and M. I. Nadiri [1988c], "Investment, Depreciation and Capital Utilization", NBER Working Paper #2571, April.

Berry, Steven [1994], "Estimating Discrete-Choice Models of Product Differentiation", *Rand Journal of Economics*, 25(2), Summer, pp. 242-62.

Betancourt, Roger R., and Christopher K. Clague [1981], *Capital Utilization: A Theoretical and Empirical Analysis*, Cambridge University Press.

Binswanger, H. [1974], "The Measurement of Technical Change Biases with Many Factors of Production", *American Economic Review*, 64, December, pp. 964-76.

Blackorby, C., D. Primont and R. R. Russell [1978], *Duality, Separability and Functional Structure: Theory and Economic Applications*, North Holland: Elsevier Press.

Blades, Derek [1983], OECD Working Paper #4, "Service Lives of Fixed Assets", March.

Blinder, Alan S. [1982], "Inventories and Sticky Prices: More on the Microfoundations of Macroeconomics", *American Economic Review*, 72, June, pp. 334-48.

Boskin, Micharl J., Ellen Dulberger, Robert J. Gordon, Zvi Griliches and Dale W. Jorgenson [1996], *Final Report of the Advisory Commission to Study the Consumer Price Index*, S. PRT. 104-72 Washington D.C., U.S. Government Printing Office, December.

Bresnahan, Timothy F. [1989], "Empirical Studies of Industries with Market Power", in the *Handbook of Industrial Organization, II*, (R. Schmalensee and R.D. Willig, eds.), Elsevier Science Publishers.

Bresnahan, Timothy and Robert J. Gordon (eds.) [1996], *The Economics of New Goods*, NBER Studies in Income and Wealth, Vol. 58, University of Chicago Press.

Brown, Randall S., and Laurits R. Christensen [1981], "Estimating Elasticities of Substitution in a Model of Partial Static Equilibrium: An Application to U.S. Agriculture 1947 to 1974", in *Modeling and Measuring Natural Resource Substitution*, (E.R. Berndt and B.C. Fields, eds.), MIT Press, pp. 209-229.

Brynjolfsson and Hitt [1996], "Paradox Lost: Firm-Level Evidence on the Returns to Information Systems Spending", *Management Science*, 42, pp. 541-558.

Burnside, Craig [1996], "Production Function Regressions, Returns to Scale, and Externalities", *Journal of Monetary Economics*, 37(2), April, pp. 177-201.

Burnside, Craig, Martin Eichenbaum and Sergio Rebelo [1993]. "Labor Hoarding and the Business Cycle", *Journal of Political Economy*, 101(2), April, pp. 245-273.

Burnside, Craig, Marti Eichenbaum and Serfio Rebelo [1995], "Capital Utilization and Returns to Scale", in the *NBER Macroeconomics Annual*, (Ben S. Bernanke and Julio J. Rotemberg, eds.), University of Chicago Press.

Caballero, Ricardo J., and Adam B. Jaffe [1993], "How High are the Giants' Shoulders: An Empirical Assessment of Knowledge Spillovers and Creative Destruction in a Model of Economic Growth", NBER Working Paper #4370, May.

Caballero, Ricardo J., and Richard K. Lyons [1992], "External Effects in U.S. Procyclical Productivity", *Journal of Monetary Economics*, 29, pp. 209-225.

Campbell, Harry F. [1976], "Estimating the Marginal Productivity of Agricultural Pesticides: The Case of Tree-Fruit Farms in the Okanagan Valley", *Canadian Journal of Agricultural Economics*, 24(2), pp. 23-30.

Carpentier, Alain and Robert D. Weaver [1996], "Intertemporal and Interfirm Heterogeneity: Implications for Pesticide Productivity", *Canadian Journal of Agricultural Economics*, 44, pp. 219-239.

Carrasco-Tauber, Catalina [1988], "Pesticide Productivity Revisited", Master's Thesis, University of Massachusetts, Amherst.

Carrasco-Tauber, Catalina, and L. Joe Moffitt [1992], "Damage Control Econometrics: Functional Specification and Pesticide Productivity", *American Journal of Agricultural Economics*, February, pp. 158-162.

Cassels, J.M. [1937], "Excess Capacity and Monopolistic Competition", *Quarterly Journal of Economics*, 51, May, pp. 426-43.

Caves, D.W., L.R. Christensen and W.E. Diewert [1982], "The Economic Theory of Index Numbers and the Measurement of Input, Output and Productivity", *Econometrica*, 50, pp. 1393-1414.

Chamberlin, E.H. [1933], *TheTheory of Monopolistic Competition*, Harvard University Press.

Chambers, Robert G., and Erik Lichtenberg [1994], "Simple Econometrics of Pesticide Productivity", *American Journal of Agricultural Economics*, August, pp. 407-417.

Chambers, Robert G. and R.D. Pope [1994], "A Virtually Ideal Production System: Specifying and Estimating the VIPS Model", *American Journal of Agricultural Economics*, 76, February, pp. 105-113.

Chavas, J.P., and T.L. Cox [1988], "A Nonparametric Analysis of Agricultural Technology", *American Journal of Agricultural Economics*, 70, May, pp. 303-10.

Chavas, J.P., and T.L. Cox [1992], "A Nonparametric Analysis of the Influence of Research on Agricultural Productivity", *American Journal of Agricultural Economics*, 74, August, pp. 583-91.

Christensen, Laurits R., Dianne Cummings, and Dale W. Jorgenson [1980], "Economic Growth 1947-73: An International Comparison", in *New Developments in Productivity Measurement and Analysis*, (John W. Kendrick and Beatrice N. Vaccara, eds.)Studies in Income and Wealth , 44, The University of Chicago Press, pp. 595-698.

Christensen, Laurits R., and William H. Greene [1976], "Economies of Scale in U.S. Electric Power Generation", *Journal of Political Economy*, 84(4), Part 1, August, pp. 655-676.

Christensen, Laurits R. and Dale W. Jorgenson [1969], "The Measurement of U.S. Real Capital Input, 1929-67", *Review of Income and Wealth*, Series 15, 4, December, pp. 293-320.

Christensen, Laurits R., Dale W. Jorgenson and Lawrence J. Lau [1973], "Transcendantal Logarithmic Production Frontiers", *Review of Economics and Statistics*, 55(1), February, pp. 28-45.

Coelli T.J. [1994], A Guide to FRONTIER Version 4.1: A Computer Program for Stochastic Frontier Production and Cost Function Estimation, mimeo, Department of Econometrics, University of New England, Armidale, NSW, Australia.

Coelli, Tim [1995a], "Recent Developments in Frontier Modeling and Efficiency Measurement", *Australian Journal of Agricultural Economics*, 39(3), December, pp. 219-245.

Coelli, Tim [1995b], "Estimators and Hypothesis Tests for a Stochastic Frontier Function: A Monte Carlo Analysis", *Journal of Productivity Analysis*, 6, pp. 247-268.

Coelli, Tim, and Sergio Perelman [1996], "Efficiency Measurement, Multiple-Output Technologies and Distance Functions: with Application to European Railways", CREPP Working Paper #96/05, Universite de Liege, Belgium.

Coelli, Tim, D.S. Prasada Rao ajnd George E. Battese [1998], *An Introduction to Efficiency and Productivity Analysis*, Kluwer Academic Publishers.

Cohen, Wesley M., and Richard C. Levin [1989], "Empirical Studies of Innovation and Market Structure", in the *Handbook of Industrial Organization, II*, (R. Schmalensee and R.D. Willig, eds.), Elsevier Science Publishers.

Cole, Rosanne, Y.C. Chen, J.A. Barquin-Stolleman, E. Dullberger, N. Helvacian, and J.H. Hodge [1986], "Quality-Adjusted Price Indexes for Computer Processors and Selected Peripheral Equipment", *Survey of Current Business*, 66. January, pp. 41-50.

Conrad, Klaus, and Catherine J. Morrison [1989], "The Impact of Pollution Abatement Investment on Productivity Change: An Empirical Comparison of the U.S., Germany and Canada", *Southern Economic Journal*, 55(3), January, pp. 684-698.

Corrado, Carol and Joe Mattey [1997], "Capacity Utilization", *Journal of Economic Perspectives*, 11(1), pp. 151-167.

Cowing, T.G. Cowing and R.E. Stevenson (eds.) [1981], *Productivity Measurement in Regulated Industries*, Academic Press.

Cox, T.L., and J.P. Chavas [1990], "A Nonparametric Analysis of Productivity: The Case of U.S. Agriculture", *European Review of Agricultural Economics*, 17, pp. 449-464.

Crandall, R.W., [1981], "Pollution Controls and Productivity Growth in Basic Industries", in *Productivity Measurement in Regulated Industries*, (T.G. Cowing and R.E. Stevenson, eds.) Academic Press, pp. 347-368.

David, Paul A., and Theodore van de Klundert [1965], "Biased Efficiency Growth and Capital-Labor Substitution in the U.S., 1899-1960", *American Economic Review*, 55(3), pp. 357-395.

de Leeuw, Frank [1962], "The Concept of Capacity", *Journal of the American Statistical Association*, September, pp. 826-840.

Dean, Edwin R., Michael J. Harper and Mark S. Sherwood [1996], "Productivity Measurement with Changing-Weight Indices of Outputs and Inputs", Chapter 7 in *Industry Productivity: International Comparison and Measurement Issues*, OECD, Paris.

Dean, Edwin R., and Michael J. Harper [1998], "The BLS Productivity Measurement Program", presented at the CRIW/NBER/BLS Conference on *New Directions in Productivity Analysis*, March, and forthcoming in the proceedings of that conference.

Demsetz, Harold [1973], "Industry Structure, Market Rivalry, and Public Policy", *Journal of Law and Economics*, 16, pp. 1-9.

Demsetz, H. [1974], "Two Systems of Belief About Monopoly", *Industrial Concentration: The New Learning*, (H. Goldschmidt, H.M. Mann and J. F. Weston, eds.), Boston: Little, Brown and Co.

Denison, Edward F. [1962], *The Sources of Economic Growth in the United States and the Alternatives Before Us,* New York, Committee on Economic Development.

Denison, Edward F. [1979], *Accounting for Slower Economic Growth*, Washington D.C., The Brookings Institution.

Denison, Edward F. [1985], *Trends in American Economic Growth, 1929-1982*, Washington, D.C., Brookings Institution.

Denny, Michael [1980], "Comment" on Diewert's "Aggregation Problems in the Measurement of Capital", in *The Measurement of Capital*, (Dan Usher, ed.), University of Chicago Press, pp. 529-534.

Deprins, D., L. Simar and H. Tulkens [1984], "Measuring Labor-Efficiency in Post Services" in *The Performance of Public Enterprises, Concepts and Measurement*, (M. Marchand, P. Pestieau and H. Tulkens, eds.), North Holland, Amsterdam.

Diewert, W.E. [1974], "Applications of Duality Theory", in M.D. Intriligator and D.A. Kendrick (eds.) *Frontiers of Quantative Economics, II*, Amsterdam: North-Holland, pp. 106-170.

Diewert, W.E. [1976], "Exact and Superlative Index Numbers", *Journal of Econometrics*, 4, pp. 115-145.

Diewert, W.E. [1980], "Aggregation Problems in the Measurement of Capital", in *The Measurement of Capital*, (Dan Usher, ed.), University of Chicago Press, pp. 433-528.

Diewert, W.E. [1981a], "On Measuring the Loss of Output Due to Nonneutral Business Taxation", in *Depreciation, Inflation and the Taxation of Income from Capital*, (Charles R. Hulten, ed.) Washington, D.C.: The Urban Institute, pp. 57-80.

Diewert, W. Erwin [1981b], "The Theory of Total Factor Productivity Measurement in Regulated Industries", in *Productivity Measurement in Regulated Industries*, (Thomas G. Cowing and Rodney E. Stevenson, eds.), New York: Academic Press.

Diewert, W.E. [1982], "Duality Approaches to Microeconomic Theory", in *Handbook of Mathematical Economics, II*, North Holland Press.

344

Diewert, W. Erwin [1984], "Duality Approaches to Microeconomic Theory", in *Handbook of Mathematical Economics II*, (K.J. Arrow and M.D. Intriligator, eds.) North-Holland Press.

Diewert, W.E. [1986], *The Measurement of the Economic Benefits of Infrastructure Services*, #278 in the series "Lecture Notes in Economics and Mathematical Systems", Berlin: Springer Verlag Press.

Diewert, W.E. [1989a], "The Measurement of Productivity", Discussion Paper # 89-04, University of British Columbia, January.

Diewert, W.E. [1992], "Fisher Ideal Output, Input and Productivity Indexes Revisited", *Journal of Productivity Analysis*, 3, pp. 211-248.

Diewert, W. Erwin, and Catherine J. Morrison [1986], "Adjusted Output and Productivity Indexes for Changes in the Terms of Trade", *Economic Journal*, 96, September,   pp. 659-679.

Diewert, W. Erwin and Catherine J. Morrison [1990], "New Techniques in the Measurement of Multifactor Productivity", *Journal of Productivity Analysis*, 1(4), June, pp. 267-286.

Diewert, W. Erwin and Catherine J. Morrison [1991], "Productivity Growth and Changes in the Terms of Trade in Japan and the U.S",, in *Productivity Growth in Japan and the United States*, (Charles Hulten, ed.), University of Chicago Press, pp. 201-228.

Diewert, W.E. and T.J. Wales [1987], "Flexible Functional Forms and Global Curvature Conditions", *Econometrica*, 5(1), January, pp. 43-68.

Dulberger, Ellen R. [1989], "The Application of a Hedonic Model to a Quality Adjusted Price Index for Computer Processors, in *Technology and Capital Formation*, (Dale W. Jorgenson and Ralph Landau, eds.) The MIT Press, pp. 37-76.

Dulberger, Ellen R. [1993], "Sources of Price Decline in Computer Processors: Selected Electronic Components", in *Price Measurements and their Uses*, (Murray Foss, Marilyn Manser and Allan Young, eds.), NBER Studies in Income and Wealth, Vol. 57, University of Chicago Press, pp. 103-24.

Dwyer, Douglas [1995], "Technology Locks, Creative Destruction and Non-Convergence in Productivity Levels", Center for Economic Studies Working Paper, CES 95-6.

Dwyer, Douglas [1997], "Productivity Races I: Are Some Productivity Measures Better than Others?" Center for Economic Studies Working Paper, CES 97-2.

Emmons III, William M. [1997] "Implications of Ownership, Regulation, and Market Structure for Performance: Evidence from the U.S. Electric Utility Industry before and after the New Deal", *Review of Economics and Statistics*, 79(2), pp. 279-289.

Englander, A.S. [1989], "Tests for Measurement of Service Sector Productivity", presented at the International Seminar on Science, Technology and Economic Growth, OECD, June; Federal Reserve Bank of New York manuscript, April.

Epstein, L.G. [1981], "Duality Theory and Functional Forms for Dynamic Factor Demands", *Review of Economic Studies*, 48, pp. 81-95.

Epstein, L.G., and M.S. Denny [1983], "The Multivariate Flexible Accelerator Model: Its Empirical Restriction and an Application to U.S. Manufacturing", Econometrica, 51, pp. 547-674.

Färe, R., and S. Grosskopf [1990], "A Distance Function Approach to Price Efficiency", *Journal of Public Economics*, 43, pp. 123-16.

Färe, Rolf, and Shawna Grosskopf]1996], *Intertemporal Production Frontiers: with dynamic DEA*, Kluwer Academic Publishers.

Färe, R.S., S. Grosskopf and C.A.K. Lovell [1988], "An Indirect Approach to the Evaluation of Producer Performance", *Journal of Public Economics*, 37, pp. 71-89.

Färe, Rolf, Shawna Grosskopf, C.A. K. Lovell, and Suthathip Yaisawarng [1993]. "Derivation of Shadow Prices for Undesirable Outputs: A Distance Function Approach", *Review of Economics and Statistics*, 75, May, pp. 374-380.

Färe, R., S., Grosskopf, M. Norris and Z. Zhang [1994], "Productivity Growth, Technical Progress and Efficiency Changes in Industrialised Countries", *American Economic Review*, 84, pp. 66-83.

Färe, R., S. Grosskopf and P. Roos [1997], "Malmquist Productivity Indexes: A Survey of Theory and Practice", in *Index Numbers, Essays in Honour of Sten Malmquist*, (R. Fare, S. Grosskopf and R.R. Russell, eds.), Kluwer Academic Publishers.

Färe, R.S. and C.A.K. Lovell [1978], "Measuring the Technical Efficiency of Production", *Journal of Economic Theory*, 19, pp. 1 150-162.

Färe, Rolf, and Daniel Primont [1995], *Multi-Output Production and Duality: Theory and Applications*, Kluwer Academic Publishers.

Farrell, M.J. [1957], "The Measurement of Productive Efficiency", *Journal of the Royal Statistical Society*, Part 3, pp. 253-290.

Fawson, C., and C.R. Shumway [1988], "Nonparametric Investigation of Agricultural Production Behavior for U.S. Subregions", *American Journal of Agricultural Economics*, 70, May, pp. 311-17.

Feenstra, Robert C., and James R. Markusen [1992], "Accounting for Growth with New Inputs", NBER Working Paper #4114, July.

Felthoven, Ronald, and Catherine J. Morrison [1998], "The Economic Costs of Pesticide Regulation", manuscript, August.

Fernandez-Cornejo, J., C.M. Gempesaw II, J.G. Elterich and S.E. Stefanou [1992], "Dynamic Measures of Scope and Scale Economies: An Application to German Agriculture", *American Journal of Agricultural Economics* 74, May, pp. 329-342.

Ferrier, G.D. and C.A.K. Lovell [1990], "Measuring Cost Efficiency in Banking: Econometric and Linear Programming Evidence", *Journal of Econometrics*, 46, pp. 229-245.

Fischer, L.A. [1970], "The Economics of Pest Control in Canadian Apple Production", *Canadian Journal of Agricultural Economics,* 18, pp. 89-96.

Fisher, F.M., and J.J. McGowan [1983], "On the Misuse of Accounting Rates of Return to Infer Monopoly Profits", *American Economic Review*, 73(1), March.

Fixler, Dennis J. and Donald Siegel [1998], "Outsourcing and Productivity Growth in Services", forthcoming, *Structural Change and Economic Dynamics*.

Forsund, F.R. and L. Hjalmarsson [1979], "Generalized Farrell Measures of Efficiency: An Application to Milk Processing in Swedish Dairy Plants", *Economic Journal*, 89, pp. 294-315.

Forsund, F.R., C.A.K. Lovell and P. Schmidt [1980], "A Survey of Frontier Production Functions and of their Relationship to Efficiency Measurement", *Journal of Econometrics*, 13, pp. 5-25.

Foss, M.F. [1963], "The Utilization of Capital Equipment: Postwar Compared with Pre-war", *Survey of Current Business*, 43, June, pp. 8-16.

Foster, Lucia, C.J. Krizan, and John Haltiwanger [1998], "Aggregate Productivity Growth: Lessons from Microeconomic Evidence", presented at the CRIW/NBER/BLS Conference on *New Directions in Productivity Analysis*, March 1998, and forthcoming in the proceedings of that conference.

Fousekis, Panos [1999], "Temporary Equilibrium, Full Equilibrium and Elasticity of Cost", forthcoming, the *Journal of Productivity Analysis*.

346

Fromm, G., L.R. Klein, F.C. Ripley, and D. Crawford [1979], "Production Function Estimation of Capacity Utilization", Presented at the Econometric Society Meetings, Atlanta.

Fulginiti and Perrin [1993], "Prices and Productivity in Agriculture", *Review of Economics and Statistics*, 75, pp. 471-482.

Fuss, Melvyn and Leonard Waverman [1986], "The Extent and Sources of Cost and Efficiency Differences Between U.S. and Japanese Automobile Producers", NBER Working Paper #1849, March.

Gelfand, M.J. and Spiller, P. [1987], "Entry Barriers and Multi-Product Oligopolies: Do they Forebear or Spoil?", *International Journal of Industrial Organization*, 5, pp. 103-113

Gollop, F., and Mark Roberts [1979], "Firm Interdependence in Oligopolistic Markets", *Journal of Econometrics*, 10, pp. 313-331.

Gollop, F., and Mark Roberts [1983], "Environmental Regulations and Productivity Growth: The Case of Fossil-Fueled Electric Power Generation", *Journal of Political Economy*, 91, pp. 654-674.

Gollop, Frank and Gregory Swinand [1998]., "Total Resource Productivity: Accounting for Changing Environmental Quality", presented at the CRIW/NBER/BLS Conference on *New Directions in Productivity Analysis*, March, and forthcoming in the proceedings of the conference.

Gordon, Robert J. [1989], "The Postwar Evolution of Computer Prices", in *Technology and Capital Formation*, (Dale W. Jorgenson and Ralph Landau, eds.), MIT Press, pp. 77-126.

Gordon, Robert J. [1990], *The Measurement of Durable Goods Prices*, University of Chicago Press.

Gordon, Robert J. [1996], "Problems in the Measurement and Performance of Service-Sector Productivity in the United States", NBER Working Paper #5519, March.

Gordon, Robert J. and Zvi Griliches [1997], "Quality Change and New Products", *American Economic Review Papers and Proceedings* 87(2), May, pp. 84-88.

Gouyette, Claudine and Sergio Perelman [1997], "Productivity Convergence in OECD Service Industries", *Structural Change and Economic Dynamics*, 8, pp. 279-295.

Gray, Wane B. [1984], "The Impact of OSHA and EPA Regulation of Productivity", NBER Working Paper #1405, July.

Green, H.A.J. [1964], *Aggregation in Economic Analysis: An Introductory Survey*, Princeton University Press.

Greene, W.H. [1980], "On the Estimation of a Flexible Frontier Production Model", *Journal of Econometrics*, 13, pp. 101-116.

Greene W.H. [1990], "A Gamma-Distributed Stochastic Frontier Model" *Journal of Econometrics*, 35, pp. 141-164.

Greene, W.H. [1992], LIMDEP Version 6.0: User's Manual and Reference Guide, Econometric Software Inc., New York.

Greene, W.H. [1993], "The Econometric Approach to Efficiency Analysis", in *The Measurement of Productive Efficiency* (H.O. Fried, C.A.K. Lovell and S.S. Schmidt, eds), New York: Oxford University press, pp. 68-119.

Greenwood, Jeremy and Boyan Jovanovic [1998], "Accounting for Growth", presented at the CRIW/NBER/BLS Conference on *New Directions in Productivity Analysis*, March, and forthcoming in the proceedings of that conference.

Grifell-Tatje, E., and C.A.K. Lovell [1995] "A Note on the Malmquist Productivity Index: *Economics Letters*, 47, pp. 169-175.

Griffin, James M. and Paul R. Gregory [1976], "An Intercountry Translog Model of Energy Substitution Responses", *American Economic Review*, 66(5), December, pp. 845-857.

Griffiths, W.E., R.C.Hill and G.G. Judge [1993], *Learning and Practicing Econometrics*, Wiley, New York.

Griliches, Zvi [1980], "R&D and the Productivity Slowdown", *American Economic Review*, 70(2), May, pp. 343-48.

Griliches, Zvi [1986], "Economic Data Issues", in *Handbook of Econometrics*, III, (Zvi Griliches and Michael D. Intriligator, eds.), North Holland Publishing Co., pp. 1465-1514.

Griliches, Zvi [1988], "Productivity Puzzles and R&D: Another Nonexplanation", *The Journal of Economic Perspectives*, 2(4), Fall, pp. 9-22.

Griliches, Zvi [1991], "The Search for R&D Spillovers", NBER Working paper #3769, July.

Griliches, Zvi [1992] (ed.), *Output Measurement in the Service Sectors*, University of Chicago Press, Chicago.

Griliches, Zvi [1994], "Productivity, R&D and the Data Constraint", *American Economic Review*, 84(1), pp. 1-23.

Griliches, Zvi and Haim Regev [1995], "Productivity and Firm Turnover in Israeli Industry: 1979-1988", *Journal of Econometrics*, 65, pp. 175-203.

Grosskopf, S. [1993], "Efficiency and Productivity", in *The Measurement of Productivity Efficiency: Techniques and Applications*, (H.O. Fried, C.A.K. Lovell and S.S. Schmidt, eds.), Oxford University Press, New York, pp. 160-194.

Grosskopf, S., K. Hayes, L. Taylor and W. Weber [1997], "Budget Constrained Frontier Measures of Fiscal Equality and Efficiency in Schooling", *Review of Economics and Statistics*, 79(1), February, pp. 116-124.

Guilkey, David, C.A. Knox Lovell, and Robin C. Sickles [1983], "A Comparison of the Performance of Three Flexible Functional Forms", *International Economic Review*, 24(3), October, pp. 591-616.

Hall, Robert E. [1981], "Tax Treatment of Depreciation, Capital Gains and Interest in an Inflationary Economy", in *Depreciation, Inflation and the Taxation of Income from Capital*, (Charles R. Hulten, ed.), Washington, D.C.: The Urban Institute, pp. 149-170.

Hall, Robert E. [1986], "Market Structure and Macroeconomic Fluctuations", *Brookings Papers on Economic Activity*, 2, pp. 285-338.

Hall, Robert E. [1988a], "The Relation Between Price and Marginal Cost in U.S. Industry", *Journal of Political Economy*, 96(5), October, pp. 921-947.

Hall, Robert E. [1988b], "Increasing Returns; Theory and Measurement with Industry Data", manuscript, presented at the NBER Conference on Economic Fluctuations, Cambridge, Massachusetts, October.

Hall, Robert E. [1990], "Invariance Properties of Solow's Productivity Residual", in *Growth-Productivity-Employment: Essays to Celebrate Bob Solow's* Birthday, (Peter Diamond, ed.), MIT Press, pp. 71-112.

Hall,R.E., and D.W. Jorgenson [1967], "Tax Policy and Investment Behavior", *American Economic Review*, 57(3), June.

Haltiwanger, John [1997], "Measuring and Analyzing Aggregate Fluctuations: The Importance of Building from Microeconomic Evidence", *Federal Reserve Bank of St. Louis Economic Review*, January/February.

Hanoch, G., and M. Rothschild [1972], "Testing for Assumptions of Production Theory: A Nonparametric Approach", *Journal of Political Economy*, 80, March, pp. 256-75.

Hansen [1982], "Large Sample Properties of Generalized Methods of Moments Estimators", *Econometrica*, pp. 1029-1054.

Hansen, Lars Peter and Kenneth Singleton [1982], "Generalized Instrumental Variables Estimation of Nonlinear Rational Expectations Models", *Econometrica*, September, 50, pp. 1269-1286.

348

Hansson, Bengt [1988], "Productivity Measurement Under Imperfect Competition", manuscript, Uppsala University, Sweden, June.

Harper, Michael J., Ernst R. Berndt and David O. Wood [1989], "Rates of Return and Capital Aggregation Using Alternative Rental Prices", in *Technology and Capital Formation*, (Dale W. Jorgenson and Ralph Landau, eds.), MIT Press, pp. 331-372.

Harper, Michael J. and William Gullickson [1989], "Cost Function Models and Accounting for Growth in U.S. Manufacturing, 1949-86", presented at the Workshop on Price and Output Measurement, National Bureau of Economic Research, July 1989.

Hausman, Jerry A. [1975], "An Instrumental Variable Approach to Full Information Estimates for Linear and Certain Nonlinear Econometric Models", *Econometrica*, 43(4), July, pp. 727-738.

Hausman, Jerry A. [1996], "Valuation of New Goods Unver Perfect and Imperfect Competition", in *The Economics of New Goods*, (Timothy Bresnahan and Robert J. Gordon, eds.), NBER Studies in Income and Wealth, Vol. 58, University of Chicago Press, pp. 209-237.

Hayashi, Fumio [1982], "Tobin's Marginal q and Average q: A Neoclassical Interpretation", *Econometrica*, 50(1), January, pp. 213-224.

Headley, J.C. [1968], "Estimating the Productivity of Agricultural Pesticides", *American Journal of Agricultural Economics*, pp. 13-23.

Hetemaki, L. [1996], "Environmental Regulation and Production Efficiency: Evidence from the Pulp Industry", mimeo, Finnish Forest Research Institute, Helsinki.

Hetemaki, Lauri [1996], Essays on the Impact of Pollution Control on a Firm: A Distance Function Approach, Finnish Forest Research Institute, Research Paper 609, Helsinki Research Center.

Hickman [1964], "On a New Method of Capacity Estimation", *Journal of the American Statistical Association*, 59, June, pp. 529-549.

Hicks, J.R. [1946], *Value and Capital*, 2nd ed., Oxford: Clarendon Press.

Hirschleifer, Jack [1980], *Price Theory and Applications*, Englewood Cliffs, New Jersey: Prentice Hall Press.

Holtz-Eakin, Douglas [1994], "Public Sector Capital and the Productivity Puzzle", *Review of Economics and Statistics*, February, 76(1), pp. 12-21.

Howard, W.H. and C.R. Shumway [1988], "Dynamic Adjustment in the U.S. Dairy Industry", *American Journal of Agricultural Economics*, 70, November, pp. 837-847.

Huang, K.S. [1991], "Factor Demands in the U.S. Food Manufacturing Industry", *American Journal of Agricultural Economics*, 73, August, pp. 615-20.

Huang, C., and J-T. Liu [1994], "Estimation of Non-neutral Stochastic Frontier Production Functions", *Journal of Productivity Analysis*, 4, pp. 171-180.

Hudson, Edward A. and Dale W. Jorgenson [1974], "U.S. Energy Policy and Economic Growth, 1975-2000", *Bell Journal of Economics and Management Science*, 5, Autumn, pp. 461-478.

Hulten, Charles [1986], "Short Run and Long Run Cost Functions and the Measurement of Efficiency Change", *Journal of Econometrics*, 33(1/2), October/November, pp. 31-50.

Hulten, Charles R. [1990], "The Measurement of Capital", in *Fifty Years of Economic Measurement*, Studies in Income and Wealth, (Ernst R. Berndt and Jack E. Triplett, eds.), Vol. 54, University of Chicago Press, pp. 119-52.

Hulten, Charles R. [1993], "Growth Accounting When Technical Change is Embodied in Capital", *American Economic Review*, 82(4), pp. 964-980.

Hulten, Charles R. [1996], "Quality Changes in Capital Goods and its Impact on Economic Growth", NBER Working Paper #5569, May.

Hulten, Charles R. and Robert M. Schwab [1991], Public Capital Formation and the Growth of Regional Manufacturing Industries", *National Tax Journal* , December, pp. 121-34.

Hulten, Charles R., and Robert M. Schwab [1993a], "Endogenous Growth, Public Capital, and the Convergence of Regional Manufacturing Industries", NBER Working Paper #4538, November.

Hulten, Charles R. and Robert M. Schwab [1993b], "Infrastructure Spending: Where Do We Go From Here?", *National Tax Journal*, 46(3), September, pp. 261-277.

Hulten, Charles R. and Frank C. Wykoff [1980], "Economic Depreciation and the Taxation of Structures in U.S. Manufacturing Industries: An Empirical Analysis", Chapter 2 in *The Measurement of Capital*, (Dan Usher, ed.), University of Chicago Press, pp. 83-109.

Hulten, Charles R. and Frank C. Wykoff [1981a], "The Estimation of Economic Depreciation Using Vintage Asset Prices: An Application of the Box-Cox Power Transformation", *Journal of Econometrics*, 15(3), August.

Hulten, Charles R. and Frank C. Wykoff [1981b], "The Measurement of Economic Depreciation", in *Depreciation, Inflation and the Taxation of Income from Capital*, (Charles R. Hulten, ed.), Washington, D.C.: The Urban Institute, pp. 81-125.

Hulten, Charles R., James W. Robertson, and Frank C. Wykoff [1989], "Energy, Obsolescence, and the Productivity Slowdown", in *Technology and Capital Formation*, (Dale W. Jorgenson and Ralph Landau, eds.), MIT Press, pp. 225-258.

Hyde, Charles E. and Jeffrey M. Perloff [1994], "Can Monopsony Power be Estimated?", *American Journal of Agricultural Economics*, 75, December, pp. 1151-1155.

Iwata, G. [1974], "Measurement of Conjectural Variations in Oligopoly", *Econometrica*, 42, pp. 947-966

Jorgenson, Dale W. [1988], "Productivity and the Postwar U.S. Economic Growth", *Journal of Economic Perspectives*, 2(4), Fall, pp. 23-42.

Jorgenson, Dale [1998], "Investment and Growth", presented at the NBER/CRIW/BLS Conference on *New Directions in Productivity Analysis*, March, to be published in the proceedings of the conference.

Jorgenson, Dale W., Frank Gollop and Barbara Fraumeni [1987], *Productivity and U.S. Economic Growth*, Harvard University Press.

Jorgenson, Dale W., and Zvi Griliches [1967], "The Explanation of Productivity Change", *Review of Economic Studies*, 34(3), July, pp. 249-282.

Joskow, Paul L. [1989], "Regulatory Failure, Regulatory Reform, and Structural Change in the Electrical Power Industry", *Brookings Papers: Microeconomics*, 1989, pp. 125-208.

Joskow, Paul L. [1996], "Introducing Competition into Regulated Network Industries: from Hierarchies to Markets in Electricity", *Industrial and Corporate Change*, 5(2), pp. 341-382.

Joskow, Paul L. [1997], "Restructuring, Competition and Regulatory Reform in the U.S. Electricity Sector", *Journal of Economic Perspectives*, 11(3), pp. 119-138.

Joskow, Paul L. [1998], "Electricity Sectors in Transition", *The Energy Journal*, 19(2), pp. 25-62.

Judge, G.G., W.E. Griffiths, R.C. Hill and T.C. Lee [1985], *The Theory and Practice of Econometrics*, second edition.

Karier, Thomas [1985], "Unions and Monopoly Profits", *Review of Economics and Statistics*, 67, pp. 34-42.

Kendrick, John W. [1979], "Productivity Trends and the Recent Slowdown", in *Contemporary Economic Problems*, (William Fellner, ed.), American Enterprise Institute, Washington, D.C., pp. 17-69.

Kendrick, John W. [1985], "Measurement of Output and Productivity in the Service Sector" in *Managing the Service Economy: Prospects and Problems*, (Robert P. Inman ed.), Cambridge University Press

Kendrick, J.W. and E. Grossman [1980], *Trends and Cycles in Productivity in the United States*, Johns Hopkins University Press.

Klein, L.R. [1953], *A Textbook of Econometrics*, Row Peterson, New York.

Klein, L.R. [1960], "Some Theoretical Issues in the Measurement of Capacity", *Econometrica*, 28, April, pp. 272-86.

Kmenta, J. [1986], *Elements of Econometrics*, second edition, New York: MacMillan.

Knutson, Ronald D., C. Robert Taylor, John B. Penson, Jr., and Edward G. Smith [1990]. "Economic Impacts of Reduced Chemical Use", *Choices*, Fourth Quarter pp. 25-31.

Kopp, Raymond J., and W.E. Diewert [1982], "The Decomposition of Frontier Cost Function Deviations into Measures of Technical and Allocative Efficiency", *Journal of Econometrics*, 19, pp. 319-331.

Kumbhakar, S. [1990], "Production Frontiers, Panel Data and Time-Varying Technical Inefficiency", *Journal of Econometrics*, 46, pp. 201-211.

Kumbhakar, S. [1992], Allocative Distortions, Technical Progress and Input Demand in U.S. Airlines: 1970-1984, *International Economic Review*, 33, pp. 723-37.

Kumbhakar, S.C. [1997],1 "Modeling Allocative Inefficiency in a Translog Cost Function and Cost Share Equations: An Exact Relationship", *Journal of Econometrics*, 76, pp. 351-356.

Kumbhakar, S., S.C. Ghosh and J.T. McGuckin [1991], "A Generalised Production Frontier Approach for Estimating Determinants of Inefficiency in U.S. Dairy Farms", *Journal of Business and Economic Statistics*, 9, pp. 279-286.

Lau, Lawrence J. [1978], "Applications of Profit Functions", in *Production Economics: A Dual Approach to Theory and Applications*, (M. Fuss and D. McFadden, eds.), North Holland Publishing Co.

Lau, Lawrence J. [1982], "The Measurement of Raw Material Inputs", Chapter6 in *Explorations in Natural Resource Economics*, (V. Kerry Smith and John V. Krutilla, eds.), John Hopkins Press, pp. 167-200.

Lau, Lawrence J. [1986], "Functional Forms for Econometric Model Building", in *Handbook of Econometrics*, 3, (Zvi Griliches and Michael D. Intriligator, eds.), North Holland Press, pp. 1515-1566.

Lau, L.J., and P.A. Yotoupoulos [1971], "A Test for Relative Efficiency and an Application to Indian Agriculture", *American Economic Review*, 61, pp. 94-109.

Lebow, D.E. and D.E Sichel [1992], "Is the Shift Toward Employment in Services Stabilizing?", Working Paper #123, Division of Research and Statistics, Board of Gobvernors of the Federal Reserve System, March.

Lebow, David, John Robert and David Stockton [1994], *Monetary Policy and 'The Price Level'*, Washington, D.C. Board of Governors of the Federal Reserve System.

Lee, Jong-Kun, and Charles D. Kolstad [1994], "Is Technical Change Embodied in the Capital Stock or New Investment?" *Journal of Productivity Analysis*, 5, pp. 385-406.

Lichtenberg, Erik and David Zilberman [1986], "The Econometrics of Damage Control: Why Specification Matters", *American Journal of American Economics*, May, pp. 261-273.

Lichtenberg, Frank R. [1992], "R&D Investment and International Productivity Differences", NBER Working Paper #4161, September.

Lichtenberg, Frank R. [1993], "The Output Contributions of Computer Equipment and Personnel: A Firm-Level Analysis", NBER Working Paper #4540, November.

Lichtenberg, Frank R. and Zvi Griliches [1989], "Errors of Measurement in Output Deflators", *Journal of Business and Economic Statistics*, 7(1), January.

Lichtenberg, Frank R. and Donald Siegel [1987], "Productivity and Changes in Ownership of Manufacturing Plants", *Brookings Papers on Economic Activity*, 3, pp. 643-673.

Lichtenberg, Frank R. and Donald Siegel [1991], "The Impact of R&D Investment on Productivity – New Evidence Using Linked R&D-LRB Data", *Economic Inquiry*, 29, pp. 203-229.

Liu, Lili and James R. Tybout [1996], "Productivity Growth in Chile and Columbia: The Role of Entry, Exit and Learning", in *Industrial Evolution in Developing Countries: Micro Patterns of Turnover, Productivity and Market Structure*, (Roberts and Tybout eds.), New York: Oxford University Press for the World Bank, pp. 73-103.

Love, H. Alan and C. Richard Shumway [1994], "Nonparametric Tests for Monopsonistic Market Power Exertion", *American Journal of Agricultural Economics*, 76, December, pp. 1156-1162.

Lovell, C.A.K. [1993], "Production Frontiers and Productive Efficiency", in *The Measurement of Productive Efficiency* (H.O. Fried, C.A.K. Lovell and S.S. Schmidt, eds.), Oxford University Press, New York, pp. 3-67.

Lovell, C.A.K., S. Richardson, P. Travers and L.L. Wood [1994], "Resources and Functionings: A New View of Inequality in Australia", in *Models and Measurement of Welfare and Inequality*, (W. Eichhorn, ed.), Berlin, Springer-Verlag Press.

Lucas, Robert E., Jr., [1988], "On the Mechanics of Economic Development", *Journal of Monetary Economics*, 22, pp. 3-42.

Luh, Y. and S.E. Stefanou [1991], "Productivity Growth in U.S. Agriculture Under Dynamic Adjustment", *American Journal of Agricultural Economics,* 73, November, pp. 1116-1125.

McElroy, Marjorie B. [1987], "Additive General Error Models for Production, Cost, and Derived Demand or Share Equations", *Journal of Political Economy*, 95(4), August,   pp. 737-757.

McFadden, D. [1978], "Costs, Revenue and Profit Functions", in *Production Economics: A Dual Approach to Theory and Applications I*, (M. Fuss and D. McFadden, eds.) North Holland Press.

Mankiw, . N. Gregory, David Romer and David Weil [1992], "A Contribution to the Empirics of Economic growth", *Quarterly Journal of Economics*, 107(2), May, pp. 407-437.

Mansfield, Edwin [1987], "Price Indexes for R&D Inputs, 1969-1983", *Managenent Science*, 33(1), pp. 1244-129.

Marschak, J. and W.H. Andrews [1944], "Random Simultaneous Equations and the Theory of Production", *Econometrica*, 12, July/October pp. 143-205,

Meeusen, W., and J. van den Broeck [1977], "Efficiency Estimation from Cobb-Douglas Production Functions with Composed Error", *International Economic Review*, 18, pp. 435-444.

Mork, Knut A. [1978], "The Aggregate Demand for Primary Energy in the Short and Long Run for the U.S., 1949-75", MIT Energy Laboratory Report # MIT-EL 7809-007WP, May.

Morrison, Catherine J. [1982], "Three Essays on the Dynamic Analysis of Demand for Factors of Production", Ph.D. Dissertation, University of British Columbia, Department of Economics, Vancouver, British Columbia, December.

Morrison, Catherine J. [1985a], "Primal and Dual Capacity Utilization: An Application to Productivity Measurement in the U.S. Automobile Industry", *Journal of Business and Economic Statistics*, 3(4), October, pp. 312-324.

352

Morrison, Catherine J. [1985b], "On the Economic Interpretation and Measurement of Optimal Capacity Utilization with Anticipatory Expectations", *Review of Economic Studies*, 52, pp. 295-310.

Morrison, Catherine J. [1986a], "Productivity Measurement with Nonstatic Expectations and Varying Capacity Utilization: An Integrated Approach", *Journal of Econometrics*, 33(1/2), October/November, pp. 51-74.

Morrison, Catherine J. [1986b], "A Structural Model of Dynamic Factor Demands with Nonstatic Expectations: An Empirical Assessment of Alternative Expectations Specifications", *International Economic Review*, 27(2), June, pp. 365-386.

Morrison, Catherine J. [1987a], "Capacity Utilization and the Impacts of Pollution Abatement Capital Regulation and Energy Prices: A Comparison of the U.S. and Canadian Manufacturing Industries", in *Advances in Natural Resource Economics*, (John R. Moroney, ed.), 6, Greenwich, Connecticut: JAI Press.

Morrison, Catherine J. [1987b], "Capacity Utilization Under Mobilization Conditions", presented at the ICAF/FEMA conference on The Application of Economic Models for Mobilization Planning, January.

Morrison, Catherine J. [1988a], "Quasi-Fixed Inputs in U.S. and Japanese Manufacturing: A Generalized Leontief Restricted Cost Function Approach", *Review of Economics and Statistics*, 70(2), May, pp. 275-287.

Morrison, Catherine J. [1988b], "Subequilibrium in the North American Steel Industries: A Study of Short Run Biases from Regulation and Utilization Fluctuations", *Economic Journal*, 98, June, pp. 390-411.

Morrison, Catherine J. [1988c], "Capacity Utilization and Productivity Measurement: An Application to the U.S. Automobile Industry", in *Studies in Productivity Analysis*, (A. Dogramaci, ed.), Kluwer Academic Press.

Morrison, Catherine J. [1989a], "Markup Behavior in Durable and Nondurable Manufacturing: An Applied Production Theory Approach", NBER Working Paper #2941, April.

Morrison, Catherine J. [1991], "Decisions of Firms and Productivity Growth with Fixed Input Constraints: An Empirical Comparison of the U.S. and Japanese Manufacturing Industries", in *Productivity Growth in Japan and the United States*, (Charles R. Hulten, ed.), University of Chicago Press, pp. 135-167.

Morrison, Catherine J. [1992a], "Markups in U.S. and Japanese Manufacturing: A Short Run Econometric Analysis", *Journal of Business and Economic Statistics*, 10(1), January, pp., 51-63.

Morrison, Catherine J. [1992b], "Unraveling the Productivity Growth Slowdown in the U.S., Canada and Japan: The Effects of Subequilibrium, Scale Economies and Markups", *Review of Economics and Statistics*, 74(3), August, pp. 381-393..

Morrison, Catherine J. [1992c] *A Microeconomic Approach to the Measurement of Economic Performance: Productivity Growth, Capacity Utilization and Related Performance Indicators*, Springer-Verlag Press.

Morrison, Catherine J. [1993a], "Investment in Capital Assets and Markup Behavior: The U.S. Chemicals and Primary metals Industries in Transition", *Journal of Business and Economic Statistics*, 11(1), January, pp. 45-60.

Morrison, Catherine J. [1993b], "Energy and Capital" Further Exploration of E-K Interactions and Economic Performance", *Energy Journal*, 14(1), Spring, pp. 217-243.

Morrison, Catherine J. [1993c], "Productive and Financial Performance in U.S. Manufacturing Industries: An Integrated Structural Approach", *Southern Economic Journal*, 59(2), October, pp. 376-392.

Morrison, Catherine J. [1994], "The Cyclical Nature of Markups in Canadian Manufacturing: A Production Theory Approach, *Journal of Applied Econometrics*, 9, July-September, pp. 269-282.

Morrison, Catherine J. [1995], "Macroeconomic Relationships between Public Spending on Infrastructure and Private Sector Productivity in the U.S",,in *Infrastructure and Competitiveness* (Jack M. Mintz and Ross S. Preston, eds.), John Deutsch Institute for the Study of Economic Policy, Kingston, Ontario, Canada.

Morrison, Catherine J. [1997], "Assessing the Productivity of Information Technology Equipment in U.S. Manufacturing Industries", *Review of Economics and Statistics* , 79, August, pp. 471-481.

Morrison, Catherine J. [1998a], "Scale Effects and Markups in the US Food and Fibre Industries: Capital Investment and Import Penetration Impacts", forthcoming, *Journal of Agricultural Economics.*

Morrison, Catherine J. [1998b], "Concentration, Scale Economies and Market Power: The Case of the U.S. Meatpacking Industry", manuscript.

Morrison, Catherine J. [1998c],"Cost Economies and Market Power in U.S. Meatpacking", report to USDA/GIPSA (Grain Inspection, Packers and Stockyards Administration), January.

Morrison, Catherine J. [1998d], "Cost and Market Structure in the US Meat and Poultry Products Industries", manuscript, January.

Morrison, Catherine J. [1998e], "Cost Economies and Market Power in the U.S. Beef Packing Industry: A Plant-Level Analysis", manuscript, March.

Morrison , Catherine J., [1998f], Inefficiency Patterns in New South Wales Hospitals, forthcoming in the proceedings of the Conference on Public Sector Productivity and Efficiency, University of New South Wales, November 1997.

Morrison, Catherine J. [1999], "Scale Economy Measures and Subequilibrium Impacts", forthcoming, *Journal of Productivity Analysis.*

Morrison, Catherine J. and Ernst R. Berndt [1981], "Capacity Utilization: Underlying Economic Theory and an Alternative Approach", *American Economic Review*, 7(2), May 1981, pp. 48-52.

Morrison, Catherine J., Warren Johnston and Gerald Frengley [1998], "Efficiency in New Zealand Sheep and Beef Farming: Pre- and Post-Reform", manuscript, University of California at Davis Department of Agricultural and Resource Economics.

Morrison, Catherine J., and Randy Nelson [1989], "The Impacts of Obsolescence, Technical Change, and Vintage on Capacity Utilization and Productivity Growth: 1952-83", manuscript, September.

Morrison, Catherine, J., and Amy Ellen Schwartz [1994], "Distinguishing External from Internal Scale Effects: The Case of Public Infrastructure", *Journal of Productivity Analysis*, 5(1), October, 249-270.

Morrison, Catherine J., and Amy Ellen Schwartz [1996a], "Public Infrastructure, Private Input Demand and Economic Performance in New England Manufacturing", *Journal of Business and Economic Statistics*, 14(1), January, p. 91-102.

Morrison, Catherine J., and Amy Ellen Schwartz [1996b], "State Infrastructure and Productive Performance", *American Economic Review*, 86(5), December, pp. 1095-1111.

Morrison, Catherine J., and Donald Siegel [1997a], "External Capital Factors and Increasing Returns in U.S. Manufacturing", *Review of Economics and Statistics*, 79, November, pp. 647-655.

Morrison, Catherine J. and Donald Siegel [1998a], "The Impacts of Technology, Trade and Outsourcing on Employment and Labor Composition", manuscript.

354

Morrison, Catherine J., and Donald Siegel [1998b], "Knowledge Capital and Cost Structure in the U.S. Food and Fiber Industries", *American Journal of Agricultural Economics*, 80(1), February, pp. 30-45.

Morrison, Catherine J. and Donald Siegel [1998c], "Data Aggregation and Cost Structure Estimation: Empirical Implications for U.S. Manufacturing Industries", forthcoming in the *Southern Economic Journal*.

Morrison, Catherine J., and Donald Siegel [1998d], "Scale Economies and Industry Agglomeration Externalites: A Dynamic Cost Function Approach", forthcoming in the *American Economic Review*.

Munnell, Alicia [1990a], "Why Has Productivity Growth Declined? Productivity and Public Investment", *New England Economic Review* {January/February), pp. 3-22.

Munnell, Alicia [1990b], "How Does Public Infrastructure Affect Regional Economic Performance?", in *Is There a Shortfall in Public Capital Investment*", (Alicia Munnell, ed.), Federal Reserve Bank of Boston.

Munnell, Alicia [1992], "Policy Watch: Infrastructure Investment and Economic Growth", *Journal of Economic Perspectives*, Fall, pp. 189-98.

Nadiri, M. Ishaq, and Ingmar R. Prucha [1989], "Dynamic Factor Demand Models, Productivity Measurement, and Rates of Return: Theory and an Empirical Application to the U.S. Bell System", NBER Working Paper #3041, July.

Nadiri, M. Ishaq and Ingmar Prucha, [1998], "Dynamic Factor Demand Models and Productivity Analysis", presented at the NBER/CRIW/BLS Conference on *New Directions in Productivity Analysis*, March, to be published in the proceedings of the conference.

Nelson, Charles R. [1973], *Applied Time Series Analysis*, Oakland, CA: Holden-Day, Inc.

Nelson, Richard [1997], "How New is New Growth Theory", *Challenge*, 40(5), September/October, pp. 29-58.

Nerlove, Marc [1972], "Lags in Economic Behavior", *Econometrica*, 40(2), March, pp. 221-251.

Newberry, David, M., and Michael G. Politt. [1997], "The Restructuring and Privatization of Britain's CEGB – Was it Worth It?", *The Journal of Industrial Economics*, 45(3), pp. 269-303.

Nishimizu, M., and J.M. Page [1982], "Total Factor Productivity Growth, Technical Progress and Technical Efficiency Change: Dimensions of Productivity Change in Yugoslavia 1965-78", *Economic Journal*, 92, pp. 920-936.

Norsworthy, J. Randolph [1984], "Growth Accounting and Productivity Measurement", *Review of Income and Wealth*, 30(3), September.

Norsworthy, J. Randolph, Michael J. Harper, and Kent Kunze [1979], "The Slowdown in Productivity Growth: Analysis of Some Contributing Factors", *Brookings Papers on Economic Activity*, 2, pp. 387-421.

Ohta, M. [1975], "A Note on the Duality Between Production and Cost Functions: Rate of Returns to Scale and Rate of Technical Progress", *Economic Studies Quarterly*, 25, pp. 63-65.

Okun, Arthur M. [1962], "Potential GNP: Its Measurement and Significance", *Proceedings of the Business and Economics Section of the American Statistical Association*, Washington, D.C.: American Statistical Association, pp. 98-104.

Olley, G. Steven and Ariel Pakes [1996], "The Dynamics of Productivity in the Telecommunications Equipment Industry", *Econometrica*, 64(6), pp. 1263-1297.

Olsen, J.A., P. Schmidt and D.M. Waldman [1980], "A Monte Carlo Study of Estimators of the Stochastic Frontier Production Function", *Journal of Econometrics*, 13, pp. 67-82.

Parks, Richard W. [1971], "Price Responsiveness of Factor Utilization in Swedish Manufacturing, 1870-1950", *Review of Economics and Statistics*, 53(2), May, pp. 129-139.

Perloff, Jeffrey M. and Michael L. Wachter [1979], "A Production Function Nonaccelerating Inflation Approach to Potential Output: Is Measured Potential Output Too High?", in *Three Aspects of Policy and Policymaking: Knowledge, Data and Institutions*, (Karl Brunner and Allan H. Meltzer, eds.), Supplementary Series to the *Journal of Monetary Economics*, 10, pp. 113-164.

Perrin, Richard K., and Lilyan E. Fulginiti [1996], "Productivity Measurement in the Presence of "Poorly Priced" Goods", *American Journal of Agricultural Economics*, 78, December, pp. 1355-1359.

Pindyck, Robert S., and Julio J. Rotemberg [1983], "Dynamic Factor Demands, Energy Use and the Effects of Energy Price Shocks", *American Economic Review*, 73(5), December.

Pindyck, Robert S., and Daniel L. Rubinfeld [1981], *Econometric Models and Economic Forecasts*, McGraw-Hill Book Company, Second Edition.

Pieper, Paul [1989], "Construction Price Statistics Revisited", in *Technology and Capital Formation*, (Dale W. Jorgenson and Ralph Landau, eds.), MIT Press, pp. 293-330.

Pitt, M.M., and L.F. Lee [1981], "Measurement and Sources of Technical Inefficiency in the Indonesian Weaving Industry", *Journal of Development Economics*, 9, pp. 43-64.

Pittman, Russell W. [1971], "Issues in Pollution Control Interplant Cost Differences and Economies of Scale", *Land Economics*, 57, pp.; 1-17.

Porter, R.H. [1984], "Optimal Cartel Trigger Price Strategies", *Journal of Economic Theory*, 29, pp. 313-338.

Rees, Albert [1980], "Improving Productivity Measurement", *American Economic Review*, 70(2), May, pp. 340-342.

Reifschneider, D., and R. Stevenson [1991], "Systematic Departures from the Frontier: A Framework for the Analysis of Firm Inefficiency", *International Economic Review*, 32, pp. 715-723.

Richmond, J. [1974], "Estimating the Efficiency of Production", *International Economic Review*, 15, pp. 1515-521.

Roberts, Mark J. [1984], "Testing Oligopolistic Behavior", *International Journal of Industrial Organization*, 2, pp. 367-383.

Romer, Paul M. [1986], "Increasing Returns and Long-Run Growth", *Journal of Political Economy*, 94, October, pp. 1002-1037.

Romer, Paul M. [1987], "Crazy Explanations for the Productivity Slowdown", *NBER Macroeconomics Annual*, University of Chicago Press.

Ruttan, V. [1954], "Technological Progress in the Meatpacking Industry, 1919-47", United States Department of Agriculture Marketing Research Report #59, Washington, D.C., January.

Ruttan, V. [1956], "The Contribution of Technological Progress to Farm Output: 1950-75", *Review of Economics and Statistics*, 38, February, pp. 61-69.

Sato, R. [1970], "The Estimation of Biased Technical Progress and the Production Function", *International Economic Review*, II, June, pp. 179-208.

Sbordone, Argia [1997], "Interpreting the Procyclical Productivity of Manufacturing Sectors: External Effects or Labor Hoarding", *Journal of Money, Credit and Banking*, 29(1), pp. 26-41.

Schankerman, Mark and M. Ishaq Nadiri [1986], "A Test of Static Equilibrium Models and Rates of Return to Quasi-Fixed Factors, with an Application to the Bell system", *Journal of Econometrics*, 33(1/2), October/November, pp. 97-118.

Schmalensee, Richard [1989], "Inter-Industry Studies of Structure and Performance", in *Handbook of Industrial Organization*, (Richard Schmalensee and Robert Willig, eds.), New York: North Holland Press.

Schmidt, P. [1976], "On the Statistical Estimation of Parametric Frontier Production Functions", *Review of Economics and Statistics*, 58, pp. 238-239.

Schmidt, P. [1986], "Frontier Production Functions", *Econometric Reviews*, 4, pp. 289-328.

Schmidt, P. and C.A.K. Lovell [1979], "Estimating Technical and Allocative Inefficiency Relative to Stochastic Production and Cost Functions", *Journal of Econometrics*, 9, pp. 343-366.

Schnader, Marjorie H. [1984], "Capacity Utilization", *The Handbook of Economic and Financial Measures*, Homewood, Illinois: Dow Jones-Irwin.

Schultz, Theodore W [1961], "Investment in Human Capital", *American Economic Review*, 51(1), March, pp. 1-17.

Schumpeter, Joseph A. [1942], *Capitalism, Socialism and Democracy*, New York: Harper.

Shapiro, Matthew D. [1987], "Measuring Market Power in U.S. Industry", NBER Working Paper #2212, April.

Shapiro, Matthew D. [1989], "Assessing the Federal Reserve's Measures of Capacity Utilization", *Brookings Papers on Economic Activity*, 1, pp. 181-225.

Shapiro, Matthew and David Wilcox [1996], "Mismeasurement in the Consumer Price Index: An Evaluation", in *NBER Macroeconomics Annual*, 11, (Ben Bernanke and Julio Rotemberg, eds.), MIT Press, pp. 93-142.

Shen, T.Y. [1984], "The Estimation of X-Inefficiency inj Eighteen Countries", *Review of Economics and Statistics*, 66, pp. 98-104.

Shephard, Ronald W. [1970], *Theory of Cost and Production Functions*, PrincetonUniversity Press.

Shepherd, William G. [1997], "Dim Prospects: Effective Competition in Telecommunication, Railroads, and Electricity", *The Antitrust Bulletin*, Spring, pp. 151-175.

Shiskin, Julius [1977], "A New Role for Economic Indicators", *Monthly Labor Review*, Bureau of Labor Statistics, November, pp. 3-18.

Siegel, Donald [1995], "Errors of Measurement and the Recent Acceleration in Manufacturing Productivity Growth", *Journal of Productivity Analysis*, 6, pp. 27-320.

Siegel, Donald [1997], "The Impact of Computers on Manufacturing Productivity Growth: A Multiple-Indicators, Multiple-Causes Approach", The Review of Economics and Statistics, 79, pp. 68-78.

Solow, Robert M. [1958], "Technical Change and the Aggregate Production Function", *Review of Economics and Statistics*, 39(5), August, pp. 312-320.

Solow, Robert M. [1988], "Growth Theory and After", *American Economic Review*, 78(3), June, pp. 307-317.

Spiller, P., and E. Favaro [1984], "The Effects of Entry Regulation in Oligopolistic Interaction: The Uruguayan Banking Sector", *Rand Journal of Economics*, 15, pp. 244-254.

Stevenson, R.E. [1980], "Likelihood Functions for Generalised Stochastic Frontier Estimation", *Journal of Econometrics*, 13, pp. 57-66.

Stoker, Thomas M. [1986], "Simple Tests of Distributional Effects on Macroeconomic Equations", *Journal of Political Economy*, 94(4), August, pp. 763-795.

Stokes, Christopher D. [1998], Research Proposal on "Regulation in the California Electric Utilities Industry", University of California, Davis.

Teague, Mark L. and B. Wade Brorsen [1995], "Pesticide Productivity: What are the Trends?" *Journal of Agricultural and Applied Economics*, 27(1), July, pp. 276-282.

Thompson, Herbert G., Jr. [1997], "Cost Efficiency in Power Procurement Delivery Service in the Electric Utilities Industry", *Land Economics*, 73(3), pp. 287-296.

Timmer, C.P. [1971], "Using a Probabilistic Frontier Function to Measure Technical Efficiency", *Journal of Political Economy*, 79, pp. 776-794.

Tinbergen, Jan [1942], "Zur theorie der Iangfristigen wirtschaftsentwicklung" *Weltwirtschaftliches Archiv*, Band 55:1, pp. 511-49. English translation, "On the Theory of Trend Movements", in *Jan Tinbergen Selected Papers*, (L.H. Klassen, L.M. Koyck, H.J. Witteveen, eds.), Amsterdam: North Holland, 1959.

Toda, Yasushi [1976], "Estimation of a Cost Function When the Cost is not Minimum: The Case of Soviet Manufacturing Industries, 1958-71", *Review of Economics and Statistics*, 58(3), August, pp. 259-268.

Trajtenberg, Manuel [1990], "Product Innovation, Price Indexes and the (Mis-Measurement of Economic Performance", NBER Working Paper #3261, February.

Triplett, Jack E. [1987], "Hedonic Functions and Hedonic Indexes", in *The New Palgrave Dictionary of Economics*, 2, (John Eatwell, Murray Milgate, and Pater Newman, eds.), New York: Macmillan, pp. 630-34.

Triplett, Jack [1989], "Price and Technological Change in a Capital Good: A Survey of Research on Computers", in *Technology and Capital Formation*, (Dale W. Jorgenson and Ralph Landau, eds.) The MIT Press, pp. 127-214.

Tybout, James R. [1996], "Heterogeneity and Productivity Growth: Assessing the Evidence" in *Industrial Evolution in Developing Countries: Micro Patterns of Turnover, Productivity and Market Structure*, (Roberts and Tybout eds.), New York: Oxford University Press for the World Bank, pp. 43-72.

U.S. Department of Labor, Bureau of Labor Statistics [1983], *Trends in Multifactor Productivity, 1948-81*, Bulletin #2178, September.

U.S. Department of Labor, Bureau of Labor Statistics [1989], *The Impact of Research and Development on Productivity Growth,* Bulletin #2331, September.

U.S. Department of Labor, Bureau of Labor Statistics [1993], *Labor Composition and U.S. Productivity Growth 1948-90*, Bulletin #2426, December.

Usher, Dan [1975], "Review of *Accounting for United States Economic Growth, 1939-1969* by Edward Denison", *Canadian Journal of Economics*, August, pp. 476-480.

Varian, H.R. [1984], "The Nonparametric Approach to Production Analysis", *Econometrica*, 52, May, pp. 579-97.

Vasavada, U. and R.G. Chambers [1986], "Investment in U.S. Agriculture", *American Journal of Agricultural Economics,* 68, November, pp. 950-960.

Walker, Cody D. and W. Timothy Lough. [1997], "A Critical Review of Deregulated Foreign Electric Utility Markets", *Energy Policy*, 25(10), pp. 877-886.

White, Matthew W. [1996], "Power Struggles: Explaining Deregulatory Reforms in Electricity Markets", *Brookings Papers: Microeconomisc*, pp. 201-267.

Winston, Gordon C. [1977], "Capacity: An Integrated Micro and Macro Analysis", *American Economic Review*, February, pp. 418-422.

Zellner, A., J. Kmenta and J. Dreze [1966], "Specification and Estimation of Cobb-Douglas Production Function Models", *Econometrica*, 34, October, pp. 784-795.

Zieschang, K.D. [1983] "A Note on the Decomposition of Cost Efficiency into Technical and Allocative Components", *Journal of Econometrics*, 23, pp. 401-405.

Zilberman, David, Andrew Schmitz, Gary Casterline, Erik Lichtenberg, and Jerome B. Siebert [1991], "The Economics of Pesticide Use and Regulation", *Science* 253.

Index